The British economy since 1700

The British economy since 1700: A macroeconomic perspective

C. H. Lee

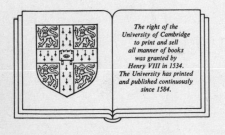

The right of the
University of Cambridge
to print and sell
all manner of books
was granted by
Henry VIII in 1534.
The University has printed
and published continuously
since 1584.

Cambridge University Press

Cambridge
London   New York   New Rochelle
Melbourne   Sydney

Published by the Press Syndicate of the University of Cambridge
The Pitt Building, Trumpington Street, Cambridge CB2 1RP
32 East 57th Street, New York, NY 10022, USA
10 Stamford Road, Oakleigh, Melbourne 3166, Australia

First published 1986

Printed in Great Britain at the University Press, Cambridge

British Library cataloguing in publication data
Lee, C. H.
The British economy since 1700: a
macroeconomic perspective.
1. Great Britain – Economic conditions
I. Title
330.941'07   HC253

Library of Congress cataloguing in publication data
Lee, C. H. (Clive Howard), 1942–
The British economy since 1700.
Includes index.
1. Great Britain – Economic conditions. I. Title.
HC254.5.L46 1987   330.941   86–14736

ISBN 0 521 32973 6 hard cover
ISBN 0 521 33861 1 paperback

WD

For Chris

Contents

Tables

Preface

To write any academic book necessitates the accumulation of many debts. This is especially true of the book which draws upon the work of many scholars in seeking to synthesize an interpretation from a diversity of topics and problems. The lengthy bibliography, which includes only those works cited in the text and omits the many others which had to be consulted, reveals this as such a study. It is appropriate to express my thanks to all these scholars, for without their work this book could not have been written.

I would like to thank my colleagues at Aberdeen and the many students who have patiently listened to my effusions and helped to keep them in touch with historical reality. More specifically I am indebted to several scholars who read all or part of earlier versions of this book, and helped improve it by their helpful criticisms: Dr R. H. Britnell, Professor R. C. Floud, Mr C. Honeywell, Professor P. L. Payne, Professor S. Pollard, Ms L. Townson, Dr P. Wardley. I am also grateful to those who made comments on papers given at various seminars in Scotland and at the University of Leeds. The observations of the publisher's assessors were stimulating and extremely helpful, as were the good offices of Francis Brooke of Cambridge University Press.

Finally my greatest debt is to my wife without whom the book would never have been written. She bought me the typewriter.

PART I

Introduction

1

British economic growth in long-term perspective

I

There has been a sustained and almost pathological interest in recent years in the problems of the British economy, ranging from television programmes and popular writing to academic debate. Recent analyses have extended the search for explanations of the current malaise beyond the limited perspective of the recent past, within which political comment and economic analysis are often confined, to investigate development in the longer term and to seek the origins of contemporary difficulties in earlier times. Thus in conventional academic investigations, Kirby (1981) and Wiener (1981) sought explanations within the past century while, at a more popular level, television series and books by Eatwell (1982) and Dahrendorf (1982) traced the skein of cause and effect back to the eighteenth century and early industrialization.

There are very good grounds for adopting a long-term perspective since few if any economic problems, or for that matter economic successes, are instantly manifest. The purpose of this study is to provide a coherent and comprehensive explanation of the economic development of the British economy from the early eighteenth century to the present day. Several reasons suggest and warrant such a study. The British economic experience is worthy of examination in its own right, as indeed is any other historical investigation. But Britain played a unique and central role in world economic development, especially before 1914, so that the British experience and contribution is important in that wider context. Furthermore, current problems can be understood only imperfectly without an awareness of the nature of this earlier phase of development. One further reason may be suggested, and it is the one which primarily stimulated this study. There has been much interest in this subject such that its literature has greatly increased in both volume and quality in recent years. As a result, much new information and many reassessments have emerged. The traditional thesis that the Industrial Revolution was the origin and essence of modern

3

economic growth has remained dominant in British historiography for over a century. Interpretations have been shaped to conform to the precepts of this model, and specialized studies commissioned and pursued in accordance with its basic assumptions. It has passed into popular consciousness and common speech as a term, an image and an explanation of the past. This long and established tradition has not survived without question or challenge, as a variety of scholarly works written during the past century can testify, but it has retained the ascendant position in explanations. The appearance of much new work suggests that the time is ripe for a review of the conventional wisdom and its underlying thesis, and a reassessment of the past development and the current problems of the British economy.

II

Before embarking on an explanation of the process of economic development during the past three centuries, it is necessary to describe in outline the main characteristics of that development. As a result of the statistical work of many scholars in recent years, it is possible to describe the main parameters of that growth with considerable confidence. There is a substantial degree of agreement amongst the majority of reconstructive studies. It can reasonably be claimed that current estimates of long-term growth are set within fairly limited bounds of error. While such estimates cannot be taken as entirely certain in detail, a state of affairs which will probably always endure, further improvement and embellishment seems likely to produce modification of these estimates rather than a complete refutation of them. They are unlikely to be replaced by a completely different set of data proposing totally different hypotheses.

The main indicator of long-term growth is the rate of growth of Gross Domestic Product (GDP). The data indicate a modest rate of growth during the eighteenth century, increasing from just under one per cent to just over it (Table 1.1). Thereafter, except for the disruptive effect of wartime, growth remained fairly steady at around two per cent per annum. 'It is almost as if the range of 2 to 2½ per cent per annum had been meted out to the British economy by divine grace – or, in the eyes of many critics, by divine retribution' (Von Tunzelmann 241). There were two phases of rather higher growth, during the first seven decades of the nineteenth century and the interwar years and in the great, but brief, boom from 1951–73. There is some lack of agreement about the timing of the earlier phase of high growth, as can be seen from the estimates for the growth of GDP for the period 1801–31 derived respectively by Crafts (2.0 per cent) and Feinstein (2.7 per cent) using different methods (Table 1.1). But the majority of commentators

Table 1.1 *British economic growth rates (per cent per annum)*

	GDP	GDP/head	Labour	Capital	Total factor productivity
1700–60	0.7	0.3	0.4	0.7	0.2
1760–80	0.7	0.0	0.7	0.8	0.1
1780–1801	1.3	0.4	1.0	1.2	0.4
1801–31	2.0	0.5	1.4	1.5	0.7
1761–1800	1.1	0.3	0.8	1.0	0.2
1801–30	2.7	1.3	1.4	1.4	1.3
1831–60	2.5	1.1	1.4	2.0	0.8
1856–73	2.2	1.4	0.0	1.7	1.5
1873–1913	1.8	0.9	0.9	1.8	0.6
1913–24	−0.1	−0.6	−2.3	0.2	1.3
1924–37	2.2	1.8	1.5	2.0	0.6
1937–51	1.8	1.3	0.1	1.3	1.4
1951–73	2.8	2.3	−0.5	3.9	2.2
1973–79	1.3	1.3	−0.1	3.5	0.5
1979–83	0.1	0.1	−2.0	1.5	1.2

Notes: Data relate to Great Britain up to 1860, to the United Kingdom thereafter. The post-1856 data for labour relate to man-hours.

Sources: N. F. R. Crafts, 'British economic growth 1700–1831: a review of the evidence'. *Economic History Review*, 2nd series, 36 (1983) pp. 187, 196 (rows 1–4).

C. H. Feinstein, 'Capital formation in Great Britain' in P. Mathias and M. M. Postan (eds.), *Cambridge Economic History of Europe*, vol. VII pt I (Cambridge 1978) p. 84 (rows 5–7).

R. C. O. Matthews, C. H. Feinstein and J. C. Odling-Smee, *British Economic Growth 1856–1973* (Oxford 1982) pp. 208, 210, 498 (rows 8–13).

Central Statistical Office, *United Kingdom National Accounts* (1984) Tables 1.17, 3.13, 11.7 (rows 14–15).

Central Statistical Office, *Annual Abstract of Statistics* (1984) p. 127.

now seem to assign the greater part of growth in this period to the years after the end of the Napoleonic Wars in 1815 (Maddison 45; Harley 1982: 286).

A better indicator of the advance of economic development is GDP per head of population (Table 1.1). Population grew at a modest rate through the eighteenth and nineteenth centuries in Britain, at rather less than one per cent annually, and at less than half of one per cent annually through that part of the twentieth century which has now passed. Population growth was sufficient to sustain the growth process, but was not so great as to swamp it in the way Malthus feared. But this modest increase in population growth meant that, in the eighteenth and nineteenth centuries, the growth of GDP per head was for most of the time at least one per cent lower than the rate of growth of GDP. Growth per head was thus under half of one per cent annually throughout the eighteenth century and averaged between one and one and a half per cent through the nineteenth century. The rate of growth per head attained by the British economy before 1815 amounted to only 10 per cent of the growth rate achieved by the poorer countries of the world in the 1970s (Williamson 1984: 688).

During the peacetime periods of the twentieth century it reached rather higher rates of increase. A very similar pattern of long-term growth is suggested in Rostow's estimates for Gross National Product (GNP), which also show a marked acceleration in the twentieth century especially after the Second World War (Rostow 1978a: 72–9).

The slowness of British economic growth in the long run is emphasized when seen in the context of the growth of the other major industrial nations. Maddison's estimates confirm the pattern and suggest that the rate of growth of GDP per head in Britain was the slowest of twelve advanced economies during the period 1820–1979 (Maddison 8). These relative rates of increase obviously altered the importance of the British economy in its international context. Throughout the nineteenth century, Britain remained the largest economy in Western Europe in terms of GDP, though Britain was overtaken by the United States during the middle decades of the century, the precise date varying according to different estimates. By 1870 there was still little difference in the size of the two economies, but the United States surged ahead in the later decades of the century so that Britain was only 37 per cent of United States size by 1914. By 1979 this figure had fallen further to under 17 per cent, and by this later date Japan, France and West Germany had become larger economies than Britain. In the twentieth century Britain also fell behind in GDP per head. But this relative decline took place, paradoxically, during the period when greater sustained growth was achieved than ever before. Most of the increase in British GNP and GDP per head generated between 1700 and the present day has been gained in the twentieth century and, according to some estimates, since 1950 (Maddison 8, 161).

III

In the very broadest terms the growth of GDP can be defined as depending on three elements, an increase in labour, an increase in capital, and an increase in the productivity of these factors of production, called total factor productivity. The principal influence underlying the increase in labour was the growth of population. The falling rate of population growth, especially in the twentieth century, has been reflected in the declining rate of labour increase and its falling contribution to growth. Changes in participation rates in employment were also important in the twentieth century, although the fall in the male participation rate was offset by the increase in the level of female participation in employment (Matthews 77). The other main influence on the input of labour has been the decline in working hours, together with the increase in holidays, which has been active since at least the middle of the nineteenth century. In recent decades the age distribution of the population has shifted in such a way as to reduce the input of labour. While in the Victorian era, and certainly before that time, increase in labour was principally a function of population increase, in the twentieth century slower population growth and the continuous reduction in the hours worked per year were most influential in reducing labour's contribution.

In contrast to the dwindling contribution of labour to growth, capital has grown at a generally increasing rate over the past three centuries, and there was a particularly high rate of increase in capital input during the period of rapid growth 1951–73. Little surprise will be occasioned by the increase in capital input since it represents a major prerequisite for any economic advance.

The derivation of the estimate for productivity increase, total factor productivity, is rather more hazardous and contentious than the estimation of labour and capital growth. Productivity is usually calculated as the residual left after the rate of growth of factor inputs have been subtracted from the rate of growth of GDP. The controversy arises from the fact that the growth rates of the factor inputs, labour and capital, must be weighted by their respective factor shares in national income. The relative size of these factor shares is thus crucial for determining the size of the productivity residual, especially as, so often in the context of historical data, these shares are based on estimates rather than certain factual knowledge. As can be seen from Table 1.2, differing assumptions about the size of factor shares produce quite different patterns in the allocation of GDP growth between labour, capital and productivity. This is most clearly demonstrated by Crafts' estimates for the eighteenth century. By adopting a factor distribution which allowed a 15 per cent share to land, not in any way an unreasonable assumption, his results leave a larger residual, productivity, than if the more conventional division between labour and capital alone is employed. Feinstein's estimate of GDP growth in the period 1801–31, higher than Crafts or Harley found, also produced a higher estimate for the contribution of productivity (Table 1.3). It was from this indicator that Williamson drew the conclusion that 'Britain's industrial revolution seems odd: whereas other nations passing through early industrialisation record high contributions for conventional capital accumulation and low contributions for total factor productivity, Britain prior to 1820 suggests the opposite' (Williamson 1984: 711–12). But this high rate of aggregate productivity increase can be diminished either by accepting the lower rate of GDP growth for the period 1801–31, following Crafts rather than Feinstein, or by assuming a different

Table 1.2 *Factor contributions to growth: three hypotheses (per cent per annum)*

	Assumption 1			Assumption 2			Assumption 3		
	Labour	Capital	TFP	Labour	Capital	TFP	Labour	Capital	TFP
1700–60	0.20	0.35	0.14	0.30	0.18	0.21	0.20	0.25	0.24
1760–80	0.35	0.40	−0.05	0.53	0.20	−0.03	0.35	0.28	0.07
1780–1801	0.50	0.60	0.22	0.75	0.30	0.27	0.50	0.42	0.40
1801–31	0.70	0.75	0.52	1.05	0.38	0.56	0.70	0.53	0.74
1761–1800	0.40	0.50	0.20	0.60	0.25	0.25	0.40	0.35	0.35
1801–30	0.70	0.70	1.30	1.05	0.35	1.30	0.70	0.49	1.51
1831–60	0.70	1.00	0.80	1.05	0.50	0.95	0.70	0.70	1.10
1856–73	0.00	0.85	1.35	0.00	0.43	1.77			
1873–1913	0.45	0.90	0.45	0.68	0.45	0.67			
1913–24	−1.15	0.10	0.95	−1.73	0.05	1.58			
1924–37	0.75	1.00	0.45	1.13	0.50	0.57			
1937–51	0.05	0.65	1.10	0.08	0.33	1.39			
1951–73	−0.25	1.95	1.10	−0.38	0.98	2.20			
1973–79	−0.05	1.75	−0.40	−0.08	0.88	0.50			
1979–83	−1.00	0.75	1.85	0.35	0.38	1.22			

Total factor productivity was estimated on the various assumptions about the distribution of national product between labour and capital as follows: Assumption 1 – 50/50; Assumption 2 – 75/25; Assumption 3 – 50/35 (Crafts' definition for the period prior to 1860). Data taken from Table 1.1.

distribution of factor shares (Table 1.2). There is no strong evidential reason to prefer any one of these estimates to another, although the Crafts data for GDP growth, showing greater growth after 1830 than earlier, are consistent both with Harley's recent estimates and the increasingly popular view that the main increase in growth was deferred until after 1815. The estimates listed under assumption 1 in Table 1.2 may well provide the best indicator of factor contributions to growth before 1860. This suggests that growth in GDP was primarily contributed by the growth of labour and capital inputs in the eighteenth century, followed by a greater increase in the contribution of both capital and productivity thereafter.

From the mid nineteenth century, the trend of income distribution favoured labour rather than capital. Total labour income increased from about 55 per cent in the second half of the nineteenth century to reach 65.1 per cent by 1937 and 72.8 per cent by 1973 while the remaining share left for property income fell accordingly, mainly affecting farm income and profits (Matthews 164). This suggests that the estimates made under assumption 2 in Table 1.2 are more plausible for the twentieth century.

Thus, in more recent times, the contribution of labour to growth was substantial only in the period 1873–1913, and 1924–37 when there was a marked shift in the age distribution which favoured increased labour utilization. But in the middle decades of the nineteenth century and during the most recent past labour has made a minimal or even negative contribution to growth. Capital inputs and total factor productivity have comprised most of the growth stimulus. Indeed in the mid Victorian period and since the late 1930s, productivity increased at a higher rate and contributed more to aggregate growth than at any other time.

IV

A rather fuller description of growth and its component parts can be found by disaggregating output growth between the sectors which produce it. Data limitations are such that prior to the mid nineteenth century such disaggregation is possible only to the very modest extent of three large sectors, each containing a considerable variety of growth and decline within it. Even such data are based as much on intelligent guesswork as hard evidence, and the most persuasive aspect of these recent estimates lies in the fact that they report results similar to each other and consistent with other evidence. The relative contribution to the growth of GDP provided by each sector is found by multiplying the rate of growth of the sector by its share of GDP. Thus, for the period 1700–60, Crafts estimated that the rate of growth of agriculture was 0.60 per cent annually and that its share in GDP was 37 per cent. The product of these two estimates yield the weighted growth rate of 0.22 per cent annually (Table 1.3). Such estimates depend not only on the accuracy of the estimated sectoral growth rates but equally on the accuracy of the estimated sector shares. Thus, for example, the Deane/Cole sector share estimates for the eighteenth century allocate a greater proportion to agriculture and less to industry than do Crafts' estimates. Since the rate of growth of GDP is the aggregate of all the weighted sectoral growth rates such a change in sector shares alters, in this instance reduces, the rate of growth of GDP (Deane/Cole 156, 161).

Both the series of sectoral growth estimates derived by Crafts and Harley reflect a similar pattern of growth. Both the industrial and service sectors contributed substantially to aggregate growth. The industry sector was so broadly defined that it included mining, construction, and public utilities as well as manufacturing, so that any comparison with the fuller disaggregation possible for the period after 1860 should combine these four sectors together. Higher rates of growth in GDP appear to correlate well with periods in which manufacturing made a greater contribution to growth. But the overall slow rate of aggregate growth is also reflected in the modest

Table 1.3 *Weighted sectoral output growth rates (per cent per annum)*

	Agriculture	Industry	Services	GDP
1700–60	0.22	0.14	0.33	0.69
1760–80	0.04	0.38	0.28	0.70
1780–1801	0.24	0.53	0.55	1.32
1801–31	0.31	0.96	0.70	1.97
1700–70	0.19	0.16	0.21	0.56
1770–1815	0.26	0.40	0.65	1.31
1815–41	0.36	0.99	0.88	2.23
1831–60	0.36	0.97	1.17	2.50

Note: The growth rate of each sector was weighted (multiplied by) the size of that sector in GDP.

Crafts' sectoral weights were used for each date set, except for the 1831–60 period when the weights used in Table 1.4 were applied.

Sources: N. F. R. Crafts, 'British economic growth 1700–1831: a review of the evidence'. *Economic History Review*, 2nd series, 36 (1983) pp. 187, 189, 191, 193 (rows 1–4).

C. K. Harley, 'British industrialisation before 1841: evidence of slower growth during the Industrial Revolution'. *Journal of Economic History* 42 (1982) pp. 284–6 (rows 5–7).

C. H. Feinstein, 'Capital formation in Great Britain' in P. Mathias and M. M. Postan (eds.), *Cambridge Economic History of Europe*, vol. VII, pt I (Cambridge 1978), p. 84 (row 8).

weighted growth rate of the manufacturing sector, never reaching one per cent until the present century. For much of the entire period from the early eighteenth century until the present day the service sector kept pace with manufacturing in its contribution to growth, and often exceeded it. Only in the early part of the nineteenth century, before the advent of the railways, and during the interwar years in the twentieth century was the contribution of manufacturing greater than that of services by any marked amount.

The estimates of sectoral growth derived by Crafts and Harley revealed a varied pattern of growth within manufacturing during the century and a half before the railways. These calculations reveal substantial increases in output. According to Harley, they occurred mainly in cotton and metal manufacture, followed by mining, construction, paper and printing, and clothing (1982: 272). Crafts' estimates of value added by industrial sector suggest that between 1770–1831 cotton manufacture accounted for £24.7 million and construction for £24.1 million of a total value added for industry of £90.1 million. The combined textile industries accounted for almost half the total value added, while coal and iron generated only modest increases (Crafts 1983: 180). Apart from the dramatic growth of the cotton industry from a negligible minor branch of textiles to the position of a major manufacturing industry by 1840, growth in industry took the form of a broad expansion of established manufactures.

Output data are considerably more reliable by the Victorian period. By then the service sector not only played a greater role in generating growth of GDP but exceeded the contribution of manufacturing. There was considerable growth in all services, but most notably in distribution and transport and communications (Table 1.4). The increasing importance of services continued into the twentieth century and commerce, the professions, and financial services, including banking and insurance, were major growth sectors, continuing their growth even through the 1970s. Disaggregation of manufacturing by sector is difficult prior to the first Census of Production published in 1907. But the major sectoral contributions to growth can be inferred in general terms. In 1907, the combined textiles, clothing and leather industries accounted for 32.0 per cent of manufacturing production, while the combined metal and engineering industries comprised a further 33.0 per cent. Had these aggregate sectors grown at the same annual rate as all manufacturing, that is 2.6 per cent between 1856–73 and 2.0 per cent between 1873–1913, then their weighted sectoral growth contributions would have been about 0.9 per cent and 0.7 per cent respectively. Similarly, the other main sector, food, drink and tobacco, which comprised 19.7 per cent of manufacturing output in 1907, would have contributed 0.4–0.5 per cent to aggregate growth. Together, these three main sectors made up the bulk of manufacturing production and growth in the Victorian period, although it is likely that textiles grew at a rate below the manufacturing average and the engineering industries above it. After the First World War the contribution of particular manufacturing sectors to growth can be estimated with greater surety (Table 11.2). Within the context of higher growth rates in manufacturing than hitherto, the relative contribution of textiles declined while that of engineering, especially its newer branches, increased as did that of vehicle production and chemicals. After 1973, within a context of accelerating industrial decline, most sectors of industry experienced contraction in output.

Changes in the structure of national output were largely replicated by shifts in the allocation of employment between different sectors as a result of differential growth. Employment growth was particularly rapid in the nineteenth century, indicating the importance of increased labour to the growth of production. But the rate of increase in employment was much lower in the twentieth century, and declined absolutely in the 1970s. Estimates of sectoral employment before the mid nineteenth century are, of course, less detailed or accurate than the data contained in the later Census of Population surveys. The most recent and detailed estimates for the eighteenth century have been made by Lindert (Tables 1.5 and 1.6). In

Table 1.4 *Weighted sectoral output growth rates (per cent per annum)*

	1856–73	1873–1913	1913–24	1924–37	1937–51	1951–64	1964–73	1973–79	1979–83
Agriculture, forestry, fishing	0.03	−0.01	−0.05	0.06	0.08	0.12	0.11	0.01	0.03
Mining, quarrying	0.19	0.12	−0.05	−0.02	−0.05	−0.02	−0.07	0.55	0.23
Manufacturing	0.61	0.51	0.14	1.04	0.81	1.14	1.11	−0.21	−0.70
Construction	0.11	0.04	0.11	0.22	−0.08	0.23	0.11	−0.11	−0.12
Gas, water, electricity	0.02	0.06	0.05	0.16	0.08	0.13	0.15	0.00	0.00
Transport, communications	0.21	0.24	0.10	0.15	0.19	0.18	0.28	0.09	0.01
Commerce	0.59	0.52	−0.50	0.44	−0.05	0.74	0.75	0.46	0.43
Public and professional services	0.12	0.22	0.08	0.16	0.39	0.21	0.27	0.40	0.17
Ownership of dwellings	0.12	0.10	0.02	0.09	0.03	0.07	0.09	0.11	0.05
GDP	2.00	1.80	−0.10	2.30	1.40	2.80	2.80	1.30	0.10

Note: The growth rate of each sector is weighted by its share in GDP.
Sources: R. C. O. Matthews, C. H. Feinstein and J. C. Odling-Smee, *British Economic Growth 1856–1973* (Oxford 1982) pp. 222–3, 228–9.
Central Statistical Office, *United Kingdom National Accounts* (1984) Table 2.4.
Central Statistical Office, *Annual Abstract of Statistics* (1984) pp. 14, 254.

Table 1.5 *Growth rates: employment and structural change (per cent per annum)*

	Employment	Structural change
1700–1801	0.27	0.65
1755–1851	1.73	0.80
1801–1901	2.25	0.68
1851–1951	0.86	0.98
1901–1981	0.33	1.26
1700–1755	0.11	0.69
1755–1801	0.46	1.41
1801–1851	3.05	1.75
1851–1901	1.11	0.89
1901–1951	0.62	1.40
1951–1981	−0.14	1.26
1841–51	3.15	1.90
1851–61	1.16	1.08
1861–71	1.23	1.31
1871–81	0.70	0.84
1881–91	1.31	0.90
1891–1901	1.17	1.29
1901–11	1.17	0.86
1911–21	0.36	4.15
1921–31	−0.05	1.99
1931–51	0.79	1.32
1951–61	0.51	1.52
1961–71	0.19	1.33
1971–81	−1.10	1.98

Notes: Data relate to England and Wales to 1841, Great Britain thereafter. Estimates for 1755–1851 and 1801–1901 based on estimated employment size for Great Britain. Structural change is defined as the sum of deviations of sectoral rates of growth from the total rate of growth, weighted by the size of the sector. For rows 1–11 the analysis was based on a ten sector disaggregation; for rows 12–24, it was based on a 27 sector disaggregation. The large structural change in the periods of 1755–1801, and 1801–51 is strongly influenced by the diversion of employment to wartime service in 1801. Similarly the very high rate of structural change in the decade 1911–21 is partly due to improved census classifications whereby the general 'not classified' category was substantially reduced. Without this accounting effect, the estimate of structural change is rather less than three per cent.

Sources: P. H. Lindert, 'English occupations 1670–1811', *Journal of Economic History*, 40 (1980) pp. 702–4.

C. H. Lee, *British Regional Employment Statistics 1841–1971* (Cambridge 1979).

Central Statistical Office, *Annual Abstract of Statistics* (1984) pp. 110–13.

Table 1.6 *Weighted sectoral employment growth rates (per cent per annum)*

	1700–1801	1755–1851	1801–1901	1851–1951	1901–1981
Agriculture	−0.08	0.38	0.19	−0.08	−0.09
Mining	0.08	0.08	0.14	0.03	−0.04
Textiles/clothing	0.07	0.51	0.35	−0.04	−0.14
Other manufacturing	0.03	0.27	0.50	0.33	0.16
Construction	0.05	0.09	0.19	0.08	0.01
Commerce	0.01	−0.09	0.03	0.27	0.33
Professions	0.02	0.06	0.09	0.08	0.24
Other services	−0.11	0.34	0.54	0.15	−0.01
Government/defence	0.15	0.02	0.04	0.12	0.08
Not classified	0.05	0.07	0.18	−0.08	−0.21
Total employment	0.27	1.73	2.25	0.86	0.33

Sources: Table 1.5.

reconstructing eighteenth-century employment, Lindert found a much higher proportion in manufacturing than had been suggested by earlier writers who had tended to accept the version of Gregory King. He had depicted late seventeenth-century Britain as a mainly agricultural society with little industry and a modest commercial sector. By contrast, Lindert's estimates for employment in England and Wales in 1700 suggest that agriculture accounted for only 20 per cent of the total, while mining, manufacturing and construction together accounted for a similar proportion (Lindert 702–4). Like Harley's estimates for output, these employment data indicate a greater level of industrialization in 1700 than has customarily been assumed. By implication they indicate a much slower rate of industrial growth during the later eighteenth century. Lindert's data indicate considerable importance in employment growth during the eighteenth century in agriculture and textiles, including clothing, and these were the main growth sectors until the middle of the nineteenth century. This is demonstrated by their weighted sectoral growth rates (Table 1.6). Agricultural employment increased from well under half a million in 1700 to a peak of two million workers in 1851, declining thereafter to reach 352,000 in 1981, a number probably quite close to that of three centuries earlier. Textiles and clothing also experienced a considerable increase in employment from under 100,000 at the beginning of the eighteenth century (probably 60–70,000 for Great Britain on the basis of Lindert's estimate for England and Wales) to a peak of 2.7 million workers on the eve of the First World War. By 1981 this sector had lost two million of those jobs. On a rather more modest scale, mining followed a similar pattern with a moderate increase in employment during the eighteenth and early nineteenth centuries and a very substantial growth in the Victorian period. This industry had a net gain of over one million jobs between 1841 and its peak employment year of 1921, and suffered a net loss of similar size by 1981. Thus, in the two centuries prior to 1914 these three employment sectors together gained some four to five million new jobs. By the last quarter of the twentieth century four million of them had disappeared. Employment that had taken two centuries to build up was lost in little more than half a century. The considerable combined contribution of these sectors to employment growth and decline is clear (Table 1.6).

While agriculture, textiles and mining accounted for half of the total increase in employment in the period 1700–1850, expansion was the characteristic of most other sectors. There was growth in the rest of manufacturing, in construction and public utilities, and in services. In the Victorian period there was a total increase of 1.5 million jobs in the metal working and engineering industries, most notably in iron and steel manufacture, shipbuilding and branches of mechanical engineering such as textile machinery, agricultural machinery and railway equipment. Growth in these sectors continued in the twentieth century, a net increase of a million jobs by 1981, but with a considerable restructuring within engineering. Electrical engineering and the motor industry represented considerable areas of expansion while most of the branches of engineering which had had their heyday in Victorian times reduced their employment capacity. In construction the main increase in employment was generated in the years before 1914 by which time the industry employed 800,000 more than it had in 1841. In the twentieth century employment in this sector has remained fairly stable.

The various and diverse service sectors were well represented in the growth of employment before 1850, although not so impressively as agriculture or textiles. Since the mid nineteenth century, however, services have increasingly dominated the growth in employment. In the Victorian period there was an increase of over one million jobs in transport and in miscellaneous services, of which domestic service was the main component. In sum, service employment increased by over four million jobs between 1841 and 1911. In the present century, as other sectors reduced employment or remained stable, several services increased greatly. While total employment in 1981 was 2.4 million jobs greater than it had been in 1911, the service industries had increased in that time by 5.9 million jobs. Principal increases were found in the professions by 2.9 million, in banking and financial services by 1.0 million, in government and defence by 1.1 million, and in the distributive trades by only a little less than a million, although this last sector was contracting in the 1970s. The overwhelmingly important role of these commercial and professional sectors in twentieth-century employment growth is indicated in Table 1.6.

The long term trends in employment change, and the large increases and decreases involved, have tempted historians to infer substantial structural change. This has been particularly persuasive for the later eighteenth century. One appropriate measure of the size of structural change is found by summing the deviations of sectoral growth rates from the national growth rate, each weighted by its sectoral share. For twentieth-century output data, the rate of structural change turned out to be extremely small (Matthews 255). Applied to Victorian output data, structural change in that period was even less impressive, remaining below one per cent compared to the 1.2–1.6 per cent range achieved in the twentieth century. Structural change in employment, which can be measured over a much longer period, proved to be similarly modest. Structural change remained well below two per cent annually, except during the First World War when the estimate was further inflated by changes in data measurement (Table 1.5). While there were large increases and decreases in employment in several sectors, that process took place over a very long period. An increase of a million jobs in an industry over the course of a century, if evenly spread, would require only an addition of 10,000 jobs per year. The low level of structural change found is consistent with the generally slow rate of growth of the economy, while the inclusion of most sectors in the process of employment increase indicates balanced growth rather than unbalanced growth characteristic of an economy impelled by a few leading sectors.

Taking the very long run, there was a higher level of structural change in the twentieth century than earlier. The apparent contradiction of this by the measure of structural change for half century periods, which suggests a higher level of change between 1755–1801 and 1801–51, is exposed by reference to Lindert's data. Much of the apparent structural change implied in these calculations is produced by the sharp fall and later recovery in agricultural employment and, conversely, the big increase in the army and navy during the protracted Napoleonic Wars. The 1801 benchmark, falling within that war period, thus reflects a wartime distortion of employment and not a secular change in structure occasioned by normal peacetime activities.

The estimates of structural change for decadal periods from 1841 onwards are based on a much greater level of sectoral disaggregation. But these estimates also show a very small rate of structural change, with an obvious increase in the twentieth century. The reason for this is not difficult to find. Growth in employment prior to 1914 took the form of differential additions to the various sectors in the economy within the context of a high rate of employment growth, especially during the nineteenth century. Agriculture was the only major sector to experience an absolute and long-term decline in employment before 1914. In the twentieth century there were two additional forces in action as well as the differential sectoral employment growth which, of course, continued. Firstly, there was a much slower rate of aggregate increase in employment, eventually dwindling into a net decline. Secondly, many more sectors followed the precedent of agriculture in shedding labour on a very large scale. Several sectors experienced substantial employment losses while other sectors registered considerable increases. The aggregate net increase in employment was very small as the two forces of employment growth and contraction virtually cancelled each other out. It is hardly surprising, therefore, that structural change in the present century has been greater than in earlier centuries.

V

The outline of British economic growth in broad aggregate terms as described above provides the context for explanations of that process and stimulates most of the basic questions. The rest of this study is devoted to the search for a coherent explanation of the nature of British economic development. The pattern of growth over these three centuries immediately raises the problem of how best to divide into historical periods such a long phase of development while keeping the periods short enough to be manageable but yet cohesive. This is an especially important issue because past explanations of British development have been sought very largely in the context of a very definite scheme of periodization, and which itself developed into an explanation of the process of historical economic growth.

At the heart of this tradition lay the notion of an industrial revolution as a fundamental discontinuity in history and hence a major, even the major, turning point. Thus Cipolla (1962) averred that, 'The Agricultural Revolution of the eighth millennium B.C. and the Industrial Revolution of the eighteenth century A.D., on the other hand, created deep breaches in the continuity of the historical process. With each of these two Revolutions, a "new story" begins: a new story dramatically and completely alien to the previous one . . . Each "Revolution" had its roots in the past. But each "Revolution" created a deep break with the very same past' (Cipolla 31). In similar vein Landes wrote that this Revolution marked 'a far more drastic break with the past than anything since the invention of the wheel' (Landes 42).

This perception of a crucial phase of transformation, which became firmly located in Britain and set generally within the century after 1750, generated both vivid description and explanatory mechanisms. In the late nineteenth century Cunningham provided such a description, 'We have no adequate means of gauging the rapidity and violence of the Industrial Revolution which occurred in England during the seventy years from 1770 to 1840 . . . Despite the gradual economic development, it seems likely though that, while centuries passed, there was little alteration in the general aspect of

England; but the whole face of the country was changed by the Industrial Revolution. In 1770 there was no Black Country, blighted by the conjunction of coal and iron trades; there were no canals, or railways, and no factory towns with their masses of population' (Cunningham 613). Such descriptions heighten the drama and the uniqueness of the revolutionary break. Indeed in the 1950s, Coleman was very critical of other historians who purported to find industrial revolutions in other periods, in the thirteenth-century textile industry or the sixteenth-century coal trade, on the grounds that the term was thus devalued. Historians should, he argued, 'reserve it for the initial – and in the long focus of history – comparatively sudden and violent changes which launched the industrialised society into being, transforming that society in a way which none of the earlier so-called industrial revolutions ever did' (1956: 20). More recently, Rostow's famous explanation, using the analogy of an aeroplane take-off to describe the crucial industrial breakthrough, was not only cast in the traditional framework but identified a twenty-year period in which the revolution was accomplished and the take-off achieved. In the British case this period was defined as 1783–1802. 'The hypothesis is, then, a return to a rather old-fashioned way of looking at economic development. The take-off is defined as an industrial revolution, tied directly to radical changes in methods of production, having their decisive consequences over a relatively short period of time' (Rostow 1963: xvii).

For all the proponents of discontinuity, the new industrialization of the eighteenth century was both precursor and essence of change. Engels argued that the invention of the steam engine and the development of new machinery for manufacturing cotton in the second half of the eighteenth century brought the revolution. These inventions enabled machines to replace manual labour and factory based production to replace cottage industry. Thus was created the first industrial proletariat, an exploited and deprived mass whose poverty stood in stark contrast to the massive accumulations of wealth generated by the new industrial system and enjoyed by the capitalist classes (Engels 37ff). Toynbee's famous lectures given at Oxford in 1881–82 and published a few years later were close to Engels in concern and interpretation. Economic and social life were transformed by the Industrial Revolution as the cash nexus replaced personal relationships. 'The essence of the Industrial Revolution is the substitution of competition for the medieval regulations which had previously controlled the production and distribution of wealth' (Toynbee 85). Writing some eighty years later, E. P. Thompson stood in the same academic tradition when he advanced the explanation that new forms of industrial organization induced alienation between different sections of society and led to the formation of the working class between 1790 and 1830, forged under the twin pressures of economic exploitation and political repression (E. P. Thompson 212–13, 217).

The Marxist version of the Industrial Revolution perceived the change it brought as entirely detrimental and effected through the gross exploitation of the many by the few. But an alternative thesis which embodied the Industrial Revolution as the central event in economic change took a much kinder, indeed an enthusiastic view, of capitalist development. This version concentrated not on social relationships but on the transformation of industry wrought by new technology, and stressed the potential for increased production and wealth inherent in the new system. Mantoux was one of the earliest writers to express this, writing in the early years of the twentieth century, and set the Revolution in the four decades after 1760. By the end of that century, 'the great technical inventions including the most important invention of all, the steam engine, had all become practical realities . . . great empires of industry had begun to grow up, a factory proletariat made its appearance, the old trade regulations, already more than half destroyed, made way for the system of laissez faire . . . the stage was set; there was nothing left but to follow the working out of the drama' (Mantoux 42). This version has retained support and in recent years has been reaffirmed by some scholars (Hicks 145, 148; Gaski 232). The long progress of economic development 'operating erratically, but cumulatively, over a long period of time and in many places, reached a critical point in Britain, around the 1760s, yielding a series of inventive break-throughs and their rapid introduction into manufacturing, starting in the 1780s' (Rostow 1975: 190). Thus there was a fundamental discontinuity in British economic development, the essence of which was the advance of industrialization, and this represented the beginning of a new era for the entire world as the impulse of the first Industrial Revolution eventually spread out to other countries.

The establishment of a crucial phase of discontinuous transformation, defined by various authorities as different sub-periods within the century after 1750, necessarily determined the way in which both earlier and later periods were regarded. Prior to 1750, interest was mainly focused on the preparations for the break-through, identification of various preconditions and arguments as to whether or not they were necessary. The identification of economic advance before 1750 gave support to the advocates of a slow and lengthy period of preparation, and consequently eroded enthusiasm for the rather cataclysmic version of events favoured by Victorians like Engels, Toynbee and Cunningham. But the essential discontinuity was not abandoned. Pre-industrial preparatory development might be substantial, even impressive, but in the context of the later Revolution it remained essentially trivial (Flinn 94, Landes 3).

After the main impact of the Industrial Revolution faded, by 1830 or 1850, the historian's problem became how to explain the continuation of the process. Hobsbawm expressed this concern in vivid terms, 'how the material for the economic explosion was accumulated, how it was ignited; and we may add, what stopped the first explosion from fizzling out after an impressive initial bang?' (Hobsbawm 40). Subsequent economic performance was to be evaluated by the historians by the yardstick of the rate of growth achieved in the Industrial Revolution and especially by the ability of the economy to maintain the business supremacy and economic advantage won by Britain. Falling growth rates in the Victorian years, growing rivalry from American and German industry, together with the complaints of contemporary industrialists about the great depression in the 1870s and 1880s, led to the characterization of the period as one of decline. 'In essence, the vantage point from which the development of the nineteenth century economy is normally viewed is that from the "culmination" of the industrial revolution; that is, the period of Britain's supremacy based on the staple industries . . . Most approaches to the industrial revolution are implicitly teleological. The "goal" is basically the industrial structure that emerged at the height of Victorian prosperity, and the threads of that structure are then sought in the past . . . Thus the faltering of industrial activity from the 1870s and the economic problems of the inter-war period are almost inevitably discussed within the framework "what happened to the industrial revolution?" rather than "how is the recent economic structure to be explained?". This is because we have pre-selected the historical threads, and "base weighted" the study of British economic history' (Falkus 45–6). Hobsbawm voiced the preoccupation of many historians in the 1960s when he wrote, 'This sudden transformation of the leading and most dynamic industrial economy into the most sluggish and conservative, in the short space of thirty or forty years (1860–1890/1900) is the crucial question of British economic history' (Hobsbawm 178). Mathias described the late Victorian economy in similar terms. 'After a successful and active industrial youth, it seemed that the country's economy was settling down to a less strenuous, less competitive, but still comfortable middle-age' (1969: 257). Less indulgently, Landes painted a scornful picture of Britain 'basking in the complacent sunset of economic hegemony' (Landes 336).

While the interwar period has often been treated as an extension of late Victorian decline, and described as such, the more recent past has usually been ignored by historians. This neglect has been encouraged by the rigid predetermination of subjects and problems within the framework of the Industrial Revolution model. Such strands of investigation do not always stretch into the twentieth century in the same form in which they have been cast in an eighteenth-century context. One solution is to adopt different analytical frameworks for different historical periods. 'It may well be that the long-run growth factors operating in the relatively simple fragmented and competitive economy of the nineteenth century have given way to a more complex variety of factors in which short-run disruptions and resulting adjustments have become the dominating elements in economic activity. From the perspective of recent times the industrial revolution stands out as just one, albeit dramatic, landmark in the modernisation of society. New forces operated from about 1880 which in time moved the economy to a fundamentally different path, but a path which leads more securely to the present' (Falkus 62). Implicitly accepting the validity and practicality of this notion, recent texts and interpretations have tended to concentrate either on the period 1750–1914 or on part or all of the century after 1880.

The two main ingredients of the Industrial Revolution thesis are the fundamental discontinuity effected by the Revolution and the primacy of industrialization in that process and indeed as the essence of modern economic development. From these basic assumptions is derived the periodization and the important areas of investigation. In fact there has been a considerable modification in recent years of the dramatic presentation of earlier writers, and Rostow's reversion to a strong affirmation of discontinuity was widely criticized. Modification has not meant the abandonment of the essential thesis, rather that the Industrial Revolution retains its basic characteristics but is presented as a more gradual transformation, a revolution in slow motion. 'If one takes a long-term view of British economic development, say from 1700 to 1900 (or from 1750 to 1850, the traditional century of the Industrial Revolution), then it becomes obvious that there was in this period a radical shift in the structure of the economy, in the composition of total output, and in the distribution of employment, which gives concrete meaning to the concept of an industrial revolution. And in the rise of output, central influence can be attributed to the great technical breakthroughs in industry of the period 1760 to 1800; it was these which allowed the acceleration of economic growth' (Hartwell 156). Mathias, too, rejected the idea of a sudden and dramatic change while affirming the notion of a fundamental change in economic structure (1969: 2–4).

The general dilution of the revolutionary trauma has moved current perceptions of growth towards the tradition of evolutionary growth, which itself has a pedigree almost as long as the revolutionary paradigm. Writing in 1890, Marshall voiced a strong preference for an explanation in evolutionary terms, while Redford in 1931, and later Lipson and Clark, all rejected the idea of industrial revolution, and much has been inferred from Clapham's failure to use the term in any of his extensive writings. 'Nothing more remote from historical truth can well be imagined than the prevailing misconception that the inventions of the late eighteenth century involved a violent break with the past and effected an abrupt revolution in the tenor and rhythm of the national life . . . If we destroy the legend that the inventions suddenly revolutionised English society and gave birth to a new industrial order we can at least put in its place a more rational interpretation in which the mechanical changes appear as a natural development in line with the course of historical evolution – the climax of centuries of steady growth' (Lipson 188–9, 216–17).

Certainly there are great conceptual difficulties involved in any thesis invoking discontinuity, not least of which lies in the difficulty in measuring such phenomena. Most obvious is the fact that 'Whether continuity is viewed as constancy of direction, or an endogeny, or a periodicity, or as a long causal chain, or as a change in the rate of change – at all times it is the ordering hand of the historian that creates continuities or discontinuities' (Gerschenkron 38). Not surprisingly the problem in satisfactorily identifying and then justifying Rostow's take-off periods has generated severe criticism (Cairncross 132, Fores 183). The increase in quantitative analysis and the compilation of new series of statistics has not helped the cause of discontinuity (Whitehead 7–9). Interestingly, a recent statistical analysis set out to test for discontinuity both in the 1740s and 1780s and found against the former while identifying 'a dramatic, positive structural change around 1780' (Hausman/Watts 407). But the structural breaks identified in this study were almost entirely in microeconomic series, such as the production of paper, printed goods, beer and candles, together with trade indicators like net imports and exports. Such indices are not in themselves sufficient to provide an acceptable measure of aggregate macroeconomic change. The two best proximate indicators of aggregate change, total production and the producers' good index, both showed some increased growth around each 'turning point' but nothing which could realistically be termed a discontinuity.

VI

While the idea of discontinuity has been largely rejected or fallen into disuse the periodization to which it gave rise is still used as a basic framework within which to investigate development. The elongated revolution proposed by Hartwell has replaced the more extravagant and theatrical concepts. But considerable difficulties remain with the basic framework. As Falkus demonstrated, the identification of strands of important elements in one period may be completely unsuitable for an earlier or later one, and the confinement of so much discussion to a limited time period and a few 'key' issues is unacceptably restricting. The extensive discussion about the climacteric of the British economy in the late nineteenth century looks rather strange in the context of much higher growth in the twentieth century. In order to gain a fresh perspective on the long process of British economic development it is essential to break away from the rigid and narrow framework of industrial revolution periodization. Its limited and limiting perspective makes it suspect, and its inability to encompass the twentieth century as well as earlier periods render it invalid. But the main objection must be simply that it fails to fit the quantitative outline of long-term development described by recent work. All the quantitative indices show a slow but accelerating rate of growth, balanced growth encompassing most sectors of the economy and a very modest, if continuous, rate of structural change. Increased growth in the early nineteenth century and a small reduction in growth rates in the later part of the century require explanation, but their dimensions hardly warrant labels like 'industrial revolution' or 'great depression'.

Organizationally, the present study is divided into two main sections of approximately equal length and dealing respectively with the periods before and after 1914. Like all other divisions, this is less than satisfactory. As a half-way mark between 1700 and the present day, 1914 is too late in terms of chronology and too early in terms of the growth of national income. Two justifications can be offered in defence of this choice. A study embracing development over three centuries needs some division since such a long period is difficult to discuss as a unity, even when continuity is emphasized in the explanation. While it is not suggested that 1914 marks a major turning point, a better case can be made for that date than for many others for in a number of ways the twentieth century is different from the earlier period. The greater rate of world economic development and industrialization, greater dislocation in war and depression, and the increased role of the state, mark the experience of the twentieth century and contrast with earlier centuries. But apart from the convenience of dividing a long time period, the choice of 1914 reflects a value judgement as to the relative importance of the different phases of British economic development. In sharp contrast to many other treatments the twentieth century is here accorded as much attention as the two centuries which preceeded it.

The appropriate analytical framework is more easily chosen and less likely to be thought controversial. Since the focus of attention is upon macroeconomic growth, the conventional identities of macroeconomic analysis provide appropriate divisions. For each of the two long time periods, there are chapters on aggregate demand, investment, aggregate supply, trade and payments and, in the twentieth century, government. There is also a chapter on regional growth, since regional variations in structure, growth and welfare played a major although often neglected part in shaping British economic development in the long run.

PART II

1700 to 1914

2

Aggregate demand: wealth and income

I

The second section of this study investigates the mechanisms of economic growth in the eighteenth and nineteenth centuries which underlay the changes in aggregate long-term growth described in the first chapter. Attention will focus initially on the demand side of the economy. Aggregate demand depends, of course, on the size and rate of growth of national income. But the way in which income and accumulated wealth are distributed has a profound influence on both the size and composition of aggregate demand. There are several ways in which the distribution of national income can be described. One conventional measure allocates income into factor shares. For the eighteenth century, such estimates are necessarily generalized. The share of national income allocated to employment rose from 25–39 per cent in 1700 to about 44 per cent a century later (Deane/Cole 247, 252). More certain estimates indicate total labour income remained steady at about 54–58 per cent of national income in the second half of the nineteenth century (Matthews 164). Within that fairly constant share there was some reallocation away from wages and self-employment and in favour of salaries. The residual property income share included, in the eighteenth-century estimates, rent, profit, interest and self-employment lumped together. This category also retained a stable share of national income in the Victorian period, and its fall in the first half of the nineteenth century is exaggerated by the transfer of the self-employed to labour income. Within this broad group, there was substantial change in the later nineteenth century, principally at the expense of farm property income in favour of income from abroad.

Another familiar way of describing the distribution of income is by expenditure on consumption, investment, government and trade (Tables 2.1 and 8.3). The extremely high share of income allocated to consumption, despite the reduction during the war period 1790–1820 in favour of government spending, is the most outstanding feature of this distribution. Indeed,

27

Table 2.1 *Gross national product by category of expenditure (per cent)*

	Private consumption	Gross domestic investment	Government expenditure	Foreign investment
1761–70	83.9	8.1	7.5	0.5
1771–80	82.7	9.2	7.1	1.0
1781–90	79.7	11.7	7.2	1.4
1791–1800	74.6	13.1	11.2	1.1
1801–10	74.8	10.9	15.5	−1.2
1811–20	73.4	11.1	12.8	2.5
1821–30	80.6	11.7	5.0	2.7
1831–40	84.3	11.3	3.2	1.2
1841–50	83.2	11.9	3.5	1.4
1851–60	82.5	10.1	4.1	3.3

Source: C. H. Feinstein, 'Capital accumulation and the Industrial Revolution', in R. Floud and
   D. N. McCloskey (eds.), *The Economic History of Britain since 1700* Vol. I (Cambridge
   1981) p. 136.

for most of the century and a half after 1760 consumption expenditure
accounted for over 80 per cent of GNP (Gross National Product). But these
unavoidably high levels of aggregation of data necessarily limit what can be
inferred. More revealing, but statistically even more hazardous, are estimates of the distribution of income and wealth between different sections of
society. The earliest estimates for the sectoral distribution of wealth relate
to the years immediately before the First World War, and indicate a heavily
skewed distribution such that the top one per cent of wealth holders enjoyed
79 per cent of total national wealth while the top ten per cent enjoyed 92 per
cent of the total (Table 8.1). It seems most unlikely that wealth was more
equitably distributed at any time during the previous two centuries.

Rather more reliable and informative are the estimates for the distribution of income, which are the result of recent revisionary work (Table
2.2). These estimates depend substantially on the social arithmetic, at
random benchmark years, originally conducted by Gregory King 1688,
Joseph Massie 1759, Patrick Colquhoun 1801–03, and Dudley Baxter 1867,
covering the 'statistical dark age'. Until recently, historians had accepted
Soltow's important pioneering study on these social arithmetic estimates,
together with Bowley's estimates for the later nineteenth century. Soltow
had concluded that the distribution of income remained fairly stable
between 1688 and 1867, although in comparison with other economies
Britain did have an unusually uneven distribution of income. According to
Kuznets' estimates, the share of income allocated to the top five per cent of
recipients on the eve of the First World War ranged from 43 per cent in
Britain to between 24 and 33 per cent in Prussia, Saxony, Denmark, Norway

Table 2.2 *Estimates of income distribution (per cent)*

		Top 5%	Top 10%	Top 11–35%	Top 36–60%	Bottom 40%	Gini coefficient
A:	1688	27.6	42.0	26.0	16.7	15.4	0.468
	1759	31.2	44.4	25.8	14.1	15.8	0.487
	1801/3	29.8	45.4	28.0	13.3	13.4	0.519
	1867	45.1	52.7	20.8	11.7	14.8	0.551
B:	1688	29.9	44.0	30.1	15.0	10.9	0.541
	1759	31.2	44.4	26.7	15.3	13.7	0.509
	1801/3	32.7	47.9	29.4	12.5	10.3	0.577
	1867	46.0	53.4	21.3	12.1	13.2	0.577
C:	1867	46.8	52.4	32.4		15.2	0.538
	1880	49.4	54.2	28.8		17.0	0.520
	1913	43.8	49.8	33.0		17.2	0.502

Note: Data A:England and Wales, estimates exclude paupers
    Data B: England and Wales, estimates include paupers
    Data C: United Kingdom
Source: P. H. Lindert and J. G. Williamson, 'Reinterpreting Britain's social tables 1688–1913'
    Explorations in Economic History 20 (1983) pp. 98–9, 102.

and the United States (Kuznets 208–11). In a wider context this was even more remarkable. 'Indeed, the inequalities of Victorian England exceeded those of all advanced countries since the Second World War. Of the 70-odd countries yielding postwar estimates of the size distribution of income, only a handful in the throes of rapid population growth and early development – Iraq, Mexico, Brazil and ten other countries in Africa and Latin America – can match the unequal Workshop of the World in 1867' (Lindert/Williamson 1983a: 96).

These two scholars re-examined and reworked the social tables from King to Baxter, producing a new set of estimates for income distribution (Table 2.2). Contrary to Soltow's original estimates, increasing divergence in income distribution was found for the period 1688–1867. The share of income secured by both the top five per cent and the top ten per cent of recipients increased through this period, and particularly strongly in the nineteenth century. Reallocation between the three other component sectors, the top 11–35 per cent, 36–60 per cent and the bottom 40 per cent, is less clear cut. The highest of these groups lost ground before 1759, recovered somewhat in the later eighteenth century, but declined again during the first seven decades of the nineteenth century. The lower middle income group lost most ground in that period, perhaps reflecting a degree of redistribution within the middle income groups. The bottom group actually increased its share in the first half of both the eighteenth and nineteenth centuries, while losing in the latter half of the eighteenth century. These estimates include the 'pauper host' of uncertain size. Alternative estimates, excluding paupers, produced a similar distribution in general outline but with slightly changed sectoral shares. But the main pattern is quite clear. There was increasing inequality in the distribution of income to the benefit of the top ten per cent of income earners until the 1860s. Each of the other groups lost, especially the middle income categories. From the 1860s to 1914 inequality decreased. From 1867 to 1880, the upper and lower extremes still gained at the expense of the middle orders. But from 1880 onwards, the middle orders gained at the expense of the top ten per cent while the share of those at the bottom remained virtually static. While Lindert/Williamson marked 1867 as a watershed between periods of increasing and decreasing inequality in income distribution, the phase after 1880 marked an important shift in favour of middle incomes. From the perspective of the very long run, from 1688 to the First World War, the middle income orders lost almost ten per cent of the national income which was redistributed mostly to the highest ten per cent of incomes, leaving a very modest increase for the bottom 40 per cent.

What effect did these redistributions of income, set within the context of a growing national income, have upon consumption? Different economic theories have offered considerably different predictions. There are three principal hypotheses. Keynes proposed a thesis which became known as the absolute income hypothesis, and which argued that consumers spent a relatively fixed proportion of their income, saving the rest, and that this share was determined by the absolute size of that income. The smaller the income the greater the share necessarily consumed, perhaps all of it or more, thus incurring debt. But at increasingly higher levels of income a proportionately greater share would be saved. According to such a thesis an increasingly wealthy society or one which allocated a progressively larger share of income to the better off, thus increasing the inequality of distribution, would thereby reduce the aggregate level of demand by distributing income in favour of those who would save it. Later and alternative theses have been less impressed than Keynes apparently was by society's moderation in demand for goods and services or its capacity to satiate such desires. The relative income hypothesis, formulated by Duesenberry, suggests that consumption and saving decisions are not taken in relation to the absolute level of income but relatively in comparison to the consumer spending of a peer group. Emulation is the key to spending behaviour. Thus a rising income does not necessarily imply a fall in spending. The share of income allocated to consumption may remain steady, at say 90 per cent, and will thus rise in absolute terms because additional spending will be required to keep up with the peer group. In an economy which behaved according to the relative income hypothesis, increasing inequality of income with a redistribution of spending power in favour of the better off would not reduce aggregate consumption but could increase it. Alternatively, redistribution in favour of greater equality of income could actually reduce the level of aggregate demand because pressure towards emulative spending amongst the more affluent might be reduced by their impoverishment relative to other sectors of society but not relative to their peers. While this thesis is a modification, in part a radical one, of the Keynesian thesis, the third strain of theoretical argument represents a quite different perspective. The permanent income hypothesis and the life cycle hypothesis are essentially complementary. Both argue that consumption behaviour is not determined by short-run considerations of current income, but by long-run considerations and expected life time earnings. Borrowing and overdrafts can be used together with savings to smooth out the effects of short-term fluctuations in earning or spending. Thus the relationship between consumption, the accumulation of assets, and income is determined by long-term individual or household planning. Current income is thus a poor predictor of consumption; the appropriate indicator is long-term income or wealth. Changes in the distribution of income under such a system would experience no change in aggregate consumption, since all sectors of society would continue to consume according to their long-term permanent income (Shapiro 188–92).

All the above described theories were, of course, derived in the context of twentieth-century affluent societies and not with particular regard to developing economies. Indeed it may be that all of these theories have a partial application to earlier historical situations varying according to the needs of different sectors of society. Principal interest must surround the very wealthiest section of society. The top ten per cent of incomes obtained over half the total increase in income between the late seventeenth century and 1867. It seems improbable that this exceedingly wealthy group would reduce its consumer spending in accord with the predictions of the absolute income thesis, and there is no literary evidence to support such an interpretation. Either of the other two theses offer plausible explanations. Wealthy society was very much accustomed to emulative consumer behaviour in this period, sufficient to keep up its propensity to spend. But the permanent income hypothesis, derived in the context of affluent modern societies, is probably applicable in regard to the very wealthy in the eighteenth and nineteenth centuries. Here was a group which could take a perspective on consumption well beyond the problems of immediate subsistence. Furthermore, they were able to borrow, especially those who could offer land as certain collateral for any debt, and thereby could fund current consumption out of future income or anticipated inheritance. There are important implications for aggregate consumption which follow from such a heavy concen-

tration of income, and of increases in income, into a few hands. It allowed
the growth of consumer good industries and services, and a diversification of
demand, which would have been inhibited or even prevented had there been
a more equitable income distribution and demand had been confined to
satisfying a limited range of basic needs. It may well be, therefore, that an
increase in income inequality might not only be a probable outcome of
economic growth, as Kuznets suggested, but actually beneficial to its
generation.

The propensity to spend income is obviously less variable in response to
change at the lower levels of the national income distribution, especially
before 1914. The substantial number of paupers who appear in estimates
clearly witness to that (Lindert/Williamson 1983a: 101). Throughout the
eighteenth century those in poverty were estimated to comprise over ten per
cent of the population, and at the beginning of that century to be as many as
one quarter of the total. While this proportion fell through the nineteenth
century, its scale must remain unsure until the later decades of that period.
Certainly it is reasonable to surmise that all those in the bottom 40 per cent
category spent all their income on the necessities of life, and that the niceties
of theories about the propensity to consume income are totally irrelevant to
them. The interpretation of the behaviour of the middle income groups is
rather less easy. The increase in income share of the higher middle income
group in the second half of the eighteenth century coincides roughly with
Eversley's identification of a consumer boom in the period 1750–80, and
with McKendrick's postulated consumer expansion in the later decades of
the century. How did this increased share of income affect their propensity
to spend? The permanent income hypothesis would suggest no change, but
the relative income hypothesis would indicate an increase in spending as the
share of the group increased and thereby fostered emulative spending. This
latter seems more probable. But by the same token, this theory would
suggest a reduction in the propensity to spend in the first half of the
nineteenth century as the sectoral share of income fell and emulative spending pressure diminished. For the present this must remain conjecture, but
literary evidence does not suggest decreased spending by any social group in
either of these centuries.

It seems most probable that the reallocation of income, which was so
marked between the mid eighteenth and mid nineteenth centuries, did not
reduce the aggregate propensity to spend. Indeed it most probably increased
it in view of the emulative social pressures on the highest income group, its
capacity to augment income by borrowing, and the redistribution of income
in its favour. The effects of the shift towards greater income equality in the
later decades of the nineteenth century are less certain. In the three decades
before the First World War there was a clear shift in the distribution of

income away from the top ten per cent in favour of the middle income groups. This trend can also be found in Bowley's estimates, in the relatively quick growth in what he called 'intermediate incomes', that is salaried incomes under £160 per annum and thus not liable to income tax (Bowley 16). This trend coincided with a fall in the share of national expenditure allocated to consumption which was quite marked after the turn of the century. This change reflected both a relative increase in net foreign investment, possibly a reallocation of spending by the wealthiest sections of society, and a relative increase in government expenditure. This latter was, in part, a welfare transfer in favour of the less well off. The implications for consumer spending are further confused by the possible increase in saving by the middle income groups favoured by the changes in income distribution. A growing awareness of the need to make provision for illness and a longer life expectancy could persuade such middle class people to allocate more of their income to saving for old age. If this relative shift of income to the middle classes was accompanied by a decreasing propensity to consume on their part, and the behaviour of other sections of the community remained unchanged, the trend towards greater equality of income could have stimulated a reduction in the aggregate level of current consumption. This could constitute a partial explanation of the fall in the share of national expenditure allocated to consumption in the Edwardian years. In sum, the aggregate level of consumption grew during the eighteenth and nineteenth centuries at a similar rate to that of national income. Changes in the distribution of income towards greater inequality probably increased consumer spending, while the trend towards greater income equality in the later part of the nineteenth century may have dampened down consumer spending. More important, however, was probably the effect of these changes on the composition of demand rather than on its size.

II

The very wide divergence in the share of wealth and income accruing to different sectors of society, and the increase in that disparity through much of this period, had a major influence on the composition of effective aggregate demand. It is important, therefore, to examine the sources of wealth and especially of the exceptionally prosperous top ten per cent of society. Much the greater part of accumulated wealth belonged to the landed classes throughout this period, and this same group received most of the highest incomes. These two centuries were, in fact, the era of the great landed estate, representing massive concentrations of wealth and abundant consumption. To afford the pleasures of wealthy society required at least an income of £5,000 per year at the end of the eighteenth century, so it was estimated, and twice that sum to be on the safe side. This compares somewhat starkly with the average nominal income of £91 per annum (Lindert/ Williamson 1983a: 102). If such an income was to be obtained directly from the land in rental, an estate of 10,000 to 20,000 acres was needed. Few of the great landlords had less than 5,000 acres while some estates exceeded 50,000 acres. There were about 400 families in England and Wales alone whose income ranged between £5,000 and £50,000 at this time, around an average of £10,000 per annum. A further group of families classed as gentry, with an income ranging from £1,000 to £5,000, numbered an additional 14,000 to 25,000 families (Mingay 19, 26). All such families would have enjoyed rising incomes from the mid eighteenth century onwards as land values and hence rents rose considerably. The revised social arithmetic estimates show a similar concentration of high incomes in the hands of lords, temporal and spiritual, barons and knights, although by 1801 a modest group of some 2,000 eminent merchants and bankers were estimated to receive an average annual income of £2,600 (Lindert/Williamson 1982: 393, 396, 400).

Great landowners remained the richest section of British society until the late nineteenth century. In 1882 there were 29 gross landed incomes in excess of £75,000 a year, all of which had increased during the nineteenth century and whose capital assets exceeded the wealth of the richest industrialists until after the First World War. While these gross figures may give a rather misleading impression of the disposable income of such families because of the debts incurred by many landowners, the scale is nevertheless impressive (Rubinstein 1981: 194–6). Further only one of the massive incomes listed belonged to a newcomer with recently acquired wealth, Lord Overstone, a banker. All the other families were long established landed powers whose acquisition of real estate extended over several centuries. 'In every county there was a persistent large core of very ancient families, who were usually also the richest, who set the pace and prevented any erosion of traditional social standards by the swirling periphery of transient newcomers. The system was thus flexible enough to admit newcomers, but stable enough to absorb them without discomfort . . . what influx there was of new men was mainly of professional or office-holders rather than of merchants or bankers. As for industrialists, they are simply not present, except for some brewers in Hertfordshire. The unity of the English elite society was a unity of the land and business, and not at all of land and industry' (Stone/Stone 280).

Nine landowners who died between the 1830s and the 1930s left estates worth over two million pounds (Rubinstein 1981: 202). The fact that the very large estates were established by the middle of the eighteenth century and that the following century was a prosperous one for agriculture ensured little change in ownership. But even the wealthiest were not immune to adversity, sometimes self inflicted. The Duke of Buckingham and Chandos accumulated debts worth £1.5 million in the mid nineteenth century, while both the Duke of Portland and the Duke of Hamilton had to sell off family assets. The former sold Bulstrode House and part of an estate in Cumberland worth £350,000, while the latter parted with paintings and other effects worth £400,000. Thus some land came onto the market and was available to the newly wealthy. Such estates were usually much smaller than the established aristocratic estates and were often found in the Home Counties where modest estates of very expensive land changed hands. In the eighteenth century some overseas merchants, brewers and bankers became gentrified, and in the following century the professional classes joined them. Merchant bankers such as Baring, Rothschild and Morrison, merchants like Matheson and some industrialists, including the iron manufacturing families of Guest and Baird, bought land. But their impact on landed society was small. 'Foremost is the fact that from the beginnings of the Industrial Revolution to the 1880s, the British landed aristocracy was increasingly becoming a caste-like and socially-isolated group, distancing itself from, and distanced from, the newer business magnates, who found it nearly impossible in many cases to gain full acceptance into the inner circles of high landed society . . . As far as I am aware, there is no instance of a major nineteenth-century landowner receiving more than half of his income from non-landed sources like stocks or mineral royalties, just as there is no instance of a major nineteenth-century businessman receiving more than half his income from the land' (Rubinstein 1981: 219).

Nevertheless, the landed classes did derive income, often considerable income, from sources other than the land. A venerably traditional source of income lay in the patronage of government office, appropriately known as 'old corruption'. In the early nineteenth century, sinecures such as the commissionerships for the Affairs of India, Tellers of the Exchequer, Lords of the Bedchamber, Constable of Dover Castle, Clerk of the Rolls in Ireland, or the Lord Vice-Admiral of Scotland were all worth a few thousand pounds a year. Three brothers of the Marquess of Hertford together accumulated several such duties and thereby generated a combined income of £17,000 a year (F. M. L. Thompson 72–3). In the eighteenth century, such offices provided some useful perks in addition to the basic income. While the Paymaster of the Forces received £4,000 a year in the early eighteenth century, the income was modest in comparison to the commissions on foreign loans, and the interest on cash balances maintained to pay the armed forces to which he also had access. Several estates were modernized, renovated and extended from such income (Mingay 74).

Another important means by which wealth could be acquired, whether newly sought by the aspiring upwardly mobile or as a means to restore the former glory of an impoverished family, lay through judicious marriage. The Sutherland family, unquestionably one of the wealthiest dukedoms in the nineteenth century, owed much of their financial success to the art of absorbing heiresses (Richards 1973: 5). In the late seventeenth century, one member of the Grosvenor family, who were Cheshire gentry at the time, married the heiress to land in London on which now stands Grosvenor Square, Park Lane, Victoria, Belgravia and Pimlico. By the 1880s, the direct descendant, now Duke of Westminster, had an estate worth £300,000 (Rubinstein 1981: 194). Other marriages brought wealth from land and commerce. Land in Bloomsbury and estates in Essex and Surrey bought with proceeds from the East India trade all contributed to the estates of the later Dukes of Bedford. Marriage could also provide a useful holding in the 'funds'. The grand-daughter of Sir Ambrose Crowley, ironmaster and financier, brought as part of her dowry to her marriage in 1756, South Sea Stock worth £14,000 together with £6,250 in the City of London's Orphan Stock. In return, the Earl of Ashburnham promised to spend £8,000 in purchasing and furnishing a house in London for his new wife who was also provided with a private income of £500 a year (Mingay 76–8).

Rising land values represented an obvious source of income from estates, whether from rents or farming. But estates with mineral reserves of coal or iron provided another source of income. This increased considerably in the nineteenth century, and some estates operated their own mining companies. In the 1830s, Lord Durham had ten mines worth £540,000 in operation in north east England. In 1896 he sold fourteen collieries and nineteen steamships to another northern magnate, Sir James Joicey. In the West Riding, both the Duke of Norfolk and Earl Fitzwilliam owned land on the Yorkshire coalfield. From the late eighteenth century, the Wentworth Woodhouse estate of the Fitzwilliam family developed collieries, ironworks, blast furnaces, ironstone pits, a china works and a tar works. Most operations were leased to outsiders, but some of the activities were run as part of the estate. Coal mining became increasingly important to many estates in the course of the nineteenth century. In the last three decades of that century the enormous increase in mineral income not only accounted for most of the growth in the income of the Wentworth Woodhouse estate but, by 1901, comprised 67 per cent of the total income (J. T. Ward 47–50). The great expansion of mining in the Victorian period, together with the fall in agricultural prices and rents towards the end of the century, meant that mineral income became increasingly important on many favoured estates. The Duke of Northumberland's income from minerals grew from £3,000 a year in 1800 to £25,000 by the 1850s. It remained stable for the next quarter of a century, and contributed an income just under one quarter of that obtained from farm rents. By the eve of the First World War, mineral income exceeded

£73,000 annually and contributed 40 per cent of gross income as compared to 20 per cent in 1880. When estate expenditure is deducted, mineral income contributed 60 per cent of net estate income in 1914 (F. M. L. Thompson 266, 317).

Perhaps even more desirable than fertile rural acres or land sitting on rich coal deposits was real estate in the growing urban centres, providing increasing ground rents and the possibility of building development. The financial rewards of building in London were obvious early in the eighteenth century. The Grosvenor estate in London earned some £2,000 per annum in the 1720s, but by 1779 it was generating £7,000 and rivalling the income from the family estate in Cheshire. By the turn of the century, the metropolitan estate was bringing in an income of £12,000 per annum. Other squares and streets built in Georgian London were financed by the aristocracy as investors as well as purchasers. Squares such as Bedford, Portland, Cavendish, Portman and, of course, Grosvenor were so funded. By the end of the nineteenth century these properties represented the most valuable real estate in the world, and they remained untaxed until 1909. Urban land and building development generated income and wealth elsewhere, albeit on a less gargantuan scale. The Marquess of Bute owned much of the land on which Cardiff was built, and the growth of the city itself was largely stimulated by the coal trade passing through the docks built by the Bute family in the early 1830s (Daunton 1977). The Marquess of Donegal dominated Belfast in similar fashion until financial difficulties prompted the family to sell off much of their estate. On a smaller scale, the Ramsden family owned most of Huddersfield and introduced the canal and later the railway to the town.

But residential building, following the metropolitan precedent, provided both a genteel and lucrative way of augmenting a fortune. The spa of Buxton in Derbyshire was developed exclusively by the Dukes of Devonshire, including the construction of a crescent in the 1790s intended to provide a northern rival to Bath. Eastbourne, begun in the 1850s, was largely owned and developed by the Cavendish family. Nor did they stop there but funded Burlington Arcade in London, endowed the subsequently famous scientific laboratory bearing their name at Cambridge, as well as engaging in other building developments at Barrow, Carlisle, Keighley and Chiswick. Eastbourne represented a provincial seaside version of the metropolis and 'exemplified to perfection the degree to which middle-class aspirations were in many ways a scaled-down version of aristocratic cultural values' (Cannadine 383). Between 1850 and 1893, the Devonshires spent £711,000 on their Eastbourne investment. While this may have represented a high capital outlay for a modest rate of return, it can hardly have been an investment fraught with hazard, rather another example of the Victorian preference for gilt edged securities. By 1885 ground rents from the Eastbourne estates were bringing in an income of £10,000 per year. Other aristocratic families invested in seaside estates in the Victorian period, at Folkestone, Torquay, Bournemouth, Southport, Skegness and Bexhill. Nor was this the preserve of individuals, Sidney Sussex College, Cambridge being prominent in financing the development of its estate at Cleethorpes. By the end of the century, returns on ground rents were increasing. The Ramsden family income from Huddersfield grew from £42,000 in 1869 to £63,000 by 1919. The Bute estate in Cardiff yielded £28,000 in the 1890s, similar to the return on the Calthorpe estate in Birmingham, while amongst the higher echelons the Bedford estates in London were realizing £100,000 by the 1880s and in the following decade the Duke of Westminster was receiving £135,000 from his Mayfair estate alone (Cannadine 415).

The full range of investment outlets were obviously available to the wealthy, offering numerous opportunities to augment their substantial wealth. It has been suggested that many landowners might have spread their assets more widely than hitherto in the late nineteenth century as land rents fell. One illustration would appear to be the Duke of Portland whose investments included brewery shares, collieries in Britain and overseas, investments in Asian and South American railways as well as in South African gold mines. The Marquess of Salisbury held consols, railway stock and London ground rents in his portfolio (F. M. L. Thompson 307). Like building, transport offered abundant opportunities for investment in this period. The Sutherland fortune was based in part on the fact that the family were heirs to the revenues from the Duke of Bridgewater's canal which had produced a return of over £2.2 million between 1803 and 1833 (Richards 1973: 118). Early involvement in railway stock brought in further lucrative dividends. As is well known, many landowners received ample compensation from railway companies which needed to cross their land. Other landowners were active in funding railways, especially when this facilitated the exploitation of their mineral reserves. The Earl Fitzwilliam was involved in the South Yorkshire Railway while the Furness Railway, a purely mineral line, was funded by Lord Burlington and the Duke of Buccleuch. Other landowners invested in harbours and docks to transport their coal, such as the Marquess of Bute at Cardiff, the Marquess of Londonderry at Seaham, County Durham, and the Earl of Lonsdale at Whitehaven.

The sources of income of the wealthy were many and varied from land, mineral rights and mining, farming and rents, urban building and ground rents, government office to stocks and securities. Many of these sources of income, if properly husbanded, could be used to greatly increase individual or family assets. Given the immense concentration of wealth and such a plethora of opportunities it is not difficult to see why there was such a strong redistribution in favour of the wealthy in the century after 1750. Further down the social scale, life was more modest and the sources of income more prosaic. For the vast majority of people, income was obtained entirely from employment. For much of these two centuries employment was rising, as were some wage rates and activity rates. The impact of this growth on effective demand depended on the distribution of pay between workers and employment between different sectors of the economy. Wage rates for full-time adult male workers appear to have remained fairly constant through the second half of the eighteenth century but showed substantial divergence, in favour of skilled employment, from the end of the Napoleonic Wars until mid century or a little later. Between 1781 and 1851, white collar wage rates increased by 350 per cent, while blue collar rates increased by 99 per cent and farm labourers, at the bottom of the social and economic scale, by only 64 per cent (Lindert/Williamson 1983b: 13). It might well be that, in spite of the general increase in incomes, the very poorest section of the community were left out of the general advance and might have become worse off (Crafts 1980: 186–7). Both the optimists and the pessimists in the long debate on standards of living would thus have a partial justification for their case.

While pay rates shifted in favour of skilled workers in the first half of the nineteenth century, employment growth was more oriented towards the less skilled and thus, at an aggregate level, moderated the effect of the wage trend (Williamson 1982: 15). Both effects obviously helped increase demand, but was this sufficient to produce the stimulus McKendrick suggested? Like Eversley, he focused on the period 1750–80. Eversley had argued that an upsurge of spending in that period depended on about 150,000 people rising to incomes over £50 a year. McKendrick estimated that both the effect and the number of people were greater. He suggested that the share of the total population with incomes in the range of £50 to £400 increased from 15 per cent to 25 per cent (1982: 24). Such figures would imply an increase of about three quarters of a million people in England and Wales alone on current estimates for late eighteenth-century population. 'I intend to argue that the surplus over subsistence produced by such earning would be particularly likely to be spent on the consumer industries which flourished in the early Industrial Revolution, and to suggest that such spending had a disproportionate effect on boosting home demand because of the consequential effects it had on class competition, social emulation and emulative spending' (McKendrick 1974: 187). Williamson's estimates for the income of a skilled textile worker suggest an income of £40–50 in the later eighteenth century and £58–67 between 1815 and the middle of the nineteenth century (1982: 48). McKendrick's argument must rely heavily on textile employment for two reasons. It was the main employment growth sector outside agriculture which was the most lowly paid, and the thesis relies on an increase in family rather than adult male income. It was the increased employment opportunities for women and children which, in McKendrick's view, enabled family incomes to pass the £50 mark (1974: 172–3, 184). Even though such additional workers earned substantially less than the adult males, several workers could increase the family income to as much as four times the normal male income. The thesis is certainly plausible, but the post 1815 period seems more likely to have produced such a stimulus than the later eighteenth century. Certainly Eversley's estimate appears to be both too small in numbers and too early in time. The post 1815 period witnessed both an increase in textile production and employment considerably greater than hitherto and, as indicated in chapter 1, witnessed an increase in the rate of growth of aggregate GDP much more impressive than any earlier acceleration.

The later decades of the nineteenth century saw another shift in the structure of incomes. From the middle of the century sectoral income differentials fell and and there was a marked trend towards convergence between different employment incomes. The trend in employment augmented rather than offset this effect as it had earlier. There was a rising skill level in the majority of employment sectors and this combined with the decline in the size of the lowest skill group, agricultural labourers, to push upward the average level of skill. But it was the wage effect rather than the employment mix which brought about the convergence in wage rates (Williamson 1982: 20–2). This upward shift in average incomes in the later nineteenth century probably contributed to the shift in income distribution in favour of the middle classes. There was a considerable increase in the number of white collar workers in the second half of the nineteenth century, one estimate puts the number of such workers at 144,000 in 1851 and 918,000 in 1911 (Crossick 19). Despite the convergence in incomes, professional employment was far more remunerative throughout these centuries than even the leading skilled manual occupations and, consequently, was far more potent in creating demand. Williamson's estimates for male earnings in the first half of the eighteenth century placed professional people such as solicitors, barristers, engineers, clergymen and government servants at the top of the wage league, and far above agricultural workers and labourers (1982: 48). A similar pattern appears in Routh's estimates for annual incomes on the eve of the First World War, as indicated by group averages of £328 for higher paid professionals, £106 for skilled manual workers, and £63 for unskilled manual workers. While the peak of manual income was represented by railway engine drivers earning £119 and coalface workers earning £112 per annum, professionals such as lawyers and doctors received four or five times as much, while the upper realms of the Civil Service found Principals paid £855 and Deputy Secretaries paid £1,500 (Routh 63, 73, 101, 120). The growth of industrial incomes in the nineteenth century and, on a larger scale, the growth of professional services augmented aggregate demand. But before the First World War the very wealthy continued to dominate in spending power. By 1913 the top ten per cent of incomes still accounted for almost half the total national expenditure.

III

The small and affluent group which comprised high society enjoyed wealth on a scale sufficient to support a standard of living far beyond the basic necessities of life. Indeed the massive concentration of wealth paid for an opulent lifestyle for the privileged members of fashionable society, and in so doing provided a large and diversified effective demand. The high point of the social year was the London season which drew the upper echelons of society from the shires for the winter months. Expenditure was considerable for maintaining or renting a suitable metropolitan property, paying for balls and receptions, and the shopping spree which could only be properly indulged in the capital. Eighteenth-century expenditures included a supper and masked ball provided by the Duke of Devonshire at a cost of a thousand pounds, while the second Duke of Kingston spend two thousand pounds in a fortnight in 1752. The Duke of Bedford kept over forty servants at his London house, and their wages alone totalled £860 per annum (Mingay 158). For the summer months rural society had to suffice, indeed the lesser gentry had to make do with its pleasures for the entire year. But this could also be expensively lavish both in the provision of necessary comforts and requisite hospitality.

One of the most obvious manifestations of conspicuous consumption lay in building, including new construction, renovation, extension and interior decoration. During the eighteenth century, Chatsworth was rebuilt at a cost of over £40,000, while Audley End cost over £100,000 to build and the Marquess of Rockingham spent £83,000 on Wentworth Woodhouse over a twenty year period (Mingay 160). To the cost of renovation must be added the necessary expenditure incurred in running such a household, providing entertainment, and maintaining the home farm and the usual stables and kennels. Costs ranged from a few thousand a year to over ten thousand pounds for a substantial establishment in the eighteenth century. Construction continued unabated into the nineteenth century. The Stafford family, later to acquire the Dukedom of Sutherland, spent over £150,000 in completing and extending Stafford House in London, and a further £50,000 on decoration and furniture between 1827–40, in addition to the purchase cost of £80,000. At the same time the family spent heavily on their country estates. Lillieshall House was rebuilt at a cost of £80,000, construction work at Trentham cost £123,000, reconstruction at Dunrobin amounted to £60,000, and Cliveden House was built for £30,000, and then rebuilt after being destroyed by fire, all between 1825 and 1850 (Richards 1973: 16). But all this spending fell well within the compass of the family income which, apart from two million pounds in returns from the Bridgewater Canal Trust in the first three decades of the nineteenth century, included interest from investments in government stock which brought it £34,000 in a single year, 1833 (Richards 1973: 288). Between 1852 and 1866 Alnwick Castle was reconstructed at a cost of £320,000, providing employment for 800 men at the peak of activity (F. M. L. Thompson 92). Illustrations of this kind abound in the literature. Besides providing a most congenial lifestyle, such properties were good investments. The Duke of Northumberland received £497,000 in compensation in 1874 when his house in the Strand was bought by the Metropolitan Board of Works to be demolished in order to widen the street (F. M. L. Thompson 104–5).

Such building was but a part of the affluent life. An appropriate range, volume and quality of consumer goods constituted necessary acquisitions. Food, drink, fashionable clothing, furniture, carriages and works of art, all found a ready market. Great occasions such as births, marriages and funerals were celebrated with costly ostentation, and were augmented by lavish entertainment. Sport, in particular, comprised an important and very expensive social activity for the wealthy. In the later eighteenth century, Lord Grosvenor spent £7,000 per year on horse racing while, at the turn of the century, the Earl Fitzwilliam spent £2,000 to £2,500 on his ordinary riding horses, £500 on his kennels, and a further £1,500 to £3,000 on his racing stables at Wentworth Woodhouse (Mingay 151, F. M. L. Thompson 97). Hunting was an expensive sport, and cost the Duke of Cleveland up to £1,500 per annum in the mid nineteenth century. Gambling was a popular sport about which few figures for 'expenses' have been computed. The social round extended beyond London and the native shires to include the seaside and spa towns. From Bath and Tunbridge Wells, the height of eighteenth-century fashion, the number of watering places increased in the following century, from Scarborough and Harrogate in the north to Brighton and much of the south coast, often founded and funded by the aristocracy themselves.

The maintenance of such a lifestyle, apart from considerable finance, needed a large host of servants. Even the better off gentry kept over a dozen. The Best family, brewers of Chatham with an income of about £6,000 a year in the late eighteenth century, kept a house in Chatham and one at Boxley on the North Downs. Thirteen servants were employed at the latter (Mingay 216, 230). While the very wealthy employed more servants, they did not always do so in direct proportion to their wealth. Even so, domestic service remained a major form of employment throughout the nineteenth century and servants were employed in many middle-class households at the end of the century.

Below the extensive and varied consumer demand peculiar to the highest levels of society, demand focused heavily on the basic necessities of life. At the lower levels of income in advanced economies as well as in the greater part of developing societies, much of household income is usually devoted to food and drink. Various estimates suggest that the share of expenditure so allocated, for all households in Britain, fell within the range 50–75 per cent in the eighteenth and nineteenth centuries. Even for the poorest households the share of spending so disposed did not exceed 70–75 per cent (Shammas 91). Certainly spending on food fell as a share of total spending as income rose. A sample taken by the Board of Trade in 1889 indicated the share at 87 per cent for incomes in the £28–40 range, falling to 50–60 per cent for incomes between £40–100, and less than 45 per cent for higher levels of income (Fraser 34). Another survey taken in 1901 showed spending on food, drink and tobacco falling from 50.4 per cent of spending at £78 per annum to 27.8 per cent in the country or 33.9 per cent in town for an income of £1,800 (Minchinton 1973: 121–2).

But even in the eighteenth century there was a strong trend towards the consumption of a more diverse range of foodstuffs. In the seventeenth century, new commodities made their appearance in the national diet, including tea, rice, potatoes and sugar and even became incorporated in poor-house catering. During these centuries there were several changes in preference as, for example, brown bread lost favour while meat, fish, potatoes, biscuits and cakes grew in popularity. By the eve of the First World War, almost one third of food expenditure went on meat, poultry and eggs, while another third was spent on bread, cereals and dairy products. Sugar and confectionary comprised another important expenditure as did vegetables. While there was a marked increase in several foodstuffs, drink was not neglected. The return from duty on gin increased tenfold during the first three decades of the eighteenth century. Rising grain prices turned attention back to beer, and the average annual consumption increased to 33.9 gallons per head by 1800 (Minchinton 1973: 134). Changes in fashion pushed this average down and then up again in the course of the next century. Tea provided a popular alternative, or complement. Falling prices helped by reduced duties helped extend the market for tea and per capita consumption increased from 1.4 lb to 6.2 lb in the course of the nineteenth century. Sugar also became cheaper and more popular, consumption rising from 6–8 lb per person in the mid eighteenth century to 78 lb per head by the First World War. Tobacco similarly doubled its per capita sales in the nineteenth century. But not all products were exotic commodities from the new world, nor did they all increase in sales per head. In the late nineteenth century, per capita consumption of wheat and potatoes fell, while there was a large increase in consumption of meat, bacon, milk, butter, sugar and tea.

While food accounted for the greater part of most household budgets, other essential expenditures included clothing, accounting for 10–15 per cent of spending, and housing, rates and rent which accounted for up to one third of spending. In these commodity ranges too, there was a considerable variation in spending patterns between income groups. According to the late nineteenth-century surveys, spending on clothing represented a small share of the outlay of the lowest incomes, as little as two per cent at the very bottom, ranged between 9–15 per cent of intermediate income spending and then fell relatively but not, of course, absolutely for the higher incomes. Lower income groups spent a greater share of their income on housing than did the more prosperous. At the end of the nineteenth century, this ranged from one eighth of a middle-class income of £2,000 per annum to one third of a working man's income (Fraser 44). In the 1901 survey, basic provision for food, shelter and clothing absorbed virtually all of the lowest quoted income of £78 per year, although there must have been many family incomes which fell considerably below that figure. Higher incomes were able to purchase a wider range of goods and services. From £150 and upward, such spending included between 5–15 per cent on servants' wages and accommodation, and 6–8 per cent on holidays and travel. Newspapers, books, stationery, entertainment and charity were all encompassed within such incomes, as indeed was provision for medical attention, and allowances for spending by wife or husband. By the later Victorian years, the growth of professional and middle-class occupations and incomes represented an important broadening of the consumer society which a century earlier had been so limited in numbers.

IV

Consumer spending remained the major sector within the national income expenditure categories throughout this period. Two of the other divisions, trade and investment are considered in other chapters. The remaining category is government spending. Historians have often taken the view that government was economically passive for practical purposes prior to 1914 and that active involvement by the state in economic affairs, at least in Britain, was postponed until the twentieth century. There is much to support this view, especially if government intervention is defined as intentional involvement rather than as a by-product of some other activity. But in the eighteenth and nineteenth centuries, government did exert a considerable influence upon economic development. This came principally from the frequent wars engaged in during the eighteenth century, and the resultant need for the government to pay for them in an age before the benefits of income tax had been discovered. Most government revenue came from indirect taxation, from customs dues and the land tax. The former influenced demand for some consumer goods and restricted the consumption of some taxed imports, while the effects of the latter seem to have been borne and accommodated without too much difficulty. But the government needed an income well in excess of the proceeds from such taxation, and had to resort to the money market to secure such funds, to such a degree that government stock became known as the 'funds'. Until the Napoleonic Wars, which generated a need for money on a much larger scale than before, additional expenditure was met by borrowing, sometimes as much as three quarters of the required sum. This had an extremely important influence on the growth of the financial market and its constituent institutions, as well as bringing about some redistribution of income (Mathias/O'Brien 623–4). But the longer and much more costly Napoleonic Wars needed taxation on incomes, and over half the cost of that war was met out of taxation, consequently diverting resources away from more productive use. Indeed the size of the war debt has been estimated at 11.5 per cent of national income in the 1790s, and 8.5 per cent between 1791 and 1820, compared to 5.0 per cent over the three previous decades (Williamson 1984: 697–8). Williamson has argued that the cost of the war was so great that it diverted resources on such a scale as to 'crowd out' the process of industrialization. Without the war, he estimated, there would have been a greater growth of manufacturing output and trade which in turn would have increased the rate of growth of income by 1.51 per cent per annum during the war period. As for government spending, both the beneficial effects in stimulating the growth of the financial markets and the deleterious effects in diverting resources to war were, in the eighteenth century, the result of political rather than economic activities. Since the two were often extremely closely linked any computation of the net effect of government action on economic development is extremely difficult.

While the Napoleonic Wars greatly increased the ratio of government spending to national income to a peak of 29 per cent in 1814, it fell sharply after the war and remained stable at 9–11 per cent until the 1890s (Veverka 114, Peacock/Wiseman 37). At the end of the Napoleonic Wars, the principal recipients of government spending were the military, servicing the accumulated national debt which was largely a legacy of war, and local government expenditure on poor relief. The decline in the ratio of public spending through the greater part of the nineteenth century was mainly a result of reduced military spending, only the Crimean War breaking the long peace. This reduction was sufficiently great not only to reduce the overall spending ratio but also encompassed a fivefold increase in local government spending. A large range of additional responsibilities were imposed on local government, including road construction and maintenance, housing and sanitation, public health, and some elementary educational provision. Much of the payment made by central government took the form of transfers, either to individuals or institutions, as in the case of the main item, debt repayment, or in educational grants and subsidies to local government. The direct share of government spending in the economy was thus rather less than suggested by the ratio of expenditure to national income.

In the 1890s and until the outbreak of the war, there was a considerable increase in government spending. At constant prices, it increased from £133 million in 1890 to £284 million by 1913 (Peacock/Wiseman 164). The growth of government spending as a share of GNP coincided, of course, with a fall in the share of consumption expenditure (Table 8.3). Part of this increased spending was prompted by rearmament, especially of the navy, as well as funding the war in South Africa. But over half the increase in total government expenditure after 1890 came in the local authority sector, and represented a major increase in social service provision, including housing. The Housing Act of 1890 permitted local authorities to use income from the rates to build housing for let. By 1914 London, the city in which the greatest progress was made, had a public housing stock which comprised five per cent of the metropolitan total. These modest developments in welfare probably indicate a small redistributive effect in income towards the poor. Income tax encompassed only five per cent of incomes, those over £160 per annum, but which comprised together over half the national income. Local rates were also levied on the better off. In so far as such revenues were diverted towards housing and similar social and educational services, they represent a growing welfare provision. The fall in the ratio of consumption to national income during the Edwardian years probably indicates a transfer rather than a net decline in consumption. Between 1890 and 1910 government spending per head on social services increased by over one pound, almost twice the increase achieved in the previous century (Ververka 119).

V

The concentration of British wealth in long-established accumulations and the similarly skewed distribution of national income, shaped the aggregate demand of the economy in the two centuries before 1914 as much as did the overall growth of income and wealth. A more equitable distribution, in the context of the lower average incomes prevailing in the eighteenth century would have been unable to generate such a diverse demand for goods and services. The growth of aggregate demand and its importance to development is not really in dispute. But there has been much debate as to the role played by demand in generating growth and its relationship to the supply side of the economy, differences of interpretation emerging from different schools of economic theory. Keynesian economics attributes an element of autonomy to demand, and has often been criticized for neglecting or dismissing supply side forces. By contrast, neoclassical economics regards demand as strictly derivative from supply, and thus without any autonomous influence on economic change. From this perspective, increased demand for one product does not increase total demand but simply switches demand from one commodity to another. Neoclassical economics does allow two circumstances in which demand might have an exogenous effect; by external demand, as in export-led growth, or in a situation in which productive resources are massively underemployed, as in the depression of the 1930s which gave rise to Keynesian economics.

Eighteenth-century Britain has recently been interpreted from the neoclassical perspective in two influential essays. Mokyr's principal concern was to refute the long popular notion that the Industrial Revolution resulted from a growth in demand, as argued by Gilboy in the 1930s. 'Necessary concomitants of the growth of large-scale production, and especially of its initial stages, are (1) changes in the shape of the demand schedule, to use Marshallian terminology, or in the nature of demand, of the various layers of consumption within the general population; (2) a shift in the demand schedule of the group, or an increase in demand; (3) the introduction of new wants; and (4) mobility of individuals within and between the various classes of the population . . . If any one of these factors is present, the others are likely to emerge. They are all interrelated. They mark a society which is socially unstable, in which standards of living are changing, and in which class lines are not clearly drawn' (Gilboy 125). Mokyr investigated the plausibility of this thesis by defining possible sources of exogenous change in demand and debating their effectiveness. Three candidates for demand induced change were canvassed and rejected: agriculture because its growth would only signify a shift in demand between commodities not an overall increase, foreign trade because it was not sufficiently large in the eighteenth century, and population because it too was limited in its influence. Hence, he concluded, change must have stemmed from shifts in supply. 'Cost-reducing and factor-increasing changes occupy the centre of the stage: supply rules supreme. Technological change, capital accumulation, improvements in organisation and attitudes, all made it possible to produce food, clothing, pots and toys cheaper and better' (Mokyr 1977: 989). Much the same argument was reiterated by McCloskey, although he did admit the possibility that demand might exert an autonomous effect through economies of scale in some sectors of the economy. 'If potential economies of scale were scattered about the economy at random then what was gained on the swings might be lost on the roundabouts. If they were located in the sectors made relatively larger by demand then there may have been a net gain to the nation. We do not know' (1981a: 121–3).

Neoclassical economics, which identifies demand forces as thus subservient to those of supply, makes the assumption that the economy customarily enjoys full employment. But prior to 1914, the assumption of full employment is highly improbable. Even in the Victorian period the utilization of skilled labour only approached capacity at the peak of trade cycles, while the prevalence of large reserves of unskilled workers, available for casual employment for brief periods, was a common and well-known phenomenon. Underemployment and short-time working were common, and the Victorian censuses reveal quite clearly the low activity rates of the period, especially amongst women. Only later, in the rapid growth of the 1950s and 1960s, was the state of full employment actually achieved.

The abandonment of this improbable assumption does not remove the validity or importance of supply side factors in the economy, but it does remove their exclusive claim to generate all growth, as suggested by Mokyr. His narrow argument is a gross and unwarranted exaggeration. In a less than full employment economy, which Britain almost certainly was throughout the eighteenth and nineteenth centuries, there must be an autonomous role for demand side forces. But this is not to assert the supremacy of demand over supply. Indeed Gilboy did not ignore or dismiss the importance of supply side forces. A more realistic perspective suggests that both demand and supply contributed to change, primarily through their being inextricably linked together.

Equally important as the aggregate size of demand was the composition of that demand which was far from being homogeneous. The extremely skewed distribution of wealth and income allowed a small proportion of society to live at a level of considerable affluence and to exert an effective demand disproportionate to their number. For these wealthy people the choice between spending and saving was very real, and thus an autonomous increase in demand was a distinct possibility. Furthermore, the nature of their consumption patterns suggests that reduced prices for basic goods like food, clothing, pots and pans, as instanced by Mokyr, would have made little difference to them. Of course, as the process of growth generated increased employment and incomes so effective demand was increased and diversified. Both demand and supply contributed to that growth. There is no need to call upon technological change alone, or any other means of disturbing supply side equilibrium, to explain eighteenth- and nineteenth-century economic growth.

3

Investment and the financial system

I

All explanations of economic development allow a central role to capital formation and investment from the Marxist thesis of primitive accumulation to neoclassical economics. The mark of a developing and developed economy as compared to an underdeveloped economy is often described in terms of differences in the ratio of investment to national income. An upward shift in that ratio, swift or gradual, is generally regarded as both symptomatic of development and a necessity for it. Thus Lewis stated that the 'central fact of economic development is rapid capital accumulation' and the main problem therefore was how the savings ratio could be increased from 4–5 per cent to 12–15 per cent of national income (Lewis 155). This could be achieved, he argued, only by having abundant labour available at subsistence wages so that all accumulation could be profit for reinvestment. This type of exploitational theory perceives the shift of income from consumption to investment as being at the expense of the poorer sections of society for whom the benefits of economic advance are deferred far into the future. Rostow's famous thesis also embodied a marked increase in the investment ratio as a central feature of the economic take-off. Unlike Lewis, however, Rostow did not envisage the required increase from five to ten per cent in the investment ratio coming from a reallocation of national income from consumption to saving. Rather he saw it as a dynamic effect of the growth of the economy, the additional investment coming from the increase in national income generated by the growth process. Thus the investment ratio can increase without cutting the value of income allocated to consumption and, therefore, without reducing living standards (Rostow 1963: 16). Growth in the short-run and in the early stages of development will be helped considerably if the economy possesses funds already accumulated which can be diverted to investment from either saving or consumption. So the size of the initial capital stock becomes an important element. Those theses which tended to stress the need to transfer resources from consumption to saving during the early phases of development assumed a poor society with limited capital accumulation or 'idle balances' of wealth.

There are thus two initial problems with regard to the financing of growth in the earlier stages of development. How much of the needed capital is available to effect the required increase in the investment ratio, and can this investment be provided without a cut in consumption? Deane (1973) derived estimates for the investment ratio which suggested a very low, albeit slowly increasing, ratio obtaining in the eighteenth century. Feinstein's later estimates conformed to a more traditional picture (Table 3.1). While Deane's estimates suggested an investment ratio rising from three to five per cent only in the course of the eighteenth century, Feinstein's data indicate both a higher level in mid century and a greater upward shift in the later part of the century. Crafts' more recent estimates support Deane rather than Feinstein, with an investment ratio rising from four per cent at the beginning of the century to eight per cent by the end (Crafts 1983: 195). There is thus a four to five per cent difference between these investment ratios in the eighteenth century. But by the early nineteenth century there is considerable agreement between the different series. Thus Deane and Crafts find a marked increase in the investment ratio in the first half of the nineteenth century, after the end of the war period in 1815, while Feinstein's increase comes in the later eighteenth century. In either case, the increase in investment ratio is a modest one and is spread over a lengthy period of time. Even the higher rate of change suggested by the Feinstein estimate could have been encompassed without difficulty within the moderate growth of the economy. In fact, the allocation to investment of one quarter of the additional national income created in the second half of the eighteenth century would have been enough to raise the investment ratio by the amount actually achieved. During the first half of the nineteenth century only 15 per cent of the increase in national income would have sufficed. Even in the period of biggest increase in the investment ratio (from the 1760s to 1780s by Feinstein's estimates) less than half the increase in national income would have been enough to augment the investment ratio. There is little doubt, therefore, that even a slow-growing economy like Britain could comfortably finance its increase in investment ratio out of additional income. There was no need to shift spending from consumption to saving to increase investment. Immiserization was not a prerequisite for economic advance, nor a necessary concomitant to it.

Part of the reason why it was so relatively easy for Britain to pay for growth from the modest increases in national income was due to the relatively small increase in the investment ratio. Having attained a level of 13–14 per cent by the late eighteenth or early nineteenth century, the investment ratio remained stable for the rest of the period before the First World

Table 3.1 *Investment ratios (per cent of GDP)*

	Gross domestic fixed capital formation	Stocks	Foreign investment	Investment ratio
1761–1780	6.9	1.5	0.8	9.2
1781–1800	10.4	2.0	1.2	13.6
1801–1830	10.3	1.1	1.7	13.1
1831–1860	10.4	0.9	2.2	13.5
1856–1873	7.2	0.9	4.5	12.6
1873–1913	8.5	0.9	5.0	14.4
1913–1924	5.9	−1.5	4.8	9.2
1924–1937	11.0	0.5	1.6	13.1
1937–1948	7.3	0.7	−4.1	3.9
1951–1964	17.7	1.3	0.6	19.6
1964–1973	21.1	1.1	0.3	22.5
1973–1979	22.1	1.0	2.1	25.2
1979–1983	20.5	−1.4	2.5	21.6

Sources: C. H. Feinstein, 'Capital formation in Great Britain' in P. Matthias and M. M. Postan (eds.), *Cambridge Economic History of Europe* vol. VII Part I (Cambridge 1978) p. 91.
C. H. Feinstein, *Statistical Tables of National Income, Expenditure and Output of the UK 1855–1965* (Cambridge 1972) Tables 5, 6, 40.
R. C. O. Matthews, C. H. Feinstein and J. C. Odling-Smee, *British Economic Growth 1856–1973* (Oxford 1982) p. 442.
Central Statistical Office, *National Income and Expenditure 1963–73*, Tables 14, 57.
Central Statistical Office, *U.K. National Accounts* (1984) Tables 1.5, 10.7.

War. By comparison with other developing countries in the nineteenth century, this was a low investment ratio (Rostow 1978a: 79–82). Indeed this level of investment was similar to that enjoyed in more recent times by countries such as Paraguay, Malaysia and El Salvador (Yotopoulos/Nugent 170–1). This low investment ratio is even more remarkable when divided into home and foreign investment. As is well known, foreign investment grew considerably in the course of the Victorian period and the scale of British overseas investment as a ratio of GDP was greater in that period than has ever been recorded by any other economy. It was one of the unique aspects of British development. Home investment throughout the eighteenth and nineteenth centuries was exceptionally low in relation to GDP, for most of the time less than half that of the investment ratio in other developing countries. Furthermore, home investment declined from about the middle of the nineteenth century.

A limited disaggregation of domestic investment is shown in Table 3.2. The period of increased fixed capital formation, roughly from 1780 to 1860, showed a fairly wide spread in investment increase, with dwellings and

Table 3.2 Gross domestic fixed capital formation by sector (per cent of GDP)

	Dwellings	Public buildings and works	Industrial/ commercial buildings	Building works other than dwellings	Plant/ equipment	Transport	Agriculture	Gas/ water	Mining	Ships & vehicles	Total GDFCF
1761–1780	1.4	0.2	0.8		0.2	1.8	2.4	0.0	0.1		6.9
1781–1800	2.3	0.2	1.8		0.8	2.1	3.1	0.0	0.1		10.4
1801–1830	3.0	0.3	2.2		0.8	1.8	2.0	0.1	0.1		10.3
1831–1860	2.0	0.3	2.0		1.0	3.3	1.3	0.3	0.2		10.4
1856–1873	1.2			3.1	1.8					1.1	7.2
1873–1913	1.6			3.4	2.2					1.3	8.5

Sources: C. H. Feinstein, 'Capital formation in Great Britain' in P. Mathias and M. M. Postan (eds.), *Cambridge Economic History of Europe* Vol. VII pt I (Cambridge 1978) pp. 40, 91.
C. H. Feinstein, *Statistical Tables of National Income, Expenditure and Output of the UK 1855–1965* (Cambridge 1972) Tables 5, 6, 40.

agriculture showing marked increases as well as industrial and commercial building and plant and equipment. The decline in the later part of the Victorian period in the investment ratio was clearly due in part to a relative fall in investment in dwellings, and it seems likely that agriculture and possibly transport also contributed. While industrial and commercial investment continued to increase, the rate of expansion was not sufficient to maintain the home investment ratio of mid century. The most puzzling question raised by such data is not how early development was financed, but rather why the growth in domestic investment was so modest, and why did it actually decline relative to national income in the later decades of the nineteenth century.

II

In spite of the modest aggregate growth in investment, there were significant increases and changes in the demand and supply of investment during these two centuries which contributed to the creation of a large and sophisticated institutional framework. While the growth of demand, supply and the institutions were closely interlinked, they will be discussed separately to make clear the main aspects of each. Demand for finance can be divided into two main components, a demand for investment funds and a demand for financial services. In the eighteenth century, much of the increased demand for investment came from the state and its need to raise funds to pay for an almost continuous succession of increasingly expensive wars. War expenditure rose from £49 million in the period 1688–97, to £1,658 million in the Napoleonic Wars from 1793–1815 (Dickson 1967: 10). Accordingly, the national debt grew from £44 million in 1739 to £820 million by 1815. The century of comparative peace which followed allowed the debt to be reduced to £620 million in 1914. Government borrowing dominated financial markets until after 1815 when the scale and diversity of investment increased considerably. Foreign borrowing became increasingly more important after 1815, initially in government loans and public utilities in Western Europe.

The first large market for investment funds independent of government borrowing was created by the advent of the railways. By the middle of the nineteenth century 'home rails' accounted for 16 per cent of nominal share values on the London Stock Exchange, while 70 per cent of investments were in government stock and six per cent in foreign investments. By the 1880s, railway shares, overseas as well as British, accounted for 40 per cent of nominal share values (Reader 43). The massive increase in investment through the stock market in the second half of the nineteenth century reflected a great increase in demand for investment abroad. Overseas investment, in constant values, increased from £4 million annually in the

1830s to £51.6 million in the 1870s and £105.4 million in the first decade of the twentieth century (Edelstein 22). Altogether between 1865 and the First World War, £4,082 million was raised in foreign securities in London (Cottrell 1975: 27). As already noted, Britain placed a higher share of investment abroad in the Victorian period as a share of GDP than any other country. Between 1870 and 1914 this averaged over five per cent, compared to French and German foreign investment which was under three per cent (Edelstein 3).

The pattern of this growing foreign investment is well known. In the early nineteenth century, government loans predominated, while the railways in both Europe and the United States provided a powerful source of demand from the 1830s. By 1847, the stock of forty foreign railway companies was quoted on the London Stock Exchange. After mid century the bulk of foreign investment went into railways and public utilities such as gas, water and electricity, into telegraph and telephone systems, and into docks and tramways. Between 1865 and 1914, 69 per cent of all new issues overseas related to such investments, and 41 per cent alone was devoted to railway plant and equipment. Primary product exploitation, agriculture and mining, together with finance, trading and real estate ventures accounted for most of the remainder with manufacturing attracting only four per cent of the total (Edelstein 37–8). The geographical pattern of foreign investment reflected the expansion of the western economies into the thinly populated but resource rich regions of North America and Australasia, which took 34 per cent and 11 per cent respectively of new issue investment between 1865 and 1914. Other investment in Latin America, Asia, and Europe also represented a response to demand for social overhead capital. The 'lumpiness' of social overhead capital projects, and of urban growth in areas of recent settlement which were having to accommodate considerable inflows of migrants, meant that investment went in periodic surges to different areas. In the middle decades of the century investment went mainly to the United States, in the 1860s and 1880s Australia attracted substantial funds, while in the Edwardian years South Africa and Canada were important sources of demand. Indeed Canada absorbed one third of net lending from Britain between 1900 and the First World War. Not all overseas investment was devoted to economic development. Some government loans contributed to good living in high places and, subsequently, to interest payments on the accumulated debt, as in Egypt and Turkey. In general, however, foreign investment replicated home investment where railways became a favoured safe security by the later nineteenth century, together with public utilities, transport and municipal developments. There was a belated spurt of industrial investment raised on the financial markets in the later nineteenth century. In 1882, only £64 million worth of industrial shares were quoted on the

London Stock Exchange in a total of £5,800 million worth of quoted securities. But the two decades prior to the war witnessed over a billion pounds channelled into industrial projects through the financial markets, helped by the creation of large businesses through the spate of amalgamations in brewing, chemicals, textiles, banking and insurance.

While the scale and disposition of funds raised through the financial institutions can be estimated with reasonable accuracy, such is not the case for investment obtained in less formal ways. It is commonplace that many industrial concerns in the nineteenth century as well as in the eighteenth raised their capital informally from friends, relatives, business colleagues and through agencies such as lawyers and bankers. Their contribution to the development of the financial system was a less direct one than that of the large government loan, but was still significant and will be considered more fully below. As well as a growing demand for investment funds, there was a parallel growth in demand for financial services which contributed to the development of the institutional framework. Insurance was a major part of this. The buoyant international trade of the later seventeenth century generated an increased need for marine insurance, which continued to grow through the succeeding two centuries. The need for fire insurance had been demonstrated by the Great Fire in London in 1666. In both branches sums insured increased very considerably (Supple 107). Life assurance did not develop much until the later years of the eighteenth century because of the difficulty encountered in computing appropriate premiums. When established in the nineteenth century, life assurance soon became a major branch of the financial system. Not only was there a great increase in the number and value of policies but the fact that such funds were, hopefully, a longer term investment than fire, accident or marine insurance meant that the funds of the life assurance companies grew particularly large. From a modest £28 million in 1837, these accumulated funds increased to £125 million in 1877 and to £315 million by 1913 (Supple 309). The demand for insurance indicated a growing capability and need to provide against ill fortune. In the later nineteenth century there was a rapid growth in small scale industrial insurance policies providing working men with cover against inability to work and a nest egg for retirement. The Prudential Company was pre-eminent in this branch of insurance, and was responsible for over seven million policies by the late 1880s together worth £66 million (Morrah 53).

The growth of insurance is an indicator of growing prosperity. So too were the friendly societies and building societies, also growing rapidly in the Victorian period but with origins in the previous century and offering additional financial services. By 1850 there were about 1,500 building societies in existence providing help towards the finance of home ownership. Savings banks protected the savings of the provident, while conventional banking services were needed by any growing market economy and consequently proliferated in number and variety as the economy developed.

III

Demand for investment and financial services came from government, from business, from consumers and from abroad on an increasing scale. Where did the funds come from to meet this demand? Was there, as some historians believed, a necessary shift of funds from consumption to saving? The data on income growth and the investment ratio indicated that such funds could have been provided out of increased national income. There is also supporting evidence that Britain in 1700 was a wealthy country with substantial accumulations of wealth. The flotation of the Bank of England in 1694 provides a telling illustration. The entire subscription of £1.2 million was taken within twelve days of being put on offer, and paid up in six months, a sum estimated at 2.5 per cent of the entire national income. But funds were also forthcoming in the first two decades of the eighteenth century for other public corporations. A large loan floated for the East India Company, a subscription for the South Sea Company, and additional funds for the Bank brought the share capital of the three corporations to £20 million by 1717 (Morgan/Thomas 29–30). Such a scale of investment suggests both ample funds and idle balances. Funds for eighteenth-century investment came from a small section of the community, estimated at no more than 25,000 persons by a contemporary in 1737, who were 'widows, orphans under trust, single women, and those never educated in any trade or business or who are past it' (Dickson 1967: 250). They were also inhabitants of London or the Home Counties. The subscription for the Bank of England in 1694 obtained almost 90 per cent of funds from London, Middlesex, Surrey and Hertfordshire. Not all subscribers were members of leisured society. The mercantile interests of the City of London were the principal contributors, supported by the legal profession and the clergy.

Wealthy individuals continued to represent a significant source of funds for investment until the First World War. The 1851 Census of Population listed 23,000 men and 121,000 women as 'annuitants' under occupation category. Not all investments by individuals were modest and required only to provide a reasonably comfortable standard of living for the annuitant. The estate of the Sutherland family generated an income of £120,000 per annum for the Duke for much of the nineteenth century. Had £100,000 of that been invested in consols, it would have accumulated to over £26 million by the 1870s (Richards 1979: 46). This enormous income was invested in a variety of ways, apart from providing a lavish life style for the family, usually according to the whim or prejudice of the current Duke. Sutherland investments ranged from government stock, land in the Scottish Highlands, works of art, and shares in the Liverpool-Manchester railway to investments abroad covering most areas of the globe. On a considerably more modest scale, prosperous merchants and industrialists invested part of their substance. Morris's studies of woollen merchants in Leeds in the early nineteenth century suggested a property cycle whereby the prosperous middle class man, around the age of forty, began to accumulate assets to generate a rentier income, even if they yielded a lower rate of return than had his business. Robert Jowitt, whose capital in the family wool stapling business grew from £3,000 in 1806 to £20,000 in 1835, bought life assurance policies, shares in local public utilities and later in railway stock. Not all ventures were successful, and Jowitt lost money on two of his investments. John Atkinson, a Leeds solicitor, followed the same strategy of shifting assets from his business into investments providing a rentier income, in his case through the purchase of farms and other property in and around Leeds (Morris, 101, 104). The Greg family were prominent in the early development of the cotton industry, but by the early nineteenth century their assets were diversified into land, for security rather than for prestige, in Cheshire, Lancashire, Norfolk and Hertfordshire. At his death in 1910, Edward Hyde Greg possessed investments in railways and public utilities abroad, in cotton manufacturing, shipping companies, insurance companies, and a variety of lesser investments including shares in Harrods (Rose 91).

In the west of Scotland, successful tobacco merchants in the eighteenth century diversified their interests. Land purchase was a favoured outlet for investment. There were few aristocratic estates in the region so that land was both available and in modest plots. But the collapse of the Ayr Bank in 1772, which had considerable amounts of landed capital tied up in it, brought landed property worth £750,000 onto the market. Land was a safe asset, offered possibilities for mineral exploitation, and could also be used to raise funds on mortgage. But the gains from tobacco spread far more widely, and were invested in leather, boot and shoe manufacture, rope making, sugar processing, glass manufacture, and into iron works, coal mines and banks (Devine 19–20, 35–7). In fact the entire financial structure of the west of Scotland comprised a network of interlocking firms and families who provided cash and credit for each other and made use of the London money market by discounting bills there.

While prosperous individuals made a major contribution to the supply of investment funds, this period saw the growth of financial institutions which became major sources of investment by virtue of their accumulated resources. One of the earliest of these institutional developments came in insurance. The fact that such businesses held funds for lengthy periods, and periodically had to meet claims, gave them both the opportunity and the need to invest such funds. Safe government securities which could be quickly turned into cash without losing value represented an ideal investment in the eighteenth century. Such returns on investment contributed substantially to the income of insurance companies. At the beginning of the nineteenth century, investment income of the Sun Fire Office amounted to £30,000 per annum compared to £12,000 in underwriting profits (Dickson 1960: 73). As well as holding government securities, the Sun held East India Company bonds and gave extensive mortgages on land. The latter generated rather lower rates of return than government stocks, but since the mortgage was usually given for only 70 per cent of the value of the land there was an obvious and lucrative compensation in the event of default. As the historian of the Sun observed, 'It is clear that, if the Sun's policy was at all typical, the landed interest was receiving massive support through this period from the London insurance companies, whose funds were largely accumulated from the savings of the commercial, industrial and shopkeeping classes of the community' (Dickson 1960: 250). In 1824, the Sun had loans outstanding on mortgage to the value of £270,000 and a further £30,000 on annuities. Together with government securities, these comprised most of the company's investments prior to the mid nineteenth century. The Royal Exchange Assurance was another major institutional investor in the eighteenth century, and it too looked primarily to Bank of England stock, the East India Company and government securities.

The growth of insurance in the nineteenth century greatly increased the importance of insurance companies as investors. By 1913, their assets exceeded £500 million, above five per cent of national income. While government consolidated stock, soon known as consols, provided a secure basis for their investments, there was considerable diversification in their investments in the nineteenth century. The Royal Exchange Assurance gave loans to estate developers in London in the middle of the century, mainly in the Paddington area, and added railway shares to the company portfolio. The Sun Insurance Company diversified its investments into railways, which accounted for 25 per cent of its holdings by the end of the century, and also into London docks and water works, and American and colonial bonds, although consols remained a substantial investment (Dickson 1960: 262–3). The Prudential Assurance, the first business to enter industrial insurance in the middle years of the century, had become by 1915 'absolutely the highest shareholder in the Bank of England, as it was in the River Company; the most extensive owner of railway securities as well as of freehold ground rents; the most considerable holder of Indian and Colonial bonds and stocks; one of the greatest London ground rent landlords owning more than half a square mile of the metropolis, and probably the greatest owner of freehold property in the United Kingdom' (Clayton 123). The Standard Life

Assurance Company, founded in Edinburgh in 1825, had developed the largest insurance business in Britain by the 1870s but was becoming increasingly worried by the declining rate of return on investments. Falling agricultural rents had reduced mortgage income, while consols were offering low rates of return. This situation stirred the company to look abroad for investments. In the later decades of the nineteenth century, Standard Life developed strong links in Canada, investing in land mortgages, and municipal securities to the extent of about £1.6 million by 1900 (Treble 183). A diversity of investments were retained in Britain, including Fife County Council, the Barrow Shipbuilding Company, Denaby and Cadeby Main Colliery, and the Irwell Bank Spinning Company. In spite of this diversification of investments, by the eve of the First World War the assets of British insurance companies still retained their traditional pattern with half in government securities and much of the remainder in mortgages, property, loans and cash (Morgan/Thomas 175).

Banking firms were also important institutional investors. In the eighteenth century, Taylor and Lloyd of Birmingham invested in East India bonds, South Sea annuities and shares in the Birmingham canal (Sayers 10). The Bank of Scotland, founded in 1695, was forbidden to lend to the government so that Scottish banking was from the outset dependent on commercial business. Mortgages on land offered business as good as they did in the south, while loans and credit financed both industry and public utilities. The Royal Bank of Scotland lent to the Forth and Clyde Navigation, while the Aberdeen Banking Company lent money to the town for harbour improvements (Checkland 1975: 232–3). In the following century, banks were involved in investing in railways, docks and harbour improvements. Glyn's Bank financed so much railway development that it became known as the Railway Bank, although it invested in construction projects in London in the 1820s and 1830s (Fulford 119, 133). Bank funds also went abroad. The Perth Banking Company invested in the United States, but lost over £30,000 there on bank stock in the 1840s. Records of two Paisley banks show that in the 1830s they held British, French and Dutch government securities as well as stock of the Bank of England and other Scottish and Irish banks (Munn, 135, 168).

Other financial institutions were also investors. Some building societies did not confine their lending to house purchase. The Sheffield and South Yorkshire Building Society advanced money to local factory owners, although most reserves were kept in mortgages (Cleary 74). But before 1914 the insurance companies remained the principal institutional investors, and, as the century progressed, they shared the reorientation of British investment overseas. The London and Lancashire Insurance Company had investments in Brazilian railways, Hungarian Gold Rentes, the Moscow-Jaroslav

Railway, Manchurian railway bonds, Siamese government bonds, the Honan Railway Gold Loan, City of St Petersburg bonds, and its principal investment in United States prior stocks and bonds by the late nineteenth century (Francis 64). Thus the supply of investment funds, which for much of the eighteenth century had come direct from a small and wealthy section of society, the landed gentry and the London middle classes, was by the following century increasingly channelled through institutions like banks and insurance companies. As increasing numbers of people took out insurance policies or borrowed from building societies, so the pool of institutional investment funds grew and drew on a greater proportion of society. As the supply and demand for investment grew, so the institutional framework developed in size and complexity.

IV

While the financial system in 1700 was much smaller and limited than it became in the course of the subsequent two centuries, it was nevertheless capable of mobilizing substantial funds. The key essentials of a financial market, dealing in securities by specialists, legal recognition of transfers, a banking system, and sufficient wealth available for investment, were all conditions fulfilled in London by the late seventeenth century. Growth was stimulated by the government requirement for funds through direct loans by the issue of government stock, and through the granting of monopolies like the Bank of England and the East India Company who were allowed to raise funds in order to lend to the government. Similarly the granting of monopoly status to the London Assurance Company and the Royal Exchange Assurance Company in 1720 was conditional upon their lending the government £300,000, a loan which was eventually written off as a bad debt. The major institutions in eighteenth-century finance, like their principal client, were metropolitan based. Many of their investors were inhabitants of London and its close environs. A list of holders of four per cent consols in 1780–93 revealed a strong concentration of ownership in Middlesex and Surrey, followed by Berkshire, Hertfordshire and Kent, with lesser concentrations in Bath and Bristol (J. R. Ward 141–2). Even at the end of the nineteenth century, ownership of gilt edged securities remained strongly concentrated in the Home Counties. Much the same was true of eighteenth-century insurance. In the 1790s, only 18 per cent of shareholders in the Sun Fire Office were resident outside the Home Counties (Dickson 1967: 297). The majority of eighteenth-century policies for insurance, fire and marine, were taken out in London and the South East. Not surprisingly, dealing was largely confined to London although the Stock Exchange did not achieve institutional form until 1802. Commercial banking and insurance were similarly concentrated in the capital.

Besides its government stimulated development, the City of London had strong international links in the eighteenth century. Since the previous century there had been a strong increase in multilateral payments in European trade, providing facilities for short-term lending and for clearing international payments. By the early eighteenth century this was established through much of Western Europe (Sperling 459). In the course of the eighteenth century, the London money market became increasingly integrated with the Amsterdam money market, which retained its international pre-eminence throughout the century (Eagly/Smith 210–11). Indeed Britain attracted some investment from Holland in this century, mainly government and bank stock, which accounted for as much as 15 per cent of all such holdings in 1750. The Dutch share fell sharply in the later decades of the century when there was a large increase in the national debt (Riley 123–5).

While metropolitan financial institutions remained dominant through the eighteenth century, London insurance companies covering property worth £190 million in 1802 compared to £15 million covered by their provincial counterparts, there was no lack of institutional growth outside London. Most obvious was the appearance of country banks in the second half of the century, growing from about a dozen in 1750 to 300 by the end of the century and to over one thousand by the 1840s. These banks were linked to the metropolitan centre of the financial system through private City banks which held deposits and discounted bills for their provincial correspondents. This function has often been accorded pride of place in accounts of the development of the financial system as the means whereby the City 'alternatively holding surplus funds and discounting bills for country correspondents, [they] linked the wealthy agricultural counties of East Anglia and the South West with the capital-hungry counties of the Industrial Revolution, to the benefit of all' (Cameron 8–10). Country banking firms emerged from a variety of backgrounds. Taylor and Lloyd of Birmingham started in 1765 with both money and personal connections in the iron trade, while Garfitt Claypons of Boston was started by a corn merchant, Wrights Bank of Nottingham by a Baltic trader, and Haydon Smallpiece of Guildford by a draper. Other banks were established by brewers, wool merchants, grocers, coal factors and revenue collectors (Sayers 2–6). Profits made in the Glasgow tobacco trade helped found the Ship Bank and the Glasgow Arms Bank in the 1750s (Devine 13). Since partnerships were restricted by law to six members, many country bankers were involved in other activities. In areas such as the West Riding, attorneys acted as financial intermediaries and suppliers of credit, channelling local funds into transport and public utilities in the same area and thus enabling a healthy local capital market to flourish (Miles 140). A very similar type of finance operated in Lancashire where mortgages could be raised on all kinds of assets through the offices of lawyers (Anderson). As well as raising funds for infrastructure improvements such as roads, river navigations and canals, these provincial financial intermediaries had links with industry. Taylor and Lloyd lent to the iron industry, and the provision of bank loans and credit to industry was not as uncommon as was once thought. By the end of the century, discounting inland bills for provincial banks had become an important part of the business of the City of London. In spite of the emphasis placed by many scholars on the role of the country banks in funnelling funds from agricultural areas, flushed with surplus money after the harvest, to provide short-term credits in industrial regions, there is no clear evidence of the scale or importance of such flows. Nor is it obvious that agriculture was a net donor of investment since, as Dickson has shown, there was a substantial flow of funds into rural areas in the form of mortgages.

The growth of the railways and Victorian industrialization provided a great stimulus to the growth of provincial financial institutions. The railways provided the first non-government demand for funds on a scale sufficiently large to warrant a major extension of the institutional network. In response to railway development, stock exchanges were established in Liverpool and Manchester in the 1830s and in most of the major provincial cities in the railway boom of 1844–45, some of which were short lived. These local stock exchanges were able to mobilize regional finance on a substantial scale. Much of the investment for early railway ventures was raised locally. While there was a London interest in the Liverpool and Manchester Railway, most of the capital came from Liverpool. The same city provided half the investment for the London to Birmingham line. While the railway boom created the provincial stock exchanges, the development of a more settled market in railway securities, and a more extensive one given growth overseas, shifted the dominant role in such securities to London. The provincial stock exchanges returned to the traditional role of pre-institutional brokerage in local capital markets (Reed 1975: 174, 182). There was, of course, an active market in joint stock company shares in the provinces before the 1840s. Some had overseas links like the Aberdeen interests in investment companies in Australia and the United States (Michie 1981: 60). Stock exchanges provided a better means of communication and harmonization of procedures than the disparate activities of lawyers and country bankers. Provincial stock exchanges consolidated their position through specialization in local activities, and received a boost from the increase in company promotions in the 1870s and 1880s from the conversion of private companies to public companies following the introduction of limited liability. One contemporary even claimed that they were as important as London for home securities in 1885, a view which certainly could not have been sustained a few years later (W. A. Thomas 1973: 114). The Oldham Stock Exchange became the main centre for joint stock flotations in the cotton industry, while Sheffield specialized in the conversion of iron companies from private to public. By the 1880s, 44 iron companies had had shares issued on the Sheffield Stock Exchange worth a paid up capital of £12 million. Amalgamations in the cotton industry, conducted through the Manchester Stock Exchange, formed nineteen new companies between 1897 and 1904 with a combined capital in excess of £45 million (W. A. Thomas 1973: 124, 135). Such local specialization was general. Liverpool retained an interest in shipping and insurance shares throughout the century, while the boom in cycle shares in the 1890s was centred on Birmingham. Some provincial stock exchanges maintained interests in overseas ventures, as did Leeds and Sheffield in mining and railways. Scottish stock markets had substantial interests in land mortgages overseas. Big increases in local authority borrowing in the later decades of the nineteenth century also generated considerable business on provincial stock exchanges.

But London remained the heart of the national financial network. While the importance of government borrowing declined in the nineteenth century, the massive increase of international lending, together with growth at home, greatly increased the metropolitan financial market. The nominal value of industrial, commercial and financial shares quoted on the London Stock Exchange increased from £125 million in 1853 to £1,500 million by 1914 (W. A. Thomas 1973: 114). Such a substantial increase in activity necessitated specialization, especially when so much of the additional business was overseas. Indeed it was the growth of international investment which allowed the emergence of merchant banking on a large scale. Many of the major firms had their origins in continental Europe and were merchant houses prior to becoming bankers. Barings came originally from Bremen, Rothschilds from Frankfurt, and Schroders and Warburgs from Hamburg. Such firms were prominent in European trade and finance in the eighteenth century. Many were drawn to London during the disruptive phase of the Napoleonic Wars, but retained their continental business connections which often overlapped with kinship and friendship. These businesses were always in the forefront of overseas investment, each taking a different regional specialization, Barings in the United States, Rothschild in Europe, while Lazards concentrated on the Far East. While the share of overseas investment funded by merchant banks appeared to decline in the later part of the nineteenth century, this was because many of the new institutions such as investment trusts were in fact funded by the merchant banks (Cottrell 1975: 31). Between 1860 and 1890 alone, Barings raised 500 million dollars and

£40 million for American and Canadian government loans. When Barings were faced with disaster in 1890, as a result of buying heavily in Argentinian government stock just before the value was severely diminished by a revolution, the City of London raised £17.5 million to provide security for the firm. Private banks, discount houses and provincial banks all joined the rescue operation. Even greater than Baring was the house of Rothschild which brought out government loans worth £1,600 million during the nineteenth century (Wechsberg 343).

Private banks in the City, and stock brokers, comprised important links in the financial network. Glyn's Bank grew initially by acting as London agents for country bankers in Scotland, West Yorkshire, Northumberland, Warwickshire, Kent and Dorset. By the 1840s the bank was heavily involved in railway shares, second only to Barclays. Later in the century the bank invested in Canada for clients and on its own behalf. Stockbroking firms traded in the market for themselves and for clients. Foster and Braithwaite represented provincial banks in York, East Anglia, Devon and Cornwall. In the second half of the century they were active dealers in British and American railway shares, banking, insurance, property, shipping, telegraph, and utilities. The firm also acted as a promoter of companies, and took a prominent role in the electricity supply industry towards the end of the century. Indeed one of the partners, Joseph Braithwaite, was himself a leading figure in the industry. In 1880, Foster and Braithwaite acted as brokers in issuing £400,000 worth of shares in the Anglo-American Brush Electric Light Corporation which unfortunately soon collapsed. But in the following decade the firm was more successful with several flotations in electrical engineering and urban electricity supply. These included the Brush Electrical Engineering Company, British Electric Traction, and the City of London Electric Lighting Company. The firm acted in the share market for private banks in the City, for branches of banks, including Barclays, and for individual clients including clergymen, army and navy officers, and at least one economic historian, J. H. Clapham (Reader 100, 109). The business of Capel and Company was similar. They were involved in large scale transactions in exchequer bills on behalf of private banks like Coutts who used such bills as a means of keeping liquid short-term reserves. Capel also acted for the Royal Bank of Scotland, purchasing railway bonds for that institution in the 1850s. In the second half of the nineteenth century, Capel also traded extensively in railway shares and foreign issues, although their link with the private banks meant that government securities remained an important part of the business. A balance sheet for 1906–7 indicated that half the commission income in that year came from work on behalf of bankers, and that Capel's own investments included railways, docks and tramways, both at home and abroad (Reed 1975: 69). As the Foster and Braithwaite interest in electricity supply extended to active participation in the industry, so Capel and Co. included one partner who was a director, and later chairman, of the Hull and Barnsley Railway, as well as holding a directorship in the South and East Coast Railway.

Institutional development necessarily included a considerable growth in the banking system. Following legislation in 1826, joint stock banking was able to develop in England and Wales, although the provincial joint stock banks remained smaller than their metropolitan counterparts. The largest of these, the Liverpool and Manchester District Bank, had £11 million in deposits by the 1880s less than half the deposits of the London and County Bank, the National Provincial Bank or the London and Westminster Bank. All the provincial banks had to discount heavily with a London agent in order to obtain a sufficient volume of liquid funds. Thus in the nineteenth century, as earlier, the bill brokers were the essential link between the provinces and the metropolitan financial markets. Nishimura concluded that poor communications in the early part of the century required businesses to maintain large inventories and thus required long credit until the 1870s. The strong demand for money which this necessitated was met by discounting bills of exchange in London. As improved transport and telegraph reduced the role of the middleman and the need for large inventories, so the demand for money fell. More overdrafts and less bills to discount rapidly reduced the volume of bills of exchange in the home market (Nishimura 77–8). This was not, however, the end of the bill discount market. Foreign bills of exchange, which had accounted for only 14 per cent of the total in the 1840s, became increasingly important in response to the development of international finance. These various components of the financial system, which were only tenuously linked in the first half of the nineteenth century, became more and more integrated as the century progressed (Michie 1985). The joint stock banks supplied cash to bill brokers to enable them to discount bills which had been accepted by merchant banks. By the last quarter of the century, there was thus created a new mechanism in international finance based almost exclusively in London. Since sterling was the main international currency, these institutions could choose between home and overseas outlets for their investments (De Cecco 85–6).

The financial network spread much wider than the banks and stock brokers. Some mercantile firms acted as agents to raise investment. Harrison Crossfield raised capital for tea estates and tobacco companies in Java and India, and for Malayan rubber estates, Japanese silk firms and Borneo timber firms. Further, the growth of the financial system was enhanced by the expansion of some of its more prosperous component parts. Here again, the insurance companies were prominent. By 1913 their funds equalled those of savings banks, friendly societies and building societies together, as they absorbed the savings of the growing middle classes. Increased business in the nineteenth century produced a spread of both business and companies from the heavily metropolitan bias of eighteenth-century development. Especially notable was the growth of insurance in Liverpool with substantial business in the United States, so that by the end of the century the three major fire insurance companies in Liverpool enjoyed a premium income well in excess of their metropolitan rivals (Supple 215). Indeed the growth in insurance followed the surge of investment overseas. Some insurance companies increased their overseas branches, as did the Sun Life Assurance Company. An alternative strategy was followed by the London and Lancashire Insurance Company, which was only founded in 1861. Income from premiums increased from £0.42 million in 1880 to £2.56 million in 1914, most of it by overseas expansion through the take-over of established local businesses. In the 1880s the firm acquired the Baltimore Fire Insurance Company and the Howard Company of New York. In the 1890s it added the Anglo-Nevada Insurance Company, the Insurance Company of Cape Town, the City Mutual Fire Insurance Company of Sydney, and in Canada, the Mercantile Company of Waterloo and the Quebec Fire Assurance Company. Similar acquisitions were made in Buenos Aires and Montevideo. British firms were also absorbed and, as a product of these additions, marine and accident insurance were added to the existing fire insurance of the parent company (Francis 41–54). The scale of activity in investment and the activities of the financial institutions, which was possible only because of the massive increase in international business after 1850, generated greater specialization in the different parts of the financial network. It also provided an element of self-sustaining growth. This richly diverse but highly integrated financial network was the essential centrepiece not only of the British economy but of the rapidly growing international economy. Indeed, the metropolitan centre of the financial system developed a markedly international outlook and specialization in the Victorian period.

V

In spite of the abundant evidence of growth and increased sophistication in British financial markets during the two centuries before 1914, a great deal of criticism has been levelled in recent years against the performance of such markets. This relates, of course, to the relatively low investment ratio in Britain especially in gross domestic fixed capital formation which, in the later nineteenth century, was exceptionally low. It has become generally agreed that the economy was not short of funds for investment during this period, so that attention has become firmly fixed on the question of the efficiency of markets in allocating financial resources. This debate has been framed within the assumption that industrialization represents the essence of development so that the problem of investment allocation becomes one of supplying industry with sufficient funds. Almost by definition, any diversion of investment to other uses has been perceived as inefficient. In an international context, Mokyr criticized the Amsterdam money market for investing in foreign government stock in the seventeenth and eighteenth centuries. Since this investment could have financed an industrial revolution, he argued, it represented a missed opportunity and the 'absent link' between industry and finance indicated inefficiency within the economic system (Riley 6–7). A similar strain runs through British historiography. Almost half a century ago, Postan observed that Britain in 1700 was wealthy enough to finance several industrial revolutions. 'What was inadequate was not the quantity of stored-up wealth, but its behaviour. The reservoirs of saving were full enough, but conduits to connect them with the wheels of industry were few and meagre' (Postan 71). Exactly the same theme and underlying assumptions have characterized Kennedy's severe criticism of the late Victorian capital markets. 'The institutional arrangements in British capital markets before 1914, while offering very good facilities for the trading of first-class securities, provided especially inadequate information on the riskiest investment possibilities and failed to encourage or facilitate efficient diversification of wealth-holders' assets' (Kennedy 1976: 152). Inefficiency came, he argued, from segmentation of markets which, through imperfections in the distribution of information, allowed differences to exist between the risk adjusted rates of return on different investments. In addition, the fact that the British capital market had developed institutionally during early industrialization, and was thus geared to ensure stability rather than growth, was another source of weakness. Thus the market was biased against small and risky investments but which were most profitable from an economy-wide viewpoint. The effect of this on the development of modern industry, as instanced by the experience of the motor industry in the decades before the First World War, was most unfortunate. 'What was required was a steady, rational, courageous flow of funds to an industry which had technical troubles but also a huge market. What it got was waves of money carelessly supplied, followed by an equally unreflective withdrawal when problems appeared, problems magnified by the previous carelessness' (Kennedy 1976: 173). From the same kind of perspective, the very high level of foreign investment in the second half of the nineteenth century represented a massive drain on the economy, bolstering foreign industrialization at the expense of British manufacturing.

There are two main lines of criticism here, that the financial markets allocated investment inefficiently and that, as a result, industry was deprived of necessary funds especially in what would be called 'sunrise industries' in modern jargon. A recent study has investigated the efficiency of eighteenth-century financial markets in Britain, efficiency being defined as the speed and effectiveness with which the market responded to the changing profitability of companies by adjusting share prices. Mirowski tested the thesis using data on the Million Bank, the London Assurance Company and the East India Company. His results suggested that while not perfectly efficient the market responded to this test with a significant degree of success, leading to the conclusion that the eighteenth-century financial market was not underdeveloped or inefficient but rather underutilized (Mirowski 574–6).

Edelstein's extensive study of Victorian financial markets suggested the same kind of efficiency as Mirowski found in the previous century. He found that opportunities for investment in the domestic market did have a strong endogenous effect on the scale of overseas investment, and that this was primarily associated with the gradual decline in population-sensitive investment. A decline in the rate of increase in births from the 1870s, and a similar and related fall in the growth of urbanization and thence social overhead capital, contributed to this. As for industry, profitable and well-established manufacturers were able to satisfy their modest investment needs. The lack of interest in science and technology for either education or research, both at a public and private level in Victorian Britain, meant that there was little demand for capital intensive investment similar to that in Germany or the United States. Thus investment sought outlets overseas in part because of the dearth of opportunities in the home market. The kind of population-sensitive demand for social overhead capital which was diminishing in the British market was very strong in international markets in the Victorian period (Edelstein 232, 310–11). In the 1850s and 1860s the United States offered a strong demand of this kind, and later decades saw similar demand in Canada, Australia, South Africa and Argentina. From the 1890s until the outbreak of war, the United States absorbed substantial additional British investment into growing American industrial production. So investors hardly deserve the strictures of their critics, especially as Edelstein's calculations indicated that the average rate of return on overseas assets from 1870 to 1913 was 5.72 per cent annually compared to the average return of 4.60 per cent in the domestic market (Edelstein 126). If investors and markets operated rationally in peace time, what about the effect of government borrowing in the Napoleonic Wars? Did the state crowd out industrial growth and delay the Industrial Revolution? The fact that both Morowski and Edelstein found a lack of demand in the home market runs counter to Williamson's assumption (1984, 1985) that the economy was running at full employment in the 1790s. There is no evidence that industry was deprived of

investment by increased government demand for funds. The cotton industry, as is well known, did not depend on the institutional capital markets for
its investment, nor was there any marked slackening of the growth of the
industry in the war period. The problems the war created for the cotton
industry were mainly dislocations in trade rather than loss of desired investment. As for the other high growth industry, iron manufacture, it was stimulated by war demand. It seems likely that the increased government borrowing in the Napoleonic Wars, and for that matter the heavy government
borrowing through most of the century, absorbed idle funds and did not
crowd out any industrial growth. Without the quarter of a century of warfare, the development path of the British economy would have been rather
different, but it is by no means certain that its rate of growth would have
been any greater.

The second line of criticism, that industry was generally underfunded, is
rather more difficult to resolve. When industry resorted to the institutional
financial markets, investment could be obtained. Even when share
flotations were undersubscribed or abortive, as sometimes happened in the
case of motor or cycle companies, there were alternative means by which the
market could and did provide the required capital (Harrison). Nor were the
institutions completely averse to taking risks. In the late nineteenth century
many of the overseas ventures, like mining or plantations, were just as risky
as home investments (Michie 1981). Even there, firms like Foster and
Braithwaite were prepared to involve themselves in new ventures like electricity supply. It was also possible to raise very large sums for industry. The
London Stock Exchange was involved in numerous conversions from private to public companies in the brewing industry in the 1880s. The Guinness
share flotation of 1886 was handled by Barings and the six million pounds
sought was heavily oversubscribed (Cottrell 1980: 168). But for the most
part, British industry sought its investment elsewhere and was not crowded
out of the financial markets, nor as far as the evidence suggests was it
deprived of investment. Certainly the economy was not deprived of funds
because of overseas investment. Interest and dividends received by investors between 1865 and 1914 from abroad amounted to 130.4 per cent of net
foreign investment, so there was no net 'loss' of funds (Cottrell 1975: 45).

The criticism of the operation of financial markets made by historians has
much to do with the a priori assumptions about what those markets should
have done. Kennedy explicitly required the markets to take 'an economy-
wide view' and to support industries with a bright future. It may be doubted
that the motor industry in 1900 actually had a huge market, since the age of
mass car ownership was at least a quarter of a century away. But it is not the
obligation of investors or the function of financial markets to generate
national economic growth either in the short or long term. The concern of

investors and their professional advisers was properly confined to their own benefit, and the purpose of markets is to allocate resources according to the wishes of those representing demand and supply not to generate economic growth. While it is an axiom of neoclassical economics that market forces ought to allocate resources in such a way as to generate optimum growth, and that failure to do so indicates market imperfections, it is by no means clear that this was true in eighteenth- or nineteenth-century Britain. The markets seem to have functioned satisfactorily, and there is no doubt that the growth of the British financial institutional framework was a major element in international trade and investment in the rapid growth of the later nineteenth century. The nature of this development is consistent with the highly skewed income and wealth distribution and the existence of substantial investment seeking rentier income. The growth of important institutional investors is also consistent with a preference for secure investments and modest returns. Not all investment was, of course, profitable or even judicious. The affluence of the Dukes of Sutherland allowed them the luxury of substantial waste. Very heavy investment in draining land in Sutherland came to nothing, and attempts to develop coal mining at Brora, to manufacture gas from peat and to develop road locomotives were all failures.

The growth and diversification of the financial system was one of the main aspects of British economic development in these two centuries, and the principal characteristic of that system was its increasing international orientation. The criticisms levelled by historians really relate to a rather different set of problems. Why was the home investment ratio so low? If, as seems most likely, this reflected a lack of effective demand for funds in the home market, the real question is why this was so. That is a question not about the performance of financial markets but about industry itself.

4

Aggregate supply: production and productivity

I

In their analyses and explanations of long-term growth, historians have traditionally concentrated on the supply side of the economy. There is no doubt that the eighteenth and nineteenth centuries witnessed a great and unprecedented increase in production in many sectors of the economy. Between the 1750s and the First World War, raw cotton consumption increased from an annual average of 1.3 to 868.8 thousand metric tons, while pig iron output increased from 69 to 9,824 thousand metric tons between the 1780s and the First World War. Other manufactures and raw materials were produced or consumed on a similar scale of increase (Table 4.1). By 1914 there were over 20,000 miles of railway track in operation in Britain, virtually all constructed since the beginning of Victoria's reign.

Statistics such as these, especially when juxtaposing output levels at dates a century or more apart, create an image of sensational and dramatic increase. But over such a long period of time, the annual rates of growth of most of these indices are reduced to a rather modest level. The data in Tables 1.3 and 1.4 reflect the leisureliness of this growth, dispersed through most sectors of the economy, rather more realistically. By the first Census of Production in 1907, the manufacturing sector accounted for 27.7 per cent of GDP, with about one third of manufacturing in textiles and clothing and another third in metal manufacturing and engineering. Transport had become a major sector, while services as a whole accounted for over half the national income. The growth of the supply side was thus broadly based across the services and manufacturing sectors, although the share of agriculture was considerably diminished by the end of the nineteenth century.

II

Increases in supply can be generated by increasing factor inputs, capital or labour or land, or by increasing the productivity of those inputs, or by a

Table 4.1 *Industrial output of selected sectors*

	A	B	C	D	E	F
1751–60	1				4.4	
1761–70	2				5.2	
1771–80	2	36			6.4	
1781–90	8	42	69		8.0	
1791–1800	14	42	127		10.2	
1801–14	32	50	248		14.8	
1815–24	55	58	374		19.9	78
1825–34	106	66	685		22.6	94
1835–44	192	76	1,304		31.2	135
1845–54	290	89	2,250		48.4	149
1855–64	369	107	3,901		77.1	266
1865–74	476	145	5,732	490*	114.0	368
1875–84	605	156	7,390	1,360	147.3	484
1885–94	692	194	7,593	3,025	175.6	525
1895–1904	748	216	8,778	4,685	217.8	665
1905–13	869	233	9,824	6,510	267.8	759

A: Raw cotton consumption, U.K. annual average (thousand metric tons)
B: Raw wool output plus net imports of raw wool, U.K. annual average (thousand metric tons)
C: Output of pig iron, U.K. annual average (thousand metric tons)
D: Output of steel, U.K. annual average (thousand metric tons) *1871–4 only
E: Output of coal, U.K. annual average (million metric tons)
F: Tonnage of ships built in U.K. for British citizens and companies (thousand tons)

Sources: B. R. Mitchell, 'Statistical appendix' in C. M. Cipolla (ed.), *The Fontana Economic History of Europe*, 4 (1973) pp. 770, 773, 775, 780, 783.
B. R. Mitchell, *Abstract of British Historical Statistics* (Cambridge 1962) pp. 220–2.
S. Pollard, 'A new estimate of British coal production 1750–1850' *Economic History Review*, 2nd series 33 (1980) p. 229.

mixture of increased inputs and greater productivity. It is generally agreed that increases in land supply did not play an important part in British growth during these centuries, except during the Napoleonic Wars when loss of food imports necessitated an increase in the area of cultivation. Increases in capital contributed only a modest increase to the growth of GDP, before the First World War, as indicated by the very low level of investment in the domestic economy, and the similarly low rate of growth in gross domestic fixed capital formation.

Data for the late nineteenth century indicate that investment in manufacturing was rather low, and it is not likely that it was greater before that time. The fifty largest manufacturing firms in Britain in 1905 possessed an average capital of £4.4 million, compared to their American counterparts' £16.4 million average (Payne 539–41). The largest British manufacturing firm,

Imperial Tobacco Company, would have ranked only eighth in the United States. Even more surprising is the smallness of most British manufacturing firms in terms of capital, only a dozen reaching £5 million. Several of these were the result of late nineteenth-century amalgamations which produced United Alkali, the Calico Printers' Association, the Fine Cotton Spinners and Doublers, and the Bleachers' Association, all of which came in the top ten manufacturing companies. A large minority of the fifty largest companies were brewers, seventeen in all, with capital ranging from £2 million to £15 million. Even in the eighteenth century, this industry had produced some of the major companies in British industry. One major factor in the growth of such large companies in this industry was the growth in tied houses in the later eighteenth century, as brewers sought to safeguard and control outlets for their product. The capital tied up in loans and leases to publicans for the three major London porter brewers increased from £90,000 to over one million pounds between 1790 and 1830. By the latter date two of the main metropolitan brewers, Truman and Barclay, had assets worth £840,000 and £1,030,000 respectively (Mathias 1959: 77, 301). The brewers were one of the few industrial groups who sought capital on the Stock Exchange on a large scale in the later years of the nineteenth century. The fact that so many manufacturers did not do so indicates both their small scale of activity, such that they were able to find investment privately or out of profits, together with a preference for avoiding public investment which could threaten ownership and control of the existing partners or family. The tradition of the small private firm militated against seeking or accepting investment on a scale sufficient to produce very large firms with a few exceptions like the breweries.

Another indicator of the importance of capital is its relationship to employment. Most of the very largest manufacturing firms, as enumerated by Payne, had a very modest capital input per worker employed. The Imperial Tobacco Company was by far the greatest with £2,924 capital per worker, followed by Arthur Guinness £1,690, Lever Brothers £1,333 and Wallpaper Manufacturers £1,210 (Payne 539–41, Shaw 52–3, 60). Many had ratios much less than this. Surprisingly this was true of most of the heavy industry representatives. The two great armaments and shipbuilding firms, Vickers Sons and Maxim and Sir W. G. Armstrong Whitworth and Company, had a capital to employee ratio of £331 and £213 respectively. Guest, Keen and Nettlefold (GKN), John Brown, Cammell Laird and William Beardmore, all in the steel and heavy engineering industries, ranged from £182 to £664 per worker and the same range covered most of the larger textile firms, J. and P. Coats providing the only exception with an investment ratio of £880. In some areas of industry investment per worker was actually falling in the late nineteenth century, a peak of £118 per employee being reached in the coal industry in 1889 before falling to £108 by 1913 (Mitchell 1984: 43). The ratio of fixed assets to labour in Courtaulds fell from £67.2 in 1886 to £47.1 by the turn of the century, after having increased through the earlier part of the century (Coleman 1969: 230–1). In an international context, even the more capital oriented industries had less capital per worker than their main competitors. The British alkali industry averaged £111 per worker in 1852, when the average in the United States chemical industry was £415. By 1905 the main British chemical firms were United Alkali with £938 per worker and Brunner Mond with £575, compared to the American average of £1,007 (Haber 18, 55, 143, Payne 539–41).

Concentration on manufacturing is rather misleading since nearly all the biggest businesses in Victorian Britain were to be found in the service sector. By 1914 there were 36 companies with capital over £10 million. Most of these were railway companies, 20 in all, including the ten largest companies with a capital value over £50 million. Even these were dwarfed by the Midland Railway with a capital of £203.7 million and the London and North Western Railway with £124.9 million (Holmes). The railway companies were, of course, a major source of demand for finance which thereby had an important formative influence on the growth of the money markets especially in the provinces, and railways comprised an important part of gross fixed capital formation in the middle decades of the nineteenth century. The limited data available suggest a high capital/worker ratio on the railways. In 1914, the ratio for the London and North Western Railway was £1,469 per worker, while for the North Eastern Railway the ratio in 1913 was £1,476 (Irving 75–6, 288). Here too, there is evidence of a greater increase in labour than capital, as the ratio for the North Eastern had been as high as £1,708 in 1884.

While railways dominated big business in scale of capital before 1914, the next major group was provided by the banks, which accounted for one quarter of the firms with capital of over £10 million in 1914. Only seven other companies had a capital greater than this. They were British American Tobacco (BAT), Imperial Tobacco, J. and P. Coats, Lever Brothers, the Manchester Ship Canal Company, the Gas, Light and Coke Company and Shell. Even the middle range of companies from £5–10 million capital was dominated by railways and banks. Altogether 68 firms exceeded £5 million capital by 1914, including 27 railway companies and 18 banks, but only 10 manufacturers. Quite clearly, separation from the main financial markets and outside investment necessarily resulted, for most of British manufacturing industry before 1914, in capital light production.

III

The other main input in the production process is labour. The aggregate growth data indicate the considerable growth of labour and its importance in aggregate growth (Table 1.2). The period from the middle of the eighteenth century to the First World War experienced a relatively high rate of employment growth which was widely spread throughout the economy (Table 1.6).

Much of the growth in economic activity in these centuries, required considerable increases in labour. The growth of population and urbanization generated demand for construction and utilities, and for services such as transport and distribution all of which were major employers. Between 1851 and 1911 alone, as indicated in the Census of Population data, employment in construction and utilities increased by over 700,000, while transport and distribution each increased by over one million jobs. By the eve of the First World War, these sectors together comprised about one quarter of all employment. By then, three quarters of the housing stock of 7.5 million had been built in the nineteenth century. So had most of the commercial and industrial building, ranging from factories and offices to theatres and churches, and infrastructure like roads, docks, harbours and railways. Construction accounted for one third of capital formation in the domestic economy in the nineteenth century, and most of the increased production was achieved by increasing the labour force. The technology of building remained largely unchanged and production depended on a host of skilled and specialized craftsmen such as brickmakers and bricklayers, joiners, plasterers, plumbers, painters, and many unskilled labourers. Indeed, the host of unclassified labourers in the census estimates of employment suggest that the numbers actually assigned to construction were almost certainly underestimated.

Distribution was heavily labour intensive. For much of the eighteenth and nineteenth centuries, traditional methods of distribution prevailed in markets and fairs operated predominantly by individual stall holders. In London in the middle of the nineteenth century, there were over 43,000 street sellers vending fruit and vegetables, fish, and confectioneries from fruit tarts and plum duff to Chelsea buns and currant cakes. Eels, whelks, oysters, soup, sandwiches, baked potatoes, meat puddings and pies could all be bought in the street. For such vendors, overheads were modest indeed. A barrow, baskets, scales and weights could all be hired for a few pence and stock could be obtained on credit or with a loan from a moneylender (Fraser 95). In the course of the Victorian era this form of distribution was slowly replaced by shops, which grew in numbers, size and variety of stock retailed. Shops with multiple branches developed, as did the combination of many shops under one roof in the departmental store. Thomas Lipton started business as a grocer in Glasgow in 1871, but within a decade had bought four shops in that city and obtained outlets in Paisley, Greenock, Dundee, Edinburgh and Aberdeen. In the 1880s, Lipton established branches in major cities as far south as Bristol and Cardiff. Departmental stores were a natural extension of drapery shops, carrying an increasing range of stock and concentrating on the middle class market. By the middle of the nineteenth century, Knightsbridge and Kensington were established as fashionable areas and soon boasted stores such as Harvey Nichols, Derry and Toms and Harrods. By the 1880s, Lewis's had expanded from Liverpool to establish branches in Manchester and Birmingham. All these forms of distributive activity were heavily labour intensive, as contemporary photographs show. By the First World War, Harrods had 6,000 employees and Whiteleys 4,000 making them, as employers, comparable to some of the larger manufacturing companies (Shaw 52–3).

Transport was, of course, closely linked with the growth of construction and distribution. While transport was a major consumer of capital, producing in the railways the most capital intensive sector in the economy, it nevertheless exerted a substantial demand for labour. In the early eighteenth century, the coal trade between the Northumberland and Durham ports and the main market in London was estimated to provide a livelihood for between 25,000 and 50,000 people, including the dependants of the workers (Wrigley 60). Another estimate suggested that in 1700, one quarter of the entire population of London depended on the port for its livelihood (R. Davis 1972: 390). The total net tonnage of shipping registered in London increased from 650,000 tons in 1700 to 5,480,000 by 1850 (R. D. Brown 194). Growth of trade with the Americas generated substantial increases in the trade of the western seaports, especially Bristol, Liverpool and Glasgow. All forms of transport increased in the nineteenth century, overseas and coastal shipping, internal transport by road, water and railway, and by the later decades was further intensified by the appearance of the early commuters from the suburbs. By 1911 transport employment was exceeded only by the textile and miscellaneous service sectors, and was only just short of employing 1.5 million people.

While such services provided employment in response to the logistical needs of a larger and more urbanized population, so other services grew in response to rising affluence. Such services are usually labour intensive since the quality of service provision is directly related to the number of those providing it. This is obviously the case with regard to domestic service, the main component of the largest employment category, miscellaneous services, which numbered almost 2.9 million workers in 1911 and accounted for 15.8 per cent of all employment (Lee 1979). The number of female domestic servants alone numbered 1.4 million in 1911 and had increased by over half a million since 1851. In 1911 servants comprised a markedly larger share of the British population (3.8 per cent) than they did in other advanced countries like Germany (2.7 per cent), France (2.4 per cent) or the United States (2.0 per cent) (McBride 118). Professional employment grew considerably, especially in the latter half of the nineteenth century. Most of these jobs were labour intensive and high income activities, ranging from traditional professions like the law and medicine to the rapidly increasing teaching profession. The growth of other services reflected the growing affluence and diversity of society. Entertainment was one such area. Following the periodic flight of the eighteenth-century gentry to the seaside and spa resorts, the same fashion was adopted on more modest scale by the middle classes in the following century. By the end of Victoria's reign the working classes had joined the trek to the seaside to resorts like Blackpool and Bridlington, Southend and Yarmouth which attracted workers for day excursions, weekends and eventually week-long visits. Cheap lodging, food and drink, funfairs and amusements were all required, as were the special excursion trains provided by the railway companies. This was no small business. The incomplete estimate of the savings of 200 Lancashire holiday saving clubs reached £228,000 in 1906 (Walton 254). Blackpool one of the beneficiary boom towns increased its population tenfold between 1871 and 1911 to reach 61,000, and Southend's experience was very similar (Mitchell 1962: 24–7). Hotel, restaurant, transport and distributive services were all stimulated by the growth of popular entertainment. Ten to fifteen thousand people was a common crowd at horse races in the later nineteenth century, while seventy or eighty thousand might turn out at a major Bank Holiday event. There was a capital input too; the value of investment in racing blood-stock increased from £1.7 million in 1877 to £7–8 million in 1913 (Vamplew 47). Professional football was also able to command large attendances, including 30,000 to see the first match played under floodlights at Sheffield in 1878. Theatres and pubs offered other entertainments, and were particularly densely packed in the main urban centres.

The increasing affluence and diversity of society, together with its size and complexity generated the demand for a host of labour intensive services. But the labour inputs into manufacturing were equally impressive in this period. Data prior to 1851 are less than completely accurate, but a comparison of Lindert's employment estimates for the eighteenth century with the 1851 Census of Population gives a clear and acceptable indication of the main employment trends during that period. There was an aggregate increase in employment in excess of eight million people. About one quarter of that increase went into textiles and clothing manufacture while almost as many were absorbed by agriculture (Tables 1.5 and 1.6). There was a big increase in mining, by some 400,000 in the century after 1750, with services taking much of the remaining increase. Employment data for the Victorian period are both more reliable and available in greater detail. The largest employment sectors in mid century, agriculture and textiles/clothing both of which had over two million workers, did not play a major part in the employment growth of the later nineteenth century. Agriculture became the first sector to shed labour, some 600,000 by the First World War, while textiles/clothing gained a further half million workers. The main increase in this period was generated in metal manufacture and the engineering trades, which together increased by 1.2 million workers, and mining which gained about 0.8 million new employees. Many of these manufacturing activities were labour intensive, as reflected in the small capital investment per worker ratios prevailing in the largest firms in the early twentieth century. Mining and agriculture retained their labour intensiveness for most of the period. Steel making remained surprisingly modest in both labour and capital relative to the raw material input. The diversity of specialized and labour intensive activities in shipbuilding resembled the building industry. The emphasis on labour inputs rather than capital necessarily determined the structure and productivity of most sectors of the economy before 1914.

IV

The relative reliance on labour inputs rather than capital in much of industry had a profound effect on the structure of production. Only a few firms were relatively large in both scale of capital investment and workers per plant, such as the Imperial Tobacco Company which averaged 2,000 workers per plant and a capital/worker ratio of £2,924 in the 1900s. Only Lever Brothers, Guinness and Dunlop Pneumatic Tyres enjoyed a labour force of over one thousand per plant and capital/worker ratio in excess of a thousand pounds. The majority of firms in the recently formed textile amalgamations were relatively small, the Fine Cotton Spinners and Doublers Association averaged 600 workers per plant, the Calico Printers Association averaged 788, and the Bradford Dyers only 188. By contrast some of the engineering, shipbuilding and armaments combines blended very small capital investment per worker with a large labour force per plant. Armstrong Whitworth had a labour force of 25,000 spread over four plants, John Brown employed 16,205 in three locations, while Vickers Son and Maxim averaged 2,812 workers per plant, and William Beardmore averaged 2,250. None of these firms had a capital per worker ratio greater than £664.

The essence of industrial production in the nineteenth century and earlier lay in specialization, and the capital/labour variations quoted above reflect different forms of specialization of the productive process. The fact that specialization was possible on a wide scale reflects the buoyancy of markets throughout this period, to which export demand made a major contribution. Two types of specialization can be identified, although they obviously merge into one another. Most immediately apparent was specialization of workers by craft skill. While manufacturing prior to the twentieth century in Britain had a modest capital investment in most sectors, it still required a substantial input of skill. Often this was provided by skilled manual labour. Mechanical engineering was typical of this, and one of the main branches of that sector was the manufacture of textile machinery, in which Britain retained a world leadership through the nineteenth century. The high quality of textile machinery was achieved through craft skill. Spindles were made using grindstones and emery cloth to achieve accuracy on extremely small components. 'By and large, the technology was one of skilled repetitive work using conventional machine tools combined with considerable numbers of special-purpose tools designed and made by the textile machinery firms themselves. However distinguished their role in world textile engineering generally, and despite the size of their output, their machining techniques were a mixture of the conventional – not to say old-fashioned – and the highly specialized. The industry did little after 1850 to advance engineering technology in general, nor was it an important centre for general engineering training' (Saul 1970: 146). Even so, spindles were produced in runs up to 10,000 by the end of the century, and the industry produced the very latest machinery, such as the ring spindle spinning machine, even if there was little demand for it in the domestic market. The use of skilled specialist workers allowed industry to respond with great flexibility to the specific needs of their customers. This is well illustrated by the second largest branch of engineering in the nineteenth century, the manufacture of railway rolling stock. In fact, British railway companies differed from most overseas railways by manufacturing and repairing their own locomotives. Private firms, in contrast to their German and American counterparts, found themselves largely excluded from their domestic market and hence were almost totally reliant on exports. The main markets were in the Empire and South America, but the great majority of railway engineers who ordered rolling stock were expatriate British who prescribed in detail the equipment they wanted built. Thus an entirely different technical product was manufactured in British workshops than the standard all-purpose German or American engine. While a major overseas manufacturer, like Baldwin of Philadelphia, produced a basic engine in large numbers with plenty of standardized spare parts, British manufacturers, on a smaller scale of production, made expensive and high quality engines to the specific designs of their customers.

A highly skilled labour force provided the ability and flexibility for industries such as engineering to produce high quality machines in relatively small batches. The same type of specialization was also characteristic of shipbuilding. A large number of separate skilled and semi-skilled jobs were characteristic of the shipyards, and over half the workers were skilled men (Pollard/Robertson 153, 178–80). Many yards specialized in certain types of ship from ocean going liners to tugboats. Increasing demand allowed this;

merchant shipping tonnage built in Britain increasing by over one million net tons between 1860 and 1913. This does not, of course, include the substantial Admiralty contracts which enabled firms like Armstrong Whitworth and Vickers Sons and Maxim to specialize in warships. Thus each yard assembled and trained a workforce to produce a particular kind of ship. Extreme specialization of function allowed shipyard owners to employ in sequence the appropriate squads of workers as the ship was built, each group paid and hired on a daily or even hourly basis. Labour intensive manufacture was not inefficient. It was estimated that in the decade before 1914, the average output of British shipyard workers was twelve tons per year, twice that of their American competitors and four times that of German workers (Pagnamenta/Overy 126).

Specialization of craft skills enabled such industries to produce high quality specialized ships and machinery. Other industries became increasingly specialized in their product in response to the massive demand increase in the Victorian period and particularly after 1850. This form of specialization was clearly marked in the textile industries. The rapid growth of cotton manufacture in the three quarters of a century before 1850 was dominated by the spinning factory and the cottage based handloom weavers. As the powerloom displaced the handloom in the weaving side of the industry, it was mainly adopted by spinning firms as an extension to their business. There was thus an increase in vertical integration of the two main manufacturing processes, and 75 per cent of powerlooms installed before mid century were in combined mills as was a similar proportion of additional spinning capacity (Lee 1980a: 167). By 1850 integrated firms employed 11.1 million spindles, compared to 9.9 million operated by specialist spinners, and 199,000 powerlooms compared to 51,000 worked by specialist weavers (Ellison 72–3). The integration of the two processes was a common feature of the growth of cotton production abroad. The advantage of such a structure of production lay in the extension of costs, and especially fixed cost overheads, over as large a volume of output as possible. Since, in the first half of the nineteenth century, powerlooms were relatively cheap to buy and install, often into unused mill capacity, combined manufacture spread overheads. This increased the number of markets available and offered a sensible defensive strategy in face of volatile markets and falling profit rates.

The unusual feature of the British cotton industry was its departure from combined production in the second half of the nineteenth century. Integrated production did have disadvantages as well as benefits. The main drawback lay in the fact that it required the maintenance of a fixed yarn/ cloth ratio otherwise some productive capacity would lie idle. This not only required careful management of the production line, but restricted manufacturers to a small range of yarn and cloth types. Specialization of production into either spinning or weaving offered a greater flexibility of operation within the single sector. The occasion for this was a massive increase in demand around the middle of the century, particularly for low quality cloth for the Asian market. The big increase in demand generated several separate but linked forms of response. Most obvious was the appearance of the Oldham Limiteds mainly from the mid 1860s onwards, specialist yarn spinning firms of an unprecedented size. Specialized weaving increased on a much smaller scale of production. Powerlooms were cheaper than spinning machinery, longer lasting and more adaptable which meant that very little capital was needed to set up production. While combined firms continued to operate and increase in capacity, the rate of expansion of this section of the industry was much slower than hitherto. Apart from the advantage of product specialization in a booming market, the coordination problems inherent in combined operation may well have reached the point at which they became uneconomic particularly as economies of scale were not great in cotton manufacture. Variations in the spindle/loom ratio in 1884 ranged from 57.1 to 66.7, suggesting that the full cost savings from vertical integration were often not being realised and that combined firms often did little more than house two distinct manufacturing processes under the same roof (Chapman/Ashton 493). In the weaving boom during the twenty years after the end of the American Civil War, in Burnley alone thirty combined firms closed down their spinning section (Farnie 164). The Ashworth family firm, which had commenced as a spinning concern in the 1840s and proceeded to combined production, closed the spinning section in the 1880s and became a specialist weaving business (Boyson 77–82). The trend away from integrated production after the middle of the century was not confined to cotton. In the worsted industry the same shift took place as a result of a great increase in demand, especially in the multiplication of fabrics for fashionable clothing, including mohair, alpaca and cotton.

The combination of labour intensive production and specialization of skilled input and output allowed small firms to prosper and enabled some industrial growth to be accomplished by the entry of new firms and the proliferation of small businesses. This had been a prime characteristic of growth in all textile manufactures in the eighteenth century, especially in the West Yorkshire woollen manufacture where the domestically located production, combined with agriculture, could be very considerably increased simply by augmenting the number of weavers. Much the same was true of the growth of handloom weaving in the cotton industry prior to the 1830s. Even in the later nineteenth century many branches of textile manufacture, as in woollens or specialist cotton weaving, remained characterized by very small units of production. In the coal mining industry, expansion also involved a considerable proliferation of pits, many of them very small. On the eve of the First World War, 3,289 colliery undertakings were operated by 1,589 separate firms. As late as 1924, when many of the smaller pits had been closed, almost one third of those still being worked employed less than fifty men.

One dimension of specialized growth, which became significant later, was the extreme geographical concentration of production. Not only did the cotton industry become concentrated in Lancashire, but spinning became the speciality of towns like Oldham and Bolton and weaving became specialized in the north east of the county. Even within this grouping there was further specialization so that coarse and plain cloth was made in Rochdale and in Rossendale, medium plain goods in Blackburn and Bury, light fancy goods in Preston, Chorley, and Ashton, and heavy fancy goods in Bolton and Bury. Similarly across the Pennines, worsteds and woollens were geographically separate, and while Bradford was the centre of the cloth manufacture, Leeds was pre-eminent in clothing manufacture. Regional specialization was also a long established but increasing aspect of agricultural production. Differences in geological conditions encouraged this development. Hence mixed farming was practised intensively on the light lands of eastern and southern England and in the Lothians in Scotland. In the clay areas of the north and west of England pastoral and dairy farming were a more suitable specialization. The impact of imported wheat on farming was thus felt more severely in the corn counties of the south east as the value of British wheat production fell from an annual average of £26.6 million in the early 1870s to £8.4 million by the later Edwardian years (O'Grada 180). While butter and cheese production were also affected by competition from European and New Zealand imports, farmers close to major cities were able to shift their dairy production to milk. In London and Manchester, ninety per cent of local dairy produce was sold as milk. Elsewhere, as in Wales and the South West, the absence of such large local markets for milk obliged dairy farmers to persist with butter and cheese production.

While specialized production and relatively small units of production remained prevalent until the First World War, there was a spate of amalgamations and some vertical integration in the later decades of the nineteenth century. Some of this amalgamation was more apparent than real. Amalgamations in the textile industries, such as the Fine Cotton Spinners and Doublers, were federations of companies rather than integrated businesses. The members of the amalgamation retained a great deal of independence and their representatives on the large board of directors sought advantage for their own firm (Payne 527–30). They were thus cartels rather than integrated combines. Much more real was the growth of integration in shipbuilding. Armament firms like Armstrong Whitworth integrated shipbuilding into their business in order to obtain lucrative and secure naval contracts. More defensive was the backward integration into steelmaking by firms like Cammell Laird and John Brown. Palmer's of Jarrow integrated shipbuilding with steel manufacture, coal mines, gas works, bridge building and iron ore mining (Pollard/Robertson 90). Integration in consumer industries was often a small step combining under a single ownership processes which had long been closely interrelated. The preparation and distribution of food and drink had long been closely and obviously linked with agriculture. Hops and barley were the main ingredients in beer production, the latter selling far more than any other cereal according to Gregory King's estimate for the late seventeenth century. The used grains returned to agriculture for cattle feed, while the grounds were used for fertiliser and excess yeast supplied to bakers and distillers. In the eighteenth century, 'the London breweries, and still more the London distillers, who fattened many thousands of pigs and cattle annually about their works on the "wash" and the grains, became part of a division of labour between industries quite beyond that of their own integrative pattern from barley-farmer to publican; and in such ways the London brewing trade provided important constituents for the production of Londoners' bread, beef and milk and even their gin – quite apart from that central item of diet which the industry ostensibly existed to supply' (Mathias 1959: 42). By the late nineteenth century Thomas Lipton had extended vertical integration to encompass fruit growing in Kent, jam and biscuit manufacture in London and distribution through a large number of shops. Other food processors also integrated several production lines. Biscuit makers like MacFarlane Lang and Huntley and Palmer were originally bakers, Crosse and Blackwell extended their range from pickles, sauce and ketchup, their eighteenth-century trade, to encompass jams, table jellies and preserved salmon, while J. J. Coleman of Norwich made mustard, blue, starch, chocolate, vinegar, beer and patent wine (Fraser 167–72). Lever Brothers also combined activities ranging from chemical manufacture to food processing as their product range increased.

V

The organizational structure of the economy, distinctive as it was, conditioned the kind of technical advance which could be incorporated into the productive process and hence the contribution of productivity to growth. The contribution of Total Factor Productivity (TFP) to the growth of GDP was not impressive in the eighteenth or the nineteenth century, although it did register a rather higher growth contribution in the mid nineteenth century. Even so, it is hard to dispute the conclusion that 'there was no substantial phase in the nineteenth century during which the trend in the rate of growth of TFP was upward' (Matthews 213). Certainly the growth of TFP was poor compared to twentieth-century performance. The weighted sectoral share of TFP in GDP fell sharply in the later decades of the nineteenth century, agriculture, mining, manufacturing and construction all bearing a share. In the coal industry there is general, although not universal, agreement that productivity was declining in the late nineteenth century. The exhaustion of the easily exploited seams of coal forced the mining of deeper and more difficult seams which required more labour and led to a fall in output per man year from 319 tons in 1884–88 to 257 tons in 1908–13 (Taylor 1968: 46). The factors which contributed to this included falling capital per worker (cramming more men in the same area, more men employed to offset the effects of irregular attendance, and the opening of small ill-equipped collieries), a decline in the quality of coal bearing land, increasing age of mines and depth of workings (Mitchell 1984: 325). Output per man year thus increased up to the final third of the century, and then probably declined. Coal cutting machinery was introduced relatively late into British mines, mainly because seams were too thin, although many mines were below the threshold pit size of 40–80 men required to justify the adoption of such machinery (Greasley 253).

Because of its large size in relation to the rest of the economy, agriculture exerted an important influence on aggregate productivity growth in the eighteenth century although it declined in the Victorian period. While there was a substantial increase in agricultural output, and thus of output per acre since there was little increase in the area of land cultivated, the rate of increase was only 0.3 per cent annually during the eighteenth century. Labour productivity grew at the same rate as output per acre (Jones 1981a: 70–7). Estimates of total factor productivity in the nineteenth century indicate a prevailing rate of 0.3 per cent, rising to 0.5 per cent in the middle decades of the century (Hueckel 192, O'Grada 179).

This fairly constant and extremely modest rate of productivity growth was achieved in the eighteenth century primarily by organizational changes. The enclosure of open fields and the concentration of ownership into fewer hands has long been recognized as an important element in such change, and plausible estimates by McCloskey have demonstrated a productivity difference of about 13 per cent between open field and enclosed systems (1975: 160). Others have suggested an increase in fifty to one hundred per cent in the productivity of land when enclosed. Recent estimates suggest that most of the enclosing of land was completed by the beginning of the eighteenth century, and that the previous century witnessed the main reorganization of that kind (Wordie 502–5). The other major organizational change, which also had its origins in the seventeenth century, was the growing adoption of mixed farming. More livestock meant more manure for fertiliser which, in turn, helped increase the productivity of arable land. This allowed the cultivation of a wider range of fodder crops, and maintained larger herds of animals than hitherto. The introduction of new breeds of sheep and cattle producing more meat and less bone, and more quickly as the age of slaughter fell, reduced the cost of feeding, and increased the amount of meat per animal.

Increased agricultural production required substantial additions to the labour force until the middle of the nineteenth century. By the First World War, employment had fallen by about 30 per cent from its mid century peak, while the level of output remained fairly constant (O'Grada 177). For the first time, labour saving machinery made a contribution to productivity increase and accounted for much of the reduced employment. The reaping machine saved two to three days' work per person per acre as against traditional methods of reaping, while the threshing machine increased labour productivity by a factor of four or five. These two innovations together accounted for half the reduction in the rural labour force and illustrate the labour intensity of traditional agriculture. Agricultural employment was also affected by the increasingly effective competition of imported food in British markets, cutting the value of crop production in half in the later decades of the century and creating unemployment in that part of the industry. The pressure of foreign competition, together with the diminishing role of agriculture in the national economy as other sectors grew faster, explains the decline in this sector's contribution to total factor productivity in the late Victorian period. Half of the fall in TFP in national income between 1856–73 and 1873–1913 was attributable to agriculture. This should not be seen entirely in terms of the inadequacy of British agriculture. Apart from the cost advantages of large scale wheat production in the Americas, some of the increases in food imports represented a diversification of diet through the purchase of products whose cultivation lay outside the capabilities of British agriculture and climate.

Since it might be expected that agriculture should make only a modest contribution to productivity, and that mining with its finite resources should be similarly restricted, the principal hope for productivity increase must focus on manufacturing. But this was modest in the middle of the nineteenth century, and actually declined in the late Victorian decades. Nevertheless, productivity in major manufacturing sectors like steelmaking and textiles was closely related to the adoption and improvement of technology. In the steel industry at the end of the nineteenth century only one third of total costs were spent on labour and capital, the bulk being raw material inputs of iron ore and coal. Ore and coke together comprised 75 per cent of the cost of pig iron which in turn constituted half the cost of open hearth steel and two thirds the cost of Bessemer steel (McCloskey 1973: 74–5). Technological improvement to reduce costs by more efficient use of raw materials was thus central to the achievement of productivity increase, as it had been in the eighteenth-century iron industry (Hyde 206).

In several sectors of industry, the dominant technology appeared to reach the limit of its potential development by the late nineteenth century. McCloskey estimated that productivity in pig iron manufacture fell after 1890, while productivity advance in Bessemer steel manufacture ceased in the 1880s, and wrought iron and cast iron similarly reached a technological limit about the same time. Similarly the basic machinery of cotton spinning, the self-acting mule, reached a technical peak of efficiency in the late nineteenth century. Much historical debate has thus centred upon the relative efficiency of British manufacturing, and specifically has questioned why industries like steel and textiles were not quicker to adopt newer technologies, like open hearth steel production and ring spindles in cotton manufacture, when compared with their competitors overseas. Amongst other problems, this debate has revealed the difficulties involved in estimating productivity, and the even greater obstacles involved in having such estimates generally accepted. Indeed there is even a problem in evaluating the 'significance' of a productivity estimate. Analysing the records of the Leeds engineering firm of Greenwood and Batley, Floud calculated a labour productivity increase of 2.3 per cent and a total factor productivity increase of 1.0 per cent between 1856 and 1900. Furthermore, productivity changes can conceal contradictory shifts. 'These two movements, the increase in the production of cwts per man-hour, and the fall in production of machines per man-hour, may be explained by the same factor, which stems from the nature of the machine tool as both the input and the output in the manufacturing process. It is likely that machine tools were, gradually, becoming more versatile and more efficient, but they were also becoming more complicated: they therefore took longer to make, although they themselves allowed the metal of which they were made to be machined more quickly and easily' (Floud 1976: 202). It is not surprising, therefore, that contradictory conclusions about the rise or fall of productivity have been offered by different scholars. In steelmaking, McCloskey concluded that British producers were as productive as their major foreign competitors (McCloskey 1973: 114ff). More recently, R. C. Allen has suggested that British steelmaking was more efficient than its German and American rivals in the middle of the century, by virtue of greater technological efficiency and lower raw material prices, but that the position became reversed by 1900. By the Edwardian years, he estimated, German and American steelmakers were 15 per cent more efficient than their British rivals (Allen 915). Rising costs of imported iron ore and failure to invest in new plant contributed to this. But the reluctance to invest in new capacity was neither irrational nor foolish. Allen agreed with McCloskey and Temin that the British steel industry faced a slow growth of demand such that new capacity was not warranted (R. C. Allen 937, Temin 1966: 149). The rapid growth of steel-making in the United States and Germany, in the later decades of the nineteenth century, reflected a buoyant demand in those markets, helped by the protection of high tariffs. Even a massive price reduction by British manufacturers would not have been enough to make substantial inroads into those markets, and certainly not enough to increase the productive capacity of the British industry to match German and American steelmaking. The scale of production, and thence the level of productivity attained, in the British steel industry was restricted by the smallness of the home market, itself a function of the slow growth of the economy and the weak demand for steel as a result of the slow growth of industry. Even the fact that British steel makers supplied almost one quarter of overseas demand in countries other than the United States and Germany by 1913 was not enough to compensate for the weakness of the domestic demand.

The cotton industry retained its pre-eminent position in world markets until the First World War, although the productivity performance of this sector has been the subject of debate. Not surprisingly, the main productivity gains were found in the middle decades of the nineteenth century. The self-acting mule increased efficiency in spinning as it was improved to operate on increasingly fine qualities of cotton, and the powerloom was an obvious improvement on the handloom. Thus there was a steady increase in output per spindle in yarn production and in output per loom in the weaving section of the industry. Greater efficiency was also contributed by mechanical handling of the preparatory stages of manufacture, by the increase in machine size and speeds to reduce manpower per unit of production (Blaug 365–6). Such technical advance did not even necessitate heavy investment. Hand mules could be converted to become self-acting, and spinning machines could be modified to carry more spindles. But the possibilities for increased productivity on mule spinning and powerlooms were virtually exhausted by the late nineteenth century. The industry has been criticized by historians for its slowness in adopting newer technologies such as the ring-frame in spinning and the automatic loom in weaving. By 1913 the British cotton industry had only 19 per cent of its spinning capacity in ring-frames, compared to 87 per cent of American spindleage, and only 1–2 per cent of weaving capacity in automatic looms compared to 40 per cent in the United States (Lazonick 1983: 198).

The advantage of the ring-frame over the mule lay in the fact that it could be operated by unskilled labour and thus saved labour costs, while the mule needed a skilled operative. On the other hand, the ring-frame needed good quality cotton and increased costs in that way. The differential shift towards ring spinning in America as opposed to Britain reflected the different structures of the cotton industry on either side of the Atlantic. In Lancashire the skilled spinning operatives were strongly organized and able to resist any attempt to introduce ring-frames which would have threatened their livelihood. But they were not averse to increases in the intensive working of existing machinery by lengthening mules or speeding up their operation, much of the cost of which could be passed on to their subordinates. Both sides of the spinning industry had a vested interest in a more intensive working of existing technology, and this was achieved mainly by 'bad spinning' or the use of poor quality cheap cotton. This practice could produce substantial reductions in productivity as a result of frequent breakages of poor cotton. Ironically, reduced productivity was compatible with cost reduction through more intensive working (Lazonick 1981: 496ff). By contrast, in the American spinning industry labour was both less unionized and more mobile. It was also less skilled. Both sides of industry had an interest in replacing mules by ring-frames. Consequently the American industry used better quality cotton and thence achieved greater productivity. 'On this basis we find that labour productivity in spinning 32s around the turn of the century was about 40 per cent higher in Fall River than Oldham even though work intensity (that is, the pace of work) was apparently lower in Fall River. The use of better quality cotton in Fall River permitted about 40 per cent more spindles per experienced worker without any deterioration in work conditions' (Lazonick 1981: 509–10). Different strategies in weaving also reflected the comparative advantages in the spinning sector. The breakages which resulted from the use of poor yarn were less costly with powerloom weaving than with the more expensive automatic loom. This latter machine, like the ring-frame, needed high quality raw material to enable a high throughput by which means low unit costs could be achieved (Lazonick/ Mass 14–15). The automatic loom was also labour-saving in that operatives could attend more machines than in powerloom working. Whether adherence to traditional technology for valid reasons resulted in rising or falling productivity in the British cotton industry is disputed. Sandberg inclines to the view that a modest rate of increased efficiency obtained up to the First World War, while Lazonick has argued that labour productivity stagnated in the two decades prior to the war because workers could not be induced to work harder to compensate for poor material worked on outmoded machinery (Sandberg 116, Lazonick/Mass 20–32). But neither interpretation would doubt the declining capability of this major industrial sector to generate productivity increase on a scale sufficient to have a marked effect on aggregate industrial productivity.

VI

The characteristics of the supply side of the British economy in the eighteenth and nineteenth century are quite clear. Modest capital inputs limited the potential of technologically oriented increases in production. But limited capital inputs, especially in manufacturing, with its corollary of relatively small businesses, enabled owners to retain control because they did not have to seek very large investments which would have obliged them to become public companies. Small private firms with limited capital could obtain their modest investment needs from friends and family and thence retain their independence. This necessitated specialization of production, a possibility realised by virtue of the massive growth of overseas markets especially after the middle of the nineteenth century in sectors like textiles, shipbuilding and several branches of engineering. Relatively low reliance on capital or productivity meant that production leaned heavily on labour inputs. This had a particular advantage in the context of business fluctuations which were especially prevalent in shipbuilding and its supplier industries, but affected virtually all sectors of production. Since workers were employed for very short periods, often by the day or even hour, they could easily be dismissed. Labour could thus be treated as a variable cost, and production which combined little capital and technology with considerable labour enabled manufacturers to carry a high variable cost component in their operations. The labour force thus paid the price of trade recessions, and manufacturers were able to insulate themselves from such vagaries of commercial fortune. The extent of this varied between industries. It was very much a characteristic of shipbuilding and engineering, rather less important in textile manufacture.

The characteristics of production before the First World War reflected an economic structure which had considerable limitations. To some degree those limitations were manifest in the low rate of growth of the national income. With such a low productivity growth, the growth of GDP was necessarily modest, and such a low rate of growth in GDP could only have been consistent with high productivity had there been no growth or contraction in factor inputs. The productive increases which were achieved, particularly in manufacturing, depended on a buoyant external demand to sustain specialized firms and cheap labour to keep down costs. Such industries were thus vulnerable to the appearance of a rival with even cheaper labour, like the Japanese cotton industry which had begun to develop in the later nineteenth century. It was also vulnerable to technological developments which could not be exploited through skilled manual work. It is generally agreed that the highly skilled manual worker was the essence of much of British manufacturing, and the justification for adherence to labour intensive manufacture (Harley 1974, Musson 1980: 99). But in industrial sectors where technical advance was embodied in machinery rather than workmen, the British tradition of manufacture limited or even precluded involvement and success. Britain remained peripheral to the two main technological developments of the second half of the nineteenth century, the development of the internal combustion engine and the creation of a generation of machine tools designed to mass produce interchangeable parts. While British engineering was eminent in the manufacture of textile machinery, steam engines and boilers, it lagged behind the United States in light engineering, sewing machines, small arms, clocks and watches and the technological skills later applied to electrical engineering and the motor car. These technologies were imported in the installation of American arms manufacturing machinery at the Enfield Arsenal in the 1850s and the establishment of a Singer Sewing Machine plant on Clydeside in the 1870s. In some cases, British developments in new sectors were inhibited by the success of earlier technologies. The efficiency of the gas industry and a fully developed railway system based on steam power together hampered the introduction of electric power and traction by providing an established and acceptable alternative (Byatt). Electrical engineering in the Victorian years entered Britain primarily in the form of branches of American or German companies. Even when new industries emerged they bore the traditional orientation towards labour intensity. The motor industry was ideally suited to mass production with emphasis on assembly line production of inter-changeable and standardized parts. But in the British industry no firm managed a rate of production of one car per man year before 1914, well below Ford's production rate a decade earlier (Saul 1962: 43–4). In the early years of the century, American Ford workers took 300 men to make 1,700 cars, while in Britain, 250 Argyll workers made 400 cars, and 326 Albion Motors employees made 265 chassis. Not surprisingly, Ford made rapid inroads into the British market from its assembly plant established in 1911 in Manchester. 'Nothing in Britain could compete for power at the price; in 1913, the Ford had RAC (Royal Automobile Club) rating of 22.4 and sold for £135 to £220, according to the body and accessories. The Austin 10, selling at £325, was rated 14.3 and the Star 10–12, rated at 15.8 sold for £265 (Saul 1962: 24).

Concentration on skilled manual work was a limitation which had effects beyond the difficulty of competing with skilled machines. Both sides of industry had an interest in the maintenance of the existing structure, owners for reasons of business control and vesting costs in labour, the skilled workers for maintaining their craft advantage and, for the better paid, to protect their differentials. Training was essentially practical, learned on the job, with little regard for theory or technology. Thus in steelmaking: 'It was an art not a science. It was termed black magic because of the knowledge they [the furnacemen] had. There was no instrumentation at all. No text-books. They had to do their work by the eye. The eye was the important thing. You had to know the colour of the steel, the flame' (Pagnamenta/Overy 77). The converse of this was a scant regard for technological knowledge throughout industry. There was nothing comparable to the availability of scientific education provided by the state as in Germany where £10 secured lectures in Chemistry for a year at the University of Berlin and a further £12 the use of a laboratory. In 1899 the number of students enrolled in the laboratories of science faculties in German universities and poly-technic schools reached 20,000 (Haber 71). British chemical manufacture remained committed to heavy inorganic chemical production in the late nineteenth century, and missed many of the new developments in organic and electrochemistry. The growth of the artificial dyestuffs industry in Germany, much of which was exported to Britain, and the large scale oper-ations of German coal tar producers, with considerable investment in tech-nical development, overshadowed the British chemical industry at the time. Historians have been very critical of the poor performance of the British industry relative to its German counterparts (Lindert/Trace, Richardson 1968).

While British manufacturers lagged behind their competitors in techno-logical developments in chemicals, electrical engineering and the embryonic motor industry, some of the major industrial sectors also faced an uncertain future. Apart from cheap labour, many industries relied on cheap raw materials such as coal and iron ore. Both were freely available and used wastefully in the nineteenth century. Between 1750–1870, the British iron industry produced 125 million tons of pig iron, consuming in the process 400–500 million tons of iron ore (Hyde 187). By the middle of the nineteenth century, some iron producing regions were having to import iron ore, and this shortage became a national one by the end of the century. While imported ore was negligible in relation to product in the 1860s by the end of the century it comprised almost one third of total ore consumption and increasing costs reduced the competitiveness of the industry. Coal reserves too, although far from exhausted, were a finite resource which was used as a very cheap fuel throughout the period before 1914. Coal was also firmly embedded in the labour intensive production processes and was an essential cheap fuel for railways and steamships. Exhaustion of resources or increased costs of coal represented as great a threat to nineteenth-century technology as did rising labour costs or loss of overseas markets.

One further force was active in the later nineteenth century proscribing the effectiveness of the productive system to generate growth. It can be seen in operation in the context of the railways, the largest institutional creation of the economy other than the financial system. By the later decades of the nineteenth century the profitability of the railways was being eroded. Social pressures crystallized into political pressure as railways became regarded not simply as commercial enterprises with the goals of narrow self-interest but as public services required to be responsive to social as well as commercial considerations. External pressure, therefore, induced the railway companies to provide a level and quality of service which was not the commercial optimum. Furthermore, government legislation prevented the companies from raising their rates. The costs of uneconomic transport were borne by the railway companies themselves and contributed to falling productivity and prevented the rationalization of passenger services (Irving 277–8). This kind of social control was not applied exclusively to the railways but extended widely through the late Victorian economy. It included pressure for the maintenance of high standards of probity in commercial life, opposition to monopoly power (one of the objections made against the railway companies), support for reasonable wage levels, and support for the purchase of British-made products. In so doing, the development of social control revealed a fundamental conflict of view as to what function industry should fulfil, either that of a profit maximizer or that of a provider of social services. Such diverse pressures have operated on industry in the present century, supporting Boswell's conclusion on the nineteenth-century experience. While informal control did modify the harsher excesses of market forces 'such achievements were probably inconsistent with a renewal of economic success on the world stage' (Boswell 239, 256).

5

Aggregate supply and economic growth

I

The previous chapter explained the nature of supply side growth in the eighteenth and nineteenth centuries; the present chapter relates that pattern of growth to the overall growth of the economy. Not only have supply side factors been heavily stressed by historians, but the growth of industry and its related technology has been widely regarded as the central event in modern economic development, as well as its prime cause and vehicle. As was indicated in chapter 1, the prevailing explanatory thesis is based on the notion of an industrial revolution. Of the two central strands of this thesis, the first strand, of a sudden and revolutionary transformation, has been gradually modified by the stretching out in time of the transitional phase and by the admission of the importance of pre-revolutionary developments. In effect, therefore, this aspect of the thesis has been abandoned. But the second strand of the thesis, the primacy of industry in the development process has remained central to the traditional explanation. It has remained virtually unchallenged from Toynbee and Mantoux writing before the First World War to the recent interpretations by Landes and Crouzet. Indeed the latter defied the conventional accounting notions of economics by asserting that industrial production represented a more important indicator of economic progress or decline than national product (Crouzet 1982: 376).

The basis for an industry-led growth explanation lies in the great increase in production in industries like textiles, iron, coal and shipbuilding from the middle or later eighteenth century, this growth coinciding with the perceived increase in economic activity generally (Table 4.1). It is also bound up with the idea of British economic primacy in the nineteenth century, as the 'first industrial nation'. This status is justified and illustrated by the substantial lead gained by Britain over other western economies in the early nineteenth century in the production of several manufactures. By the 1830s, by which time reasonably acceptable comparative statistics are available, British annual consumption of raw cotton averaged 105.6 thousand metric tons, compared to 33.5 thousand for France and 3.9 thousand for Germany (Mitchell 1976: 780). In coal and lignite production, the relative output in million metric tons was, Britain 22.8, France 2.0 and Germany 1.9 in the 1830s, while pig iron output, similarly measured, showed Britain producing 0.70, France 0.24, Germany 0.11 and the United States 0.17 (Mitchell 1976: 770–3, Temin 1964: 264–7). Bairoch's estimate for total industrial product shows Britain outstripping all other countries until the later nineteenth century, reaching a peak share of world manufacturing production of 22.9 per cent in 1880 (Bairoch 1982: 275).

Just as Britain's economic primacy from the mid eighteenth century to the later Victorian years was based on manufacturing, so the 'closing of the gap' in production, as other countries caught up, became interpreted as evidence of relative British decline. British production of pig iron was overtaken by the United States after 1890 and by Germany in the 1900s. In steel production the transition came a few years earlier. By the First World War the gap had become a considerable one. Comparative steel output, in million metric tons, on the eve of the war found Britain making 6.93, Germany 16.24 and the United States 23.68. In coal production Germany was not far behind Britain by 1914. While Britain retained a substantial lead in cotton consumption in Europe, manufacturers had been overtaken by the United States in the late 1890s and consumed only 72 per cent of American consumption in 1910–13 (Sandberg 62). This shift in international manufacturing capacity led both contemporary commentators and generations of historians to depict the later decades of the century as a period of decline and depression, and seek explanations for the loss of industrial vigour and to identify the culprits responsible. As Britain's lead in manufacturing output in textiles, metals and engineering disappeared, so the national share of manufacturing output as a whole fell sharply and dropped well behind that of both Germany and the United States by 1913 (Bairoch 1982: 275, 284). But amidst the analysis and criticism, the one aspect of the problem which has remained unquestioned has been the centrality of industry in economic growth and prosperity. If that basic assumption is unsound, the entire explanation of British growth needs to be reassessed.

II

The most specific exposition of industry-led growth, as well as the most famous, is that formulated by Rostow. Not only was this explanation rooted in traditional ideas, as Rostow himself observed, but might legitimately be regarded as the clearest definitive statement of that tradition, as indicated in Chapter 1. Using the analogy of an aeroplane taxiing and taking-off, Rostow defined the crucial economic break-through as spearheaded by a leading sector. It was the transformation of this sector which in turn carried the rest of the economy into the era of modern economic growth. Curiously, in most of Rostow's case studies of national economic take-off the leading sector was found in services rather than manufacturing, namely railways. But in the first take-off, in Britain, the leading sector was identified as the cotton industry, and the means of its transformation was a radical change in production by virtue of new technology. Similarly central to his thesis were the linkages of the leading sector to other parts of the economy, generating backward effects through the demand for new inputs, lateral effects through necessary developments in the infrastructure, and forward linkages inducing new industrial development by reductions in production costs or the provision of a new input. 'It is the combination of these three types of spreading effect from rapidly growing sectors infused by new production functions which justifies empirically the notion of leading sectors in economic growth' (Rostow 1963: 7). Expounding the thesis in rather broader terms, Rostow included coal and iron technology, the steam engine and foreign trade amongst the necessary and sufficient conditions for take-off (Rostow 1960: 31). Such a narrowly based transition necessarily perceives growth as essentially unbalanced. Indeed advance in a few sectors creates further imbalances and hence generates more growth. Since industry is the focus of such developments, the most probable source of unbalanced advance is likely to be technological change. 'The wave of inventions which led to the Industrial Revolution originated in attempts to break through these two bottlenecks: to overcome timber shortage by coke, and shortage of yarn by the use of machinery. Similarly the pressing need for power led to the discovery of the use of steam to produce rotary motion' (Streeten 182). Rostow too, and more recently Hicks, placed great importance on technological and scientific advances which marked the divide between the industrial and pre-industrial worlds. 'This impact of science, stimulating the technician, developing new sources of power, using power to create more than human accuracy, reducing the cost of machines until they were available for a multitude of purposes, this surely is the essential novelty, the essential revolution, working so vast a transformation because it can be repeated one might almost say it repeats itself over and over again' (Hicks 148).

While accepting the primacy of industry in leading growth, and its underpinning by technological advance, many historians have found Rostow's leading sectors to be rather too restrictive. Accordingly a greater part of industry, or even all of industry has been cast as the vehicle of economic development. McCloskey estimated the contribution of a number of sectors to the national increase in productivity of 1.2 per cent annually over the period 1780–1860. Traditional manufactures were extremely prominent in his estimate, textiles accounting for 0.27 per cent although iron contributed only 0.018 per cent (McCloskey 1981a: 114). In all, his 'modernised sectors' together accounted for 0.52 per cent or just under half the total increase in productivity. Set more widely still is the Kaldor thesis which advanced the hypothesis that the growth in national income was a function of the growth in manufacturing output, but not closely related to growth in the other sectors, namely agriculture and services (Kaldor). Stoneman tested this thesis on British data covering the long period 1801–1969 and accepted the Kaldorian argument about the relationship between manufactures and national income but obtained results which were indeterminate as regards the relationship between the other sectors and growth of GDP (Stoneman 317). Kaldor extended his thesis to encompass Verdoorn's Law, that growth of manufacturing productivity was a function of growth of output. Linking this to the earlier proposition, the inference must be that growth of national income is related to both industrial growth and increased productivity, thus again linking technology and industrialization functionally to aggregate growth.

Before looking at the historical evidence, it is worth considering in abstract terms what is implied and required to fulfil a leading sector growth thesis. The essential features of the growth pattern will depend on the rate of growth of the national economy, the rate of growth of the leading sector, the size of the leading sector in relation to the rest of the economy, and the strength of the linkages between the leading sector and the rest of the economy. As can be seen from McCloskey's estimate, a high rate of productivity increase in a small sector, like the cotton industry, or coastal and foreign shipping another of his modernized sectors, can make only a modest contribution to aggregate change. The low rate of growth of British GDP does not actually leave a great deal to be found by way of growth stimuli. Even so, an extreme hypothesis, such as the Rostovian heavy reliance on the cotton industry in the late eighteenth century, does impose very great demands on the chosen leading sector. At that time the cotton industry comprised no more than five per cent of national income. For this sector to account for the increase in GDP growth of 0.6 per cent per annum in the take-off period, it would have had to increase its output by about twelvefold. Such a rate of increase lay beyond the capacity even of the cotton industry, raw cotton consumption increasing by a factor of about five and a half. Textiles, and mainly cotton, doubtless accounted for most of the increase in growth in the industry sector, 0.15 per cent in the late eighteenth century and 0.43 per cent in the early nineteenth century (Table 1.3). This was certainly a greater stimulus to increase in GDP growth than agriculture or services, but was only just able to lift the aggregate growth rate of the economy to two per cent. Furthermore this period, roughly from 1770 to 1840, represented the phase during which industry contributed most to GDP growth prior to

1914. The weighted sectoral growth rate of industry appears to have remained constant at a little under one per cent from the beginning of the century to the 1870s, falling to 0.73 per cent thereafter (Table 1.4). At no point in these two centuries did industry contribute half of the total modest growth rate of British GDP. As for the various leading sectors or staple industries, such as textiles and iron, their rate of growth must have remained close to that of the national economy as evidenced by the fact that their share of national income remained fairly constant. During the century after 1770, the combined textile industries ranged between 9–11 per cent of national income, apart from a brief jump to 14 per cent in 1821, while the iron industry 1801–1907 ranged within 3.5–7.6 per cent except for a brief jump above 10 per cent in 1871–81 (Deane/Cole 212, 226).

McCloskey's modernized industrial sectors together contributed 0.29 per cent of the total productivity increase of 1.19 per cent per annum between 1780 and 1860 (1981a: 114). Estimates for total factor productivity by sector for the Victorian period indicate both a lower total contribution to GDP growth and a modest share of that productivity vested in industry, 0.29 per cent in 1856–73 and 0.16 per cent in the period 1873–1913 (Matthews 229). Such data are hardly compatible with either an industry-led thesis or even an interpretation which gives manufacturing pride of place in the economy. Stoneman's test of the Kaldor thesis, it will be recalled, supported the idea that growth in GDP was a function of industrial output. But Stoneman's regression results covered the entire period from 1801–1969 (Stoneman 311). The best statistical result was obtained for the period 1856–1965, with significant parameter estimates and a coefficient of determination of 0.72. But if the same thesis is tested on the data for the nineteenth century alone, the explanatory power of the model is sharply reduced, and a coefficient of determination of only 0.37 is obtained. Quite clearly the strength of the relationship between industry and growth of the aggregate economy was much stronger in the twentieth century than hitherto. Indeed the relationship for the nineteenth century, and by inference also for earlier periods, was statistically significant but relatively weak. There is no support for an industry-led explanation here.

There are two possible ways in which the traditional explanation might be reasserted. The first lies in the argument that the crucial changes in the economy wrought by industrialization were at first so small as to be imperceptible. This is the argument advanced by Landes in rather poetic terms. 'Beneath the surface, the vital organs were transformed and though they weighed by a fraction of the total – whether measured by people or wealth – it was they that determined the metabolism of the entire system' (Landes 122). This rather beguiling suggestion allows belief in the traditional industry-led thesis even though statistical data and quantitative evidence do not support it. Indeed, it is essentially a view which requires the subjection of such material in favour of the historian's 'feeling' for a problem. But since aggregate growth can only be expressed meaningfully in terms of relative size, rate of change, and similar quantitative measurements, the refutation of such measurement makes little sense. Furthermore, this kind of impressionistic inferential explanation, by ignoring or rejecting measurement, precludes further investigation by making it unnecessary. Such an approach is unhelpful and cannot be taken seriously. The second way in which the traditional primacy of industry might be restored relates to its relationship to other sectors in the economy and most especially to the service sector. If the intersectoral linkages, as proposed by Rostow, bound the services to manufacturing in such a fashion that they could be seen to be ancillary derivatives of industrial growth then the industry-led explanation could be sustained.

III

The small amount of attention paid to the service sector is one of the curiosities of the historiography of British economic development. The size and importance of the services is not in doubt (Tables 1.3 and 1.4). Only during the first three decades of the nineteenth century was the contribution to growth of this sector less than that of industry. By the late nineteenth century the gap between these two aggregate sectors was substantial, and from mid century the services contributed over half the weighted sectoral output contribution to GDP growth. Crafts' recent estimates indicate a steady increase in the share of national income in the service sector from 42.6 per cent in 1700 to 47.7 per cent by 1870 (Crafts 1985: 62–3). By the 1907 Census of Production, the share of GDP in the service sector was 59.0 per cent (Deane/Cole 175). The scant interest shown by historians in this sector can only be explained in terms of an implicit assumption that the service sector was largely if not entirely developed in response to industrialization or, in present day jargon, was paid for by the 'wealth creating' part of the economy which was manufacturing. References to services in the main textbooks appear to accept such an interpretation. Mathias pointed out that the growth of shipping, the docks, urbanization, banking, local transport, distribution and even domestic service in Lancashire depended on the growth of the cotton industry. 'One cannot set out to increase the national income or expand the economy by increasing the number of clerks and lawyers and dock workers, even though as a result of industrial expansion these groups may rise and profit more than manufacturing groups. The initiative which determined economic expansion and the redeployment of the labour force was firmly centred in the manufacturing and the transport sectors and derived from the vast increases in productivity made possible by steam power' (Mathias 1969: 273). As Hartwell noted, many eminent textbook writers have made some reference to services, like Mathias, but have not related them to economic and structural change except in a minor and subsidiary role (Hartwell 1971: 208). Nor have recent scholarly contributions departed from this practice. The two volume history of the British economy published in 1981 contains few footnote references to the service sector (Floud/McCloskey). Even the transport system, placed alongside manufacturing in Mathias' judgement, has usually been treated as a product of manufacturing growth. Thus canals and improved river navigations which were often projected and funded by local industrial interests are stressed as important features of eighteenth-century transport. McCloskey includes canals, railways, coastal and foreign shipping among his modernized sectors, collectively comprising almost half the productivity increase of the modernized sectors (McCloskey 1981a: 114).

The greater contribution to GDP growth of the industrial sectors than services before 1830 or 1840 facilitate the exposition of industry-led growth. Rather more problematic is the Victorian period during which the sectoral contributions were reversed (Table 1.4). Growth was spread across all the services, and in the half century before the First World War service sector employment increased from 3.3 million to 7.6 million jobs and increased its share of national employment by ten per cent (Lee 1984: 140). Any explanation of industry generated services for this period must depend on an increasing ratio of service employment to manufacturing.

Two questions emerge from these data. Were the linkages between industry and services sufficiently widespread or strong to justify a simple functional dependency? If that was not so, are there other plausible determinants available to explain the growth of the service sector? There were obvious links between industry and services in which the latter was primarily a response to the former. The improvement of the Aire and Calder river navigation at the start of the eighteenth century was instigated and paid for by Leeds wool merchants and Wakefield coal owners, both of whom wanted access for their products to the port of Hull. The greater part of canal mileage, developed later in the eighteenth century, linked the industrial areas of northern and midland England, and carried cotton, coal, iron ore, chemicals and other heavy materials. The early railways were developed in industrial and mining areas, such as Lancashire and the north east, and coal was a vital commodity on many lines throughout the nineteenth century. Similarly developments in coastal and overseas shipping were closely bound up with the exchange of industrial raw materials for manufactured goods between regions of Britain and between Britain and the rest of the world.

But the complementary relationship between development in transport and industrial sectors was not a simple one-way relationship. Obviously the growth of transport in some situations preceeded industry or even was unrelated to it. Many are familiar with Defoe's graphic description of the volume and variety of consumer goods and food flowing into London from the provinces in the early eighteenth century (314ff). Apart from the coastal shipping of coal from Durham and Northumberland which had been sufficiently impressive in the sixteenth century to form the basis of one industrial revolution thesis, food and cloth came into the metropolis from most parts of Britain. Not surprisingly the major improvements in roads in the first half of the eighteenth century, were radial developments from the capital and mainly within fifty miles of it. London was at the same time by far the greatest international seaport in Britain and soon in the entire western world. Such growth was so closely intertwined with manufactures like shipbuilding and repairing, the construction of docks, wharves, warehouses and roads, as was food processing with food distribution, that it is quite meaningless to distinguish between them. While industrial development contributed to the demand for better transport, as in nineteenth-century railways and ocean going steamships, the pattern of causation can equally clearly be identified running in the opposite direction. The considerable increases in productivity in intercontinental shipping between the early seventeenth century and 1850 were hardly a simple functional response to industrialization. The decline in piracy allowed more space on board vessels to be devoted to cargo rather than to guns and fighting men, and reduced costs by cutting the size of crews needed. Further the greater volume of international trade made possible organizational improvements which reduced the time lost while ships waited idly in port for a cargo. Falling insurance rates, also a result of the decline in piracy, helped reduce costs. Intercontinental migration increased in the nineteenth century, a function of the widespread development of international trade and growth in the entire Atlantic economy, and provided a scale of activity sufficient to generate further increases in productivity (North 1968: 173). Such reductions in shipping costs stimulated industrial production by cutting the cost of exports of textiles and engineering products which were so important to the growth of those industries. The two-way process continued through the nineteenth century. Increased efficiency of marine engines allowed steamships to travel further without refuelling, thus cutting the capacity lost in carrying coal which could be turned over to cargo. Apart from increasing demand for coal, shipbuilding, and marine engineering, this advance helped reduce transaction costs on increasingly long journeys to facilitate trade and increase the markets available to manufacturers (Harley 1971). Nor was transport development entirely bound up with industrial needs. The proliferation of railway lines in the Victorian period extended well beyond the centres of industry to the far west of Wales, to Cornwall, and the Scottish Highlands. Rural and suburban Surrey and Sussex were as well served by the railway as were industrial Manchester and Birmingham.

The study of intersectoral linkages has not proceeded very far in historical analysis, partly because of data limitations. But some present day studies are relevant because they have identified sectoral links common to both advanced economies and less developed ones. Industries which exhibited both high backward and forward linkages, in the Rostovian sense, included iron and steel manufacture, coal, chemicals, textiles, paper and printing. Agriculture and mining exhibited high forward linkages only, while clothing, shipbuilding, food processing and machinery, including transport equipment, had high backward linkages. The only sectors with low linkages were fishing, transport, trade and other services (Yotopoulos/Nugent 301). This suggests strong linkages between various manufacturing sectors, but a much lower level of linkages between industries and services. Nineteenth-century data bear out this view. Many of the major industrial sectors were closely interrelated, like textiles and clothing, iron and steel with engineering, and coal providing industry with its basic fuel. As late as 1870, the greater part of steam motive power was applied in the textile and clothing industries, and much of the balance was found in metal manufacturing (Musson 1976: 437–9). In 1907, the production of British engineering was dominated by textile machinery and railway locomotives, followed by other steam engines (Saul 1970: 143). Iron and steel, engineering products and coal were all major inputs into shipbuilding.

Sectoral linkages measured in employment concentrations were very clear throughout the Victorian period, manifesting four distinct types. Textile manufacturing was consistently related to mechanical engineering, much of the employment in which was devoted to the production of textile machinery, while all the metal making and working trades were related. Mining was a distinctive type of industry sector by virtue of its employment size, although it exhibited links with metal working, shipbuilding and most branches of engineering. But by far the greatest interrelated sector encompassed 16 of the 27 employment sectors within it and included 65.2 per cent of employment in 1911. This largely homogeneous group of employment sectors comprised all the services together with a number of consumer good industries such as printing and publishing, timber and furnishing, clothing and footwear, food, drink and tobacco, as well as construction and utilities (Lee 1981: 445–6). During the course of the Victorian period this large aggregate sector grew in share of total employment by about 10 per cent, and accumulated linkages with additional sectors. The services were always the basis of the agglomeration, but links with consumer manufacturing increased in number and strength as the century progressed.

The fact that services were linked to each other but not very closely to much of manufacturing raises the question whether services could and did grow in response to demands other than were exerted by industry. Census of Population data allowed this thesis to be tested on Victorian employment linkages. Two popular notions were dispelled. Firstly, the idea is often advanced that service employment was simply proportionate to population size. If that were the case, service sector employment expressed as a ratio per 10,000 population would show no variation about the mean employment (at county or sub-regional level) and would register zero scores for both coefficient of variation and skewness. Such descriptive statistics derived for the benchmark years 1861, 1881 and 1911 indicated that only the distributive trades were closely related to population size (Lee 1984: 142). The second question is whether service employment was functionally dependent on employment in manufacturing. Such a relationship, if valid, should not be affected by growing productivity in manufacturing. In such a case, manufacturing would simply sustain more service workers. Nor is a high manufacturing employment ratio per head of population inconsistent with a high service ratio as would obviously be true if sectoral employment was expressed as a percentage of the total. But a high manufacturing and service employment provision is possible by increasing the activity rate, drawing more people into employment from the existing potential labour force or by attracting migrant workers. To test the thesis that service employment was a function of manufacturing the service ratio for each service sector was regressed against the manufacturing ratio for each of the three benchmark years. In the case of transport, distribution and banking/commerce there was no statistically significant relationship at any of the benchmark dates. In the case of professions, miscellaneous personal services (of which the greater part was domestic service), and government/defence, as well as all the services together, there was a significant but inverse relationship. This points to specialization in either manufacturing or services in different parts of the economy, but not to a simple functional relationship between them. This confirms the specialization suggested by the major sectoral linkages. This does not imply, of course, that there was no link between manufacturing and services, nor does it deny the existence of some service sector activity which was functionally dependent on manufacturing. Mathias' example of the growth of services in Lancashire in response to the demands of the cotton industry is undoubtedly valid (Mathias 1969: 245–6). Furthermore, examples can be found of wealthy industrialists migrating to Brighton and similar watering places to enjoy, in rather more salubrious surroundings, the profits of Yorkshire mills, Tyneside shipyards and Welsh coal mines. But there was clearly much more to the growth of the service sector than can be attributed to manufacturing stimuli alone.

The service sector was able to respond to a number of very potent sources of demand in both the eighteenth and the nineteenth century. The growth of the City of London as a major European financial centre in the eighteenth century, developing into the major international financial centre in the Victorian period, was the most obvious stimulus to such growth. As Rubinstein's researches have shown, fortunes accumulated in manufacturing compared pretty poorly against those made in the City in both number and size (Rubinstein 1977a, 1977b, 1980, 1981). The City drew on very traditional sources of wealth for the investment it spread across the world. Landed estates, trading profits and proceeds from government borrowing all contributed and bound together the establishment of land, government and finance into a single integrated economic and social fabric (Cassis).

Wealth was itself a major stimulus to the growth of the service sector. From the professions like the law and medicine to domestic service and all the many forms of distributive and transport service, rising incomes provided the key to expansion. The importance of concentrated wealth for the size and diversity of effective demand, as described in chapter 2, was further manifest in the burgeoning service sector. Growing middle class incomes, especially in the later Victorian years, extended the effective consumer demand of society and continued the increase of the service sector. Similarly, population increase and concentration into major urban centres increased the demand for additional distributive and transport services. So too did government, both directly through the provision of public services and indirectly by virtue of its need to borrow and pay for them. There was, throughout these centuries, a diversity of demands in addition to manufacturing growth which stimulated the massive growth of the service sector.

IV

The conventional view of the contribution of the supply side to growth needs to be modified. The notion that development was channelled through leading sectors, generating unbalanced growth, cannot be sustained. Indeed the evidence is strongly in favour of balanced growth, with manufacturing and services making a similar contribution until the 1870s. In the later decades of the nineteenth century the growth contribution from manufacturing fell quite sharply, just as that of the agricultural sector had declined after mid century (Tables 1.3 and 1.4). Within these aggregate sectors, a significant contribution to growth came from several industries and services, further supporting a balanced growth interpretation. Statistical measures of balanced growth are not very different from the method used to estimate structural change (Yotopoulos/Nugent 295, Table 1.5). Balanced growth might be expected to be associated with a modest rate of structural change. This was certainly true of the British economy which experienced a very low rate of structural change in the second half of the nineteenth century.

Balanced growth and low structural change should not cause surprise in the context of the very slow rate of growth of the British economy. Another related effect was the diversified nature of growth, reflecting a much richer pattern of development than is suggested in crude industry-led explanations. It was obviously true that industrial growth generated a demand for support services in commercial and banking facilities, transport and several other sectors. But equally obvious is the fact that such service provision did not come into existence solely at the behest of industry. Indeed it can be argued with some persuasiveness that the prior existence of many such services allowed the development of industry. It is also true that part of the growth of the service sector was largely unrelated to industry, but was a response to the older traditional stimuli of landed wealth and international commerce. The distinction between manufactures and services is an analytical convenience which, like most necessary simplifications, is a departure from reality. Much of industry and the services were closely related to each other in a variety of ways which precluded a simple one-way causal relationship.

The most intriguing problem posed by British growth in the centuries before 1914 is the recurrent theme of the slowness of growth and change. There are several other peculiarities of British development which impinge on the role of supply side forces, and especially on industrial performance. As many historians have found, many of these features became exaggerated in the later nineteenth century, as slow growth decelerated, and the contribution of manufacturing to output and productivity increase showed a marked fall. Indeed recent calculations of total factor productivity by sector in the Victorian period show manufacturing performing much more poorly in this regard than services. While productivity was very low in all manufacturing sectors other than utilities, especially after 1900, and was negative in agriculture, mining, and construction, there were substantial increases in productivity in transport and communications, commerce, and public and professional services (Feinstein 1982: 178–9). It is generally accepted that a partial explanation for industry's falling contribution to output and productivity can be identified in the exhaustion of technical advance in large sectors like textiles, together with the increasing problems of mining. For the rest there is much unresolved debate. One pertinent aspect of this problem is the low level of investment in the domestic economy and the very high foreign investment both of which were peculiar to Britain in this period. It is not difficult to show that a greater level of investment in the home economy could have generated faster growth and probably increased productivity. Using one such model, Crafts has argued that an investment rate of 12 per cent from the early 1870s would have increased consumption expenditure by 25 per cent by 1911 (Crafts 1979: 536). Other estimates could be derived in the same way to demonstrate that the economy 'failed' in generating sub-optimal growth. It may be that such is the case with most economies on most occasions. The debate about the performance of the late Victorian economy has been confused because the distinction has seldom been recognized between the actions of individuals and groups in the economy and the aggregate economy itself. It has been assumed that the good of one was identical with the good of the other. Thus the export of capital which 'ought' to have been invested in home industry is either irrational or indicative of some remiss behaviour, say by lazy or unimaginative businessmen, or some weakness in the system. The evidence for this is not persuasive and, vitally, does not recognize that the interests of the investors and their obligations were limited to their personal, family or clients interests. It is not the concern or duty of an investor to buy assets which will make the economy adopt its optimum growth path, but simply to fulfil their narrower personal ends. The problem of industrial finance and its limited scale in the Victorian period lay not with the financial markets but with industry itself. The demand for funds was simply not there on a large scale, and that was the reason for the low investment ratio at home.

The Victorian economy probably performed as well as it could, as McCloskey has argued (1970, 1979) but not because its productive resources were fully employed, which was certainly not true of labour, or even optimally allocated. But the structure of that economy was set, and its low rate of growth and productivity largely determined by the limitation of its industrial base in size and composition, and by the restricted role played by industry in wealth generation and asset holding. Insofar as the idea of an industrial revolution has any meaning, it is most realistically explained by North as the outcome rather than the cause of changes in industrial organization and specialized production stemming from the growth of markets. Further it was a phenomenon which realised its potential in technological advance at the end of the nineteenth century rather than a hundred years earlier (1981: 162–9). Redefined in this way, the crucial beginnings of recognizable modern manufacturing are identifiable in the United States and possibly Germany rather than in Britain. British industry was able to make only a modest impact on a slow aggregate growth rate in the eighteenth and nineteenth centuries because it was small in total output, small in scale of production and its reliance on labour and craft technology rather than capital and labour saving technology, confined it to limited productivity growth. The general lack of interest in scientific education, the basic theory underlying technology, the science of business organization and management, all cut British industrialists off from the potential benefits of the kind of practice adopted in American engineering or the research and development in German chemical manufacture. Far from being revolutionized by industry, the low rate of growth of the British economy before 1914 and the modest and faltering contribution of manufacturing to that growth is witness to the weakness and fragility of industrialization in the first industrial nation.

6

Foreign trade and payments

I

Britain's long-established role as a maritime trading nation, together with the desire of historians to determine the position of early British industrialization within the wider process of international economic development, has meant that the role of foreign trade, in British economic growth, has been much debated. Indeed, it remains the subject of considerable disagreement and controversy. Since economic theorists have suggested the possible influence of trade on growth ranging from highly beneficial through neutral to extremely deleterious, a very wide range of optional explanations are available. Two major problems are posed by the international context of British economic growth. Most immediate and obvious is the question, were such external relations including imports, exports and foreign investment important elements in British growth? This has been hotly debated in terms of original causation and subsequent development. Secondly, a rather wider question is suggested about the nature of economic development itself. Was this essentially a nation-based phenomenon, as traditional explanations have tended to argue, with modern economic development starting as industrialization in one country, Britain, and thence spreading to rival and competitor nations such as Germany and the United States? Alternatively, is this familiar paradigm wrong? Was economic growth in the modern world an international phenomenon from its very beginning and its history characterized by the emergence of such an international system? Both explanations contain some truth, but they do represent quite different paradigms of modern economic history and the nature of modern economic development. The explanation advanced here falls firmly into the latter of the two explanatory traditions.

II

The main aggregate indicator of the importance of exports is their ratio to national product. Eighteenth-century estimates are, needless to say, of uncertain accuracy, but all recent series indicate an increase in the export ratio through the course of the century. Indeed there is much similarity between the Crouzet and Crafts estimates, showing an increase in the export ratio from about eight per cent in 1700 to 15–18 per cent a century later (Table 6.1). This ratio fell during the Napoleonic Wars, and during the first half of the nineteenth century when so much investment was channelled into infrastructure developments like the railways, before rising to much higher levels in the Victorian period. By 1913 the export ratio stood at 30.1 per cent and, by that time, included a considerable component of export service earnings (7.6 per cent) as well as export of goods (Matthews 433). It is the very great increase in the export ratio in the second half of the nineteenth century which persuaded historians to label Britain an 'export economy' and, in contrast, to play down the importance of exports in the previous century and a half. But it is beyond dispute that for the bulk of these two centuries exports grew faster than national product, as indicated by the rise in the export ratio. Furthermore, such estimates do not include net property income from abroad which is part of the credit side of international trade and finance and which grew very considerably in Victorian Britain (Table 12.1).

The composition of exports by commodity was dominated throughout these centuries by textiles. Woollen goods accounted for 21 per cent of the increase in the value of exports between the beginning of the eighteenth century and the 1770s, while similar shares were contributed by other textile products and metal manufactures (Crouzet 1980: 62–8). Between the 1770s and 1840s the textile industries accounted for 70 per cent of the increase in exports, and about 50 per cent was contributed by the cotton industry alone. Even in the period of highest export growth, from the 1840s through to the 1870s, the main stimulus came from the textile manufactures, cotton accounting for 27 per cent of the export increase and the wool and worsted industry for a further 14 per cent. The metal manufacturing industries contributed 22 per cent. While export growth slowed down in the later decades of the nineteenth century, the export ratio for goods alone hardly increasing after the early 1870s, the increase was still dominated by the cotton industry. Almost 40 per cent of the increase in exports between 1873 and 1913 was due to the cotton industry, while iron and steel contributed 15 per cent, machinery 20 per cent and the coal industry 26 per cent (Mitchell 1962: 304–6). By 1913 these export staples together contributed a very large share of total export earnings for goods, and cotton retained the pre-eminence in exports that it had held since the late eighteenth century. Indeed it has been argued, convincingly, that the decline in export growth towards the end of the nineteenth century was a result of the failing export momentum of the cotton industry. Its capacity to increase productivity by extending and improving mechanization was by then exhausted, and with it went the power

Table 6.1 *Trade: Ratio of payments to national income (annual averages per cent)*

	Exports	Exports	Exports	Imports	Balance of visible trade	Balance of invisible trade	Balance of trade
1700	8.3	7.5/8.5	7.4	11.6			
1730			11.0	16.2			
1760	12.4	11.6	15.0	13.3			
1780	10.5	7.8	8.3	11.2			
1801	15.3	17.8	16.3	26.9			
1811			10.9	16.9			
1821		12.6	12.6	15.7	−3.3	6.2	2.9
1831			10.9	18.2	−4.1	5.3	1.2
1841		11.1	11.4	18.6	−4.7	5.6	0.9
1851			14.2	20.9	−5.6	6.8	1.2

Note: See Table 12.1 for period after 1851.

Sources: Col. 1: N. F. R. Crafts, 'British economic growth 1700–1831: a review of the evidence' *Economic History Review*, 2nd series 36 (1983) p. 197.

Col. 2: F. Crouzet: 'Toward an export economy: British exports during the Industrial Revolution' *Explorations in Economic History*, 17 (1980) pp. 78–9.

Cols. 3–7: P. Deane and W. A. Cole, *British Economic Growth 1688–1959* (Cambridge 1967) pp. 36, 282. B. R. Mitchell, *Abstract of British Historical Statistics* (Cambridge 1962) pp. 279–283. W. A. Cole, 'Factors in demand, 1700–80' in R. Floud and D. McCloskey (eds.), *The Economic History of Britain since 1700* (Cambridge 1981) Vol. I, p. 64.

to lead in export markets by cost and price reduction. Since other industries were unable to fill the role vacated by the cotton industry, the aggregate rate of growth of exports declined (Matthews 449–51).

The substantial role played by industries like cotton in the export trade was mirrored by the dependence of such industries on markets overseas. This was especially true of the cotton industry itself. Except in the 1780s, when it fell as low as 16 per cent, the share of exports in final product value of this industry always exceeded 30 per cent prior to 1800, and was over 50 per cent throughout the nineteenth century (Deane/Cole 185, 187). Loss of overseas markets would have severely curtailed the growth of this industry. Indeed, in the second half of the nineteenth century, exports took 60–80 per cent of the output of the cotton industry, a very high level of export dependency. Exports were also an important part of the sales of the woollen industries, averaging over 40 per cent through the eighteenth century and between 20–35 per cent in the following century (Deane/Cole 196, Crouzet 1980: 86). Estimates for eighteenth-century woollen production in England suggest that about 40 per cent was exported in 1700, and that the proportion rose to 67 per cent by the end of the century. The main growth in this industry took place in the West Yorkshire branch of the trade, and about 80 per cent of the increased output in that area was exported. In other words, without a substantial export demand there would have been little increase in the woollen industry in the eighteenth century (Deane 1957: 220).

Exports played an important role in providing the demand for other manufactures. In the 1740s, according to a recent estimate, 8,000 tons of bar iron were exported out of a total output of 19,000 tons (Hyde 50). The American colonies constituted an important market for iron products, especially nails, tools and hardware. During the first half of the nineteenth century, exports comprised 20–30 per cent of iron products apart from a temporary fall in the late 1820s. This proportion increased as the century progressed and averaged 40 per cent in the second half of the century, rising to a peak of 50 per cent in the Edwardian decade (Deane/Cole 225). The growth of the coal industry also depended on overseas markets. While exports were only 3–6 per cent of output in the century prior to 1850, by the 1890s the share was over 20 per cent and by the eve of the First World War it was 34 per cent (Buxton 1978: 55, 86).

The importance of industries like textiles and metal manufactures in export growth, and their dependence on export markets, has encouraged the formulation of investigations into the importance of trade in British growth in the context of export-led growth hypotheses. This has been further encouraged by the primacy accorded to industry in general and these industries in particular in explanations of industrial revolution. Indeed in that specific context, export-led growth might provide an explanation for the initial causal spark which started the revolutionary growth process. Couched in such terms, the export-led growth thesis is not very plausible. This kind of explanatory device has usually been proposed in the context of less developed economies responding to strong external demand for primary products from industrial countries, such as coffee and rubber in nineteenth-century Brazil, cotton in Egypt or India or even to explain the Canadian wheat boom at the end of that century (Caves). But to explain the industrial development of the 'first industrial nation' it seems unlikely that demand from similarly developed or less developed economies would provide such a stimulus. Accordingly, the export-led growth thesis has been rejected as a determinant of eighteenth-century growth or as a cause or prerequisite for industrialization. But unfortunately the narrow terms within which the export-led thesis has been considered has meant that the rejection of the hypothesis in its most stark and simplistic form has also meant the rejection of the international dimension in explanations of growth, certainly in the case of the eighteenth century. R. Davis, although a leading authority on seventeenth- and eighteenth-century trade, strongly espoused the traditional thesis of home-produced industrialization. 'The role of overseas trade in Britain's economic development changed during this period. It was important to the modest industrial growth that was going on before the Industrial Revolution, but made little direct contribution to the advance of the Industrial Revolution itself and was not essential in the early stages of its development' (1979: 63). The key to the whole process, for Davis, lay in the technological changes in cotton manufacture, changing supply side conditions and thereby launching a new kind of economy. The contribution of trade prior to the great revolution was simply to add strength to the preparatory phase and help 'create the base without which the industrial take-off might not have proceeded so fast or gone so far' (1979: 10). This type of argument, which was also adopted by Landes, places the thrust of its explanation on industrialization in one country, and thus has to play down the pre-industrial and international aspects of development in order to maintain the exclusiveness in place and time of the revolutionary breakthrough.

A more specifically statistical statement of the same thesis has been presented by Bairoch and Crouzet, both of whom play down the importance of trade in British eighteenth-century growth by refuting an export-led growth explanation. Comparing the increase in national income from 1700–10 to 1780–90, Bairoch estimated that external demand accounted for between five and nine per cent of total additional demand, while the home market generated the other 91–95 per cent. Thus foreign demand, he concluded, comprised a small and peripheral share of the increase in demand, although it did increase later to account for 30 per cent of United Kingdom increased demand between 1780–90 and 1860–70 (Bairoch 1973: 568–70). He thus reiterated the conclusion reached by R. Davis and Mokyr that external demand was not sufficient to produce the revolutionary explosion. Building on Bairoch's estimates, Crouzet came to a similar conclusion, assigning a modest role to the foreign trade sector prior to the 1840s while admitting the importance of trade in brief spurts such as 1740–60 and 1800–15. Thus the 'export economy' is the characterization of the phase of British development in the Victorian period, after the establishment of the Industrial Revolution on the basis of home demand. This view, in turn, supports the argument of Eversley that a substantial growth in home demand in the period 1750–80 laid the foundations of the Industrial Revolution and that the overseas market did not play a major role in that process. This explanation depends on the narrow perspective and assumptions of the Industrial Revolution hypothesis. In that context there are only two possibilities. Either the Industrial Revolution was sparked off by outside influences and was export-led in the most crude variant of that thesis, or the Industrial Revolution was caused by internal factors and trade was unimportant. When the restrictive assumptions of the Industrial Revolution theory are set aside, it can be seen that this treatment of the role of exports runs together two quite separate problems. The first is the applicability of the export-led growth model to eighteenth-century Britain and the obviously correct conclusion is that it provides a very implausible explanation. The second problem, completely obscured in the revolutionary model, is to assess the quantitative contribution of exports in particular and trade in general to economic growth. This question will be investigated further after imports and balance of payments have been discussed.

III

As the export ratio increased steadily through the eighteenth and nineteenth centuries, so too did the ratio of imports to national income (Table 12.1). As manufactures dominated the composition of British exports so food and raw materials were the principal items in the composition and growth of imports. During the first three quarters of the eighteenth century food imports were the main source of increase, especially sugar, tobacco, tea, coffee, and later grain. There was also a marked increase in the import of raw materials for manufacture, including silk, flax, hemp, wool and cotton for the textile industries, and iron, timber and tallow. There was, as part of the import trade in raw materials, a substantial trade in re-exports mainly of colonial produce to mainland Europe. This included tobacco and sugar from the Americas and silk and calicoes from the East Indies. In the eighteenth century, re-exports were seldom less than 50 per cent of domestic exports. From the late eighteenth century until the mid nineteenth century, import growth was dominated by raw cotton which alone accounted for 70 per cent of the increase between 1784–6 and 1854–6 (R. Davis 1979: 36, 41). While established food imports like sugar, wine, spirits, tea, and coffee increased, there was a greater relative growth in the import of grain, meat, butter, and dairy produce. Through the second half of the nineteenth century this pattern of imports was sustained although there was some diversification in food products imported, as refrigeration made possible the import of meat from South America and Australasia. Even so, on the eve of the First World War food still comprised almost 30 per cent of imports and textile raw materials a further 20 per cent. By this time re-exports had become a modest and static component in the balance of trade. Raw cotton still accounted for 9.2 per cent of imports, and manufactured goods and fuel were still only 5 per cent of imports, most of that being iron and steel and machinery.

The pattern of imports and their countries of origin remained fairly stable through these two centuries. In the early eighteenth century, imports were obtained primarily from north west Europe and the Mediterranean. During that century the main increases in imports were drawn from the West Indies and North America, the East Indies and Ireland. By the end of the century, the West Indies supplied 25.0 per cent of all imports, the East Indies 24.2 per cent and northern Europe 13.8 per cent. The growth of the raw cotton trade, very heavily oriented towards the southern United States, meant that America became the main source of imports by the middle of the nineteenth century. By 1913 the share of imports from the United States had increased to 18.4 per cent of the total, followed by Western Europe 13.6 per cent and Asia 12.1 per cent (Mitchell 1962: 279ff).

It is impossible to estimate the dependence of the economy on food imports as a whole, since some could be regarded as luxuries. But it is beyond doubt that the capacity to import food on a large scale, such as the transformation of the wheat surplus of the first half of the eighteenth century into a substantial deficit by the end of the century, enabled population to increase while allowing resources to be devoted to non-agricultural activities. The reliance of industries on imported raw materials is more easily evaluated, especially in the case of the cotton industry. The entire supply of raw material was imported and there was no substitute. Without that supply the cotton industry would not have existed. From the early nineteenth century, imported wool was increasingly necessary to supply manufacturers. Had wool producers been confined to the home market for their supplies of raw wool, they would have been unable to meet the demand of the home market from the 1820s let alone supply overseas markets. By the 1880s they would have been able to meet only half of the home market demand and by the end of the century they could have supplied only one quarter of it from home grown wool.

Imports of bar iron were very important to that industry through much of the eighteenth century, British manufacturers relying on supplies from Russia and Sweden. Indeed British manufacturers of pig iron were able to satisfy only 54 per cent of the home market in 1720, 43 per cent in 1750, and 60 per cent in 1788, and did not become self-sufficient until the Napoleonic Wars (Hyde 43, 67). The large increase in production in the nineteenth century meant that imported supplies of iron ore were needed even though home output increased substantially (Mitchell 1962: 129–30). Imports of iron ore, which were very small until the late 1860s, exceeded seven million tons by the First World War at about £1 per ton (Mitchell 1962: 139). During the period 1901–13 the annual average imported iron ore by weight amounted to 46 per cent of home ore production. About one third of iron ore inputs had to be obtained from abroad by this time.

IV

Balance of payments data are hard to find for the eighteenth century. Official values for trade provide an acceptable, if not entirely reliable, indicator of exports, imports and re-exports of goods. For almost the whole of the eighteenth century, imports exceeded exports but the substantial trade in re-exports was sufficient to produce a net balance of commodity trade (Mitchell 1962: 279–84). Expressed in terms of national income estimates, these data indicate a small but fluctuating surplus on trade account as a share of national income. It might be that interest on loans from abroad, principally from Dutch financiers, would have depressed this surplus towards a balance in total payments in the latter part of the century. But it seems reasonable to infer that there was no large surplus or deficit on balance of payments in the eighteenth century.

The Napoleonic Wars brought a change by depressing exports as entry into Western Europe, the main market for textiles, became increasingly difficult while imports continued to rise. The positive balance of trade proved to be difficult to restore after the war and from the early 1820s onwards there was a continuous deficit on trade in commodities. In the second half of the nineteenth century this gap widened to about six per cent of GDP by the two decades before the First World War (Table 12.1). There was, however, throughout the nineteenth century a net balance on invisible trade which was increasingly supplemented by earnings on overseas investments. As a result, except for a few years in the first half of the century, there was a comfortable surplus on current account balance of payments (Mitchell 1962: 333–5). A net balance on services in international trade, such as shipping and freight insurance charges, was sufficient to maintain a positive balance of trade until the 1870s. Thereafter, until the First World War, the trade balance fell further into deficit. But the second half of the nineteenth century brought a very large increase in income from overseas investment. By the period 1891–1913 this averaged 6.8 per cent of GDP annually. It was this substantial and rising income from abroad which turned the balance of trade deficit into a balance of payments surplus. The peculiar orientation of the British financial system to international trading services and overseas investment thus provided a handsome balance of payments surplus for an economy running a large and increasing deficit on commodity trade.

V

The debate as to the importance of trade in British economic growth during the eighteenth century has generated much disagreement, as has the related question as to the path of causality and whether it runs from growth to trade or vice versa. As explained above, many historians have been concerned with the export-led growth model, and there can be little doubt that this particular form of explanation does not fit well with the historical evidence for eighteenth- and nineteenth-century Britain. This line of argument has, however, been extended to an interpretation which gives little importance to trade, at least in the eighteenth century, in British growth. This is the inference drawn by Bairoch, Crouzet and R. Davis. To this Mokyr added the argument that export growth in Britain did not coincide with the phase of development when industrial growth was fastest, immediately after 1815, hence suggesting internally oriented growth (Mokyr 1977: 987). Even a scholar who has usually stressed the importance of foreign trade, Cole, has argued that causation ran from internal growth and increased technological efficiency to export growth. His hypothesis was that increasing industrial efficiency reduced the cost of exports relative to imports. At the same time, rising national income from internally generated growth drew in more imports. Together these two effects shifted the terms of trade against Britain, making our exports relatively cheaper as well as creating purchasing power abroad through our increased demand for imports. Trade was thus important, but the stimulus was firmly rooted in the British economy, not in overseas demand. Cole argued that the import function was especially effective in the period 1745–60 when retained imports increased by over 33 per cent. By the later decades of the century, all stimuli to trade were effective and favourable, both import demand and autonomous external demand for the new manufactures. The rapid growth of imports in this period, and in the subsequent decades, supports the Eversley thesis that growth was internally generated (Cole 1973: 333). Thomas/McCloskey reiterated this argument in the context of the eighteenth century and extended it into the nineteenth century, noting that the greatest decline in the terms of trade, in the 1830s and the 1850s, coincided with the fastest growth in exports (Thomas/McCloskey 101).

Impressive as this weight of argument is, there is much that is not beyond dispute. The fact that foreign demand comprised a modest proportion of demand and increased demand in the eighteenth century, as shown by Bairoch, does not justify the inference that trade was peripheral. It is improbable that any advanced economy, and Britain was one of the wealthiest economies in the world in the eighteenth century, would derive a very large share of effective demand from abroad. But this only refutes export-led growth. Kravis argued a similar line, that trade was unimportant to the United States in the late nineteenth century since only six per cent of national income was earned through exports. But Williamson demonstrated with a few simple counterfactual hypotheses that America's exposure to international markets fundamentally affected the nature of economic growth. Had terms of trade for agricultural produce stayed constant in the late nineteenth century rather than deteriorating, he argued, resources would have been retained in agricultural production and stifled industrialization until the 1890s (Williamson 1974: 215–16). Much of the change in the American economy, he concluded, was determined by exposure to world market conditions. The only way to evaluate the importance of trade to eighteenth-century Britain is to approach the problem in the same way. What would the scale and nature of development have been if Britain had been denied exports and, presumably, imports? The cotton industry would never have existed, since it was wholly dependent on an imported raw material. The eighteenth-century iron industry would have been much smaller, since it depended heavily on imports, and the expansion of the woollen industry would have been curbed. Since Britain was a net grain exporter for much of the century, agriculture too would have grown less. McCloskey's response is that resources would have been allocated to other activities. But there is no strong reason to believe that this would have happened. A hypothetical British economy cut off from imports of food, timber, luxury products like tobacco and sugar, as well as industrial raw materials like cotton and iron would surely have been much diminished in income and economic activity. One might add that the growth of the financial system would have been greatly hampered without the demand for funds from the government largely for the purpose of waging war against various foreigners. An eighteenth-century economy without recourse to trade would have been smaller, less diversified and must have generated less growth even than the modest rate of increase actually achieved.

Explanations of causation based on changing terms of trade are also questionable. Terms of trade are not a reliable guide to changes in trade volume. Nor does a deterioration in British terms of trade necessarily indicate an increase in British cost reduction because it does not provide any basis for inferring the change in the purchasing power of trading partners. As the eighteenth century progressed the American colonies and the West Indies traded with partners other than the mother country, so the system was far from closed. Further investigation of the causal links between imports and exports in the half century prior to 1745 suggested that no causal link existed. For the following half century there was a clear link by which causation ran from exports to imports and with no feedback effect. Prior to 1745 imports were a function of re-export trade while thereafter they were a function of growth in the export of home produced goods (Hatton 1983: 179). This does not support an export-led thesis, but does support an interpretation which accords a dynamic and partly autonomous role to both trade and home demand in the eighteenth century.

In view of the substantial increase in trade ratios in the nineteenth century and the large absolute increase in trade and foreign investment, most interpretations subscribe to Crouzet's identification of an 'export economy' in which the external sector played a major influence on the fortunes of the economy. Not only has the high rate of export growth been perceived as central to the expansion of the middle decades of the nineteenth century, but the declining rate of export growth in the years after 1873 has been depicted as important in the similar fall in the growth rate of GDP. Meyer estimated that if the rate of growth of exports between 1854–72 had continued until the Edwardian years then both industrial production and GDP would have grown much faster. He attributed the fall in the aggregate rate of growth of the economy to a slowing down of world trade (Meyer 189). Similar arguments have been advanced in suggesting that British industry had exhausted its capacity to generate productivity increases, to expand or maintain its market share, or that it was prevented from so doing by tariff barriers imposed by competitors (Temin 1966). In like vein, it has been argued that Britain was over committed to industries whose export potential was reaching the upper limit by the late nineteenth century (Richardson 1965). Crafts has emphasized the growth limiting effects of international investment. He argued that if the large and increasing volume of British investment abroad in the late nineteenth century had been deflected into the home economy then consumers' expenditure on the eve of the First World War could have been 25 per cent higher than it actually was. Thus by engaging extensively in international investment, the British economy did 'fail' in that it achieved a lower rate of growth than it might otherwise have done (Crafts 1979).

There is no doubt that the rate of export growth declined as the Victorian period progressed, from an average of 5.6 per cent for manufactures alone in the period 1830–57, to 3.1 per cent in the period 1957–73 and then to 2.0 per cent during 1873–1913 (Matthews 448). Nearly all this decline was accounted for by the falling growth rate of textiles and particularly cotton which comprised a large share of total exports. This coincided with a marked shift of British exports away from the advanced economies and towards developing countries, as new outlets in Asia were sought by the cotton industry. In the four decades before 1913, the share of British exports to Germany and the United States fell from 24–13 per cent, while the share sold in Asia and Africa rose from 17–31 per cent. The falling rate of export growth has been identified as the main source of decline in effective demand in the late nineteenth century (Matthews 321, 452). Further the shift in trade patterns and strength of export markets affected the supply side of the economy by failing to exert pressure to increase productivity and thereby reducing the level of disguised unemployment. The two main sectors in which total factor productivity decline was identified were agriculture and mining. The former can be attributed directly to the effects of foreign competition in the domestic market through the success of wheat imports. As to mining, its growth drew resources into an industry where productivity was not increasing, and where the intensification of diminishing returns pushed down its productivity growth. From such evidence it has been estimated that half the decline in the growth rate of total factor productivity between

1856–73 and 1873–1913 had its origins in international markets. Similarly the fall in GDP growth between the two periods can be explained in terms of the exogenous effects of foreign trade (Matthews 445, 464).

Against this range of arguments in favour of the central importance of international relations on the experience of the nineteenth-century economy only McCloskey seems to remain unimpressed. As with regard to the eighteenth century, his argument that nineteenth-century growth and decline were not caused by trade, hinges on the assumption of fully utilized resources, just as those of others like Meyer who attributed growth decline to trading performance assumes a less than full employment level. McCloskey is right to argue that without trade the economy could have responded to changed circumstances by adjusting the composition of its production. But the extent to which the British economy was shaped by its international trading and financial links would have meant that an extensive and painful change would have been required. But the assumption that there was full employment, and that there still would have been full employment under a 'no-trade' regime is implausible. Rather more acceptable are his arguments concerning free trade which, it was suggested, reduced national income by causing a deterioration in Britain's terms of trade (McCloskey 1981b: 170). Even though the estimated loss is a small one, four per cent of national income, it does indicate the effects of non-protectionist policies even at a time when British commodities competed well in many overseas markets. Similarly interesting are his estimates of British national income in 1913, constructed under the hypothetical assumption that German industrial production had remained constant in per capita terms at its 1870 level. His results suggest that under such conditions of reduced German trade competitiveness the British national income would have been little different in 1913 than it actually was. This is not really surprising, since the main trend of British trade in the later nineteenth century was away from sectors in which German competition was important, steel being the main exception (McCloskey 1981b: 181).

In sum the argument which minimizes the importance of the international dimension of British growth in the two centuries after 1700 comprises two elements. It is a refutation of the export-led thesis in a fairly crude form, and it seems unlikely that anyone would wish to challenge that. Secondly, it relies on the neoclassical assumption of full employment of productive resources to suggest that growth with international trade was just one of a number of developmental paths. Without trade, resources would have been reallocated within the economy to provide a modified package of goods and services. Even in such extreme circumstances there would have been some growth. But it seems highly unlikely that it would have been as much as the modest growth actually realised. Even less plausible is the assumption that resources were fully utilised. The evidence demonstrating considerable unemployment and destitution is abundant; short-term casual work was common to many industries, and cheap labour and low wages prevailed widely (Stedman Jones). The great weight of evidence testifies to the centrality of international trading and financial links in shaping British economic growth, in these two centuries, and in contributing a substantial stimulus to that growth.

VI

Placing the international dimension in a prominent position in the explanation of British economic growth suggests a further probing of the process of development. Customarily this has been approached in the context of national economy studies from the perspective of the particular economy and external relations considered only when they impinge on that national economy as flows of imports and exports. This is, of course, quite proper. But it does lead to a perspective on development which is narrow and even myopic. This has certainly been the case in the historiography of British economic development. The perspective of the Industrial Revolution wrought in the first industrial nation has necessarily placed the favoured economy, Britain, at the very centre of the world economic advance. Consequently growth elsewhere has been treated as peripheral until such time as the stream of industrial growth overflowed and the revolution spread abroad or was copied.

Since the argument here is not couched in the terms or assumptions of the industrial-revolution thesis, there is no reason to assume or expect economic development to be vested in a single country or even to originate in so narrow a compass. The fundamental question is, therefore, should growth be depicted as an essentially international phenomenon? If that is correct, and it will be argued here that it is, then the process of British growth needs to be looked at from a rather different perspective than has usually been adopted.

While the early phases of modern industrialization and economic growth can reasonably, and conventionally, be located in the eighteenth century, the process of economic development did not start then. Studies of long-run development, written in recent years, have all stressed the evolution of market based systems of exchange whose origins lay far in the past (Hicks, Jones 1981b, North/Thomas). Commercially oriented mercantile systems can be clearly identified in the various societies which successively flourished around the Mediterranean in ancient and medieval times. The cities of the Phoenicians, the Greek city states, their counterparts in medieval Italy and, later and further north, the Hansa towns, were all extensively involved in trade with outsiders. Different geographical locations gave various societies some particular comparative advantage which both encouraged and allowed further specialization of economic activity and exchange. The growth of such trading societies required money, credit, and legal protection. The growth of the market system drew more sectors of the economy into its orbit, most importantly agriculture which was the predominant activity of pre-industrial society. Successive phases of economic development represent the expansion of the market system, increasing trade and specialization and allowing the growth both of production and population. Being able to sustain a larger and wealthier population provided economies with a greater and more diverse demand, and exchange reduced transaction costs thereby stimulating demand for more trade.

These economic developments were able to generate, slowly and with setbacks, a momentum which moved steadily forward in Western Europe by the early modern centuries. There was thus a substantial increase in European population in the three centuries after 1500, and an especially high rate of increase and urbanization in North West Europe. While the population of Europe almost doubled between 1500–1750, that of the three great urban concentrations, London, Paris and the Dutch Randstad grew from 370,000 to 1,500,000 between the late sixteenth century and 1700. Such growth, unprecedented in the western world, was not attended by widespread immiserization but by increasing economic activity and affluence. Not only was agricultural produce marketed and cultivation specialized, but there was a substantial increase in industrial production. Woollen manufacture, bleaching and dyeing of linen, shipbuilding and repairing, sugar refining, pottery, paint and paper manufacture, soap boiling and starch making were but a few of the industries which were active in Amsterdam and London in the late seventeenth century. Rural industry, now generally labelled as proto-industrialization, in textiles and clothing, metal working and mining was established in Maine, Picardy, Languedoc, Saxony, Westphalia, Flanders and Twente, Ulster, West Yorkshire, the Cotswolds, East Anglia, Northumberland and Durham. Trade was the essential link, indicated by the increase in the European merchant fleet from 600/700,000 tons in 1600 to 3,000,000 tons by the late eighteenth century. This is a novel and momentous phenomenon seen in relation to the coastwise and more sporadic exchange of goods that typified earlier days. Now we see a regular flow of traffic through an immense network of trade routes that are linked together to form a European system of redistribution with Antwerp, Amsterdam, London and Hamburg constituting some of its important centres. The beginnings of an international division of labour are established, or in the words of an English economist, Dudley North in 1691: "The

Whole World as to Trade is but as One Nation or People, and therein Nations are as Persons" ' (Glamann 451–2).

The centre of European trade was established in Amsterdam by the seventeenth century and extended to southern Europe and Asia as well as across the Atlantic, although the very long distance journeys contributed only a little to the volume of European trade. But the development of a network of financial institutions was of great importance, providing the banking, insurance and investment to underpin the trading system and allow multilateral payments. Amsterdam not only linked the trade of three continents, but provided the financial services and investment to stimulate its further growth. By the second half of the seventeenth-century London had emerged as a second major centre of international trade and finance and acquired the beginnings of an institutional framework. In the second half of the seventeenth century there developed an international financial system, based on Amsterdam and London, which provided adequate facilities for short-term lending and provided a system able to clear international payments by the use of bills of exchange (Sperling). The fact that international trade was able to increase without recourse to large movements of bullion between nations indicates that there was established, in the course of the eighteenth century, an effective system of multinational payments in Western Europe. This indicates an immense step forward in the development of the market system, and the convergence of exchange quotations in the Amsterdam and London markets marks the growing integration of the parts of the system (Eagly/Smith). Indeed Sperling concluded that multilateral payments were extensive in late seventeenth-century Europe and comprehensive throughout the continent by the early 1700s.

By the eighteenth century, North West Europe was a substantial and growing integrated economy. In the course of that century trade and colonial links with the West Indies and North America added a new dimension to international trade and formed the basis of the 'Atlantic economy'. Industrialization was one of the most potent effects and manifestations of the growth of this expanding, international and wealthy economic system. 'Amongst these favoured regions, [of Western Europe] England stood out because of its ability, already apparent by the mid-eighteenth century, to integrate its industrial sector most fully into the Atlantic trading system' (De Vries 175). By the middle of the eighteenth century, Britain had become the centre of the largest free-trading market area in the world (Berrill 358–9).

There can be little doubt that Britain's growth in the eighteenth and nineteenth centuries was not only a major component in the growth of the Atlantic economy but that much of the stimulus to growth was drawn from being part of that larger international economy. The influence of international trade was pervasive throughout the economy. Many historians have identified the multiplier effects of port development and trade, from ship-building and repairing and provisioning, to ancilliary industries like flour milling and sugar boiling. To this can be added social overhead capital developments in the form of dockyards, wharves, warehouses, commercial buildings and transport facilities. Some of the trade of great ports like London was coastal, as in the massive shipment of coal from Northumber-land and Durham from the sixteenth century onwards. But ease of access to Europe, to the Baltic and Mediterranean ports, had long established London as the greatest port in the country. In the eighteenth century, the growth of the Atlantic trade brought rapid and impressive growth in the west coast ports of Bristol, Liverpool and Glasgow. Bristol was heavily involved in commerce with both the West Indies and North American colonies, as well as having links with South Wales and the South West with which it linked the midlands by way of the navigable Severn and Wye rivers. Much of the iron ore passing from South Wales to the midlands went through the city on its way to the metal workers, and then passed through Bristol again on its way to the North American market. Capital accumulated in overseas trade by Bristol merchants was invested in coal mining and iron production locally and in South Wales (Minchinton 1954, John). Here, as in London, Glasgow, Liverpool and elsewhere the close interrelationship between the development of the home market and international trade and finance is clearly manifest as integral parts of the same process. As for London, the greatest city in the western world in the eighteenth century, 'it was the fact that the growth of her trading wealth enabled London herself to grow, to develop as a centre of consumption, and to dominate English society, which formed her greatest contribution to the total process of growth in the country as a whole' (Wrigley 63).

The growth of the international economy increased markedly in the nineteenth century. According to Rostow's estimates the growth of world trade and industrial production both exceeded the one per cent rate of growth achieved in the eighteenth century, especially trade which reached a growth rate of five per cent annually in the mid nineteenth century (Rostow 1978b: 67). Both the rate of growth of the British economy and the trade ratio increased in the middle of the century while, in the second half of the nineteenth century, British finance provided the central fabric of the international economy and derived a substantial income in payment. The growth of the British economy in these two centuries was inextricably linked to the growth of the international economy whose axis lay across the Atlantic.

Several recent studies have revealed the extent to which international commodity markets were integrated by the nineteenth century. Wright's work on the cotton industry, surely the most obvious creation of an international economy, found that in the period 1830–60 the price for cotton was determined by the interaction of the American crop and the British manufacturers' demand. Cotton planters in the United States responded to the price obtainable in the British market and the cost and availability of land at home. The main force of demand for the entire system came from the rise in world income and fall in production and transport costs (Wright 79). A similarly integrated market existed in the iron industry in mid century, American domestic production responding both to home demand and the protection of a tariff imposed to keep out British imports, and to the fact that periodically the British market absorbed sufficient iron to leave little surplus for export (Engerman). On a larger scale, Temin modelled aggregate price formation in the United States and Britain for the period 1820–60 and found that more reliable results were found when the two economies were modelled as part of an integrated system rather than as separate entities (Temin 1974: 219). On a considerably more ambitious scale, Brinley Thomas has developed the thesis that there was a fully integrated international economy, operational both in the eighteenth and nineteenth centuries, which linked Britain with the United States and some colonial territories through the migration of people and investment, as well as trade flows (1973, 1978).

It makes sense, both on a priori grounds and on the basis of historical evidence, to explain modern economic growth as an essentially international phenomenon. Britain's unique and important role in that process was an essential feature of British economic growth. It is equally important to understand British growth in its international context to examine the size and dynamism of the economy in relation to other major economies. Anglocentric explanations have, of course, tended to emphasize the pre-eminence of the British economy. The comparison with the United States is particularly pertinent. The American colonial economy was much smaller than its British metropolitan counterpart throughout the eighteenth century, although its rate of growth of 3.4–3.6 per cent annually between 1710–1840 was far greater than that of the mother country. For the rest of the nineteenth century, the American economy grew at just under 4.0 per cent annually (L. E. Davis 22, 33–5). Prior to 1840 population growth was close to that of national income, leaving only a small increase in per capita income, but from the 1840s population increase lagged steadily behind and income per head rose steeply. It has been estimated that in 1840 the United States national product was approximately 66–77 per cent that of Britain's and about 64 per cent that of France, suggesting that the British and French economies were of similar size. Estimates based on Rostow's data suggest that the United States national income was about 57 per cent of that of Britain in 1800, but 22 per cent larger by the middle of the century (1978a: 72–9). Maddison's estimates for 1870 show a similar relative size (Maddison

46). Britain remained a larger economy in terms of aggregate income than either France or Germany well into the twentieth century, but was passed by the United States somewhere around the middle of the nineteenth century. By 1900 Britain was dwarfed by the United States. For most historians, British supremacy has been perceived mainly in terms of industrial superiority. The most recent estimates of world manufacturing production place Britain ahead of all other countries until the 1880s when output was overtaken by that of the United States, as it was by Germany between 1900–13 (Bairoch 1982: 296). In fact, British manufacturing supremacy lasted only from 1800–80, and even then output was less than that of China or India. In manufactures per capita, of course, Britain retained a substantial lead over other countries throughout the nineteenth century (Bairoch 1982: 294). The British economy remained a major element in the international economy throughout this period, but its phase of dominance had passed by the middle of the nineteenth century and by the end of that century it had been far outstripped in growth and income by the much larger economy of the United States. It was in that country, as North has argued, that the real revolution in manufacturing occurred in the late nineteenth century. By then Britain's main hold on the international system, and role within it, was firmly secured as a financier not a manufacturer.

7

Regional growth

In the extensive literature on the causes, effects, and nature of British
economic development, little attention has been focused on growth at the
regional rather than the national level. This is not difficult to understand
since historians have generally been impressed by the pervasiveness of the
development process in spreading, albeit in different forms, through most of
the country. Writers have thus concentrated on apparently more critical and
contentious issues. Where regional variations have been recognized their
significance has seemed obvious. So different manifestations of industrialization have included the growth of woollen textiles in West Yorkshire, the
revolutionary boom in cotton manufacture in Lancashire, coal mining and
iron manufacture in South Wales and West Midlands, shipbuilding on the
Tyne and the Clyde. These variations in industrial specialization together
represent the essence of industrial transformation but individually simply
add a little local colour to the overall picture.

Since such key industries were not found, at least on any significant scale,
in the southern half of England, little attention has been paid to those
regions in most explanations of industry-led growth. In so far as the south
did advance economically, it has been depicted as an agricultural region providing food for the industrial cities. Indeed the failure of the south to
generate industrialization has been explained in terms of its having a comparative advantage in agriculture (Jones 1965: 430). The role of London has
also been fitted into this dualistic thesis. Despite the size of the capital city,
most scholars seem to have subscribed to the view expressed by Hammond
that the Industrial Revolution was 'like a storm that passed over London and
broke elsewhere'. Even the pre-eminence of London in the national
economy in the sixteenth and seventeenth centuries, clearly delineated by
Fisher and Wrigley, has been interpreted to show that the capital city was
rooted in the pre-industrial economic order. 'Certainly the industrial revolution did not occur in London. If anything, the Industrial Revolution in

125

England accentuated "pre-industrial characteristics" in London' (Daunton 1978: 247). Thus London was central to the pre-industrial world but entirely divorced from the growth of modern industrialization. 'The obvious fact was that the capital cities would be present at the forthcoming industrial revolution in the role of spectators. Not London, but Manchester, Birmingham, Leeds, Glasgow and innumerable small proletarian towns launched the new era' (Braudel 440).

This perspective embodies two of the basic suppositions of traditional explanations of early modern growth, that there was a division between the pre-industrial and modern eras, usually identified about the middle of the eighteenth century, and that the onset of modern economic growth was realised in the growth of industrialization. Variation in regional experience was one aspect of this dichotomy. 'In common with many other countries during the early phases of economic development, England underwent the divergence of regional fortunes which has become known as the "North-South problem". During the seventeenth century, England's populous, urbanized, industrial zone still lay along the right-angle connecting Bristol, London and Norwich. By the middle of the nineteenth century the centres of intense industrial activity had shifted north and north-west, to the coal-fields of the West Midlands, the West Riding, Lancashire and South Wales' (Jones 1965: 423). These changes in location cannot be denied, although they were the result of relative growth and decline rather than of a geographical transfer of production. But, as is well known, iron making declined in Kent and Sussex, and in the Forest of Dean, but expanded in Shropshire during the eighteenth century, while woollen textile manufacture grew rapidly in the West Riding but was stagnant or declining in East Anglia and the South West. Since the explanation of British economic growth advanced here does not conform to traditional ideas of the primacy of industry in development, a re-examination of the regional dimension of growth is necessitated.

II

Within the context of British population growth in the eighteenth and nineteenth centuries there was a marked change in relative regional growth and distribution (Table 7.1). The greatest growth in these two centuries was attained by the North West (Lancashire and Cheshire) which was closely followed by Yorkshire/Humberside (East and West Ridings). These two regions were the smallest in population in 1700, accounting for only 9.4 per cent of total population. Their rapid expansion came, therefore, from a small initial base. By 1901, their share had considerably increased to 22.8 per cent of national population, and from 650,000 to over 8.4 million during

Table 7.1 *Population distribution by region (per cent)*

	1701	1751	1801	1851	1901	1951	1981
South East I	8.5	8.0	7.9	12.1	14.4	11.5	12.4
South East II	7.7	7.5	8.5	5.8	8.0	11.9	9.0
South East III	7.2	7.3	7.4	6.6	6.0	7.4	9.5
East Anglia	7.5	6.6	5.9	4.9	2.9	2.7	3.5
South West	15.5	15.0	13.0	10.7	7.0	6.8	8.0
West Midlands	7.5	7.5	8.1	8.2	8.1	9.1	9.5
East Midlands	8.5	7.5	7.6	6.8	6.5	7.1	7.0
North West	4.9	5.8	8.3	12.0	14.1	13.0	11.8
Yorkshire/Humberside	4.5	5.1	6.7	7.7	8.7	8.4	9.0
North	7.0	6.7	6.1	5.6	6.8	6.4	5.7
Wales	6.0	6.1	5.6	5.7	5.4	5.3	5.1
Scotland	15.2	16.9	14.9	13.9	12.1	10.4	9.5
Great Britain	100.0	100.0	100.0	100.0	100.0	100.0	100.0

Sources: P. Deane and W. A. Cole, *British Economic Growth 1688–1959* (Cambridge 1967) p. 103.
C. H. Lee, *British Regional Employment Statistics 1841–1971* (Cambridge 1979).
Regional definitions given on p. 40.
South East I : London, Middlesex ⎫ Home Counties
South East II: Kent, Surrey, Hertford, Essex ⎭
South East III: Rest of South East
General Register Office, *Census of England and Wales 1981* Historical tables pp. 2–3
               Census of Scotland 1981

these two centuries although some uncertainty must be attached to the eighteenth-century estimates. (These are based on the Deane/Cole data which probably underestimate growth in the first half of the eighteenth century and overestimate it in the latter half of that century. But they remain the only estimates of eighteenth-century regional population.) As a result of this growth, most other regions experienced a falling share of national population through this period, although such broad aggregates conceal large variations within regions. Thus there was a relatively high rate of growth of population in Strathclyde in Scotland, in South Wales within the principality, and in Tyneside in the North. Apart from these industrial areas, the only part of the country to register a great increase in its share of national population was London from 8.5 per cent to 14.4 per cent. The relative decline of the south of England, therefore, relates primarily to the South West and East Anglia. But the notion of a wholesale drift of population to the north is an exaggeration. The population share of the three southern regions, South East, East Anglia and South West together fell only from 46.4 per cent to 38.3 per cent during these two centuries.

The heavy emphasis placed by historians on the growth of the northern industrializing counties reflects a concern with rates of change rather than relative size. Both features are, of course, equally important and their combined effect can be seen in the weighted growth rates for regional population showing their contribution to the national growth rate (Table 7.2). The contribution to growth of the North West and Yorkshire/Humberside was much less than their growth rates might suggest because their initial populations were small, although they contributed about one quarter of the total growth for most of these two centuries. Except in the half century before 1750, for which period the data are most uncertain, the contribution to growth of these two northern regions was just less than the contribution of the South East. But apart from these two major regional population growth areas, the weighted regional growth shares suggest a fairly even dispersion of population increase, with the single exception of East Anglia throughout the two centuries and the North and Wales before 1800.

Population growth was accompanied by substantial increases in urbanization. London remained the major city not only in Britain but the western world, having outstripped Paris during the seventeenth century. From a population of about 200,000 in 1600, London grew to 575,000 by 1700 and 900,000 by 1800 (Wrigley 44). By the eve of the First World War London, including Middlesex, had increased to over 5.6 million people. No other city even approached this size, but many of the new urban centres of the North West and Yorkshire/Humberside were very large by this time. Growth in these provincial urban centres since the early eighteenth century had been very great. Manchester and Salford, which together numbered some 10–12,000 people in the 1700s, had grown to a population of 945,000 by 1911, while Liverpool increased from 5–6,000 to 753,000 and Birmingham to 840,000 during the same period. Leeds and Sheffield, similar in size to Liverpool at the beginning of the eighteenth century, were both close to half a million by the First World War, as also was Edinburgh. Glasgow too increased from a mere 10,000 in 1700 to one million by 1911. Such were the major cities in Britain at the end of the nineteenth century, and they were quite different from the major urban centres of two hundred years earlier. Pride of place in 1700 amongst provincial towns was held by Norwich, Bristol, Great Yarmouth, Newcastle, Nottingham and York. By 1911, Britain had thirty-eight cities with a population in excess of 100,000. Many of these were in the industrial regions, and included Birkenhead, Blackburn, Bolton, Bradford, Bristol, Cardiff, Hull, Leicester, Newcastle, Nottingham, Plymouth, Portsmouth, Stoke-on-Trent and Sunderland (Mitchell 1962: 25–7, Chalkin 18).

Two main aspects stand out in the pattern of population growth and urbanization before 1914. There was absolute population increase in almost

Table 7.2 *Weighted regional population growth rates (per cent per annum)*

	1701–51	1751–1801	1801–51	1851–1901	1901–51	1951–81
South East I	0.00	0.06	0.23	0.20	0.02	0.08
South East II	0.01	0.08	0.04	0.13	0.14	−0.06
South East III	0.02	0.06	0.08	0.06	0.07	0.11
East Anglia	−0.01	0.04	0.06	0.01	0.01	0.04
South West	0.04	0.07	0.12	0.04	0.04	0.07
West Midlands	0.02	0.07	0.11	0.09	0.07	0.05
East Midlands	−0.02	0.06	0.09	0.07	0.05	0.03
North West	0.03	0.11	0.22	0.20	0.06	0.01
Yorkshire/Humberside	0.02	0.08	0.12	0.12	0.05	0.05
North	0.01	0.04	0.07	0.10	0.03	−0.01
Wales	0.02	0.04	0.08	0.06	0.03	0.02
Scotland	0.06	0.09	0.18	0.12	0.03	0.01
Great Britain	0.20	0.80	1.40	1.20	0.60	0.40

Sources: As Table 7.1.

all parts of the country. Only the Scottish Highlands, Dumfries and Galloway, Rutland and Huntingdonshire experienced population contraction in the nineteenth century. Within the general increase in population, relative increase was concentrated principally in two areas, in the North West and Yorkshire/Humberside in the north, and in London and its hinterland in the south.

III

These patterns of change in regional population distribution find a counterpart in the limited and rather uncertain data from which regional income estimates can be derived. One pioneering study used tax assessments to provide an indication of wealth distribution between the English counties from the eleventh to the nineteenth century. The overall pattern appeared to be stable in terms of the rank order of counties until the late seventeenth century. But during the final period covered, 1693–1843, there was a fundamental change in the rankings. The essence of that change is seen by looking at the main positional changes. Those counties which rose by at least ten places in the rank order were Cheshire, Derby, Durham, Gloucester, Lancashire, Nottingham, Stafford, and Yorkshire, while those counties which fell by at least ten places were Bedford, Berkshire, Buckingham, Dorset, Essex, Huntingdon, Northants, Suffolk, and Wiltshire (Buckatzsch 187, 195).

Variations in regional income in the more recent past have to be inferred from similarly incomplete and imperfect sources. There exist, scattered randomly through the nineteenth century, records at county level for income tax assessment although not for all five schedules. The earliest, for 1812, provides the data for assessment under Schedule D, while the 1859–60 data relate to Schedules A, B and D and that for 1879–80 for Schedules A, B, D, and E (Table 7.3). These data do provide a general indicator of the probable average regional income since half the national income was taxed, although only four or five per cent of incomes were large enough to be liable to taxation. Another source of information on regional variations in income, albeit an indirect one, is the assessment of liability to pay the Inhabited House Duty. This tax was based on the rental value of property, or the imputed rental for freehold property. Rubinstein favoured the use of this valuation as a proxy for income on the grounds that rental might be expected to be highly income elastic, thus reflecting accurately local variations in income (Rubinstein 1980: 49–50). It seems equally likely that such valuations would be responsive to wealth as well as income, and that they could thus provide a good proxy for variations between regions in both income and wealth.

These occasional and differently composed proxies for regional affluence do provide a consistent picture of regional income variation. Most significant is the relatively high share of national income and hence income per head consistently obtained by the South East. This was particularly marked in London and Middlesex which accounted for 38.9 per cent of all income assessed to tax in 1812. Although this share fell to 30.9 per cent in 1859–60, it rose in the later part of the century to stand at 45.6 per cent in 1911. Furthermore, the missing schedule estimates undoubtedly underestimate the true share of metropolitan tax liability and income. The two missing schedules, returns on British and foreign government securities (C), and public service employment (E), related to sectors in which the metropolis was disproportionately involved. The assessment for tax under Schedule E for 1814 totalled £915,310 for London, Westminster and Middlesex compared to £9,092 for the combined assessment for Lancashire, Yorkshire, Durham, Northumberland, Stafford and Warwick (Rubinstein 1977a: 616). Similarly the tax returns for 1859–60 and 1879–80 must be regarded as biased against the metropolitan economy.

Even so the pattern of regional income indicated by these estimates is quite clear. Either in per capita terms or as a proportion of the national average, the relative affluence of the South East is beyond question. The gap between the Home Counties and almost all other regions was enormous in the nineteenth century, and showed no sign of diminishing before the 1879–80 estimate. The next highest region relative to the national average was the East Midlands, a region which contained much landed wealth in Lincoln-

Table 7.3 *Index of regional income (per head)*

	1812	1859/60	1879/80a	1879/80b	1911/12
South East	382	122	147	240	331
East Anglia	112	109	104	60	97
South West	118	94	93	100	138
West Midlands	102	89	87	80	94
East Midlands	89	114	108	60	78
North West	100	100	100	100	100
Yorkshire/Humberside	125	82	90	60	78
North	77	93	84	60	81
Wales	36	68	70	60	87
Scotland	74	80	96	60	88

Notes: Data in col. 2 relate to income tax schedule D; data in col. 3 relate to schedules A, B, and D; data in col. 4 relate to schedules A, B, D, and E. Data in cols. 5 and 6 relate to tax charged under the Inhabited House Duty.
Sources: Inland Revenue, *Report of the Commissioners of H.M. Inland Revenue*:
Parliamentary papers, 1814–15, Vol. 10; 1860, Vol. 39 pt II; 1882, Vol. 52; 1913, Vol. 28.

shire and Northants together with the 'most aristocratic county', Rutland. Sporadic assessment data for Schedule D in 1911–12 confirm the pattern. While London and Middlesex together accounted for 45.6 per cent of the total national assessment, Lancashire's share was 11.5 per cent and that of the West Riding 6.6 per cent. A similar metropolitan effect on a smaller scale is found in the assessment for Edinburgh which accounted for 23.7 per cent of the total assessment for Scotland.

The Inhabited House Duty assessments are consistent with the results of the income tax assessments. The South East sustained substantially higher levels of assessment per head than any other part of the country. In 1879–80, London, Middlesex and Surrey followed by Kent and Sussex stood out far ahead of all other counties. By 1911–12, while London, Middlesex, Surrey and Sussex remained outstandingly large, very high values were found elsewhere in the South East in Kent, Hampshire, Berkshire, Hertfordshire, Oxfordshire and Essex. High values comparable to these were found outside the South East only in Devon, Somerset and the Lothian region which, of course, includes Edinburgh.

Both sets of indicator give a consistent profile of relative regional income in the nineteenth century. Not only do they suggest a very substantial advantage in affluence in London and the Home Counties, spreading through the rest of the South East during the course of the century, they also suggest that the centres of industrial concentration fared very poorly in terms of income. This is evidenced by both sets of data. According to the Inhabited House Duty assessment for 1911–12, the lowest assessments were returned in rural counties like Cornwall and the Highlands and for industrial areas such as Staffordshire, Durham, and Central/Fife. Amongst the lowest returns under the income tax assessment for 1879–80 were counties such as Stafford, Nottingham, the West Riding, Durham, Glamorgan/Monmouth and Tayside. In the context of larger aggregate regions, industrial divisions such as Yorkshire/Humberside, Wales and the North fared very badly in comparison with the national average and, of course, the South East.

IV

Data relating to the structure of production are hard to find for the national economy prior to 1914 and there is no suitable information from which regional structures in terms of product can be derived. Analysis of regional structure must therefore be limited to employment, and the decennial Census of Population provides comprehensive and detailed information for this from 1841 onward. Regional employment structure prior to 1841 must be inferred from less standard and comprehensive sources. But Lindert's recent work on aggregate employment growth in the eighteenth century does contain some useful pointers. The sectoral contribution to aggregate employment growth is shown in Table 1.6. The considerable importance of textile and clothing employment growth between the mid eighteenth century and 1914 is quite apparent. So too is the growth of other manufacturing and mining, as well as employment in the professions and the rest of the service sector.

The availability of suitable data after 1841 allows the statistical analysis of regional employment structure (Lee 1981). Four main types of regional structure were identified in the Victorian period, and most if not all were established in the eighteenth century, at least in embryo. The most common regional structure, even in 1914, was still the rural region dominated by agriculture. Most characteristic of this type were counties such as Cambridge, Huntingdon, Suffolk, Lincoln, Rutland, Dumfries and Galloway, Grampian and Highland. There were two types of industrial region. The first was clearly primarily oriented towards textile and clothing manufacture. Most characteristic of this regional typology were Lancashire, Tayside and the West Riding, followed by Cheshire, Nottingham and Central/Fife. On the fringes of this regional structure were Derby, Leicester and Strathclyde and, later in the century, the Borders. The second industrial region was primarily categorized by mining and included Durham and Glamorgan/Monmouth, and, in the late nineteenth century, Derby and Central/Fife became significant coal producers. Each of the three regional types categorized above comprised geographically separate but similar economic structures. The fourth regional type was different in that it comprised a single region of contiguous counties initially composed of London, Middlesex and Surrey alone. As the Victorian period proceeded there was a marked increase in the number of neighbouring counties which adopted the same employment structure as the metropolitan centre, especially Kent, Sussex, Berkshire and Essex. Of the ten regions conforming to this kind of employment structure by 1911, only Gloucestershire and Lothian lay outside the South East.

Just as these regional employment types can be identified statistically, so the changing structural composition between censuses can similarly be found. Most of the textile regions were established as such by the 1870s, and doubtless an extrapolation into the early nineteenth and eighteenth centuries would show these regions forming in that earlier period when, of course, there was considerable increase in population in Lancashire and the West Riding. In contrast, the mining region typology was very much the creation of the Victorian period, as was the growth in mining employment and coal production. Growth of this type of region was greatest from the 1880s onward and was especially strong in Wales and the North. The third growth typology was the metropolitan economy of the South East. The principal adaptation of the Home Counties and then the rest of the region to the same employment structure as London itself came in the later decades of the Victorian period. Hitherto these counties had been primarily rural in composition.

The growth in textile and clothing employment nationally and the rapid population increase in Lancashire and the West Riding, in the century or so up to 1841, were obviously related phenomena. By that date employment in these closely related activities accounted for 42.0 per cent of all employment in Lancashire and 35.1 per cent of West Riding employment. These two regions together employed over half the national total of textile workers. The same two regions employed 82 per cent of the additional jobs created in textiles between 1841 and 1911. But neither region was entirely dependent on the textile industry. In Lancashire the textile and clothing trades accounted for 27.4 per cent of new jobs created in this period, but metal manufacturing and mechanical engineering comprised 10.0 per cent of new jobs and mining a further 6.2 per cent. Some of these other activities were related to the textile trades. The bulk of employment in mechanical engineering was engaged in the manufacture of textile machinery for the home and export market. Mining and metal manufacture were also related here, as in most regions where they were found together. Activity rates were relatively high in these regions since clothing and textile work offered considerable employment opportunities to women, and constituted the main source of manufacturing employment for women in the nineteenth century. Like Lancashire, the West Riding and Nottinghamshire had a mixed manufacturing structure composed of textiles, mining, engineering and iron manufacture. But some other regions which were heavily dependent on textiles enjoyed a far lower level of employment diversity. Both Tayside and the Borders had a greater dependency on this single manufacture and, in the latter case, half the additional employment in this period was generated in the textile trades.

The other major industrial type of region prior to 1914 was characterized by mining, principally for coal. This sector accounted for a large share of the employment increase between 1841 and 1911 in certain regions. In Glamorgan/Monmouth 35.9 per cent of new jobs were in mining, while in County Durham the proportion was 32.3 per cent, and in Central/Fife 35.0 per cent. Ancilliary employment was mainly in metal manufacture in each of these areas, while shipbuilding was important in County Durham and mechanical engineering created a significant number of additional jobs in Northumberland, which was also an important mining region. Unlike the textile regions, mining areas did not offer many employment opportunities for women and the activity rate of women was extremely low, thus keeping down the aggregate activity rate. The growth of mining did generate a multiplier demand for construction workers and created some employment in services, although these regions were less well provided in these sectors than the national average. Characterization of regional structure in terms of employment alone is a little misleading since those activities which were locally important but which required less heavy inputs of labour, such as shipbuilding or iron founding, tended to be overlooked. In fact, heavy industry of this kind was regionally concentrated in the areas where employment was dominated by textiles or mining.

The third of the regional growth typologies comprised a single expanding region as well as a distinct structural entity. The South East had little textile manufacturing, coal mining or iron and steel production. Its economy was characterized by a very large service sector. Between 1841 and 1911, 66.1 per cent of the new jobs created in this region were in services, and most of the others were in related consumer good manufactures. Compared to the national average, and even more distinctly in comparison with other regions, the South East had an extremely high level of service employment per head of population. In 1841 London and Middlesex had a ratio of 21.7 service jobs per hundred population compared to the national average of 13.1 and by 1911 the respective ratios stood at 27.9 and 20.7. While the metropolitan ratio was the largest in the country in 1841, by the end of the century it had been exceeded by other counties in the South East including Surrey, Sussex, Hampshire, and Berkshire. The growth of service employment in the Victorian period provided over half the increased employment in that era. One fifth of those new service jobs were created in London and

Middlesex, and a further fifth in the rest of the South East. In other words for every ten new jobs created in the entire economy between 1841–1911, one was a service job in London and another a service job elsewhere in the South East.

It was not only in the full range of service activities that the South East had such a comparative advantage in employment over other regions. While this region was not prominent in most of the heavy industries which played such a large part in the growth of economic activity in most of the provincial regions, the South East was well provided in other areas of industry. Some of these were the long-established manufactures characteristic of most sea-ports and capital cities, such as timber and furniture trades. London had for centuries been a prime destination for imported woods of all kind, and the furniture making trades had developed in the city close to their raw material supply and to their principal market, fashionable society. Paper and printing was a similarly long-established activity in London, as was the fashionable clothing trade, the major common link with provincial industry. In each of these activities, the South East acquired a relatively large share of new employment between 1841 and 1911. Overall the region obtained 31.9 per cent of all new employment. But its relative share of certain sectors was substantially greater, as in services and construction together 40.3 per cent, timber and furniture 40.0 per cent, paper, printing and publishing 44.2 per cent, clothing 37.8 per cent. Equally the South East was at the forefront of some of the newer technological advances, London having long been a major centre of engineering. Thus the region provided 48.0 per cent of new jobs in instrument engineering and 41.4 per cent in electrical engineering in this period.

Within the growth of population and employment in the British economy during the two centuries after 1700, there emerged a number of quite distinct regional structures. Data before the Victorian period are scarce and limited, but the relatively greater share of national population growth in the South East and in the North West and Yorkshire/Humberside regions complements the aggregate employment growth estimates derived by Lindert showing substantial increases in textiles and many services. There seems no reason to doubt the hypothesis that there existed, in the eighteenth century, the same form of regional specialization in services in the South East and in manufactures in the northern regions which can be identified in the mid nineteenth century from census data. This is not, of course, to propose a sharp division between service oriented regions and manufacturing regions. There were obvious multiplier effects on the service sector generated by the growth of Lancashire cotton manufacture, just as there was always a substantial manufacturing component in London and other parts of the South East. In the Victorian period both types of economy grew, both within their established centres and expanding outward. In the case of the metropolitan economy this was a literal expansion into other adjacent counties, while in the case of the textile manufactures growth was manifest by the emergence of other centres of production, as in the Borders or Leicestershire. It was mainly in the Victorian period that the third distinctive type of regional employment structure emerged. This was principally the product of coal mining expansion on an extensive scale in employment terms as well as highly localized into a number of counties. The scale of this is reflected not only in the big increase in the numbers of miners but in the increased population growth in regions such as the North and Wales.

V

The various indicators of economic structure and change at regional level, population, employment and income coalesce to provide a coherent outline of development of the major aggregate regions of Britain. They confirm the importance of industrialization in textiles, iron and steel, engineering and coal mining as the basis for development in many parts of the economy, often transforming hitherto rural backwaters such as Lancashire and the West of Scotland. Other regionally concentrated industries, such as mining and shipbuilding on the Tyne and Wear, and in South Wales, or textile manufacture in the West Riding, were completely changed by the enormous increase in the scale of their activity. This growth proliferated into new industrial development, such as textile machinery manufacture in Lancashire, a greatly expanded chemical industry in the same county and on the Tyne, and growth of iron production, coal mining, and metal working in the West Midlands. It also brought an expanded need for services, like transport and distribution as the great provincial cities flowered in their Victorian heyday. Professional and commercial services were required to supplement industrial activity, and construction and public utilities needed to house the growing urban population and provide monuments appropriate to burgeoning civic pride.

All this is, of course, very familiar to those acquainted with the large literature on British economic growth in the eighteenth and nineteenth centuries, for the process of growth has been explained in such terms. But the exclusiveness of the industry-led growth thesis does not fit very well with the evidence on regional employment growth and especially the data on regional income. There is an obvious inconsistency between the notion of the primacy of provincial industry in economic growth and the rather poor showing of all the industrial regions in terms of nineteenth-century relative incomes. These low incomes are, however, consistent with the results of Rubinstein's investigations into Victorian fortunes which indicated that cotton manufacturing and iron making were not the best ways to make a great fortune.

Some wealth generated in manufacturing was doubtless spent in areas of the country other than those in which it was earned. It has, after all, been frequently chronicled how those who made their wealth amidst the dark satanic mills of industrial Britain were eager to escape to more congenial surroundings to enjoy it. The Marshalls, who made their money in Leeds textiles, repaired to the Lake District. Sir William Armstrong made his money at Elswick on the Tyne, but built his palatial retreat thirty miles away in Rothbury. Others headed for London, the south coast of England and the Mediterranean. Thus income created in one region was spent elsewhere. But this transfer effect alone will not explain the low relative incomes in the industrial regions. The outstanding feature of British industry was the labour intensity of its production methods. In order to manufacture in this way, and still be able to compete successfully abroad, labour costs had to be kept as low as possible. This explicit policy decision on the part of many Victorian industrialists, who were able to take advantage of an abundance of labour, underlay the extreme specialization of skilled function in shipbuilding and the practice of hiring workers on an hourly basis. Similarly it underlay the orientation of textile manufacture towards the employment of females and youths in large numbers relative to the more expensive skilled male workers. The rise and fall of heavy industry in Scotland has recently been explained in terms of the comparative advantage held by these industries in Victorian times based on cheap labour, even compared to the equivalent industries in England. When national wage bargaining led to increases in Scottish industrial wages to bring them into line with their fellows south of the border, this comparative advantage was eroded (Campbell).

From the point of view of the industrialist, low wages provided a very desirable production strategy, keeping down fixed costs and passing the risk and price of variations in demand onto the workforce who could be engaged or laid off at short notice. From the perspective of the aggregate economy it is clear that one of the effects of this was to keep down income levels in the manufacturing regions, especially when the variability of employment is taken into account. The nature of British industrialization was such that low wages were imperative if prices were to be competitive in foreign markets (Table 7.3). This in turn inhibited the growth of consumer spending in these areas which would have had a multiplier effect on employment and income growth in the service sector, which was responsive to variations in income but was much smaller per head of population in the manufacturing regions than it was in the South East. Again the west of Scotland provides a potent illustration. Several historians have drawn attention to the fact that Scotland failed to attract or generate consumer good industries in the late Victorian period (Lenman 204). Furthermore, the poverty which was so widespread in the industrial areas of Strathclyde meant that many families could not afford an economic rent for housing. As a result, Glasgow had both massive overcrowding and much poor quality housing. 'In 1917 there were more than four persons per room in 10.9 per cent of Glasgow's houses, over three per room in 17.9 per cent, and over two in 55.7 per cent; the figures for corresponding English cities were 0.8 per cent, 1.5 per cent, and 9.4 per cent. The tenements which contained these "houses" contrasted with the three or five room terrace or detached houses more typical of England. The people of Glasgow were packed into their homes to a degree unimaginable even in the largest English cities' (Checkland 1976: 20). The Glasgow Improvement Trust spent some £600,000 on new tenements before 1914, but were thus able to house only 10,000 of the better off members of the working class. The poor were excluded by the high rentals charged.

Lack of spending power reduced effective demand for services, and this was reflected in the below average provision of service employment. While Scotland employed only 149.9 per thousand population in 1911, compared to the British average of 176.0, the main industrial regions, Strathclyde and Central/Fife, were far below the Scottish average with 139.6 and 114.3 respectively (Lee 1983: 32). The disparity was particularly marked in those services most responsive to income, including banking and commerce, professional employment, and personal services. Some of these activities, especially domestic service which comprised a large share of personal service employment before 1914, were low pay jobs, although the professions and commerce included some of the largest incomes. But in terms of employment alone this 'shortfall' in service employment represents a substantial loss in potential jobs and the multiplier effects of increased spending power. Some idea of the scale of this loss is indicated by the fact that had Strathclyde enjoyed the same service employment provision as Great Britain as a whole in 1911, the regional labour force would have been increased by 8.4 per cent. On the same assumption, the labour force in Central/Fife would have been increased by 14.8 per cent. Even with low pay, such an increase in employment must have substantially increased regional spending power. While these two regions represent two of the more extreme cases of low incomes and demand deficiency, the same elements were present in most of the other industrial regions of Victorian Britain, especially the mining regions. It is, therefore, not surprising that these industrial regions had relatively low incomes per head compared to the national average.

The main difference in the various estimates for regional income and wealth lies in the discrepancy between the South East and the rest of the country. Indeed each estimate for London and Middlesex suggests an average income level several times that of other regions (Table 7.3). There is no substantive evidence to support the idea that this wealth was obtained largely through transfers from the industrial regions, so that the relative affluence of the South East is not consistent with those interpretations of growth which place total or even major causal emphasis on industry. The means by which the South East acquired its affluence is therefore a most important enquiry in the context of British economic growth. The structure of this region was markedly different from that of the industrial regions principally because of the very high level of service employment per head of population. This was particularly true of those service sectors, like banking and financial services, professions and personal services which were closely related to wealth (Lee 1984). Rubinstein's investigation of the activities of those who left major fortunes indicated that metropolitan pursuits in finance and commerce were very important sources of great wealth (1977a: 602–3). Several strands of economic and social prosperity merged in the prosperous economy of the South East. As the major European city and a major international port, London attracted both business and fashionable society. Even in the eighteenth century, the wealthiest section of society spent part of its year and much of its affluence in the capital in fine houses and gracious living. Much of the unequally distributed wealth of the country was spent in the metropolitan heart of society. Even those in high society who had landed estates far from London maintained their connection with society, court and government. Throughout the eighteenth and nineteenth centuries the connection of the South East with the landed wealth of the shires was closer, and more profitable, than its links with the industrial regions. Demand was sustained for services, especially in domestic employment but including professional people like lawyers, bankers and financial advisers. The affluence of the metropolitan market extended to construction and consumer good manufacture.

Another feature in the structure of the metropolitan economy lay in the international trade which had played so important a role in the history of London since medieval times. By the eighteenth century, profits made in trade formed the basis of established City fortunes. This wealth could be augmented by investment in other trade, but increasingly other opportunities were provided by the growth of the City as a financial centre which developed from national pre-eminence to international pre-eminence between 1700 and 1914. As the government was based in the capital, so the financial network developed to service it naturally grew there. The growth of a complex network of financial institutions and specialist consultants provided outlets for the surplus funds of the wealthy, enabling them to supplement their income or replace their expenditure. Furthermore, the scale of this financial system and its international connections and expertise, fitted it for a central role in the immense growth of the international economy in the second half of the nineteenth century which brought an insatiable demand for investment. It was this international financial element of the British economy which created the really big fortunes, for the merchants and financiers of the City.

The growth of the South East was based, therefore, on the twin pillars of accumulated wealth from trade and finance and the land. The money markets and institutions of the City provided numerous ways in which such funds could be safely invested and augmented. At the same time, the metropolitan economy provided an abundance of ways in which such wealth could be enjoyed. By thus creating employment in services, of all levels of skill and shades of propriety, and consumer good manufacture, the affluent economy developed an element of self-sustaining growth. Scale too was important. As the city and its suburbs grew, especially in the late Victorian years, and spilled over into neighbouring counties like Essex, Surrey and Kent so it generated growth in housing construction, the provision of suburban and underground railways, and additional distribution services to provide the wants and needs of a very large population. As the growth of the industrial regions was limited by low incomes, no such restriction hampered the South East. Wages here were, of course, low in many jobs, and London was well-known for its large and underemployed pool of unskilled, casual labour. But the wealth of society and the high incomes of the middle class professional workers was more than enough to sustain the high level of consumer demand. The significance of unequally distributed national wealth, the growth of the financial system and the vitally important international environment of British growth are all manifest in the differential growth of the South East and its relationship with landed wealth in the shires.

Chenery's study of typologies of development in recent decades identified three main forms of growth (Chenery/Syrquin). Two related to small economies needing to export for growth, either manufactures or raw materials. The third type of economy was larger, and wealthier, and less reliant on external trade because it enjoyed a greater capacity to self-sustain growth. These categorizations apply in general terms to the kinds of regional economy developed in pre-1914 Britain. There was a substantial element of dualism in that growth. The traditional mode of explanatory hypothesis which stressed the primacy of industry has identified one of the strands of that dualism. It is the kind of growth which undisputably characterized Lancashire textiles and Durham mining. Victorian novelists frequently drew the distinction between the grim industrial north and the genteel, effete and, by inference, idle south. Thus the second aspect in the dualism of British economic growth has been ignored or played down. In fact the metropolitan economy represented not only a structurally different type of economy, as well as a geographically separate one from the industrial regions, but in terms of size and wealth was probably the greater. This is not to suggest that these two growth variants were without linkages or that they were hermetically sealed from each other. Such was manifestly not the case. But they were substantially different in structure, comparative advantage, wealth and long-term prosperity. It is hard to disagree with Rubinstein's conclusion that there was a fundamental dualism in eighteenth- and nineteenth-century Britain which ran from economic affairs to social and political divisions. The economic and geographical separateness, dividing land and commerce from industry, was reinforced by the social links between the London financiers and the landed gentry, the Anglican Church, the public schools, the ancient universities and conservative political interests. The industrial provinces, with the exception of a few wealthy inter-lopers, remained largely outside this network of influential institutions and interests, and adhered to nonconformist denominations, liberal politics and their own educational institutions (Rubinstein 1977a: 620–1, 1977b: 11, 112). The pattern of regional growth reinforces the view that national growth was richer, more diverse and, in the last resort, different from the conventional picture depicted by the Industrial Revolution explanation.

PART III

The twentieth century

8

Aggregate demand: wealth and income

I

Two main features stand out in the growth of national income in the twentieth century. In a British context alone, national income has grown faster overall than in any earlier measured period. Decadal increase was greater in the 1950s and 1960s than in any earlier period, although in the 1970s that spurt of high growth had given way to much slower advance. Even the inter-war years compared quite respectably with the best growth rates of the two previous centuries (Table 1.1). But the two world wars caused the complete disruption of normal economic activity, and in their prolonged aftermath the return to normal was slow and incomplete. The three decades after 1914 produced a massive disturbance in both British and international economic development. While the growth performance of the British economy in the present century has been good compared to earlier, and often more vaunted, periods of its economic history, the record does not appear so favourable when compared to the growth rates of other advanced industrial nations. Higher rates of growth in national income per head has seen Britain overtaken by France, Germany and Sweden during the present century, and the rapid advance of countries like Japan suggests that others may soon do the same (Rostow 1978a: 72–9). Much debate and analysis has thus emphasized the relatively poor performance of the British economy, especially in recent years.

Besides growing at an unprecedented rate, national income has been redistributed in the twentieth century in such a way as to produce very large changes in its sectoral composition. The most obvious change in expenditure was the extremely fast relative growth of the government sector fuelled by two enormously costly wars and, more recently, by the continued expansion of the public sector (Table 8.3). While gains from foreign trade and investment have contributed a smaller share of GNP than in the nineteenth century, the share of public spending in total expenditure has increased principally at the expense of consumer spending. Since the Second World War the latter has had its share further eroded by the growth of capital formation spending, at levels substantially higher than in any earlier period.

Changes in the distribution of national income by factor shares in the twentieth century strongly favoured labour income at the expense of property income. Much of that increase was concentrated in salary payments and employers' contributions. Since 1950, total labour income has accounted for over 70 per cent of GNP compared to 56 per cent just before the First World War (Matthews 164). Conversely almost all categories of property income showed a relative decline. While rent and income from abroad showed some recovery in recent years, the decline of the share of profit continued unabated, from a peak of 28.8 per cent of GNP in 1873 to 17.2 per cent a century later.

Wealth has always been more unequally distributed than income. But there has been a strong and sustained trend in the twentieth century towards a more equitable distribution of national wealth (Table 8.1). Even the considerable difficulties involved in the measurement of wealth do not undermine this conclusion, so great has been the shift away from the extremely skewed distribution which obtained at the end of the nineteenth century. But the process of change, accelerating since the 1950s, has taken place within the context of a very large increase in the stock of wealth. National wealth was estimated at £6 billion in 1911–13 and at £274 billion in 1976. While the share of the top ten per cent of wealth holders fell, they still received almost 60 per cent of the increase in wealth during this period (Atkinson/Harrison 139). The top wealth holders have thus suffered only a relative loss of substance not an absolute one. But the share of this privileged group falls even more if the stock of national wealth is defined to include pension rights, both occupational and state schemes, which almost doubles the total wealth and reduces the share of the top ten per cent in 1976 from 60 to 40 per cent (Royal Commission on Wealth Report 7: 112).

Income is usually distributed more equitably than wealth, and such has been the case in twentieth-century Britain. But like the wealth distribution, the long term trend in income shares has been towards greater equality. The relative share of the top one, five and ten per cent of incomes has fallen (Table 8.2). The middle income groups were the principal beneficiaries, while the share of the bottom 40 per cent increased only very slightly and still compares unfavourably with the share obtained by this group in the late Victorian period (see Table 2.2). The trend towards convergence, as shown by the declining Gini Coefficient, has thus come from the relatively faster growth of middle order incomes. The inequality of the income distribution has been somewhat modified by the effects of taxation which fell far more heavily on the upper income groups. The top ten per cent of incomes contributed 40 per cent of the tax revenue in 1976–77, and most of the increases

Table 8.1 *Estimates of wealth distribution (per cent)*

	Top 1%	Top 5%	Top 10%
1911–13	69.0	87.0	92.0
1923	60.9	82.0	89.1
1938	55.0	76.9	85.0
1950	47.2	74.3	n.a.
1960	33.9	59.4	71.5
1969	30.2	54.2	65.7
1976	24.9	46.2	60.6

Note: Data for 1911/13 relate to England and Wales
Data for 1923–60 relate to England and Wales
Data for 1969 relate to Great Britain
Data for 1976 relate to United Kingdom.
Sources: A. B. Atkinson and A. J. Harrison, *Distribution of Personal Wealth in Britain* (Cambridge 1978) p. 139.
Royal Commission on the Distribution of Wealth and Income, Report No. 7 (1979) pp. 93, 95 Cmnd 7595.

Table 8.2 *Estimates of income distribution (per cent)*

	Top 1%	Top 5%	Top 10%	11–60%	Bottom 40%	Gini coefficient
1938	16.6	29.9	38.8	0.0	0.0	0.464
1949	11.2	23.8	33.2	0.0	0.0	0.411
1959	8.4	19.9	29.4	55.0	15.6	0.398
1968/9	7.1	17.8	27.1	56.3	16.6	0.374
1976/7	5.5	16.3	26.2	57.1	16.7	0.372

Note: Data relate to United Kingdom, income before tax.
Source: As Table 8.1 Report No. 7 pp. 23, 165.

in taxation in this century have been in direct taxation. The main beneficiaries from the transfer effect of tax and benefits have been the increasing number of pensioner households. By the 1970s, retirement pensions accounted for 42.4 per cent of all transfer payments, while supplementary benefit took a further 11.6 per cent. The Royal Commission on Wealth concluded that these transfers, together with unemployment benefit, sickness and invalidity benefit, family allowance, rent rebate and student grants, achieved a substantial redistributive effect towards equality (Royal Commission on Wealth: Report 5: 65).

The redistributive effect of taxation reveals changes in the economic and social structure. In recent decades there has been a marked change in the

Table 8.3 *Gross National Product by category of expenditure (per cent)*

	Consumers' expenditure	Gross domestic fixed capital formation	Public authority spending	Exports-imports	Net property income from abroad
1871–80	82.7	7.9	4.8	0.9	2.9
1881–90	81.2	6.4	5.6	2.0	4.2
1891–1900	81.5	8.0	6.3	−2.2	5.3
1901–13	78.7	7.8	7.8	−0.8	5.9
1913–24	72.0	5.2	19.9	1.5	2.6
1924–37	79.2	9.4	9.7	−2.3	3.6
1937–48	64.4	6.5	32.2	−5.1	1.4
1951–64	65.9	15.4	16.4	−0.1	1.1
1964–73	58.4	20.2	20.4	−0.9	1.1
1973–79	57.4	19.1	20.6	1.4	0.7
1979–83	59.3	17.7	21.0	2.0	0.4

Sources: C. H. Feinstein, *Statistical Tables of National Income, Expenditure and Output of the U.K. 1855–1965* (Cambridge 1972) Tables 5, 14, 15.
Central Statistical Office, *United Kingdom National Accounts 1984*, Table 1.5

composition of households with a significant increase in single person households, both pensioner and non-pensioner. There has also been an increase in households without children. Taxation has thus modified the effects of social change which, if unchecked, would have increased the inequality of the income distribution. The growth in the number of pensioners, and of school leavers who defer entry into employment in order to take advantage of further education, tends towards income inequality. Together these two developments have caused much of the increase in inequality at the very bottom of the income distribution.

II

These changes in the distribution of wealth and income between sections of the community, reflected both in factor payments and the distribution of expenditure, all indicate major changes in both the acquisition of wealth and income and in its disposal. Despite the relative decline in the share of the extremely affluent, the top ten per cent of income recipients and wealth holders continue to enjoy great prosperity. Wealth accumulated in traditional forms was still of great importance in the 1970s. Holdings in excess of £50,000 accounted for over one quarter of total net wealth. It was owned by 2.5 per cent of the population, but included over 60 per cent of the value of land and government securities, and over 70 per cent of the value of listed ordinary shares and other company securities. The very wealthiest people held a greater share of their assets in land than any other group, and a more considerable share in government securities and company shares than did the less prosperous. The pattern of pre-1914 wealth holding was thus sustained. The cumulative element of wealth augmentation was illustrated by the increase in the value of estates in the twentieth century. The number of estates left by millionaires in the interwar years, landed and non-landed, was almost as many as were left in the entire previous century (Rubinstein 1981: 43, 60–5). Since the Second World War much larger estates have been bequeathed, including 29 worth over £3 million each between 1940 and 1969, and ten worth over £5 million in the 1970s. In spite of the fact that the need to practise tax avoidance has certainly reduced the number of large estates, there has been a steadily upward trend in the number of estates worth over half a million pounds (Rubinstein 1981: 228–9, 233).

The professions of those who left large estates in the twentieth century were very similar to those of their Victorian predecessors. Within the ranks of the non-landed millionaires, brewers remained prominent and in the interwar years this group equalled the combined total of cotton and chemical millionaires. There were also eleven tobacco millionaires in the interwar years, compared to three iron or steelmakers and one shipbuilder. Other services were well represented, newspaper magnates joining shipowners and, of course, bankers and financiers. Amongst those who left major fortunes in the years 1940–79, drink, tobacco and finance were well represented while seventeen out of the thirty-nine largest estates were left by either landowners or property developers. Of the seven estates which were worth over £10 million, four were connected with land and property development, one with merchant banking, one came from abroad, and the largest of all, the estate of Sir John Ellerman, reflected a vast diversity of interests beyond his nominated profession of shipowner.

The great majority of the large estates of the twentieth century were established in earlier centuries, and the long-term process of accumulation was assisted by the tax system which was far more lenient in its treatment of wealth than income. Several studies have revealed the importance of inheritance in the process of wealth accumulation. Harbury/Hitchens took four samples of wealth leavers, for males only in 1956–7 and 1965 and for members of both sexes in 1973. In each of the male samples there was a clear association between the wealth of sons and their fathers. For the richest sons, it was found that two-thirds were preceeded by fathers leaving over £25,000, while over three quarters of sons in the upper and medium wealth brackets had been left at least £1,000. So even the acquisition of moderate wealth depended to a large extent on having a father who was well into the upper echelons of the wealth distribution. After 1950 there was some weakening of this relationship. As for the female sample of inheritors, their wealth was strongly associated with the wealth of father or husband, being inherited from one or the other. Three-quarters of those who left substantial wealth were themselves the progeny of fathers whose own fortune had been large enough to include them in the top ten per cent of the wealth distribution ten times over. Further, inheritance was increasingly more important as a source of wealth as opposed to 'self-made' wealth, increasing from 28 per cent in 1902–34 to 67 per cent by 1936–73 (Harbury/Hitchens 121, 129).

Certainly inheritance has been far more influential in generating inequalities in the wealth distribution than the accumulation of assets up to the point of retirement by workers, which is characteristic of middle-class earnings. The principal factor in wealth accumulation in the twentieth century has been the rising internal rate of return, helped by rising land values, diversified investment portfolios, and appropriate marriage contracts. A study of the long-term marriage pattern of ducal offspring revealed a marked and sustained preference for keeping marriage within the peerage (Hollingsworth 24). As a result, a survey conducted in the 1950s found that one-third of the estates surveyed and two-thirds of the land acreage had remained in the same family since the nineteenth century. As Wedgwood concluded in his study of wealth in the 1920s, 'about one third owe their fortune almost entirely to inheritance (including gifts inter vivos), another third to a combination of ability and luck with a considerable inheritance of wealth and business opportunity, and the remaining third largely to their own activities' (Wedgwood 179). But as the twentieth century progressed, opportunities for making enormous fortunes from nothing appeared to become increasingly scarce.

Very large capital accumulations have been sustained and augmented by investment, marriage and by a relatively favourable treatment of wealth by British tax legislation. The rate of estate duty levied on an estate valued at one million pounds was 15 per cent before the First World War, while an estate worth £50,000 was liable to tax at seven per cent. By the 1960s these tax rates had increased to 80 per cent and 35 per cent respectively (*Royal Commission on Wealth*: Report 1: 100). But the level of exemption has also been raised through the century, effectively reducing the tax on smaller estates and making the tax increasingly progressive in its effect. As a proportion of total personal wealth, estate duty realised only one quarter of one per cent both before the First World War and in 1976–7, having increased slightly for part of the interim (Atkinson 1972: 127, *Royal Commission on Wealth*: Report 7: 107). It seems probable that successful avoidance of estate duty has limited the extent of wealth redistribution. While the share of wealth owned by the top one per cent of the population fell steadily through the century, the share of the next four per cent increased. Many have inferred that this reflected the transfer of wealth within families by gifts and bequests to avoid duty. One 1966 estimate suggested that gifts to avoid estate duty amounted to £350 million, a sum equivalent to one quarter of the total value of estates liable to duty (Atkinson 1972: 127). This thesis is supported by the fact that the frequency with which estates actually pay duty averages once in 51 years. The replacement of the Estate Duty in 1975 by the Capital Transfer Tax was clearly designed to block a popular avenue of tax avoidance, as well as to supplement the Capital Gains Tax which had been introduced in 1962. Recent decades have thus seen an attempt to tax wealth itself as well as income from wealth. During the 1970s, Estate Duty and its successor realised between £300–400 million in most years, while the return from Capital Gains Tax increased from £128 million in 1969–70 to £340 million in 1977–78 (*Royal Commission on Wealth*: Report 7: 105).

Seen within an international context, and set against very limited comparative information, the distribution of wealth in Britain appears markedly unequal. In the early 1950s the top one per cent of wealth holders in Britain owned 40 per cent of the total compared to 24 per cent in the United States, although the income distributions of the two countries were very similar to each other (Atkinson 1972: 19–20). By 1972 the gap had narrowed somewhat, with respective shares of 25.8 per cent in the United States and 32.0 per cent in Britain. But even such large concentrations of wealth have not been impervious to disaster on occasion. It has been estimated that the 40 per cent fall in share values on the London Stock Exchange in 1973–74 cost the top one per cent of wealth holders between one quarter and one third of the value of their assets (Atkinson 1983: 110).

The trend towards greater equality in the distribution of both wealth and income in the twentieth century has been the result of the increasing affluence of the middle classes, continuing an advance which was in progress in the later decades of the nineteenth century. The assets of this sector of society, worth between £5,000 and £50,000 per head in the 1970s and together comprising just over half of the total number of wealth holders, had a composition quite different from that of the very wealthy. Dwellings, building society deposits, and life assurance policies were the main form of asset holding by the middle classes. Indeed much of the increase in national wealth in the twentieth century, and especially since 1950, was a result of the growth of owner-occupied dwellings and the assets of the financial institutions most closely associated with that growth. Further down the social scale, the lowest group on the social ladder owned only 7.9 per cent of national wealth in the 1970s although they accounted for 42.9 per cent of the total population. Their assets principally took the form of national savings, life assurance policies, bank and cash deposits, building society deposits and household goods (*Royal Commission on Wealth*: Report 7: 102). For the top 10 per cent of wealth holders, the earning capacity of assets was sufficiently large to contribute a considerable part of their income, mainly through investments. For those below this level income from employment was the main and for most people the exclusive source of income. For the middle income groups, employment provided 80–90 per cent of all income. But in the lower part of the national income distribution, the share contributed by employment declined to no more than 50–60 per cent, the rest being made up by transfer payments of various kinds (*Royal Commission on Wealth*: Report 7: 42).

The growth of incomes and the consequent increase in consumer demand in the twentieth century has been a result of structural change in employment. There has been a marked redistribution of employment away from manual work into white collar jobs, together with a substantial increase in the activity rate for women. During the period 1911–79 the share of manual workers in total employment fell from 79.7 per cent to 48.1 per cent. The share of professional workers increased from 4.0 per cent to 17.1 per cent and clerical occupations from 4.8 to 16.0 per cent (Routh 6–7, 45). Within manual occupations there was an absolute decrease in skilled and semi-skilled jobs, such that the increase in unskilled work was only just enough to sustain a net increase in manual work. In the period since 1945 full employment prevailed for the best part of three decades, and this increased earnings both by the creation of additional employment and through wage increases facilitated by labour shortages. Growing employment in the twentieth century has thus generated increased affluence and consumer power for an expanding proportion of society, and on a far greater scale than before 1914.

There was substantial change within occupation and employment sectors in the twentieth century. Within the growing professions, some established traditional callings such as the law, the church and medicine grew modestly, but great increases took place in science and engineering, and in accountancy. Amongst the rather less exalted professional occupations, laboratory technicians and social welfare workers greatly increased their numbers. There was a considerable increase in many managerial and administrative occupations. Within the relative decline of skilled manual work, which meant a small absolute decline in numbers, there were wide sectoral variations. Very considerable job losses were recorded in textiles and clothing and in mining, together with some contraction in railway and sea transport. But these employment losses were countered by increases in skilled manual work in the metal making and working industries, in paper and printing, and in building, contracting and decorating, as well as in occupations as varied as hairdressing and the police force. There were even greater losses in semi-skilled employment, with substantial losses in agriculture, forestry and fishing as well as in domestic and personal services. These two broad employment categories, agriculture and miscellaneous services were, of course, the largest employers of labour before 1914. The largest part of the fall in the size of the latter sector was accounted for by the decline of female indoor domestic service, in which group well over one million jobs have been lost since the First World War. Growth elsewhere brought partial compensation for this loss in semi-skilled employment. The distributive trades continued to grow through most of the century, as did work for storekeepers, packers, and for workers in transport and communications. The pattern of unskilled work was erratic, increasing until the 1930s, declining over the next two decades, and expanding from the early 1950s. This aggregate pattern of change concealed a variety of sectoral experiences. Charwomen and office cleaners have grown steadily in numbers through the century. Building work increased in the interwar years and fell after 1950, and the growth in transport turned to decline in the 1930s. Unskilled work in textiles, mining and chemicals all declined, while opportunities appeared in metal manufacturing and engineering. Occupational opportunities have obviously grown and contracted in response to structural changes within the economy. In the context of twentieth-century advance in a high income economy such changes have favoured professional and clerical work rather than manual employment.

One of the major aspects of occupational change has been the greatly increased activity rate amongst women, presaged by the labour shortages of the two world war which saw women drafted into a wide range of hitherto male preserves. This process was further stimulated after 1945 by full employment and labour shortage for the first time in peace. Female employment grew in traditional professional sectors such as nursing and teaching, and rapidly in new sectors like social work and laboratory work. But clerical occupations provided the main growth area for female employment from 179,000 in 1911 to well over two and a half million by the present day, accounting for over one quarter of female employment. Within manual employment, female jobs represented a large part of the contraction in textiles and clothing. In semi-skilled work, the massive decline in domestic service was countered if not completely replaced by work in the distributive trades. Since the First World War female employment has almost doubled, accounting for well over half the total increase in employment. Like male employment, women's work has shifted away from manual occupations towards the clerical and professional. Manual work, which accounted for 83.3 per cent of female employment on the eve of the First World War had fallen to 53.4 per cent by 1971 (Routh 6–7).

These changes in occupational structure have added jobs primarily in higher income employment, thus augmenting consumer demand. A similar effect was created by rising female employment, often adding a second source of family income. These changes in occupation have been accompanied by changes in pay in different occupations. Prior to 1914, there was a considerable difference between the incomes of the relatively limited numbers in professional employment and the very much greater numbers employed in manual jobs, even those that were highly skilled. In the present century that gap has been eroded steadily over time and throughout the advanced industrial economies. It has taken place, of course, within the context of a general increase in pay in virtually all occupations. Average male earnings rose from £94 per annum in 1913–14 to £4,786 in 1978, while female average pay rose from £50 to £2,691 (Routh 120–1). But as multiples of the 1913–14 level deviations from the category averages indicated that amongst male workers the semi-skilled and unskilled fared better than professionals, whose earnings fell from 392 per cent of the male average to 290 per cent. But while the two lowest groups moved closer to the average wage, they still remained well below it.

The pattern of long-term changes in pay was different for female workers. There was a modest and increasing dispersion in earnings from the First World War until the mid 1930s, followed by a very substantial dispersion up to the mid 1950s, and then a trend towards greater equality emerged. The principal beneficiaries up to the 1930s were clerks and professional women, but in recent decades female unskilled wage rates have begun to catch up. Since the First World War, unskilled workers and managers have fared best in terms of female pay, followed by clerks and forewomen, and skilled manual workers. All have done better than any male occupational sector, so that there has been convergence between male and female rates in all groups with the exception of the semi-skilled. Even so, by the late 1970s women's pay remained well below that of their male counterparts. In skilled manual work the average female income was 52 per cent of the average male income and in the higher professional occupations the proportion was 81 per cent (Routh 123).

The reasons for the convergence in pay between white collar and manual workers and between male and female has generated considerable debate. One obvious help to manual work earnings came from the two world wars. Under wartime emergencies labour was diluted by the recruitment of less skilled workers into hitherto jealously guarded craft preserves, while the public control of wages in the wars gave the same cost of living allowance to all workers. During the First World War, British trade union membership doubled, principally by recruiting less skilled workers. All these factors helped erode differentials which had traditionally favoured skilled manual work. Once eroded, such differentials are not easily restored. Major changes in the structure of pay occurred in the periods 1914–20, 1934–44 and 1951–55, during each of which there was a general narrowing of pay differentials. Each period witnessed high rates of inflation, and was characterized by flat-rate claims for wage increases rather than percentage claims in order to maintain solidarity within industries or unions. Much the same was the case in the 1970s at the time of the 'social contract' between the government and the trade unions. Flat-rate increases obviously compress differentials. National wage bargaining at industry level, increasingly common in the twentieth century, has also reduced differentials by establishing standardized wage rates and reducing variations in regional wages (Phelps Brown 280–1). As in the nineteenth century, convergence in pay rates between related occupations fell while there was dispersion within the occupations themselves so that the overall level of dispersion has remained fairly stable. Routh noted that the wages of male manual workers showed very little dispersion between 1886 and 1914, while the median earnings of male workers in a sample taken from several industries in 1906 and 1960 showed little change between skilled, semi-skilled and unskilled workers (Routh 214, Phelps Brown 78). Structural change favouring the creation of more white collar employment in the higher income jobs augments aggregate demand. The increase in female activity rates and therefore of the total labour force, and the convergence of pay rates upwards have the same effect of increasing consumer spending power. The twentieth century has continued the process of extending consumer demand beyond the select band of the extremely wealthy which was clearly in progress towards the end of the Victorian years. The more equitable distribution of the national income thus effected, together with the higher sustained rate of growth of national income in the twentieth century, has not only increased aggregate demand but substantially changed it. Effective demand until the later nineteenth century comprised two main components, the varied demand of the wealthy, rich in substance but limited in number of people, and the demand of the rest of the population which was largely restricted to the basic necessities of life. The growth of the middle income groups in affluence and numbers, in the twentieth century, brought new dimensions to aggregate demand, increasing both the size and the range of goods and services falling within the spending power of an ever larger proportion of the population.

III

The aggregate pattern of consumer spending in the twentieth century subsumed a diversity of spending patterns by social groups at extremely different levels of affluence or poverty. The relative decline of the wealthiest sections of the community does not imply any absolute decrease in the substance, and the fruits of extreme affluence have contributed strongly to aggregate demand in the present century as they did before 1914. But beyond question, much of the increase in aggregate demand has come from the growing affluence of the middle classes. Their relative gain reflects a considerable absolute increase in income for these sections of society. The pattern of consumer demand has, therefore, been strongly influenced by the spending preferences of this section of society. Nowhere is this more apparent than in housing.

The growth of housing, and especially private housing for owner occupation, has been one of the major sources of demand in the twentieth century. In part, this reflects the very limited advance in this area before 1914 for the great majority of people. Almost four million houses were built in the interwar years, three quarters of them for private ownership and occupation. While the upper end of the middle-class housing market offered properties at prices up to £1,250 for a suburban semi-detached, the more popular range was £250–550 (Powell 94). Public authority housing provision was also helped by the Wheatley Act of 1924 which allowed a subsidy of nine pounds per year for forty years for housing built by local authorities. In 1930 the Greenwood Housing Act provided subsidies for the replacement of slum properties. But in the 1930s public sector housing seldom exceeded 20 per cent of total housing expenditure, and it was the private housing boom which has been generally accepted by historians as the principal stimulus in generating recovery from the depression in Britain (Richardson 1967: 155). Rising real incomes for those in work, helped by the cheap money policy of the government which kept construction costs down, and the increasing availability of funds as consols became a less desirable form of investment, all helped the housing boom. Much of the demand for private housing was located in the prosperous south of England and the midlands. In the interwar years, 50–65 per cent of unsubsidized house building for owner occupation was confined to London, the South East and the South West. By contrast, increased local authority housing provision was more characteristic of the relatively depressed industrial areas (Richardson 1967: 179). New housing had important multiplier effects in exerting a demand for plumbing, drainage, and decorating, and considerably increased the use of electricity which, at last, superceded gas lighting. The number of electricity consumers was thus raised from 730,000 in 1920 to almost nine million by the late 1930s. Housing development in new areas, and much of the interwar private building was suburban, necessitated additional social provision in the form of roads, shopping centres, schools and hospitals, hence stimulating more construction work. For most of the interwar period, non-housing construction comprised 25–40 per cent of the total.

Impressive as this growth was in comparison to earlier housing provision, it seems modest indeed when compared to the postwar housing expansion after 1945. The stock of owner occupied dwellings grew from 4.1 million in 1951 to 10.5 million in 1975, while the stock of housing rented from local authorities increased from 2.5 million to 6.2 million. There was a decline in the private rented housing sector. Even so, the total housing stock showed an unprecedented net increase of six million houses during this quarter of a century (Royal Commission on Wealth: Report 5: 143). Not surprisingly, it has been the growth of owner occupied housing in the twentieth century which has played a major role in creating a more equal distribution of wealth. The share of total personal wealth held in housing increased from 17 per cent in 1960 to 37 per cent in 1975, reflecting both the great increase in home ownership and the appreciation of this asset relative to others (Royal Commission on Wealth: Report 5: 150). It was, of course, the upper and middle-income groups which were most closely involved in house purchase. In 1975, 82 per cent of private housing was owned, or was being purchased, by persons with incomes over £3,000 per year. The bulk of properties which were fully owned belonged to retired people who had paid off their mortgages. But local authority housing and privately rented property was mainly leased by those on lower incomes. Those earning less than £3,000 per year comprised only 18 per cent of the purchasers or owners of private housing, but they leased 63 per cent of privately rented unfurnished property and 52 per cent of local authority housing. Conversely those with high incomes accounted for only a small share of public authority tenants (*Royal Commission on Wealth*: Report 5: 153).

The greater part of the national housing stock has been built in the present century, 67.3 per cent of the total stock since 1918 and 44.7 per cent since 1944. There have been significant regional variations, however, both in the rate of construction and the age of the housing stock. Twentieth century building has been concentrated heavily in the East and West Midlands, and most strongly in the South East outside Greater London. A high proportion of housing in these regions is of twentieth century vintage. It is in these regions that the main thrust of new housing construction has been felt. Other regions, like the North West, Yorkshire/Humberside, Wales and the North, have possessed a greater share of their housing stock since the nineteenth century. That fact, together with the lower levels of income and economic activity, restricted the potency of the housing boom in those areas.

Another major growth in demand in the present century, related to housing and increasing affluence, has been the appetite for consumer durables including furnishings, washing machines, refrigerators, telephones, and more recently central heating. Recent decades have seen substantial increases in ownership of many consumer durables which were limited to a relative few in the interwar years. Central heating, which was found in a variety of public buildings in the interwar years, was rare in domestic households. As late as 1964, only seven per cent of households possessed central heating, but this proportion increased to 31.0 per cent by

1970–71 and to 59.8 per cent by 1980–81 (*Regional Trends* 1983: 100). Similarly ownership of refrigerators expanded from 34 per cent of households in 1964 to 95.5 per cent in 1980–81, while ownership of washing machines increased from 53.0 per cent to 79.7 per cent, and telephones from 22.0 per cent to 73.8 per cent.

The increase in the ownership of other consumer durables reflects the increased orientation of entertainment towards the home. Radio was one of the outstanding developments of the interwar years, mass production boosting demand from the late 1920s such that the number of licence holders grew from three million in 1929 to eight million in 1936 (Richardson 1967: 120). Its postwar counterpart was television, although it was operational from 1936. This was an entertainment form in which Britain led as both producer and consumer, and the number of sets per thousand people increased from 11 to 211 in the 1950s, a far higher ratio than was achieved in any other European country. By the early 1980s no less than 96.7 per cent of British households possessed a television set. In the 1970s there was a massive transfer from black and white television receivers to colour sets indicated by a fall in licences for the former by over eight million and an increase in colour set licences by almost nine and a half million (*Monthly Digest of Statistics*, January 1984). Increased affluence has brought multiple ownership of television sets. The growth of video machines and home computers, both of which operate in conjunction with a television set, reflects the expansion of the same market. But much higher ownership rates in the United States suggests that the market is far from saturated (Deaton 126).

Apart from housing, private motoring has represented the greatest area of growth in consumer spending in the present century and for most people it comprises the largest financial commitment after housing. The number of private cars with a current licence grew from just under two million in 1938 to five and a half million in 1960 and to 15.4 million in 1981 (*Annual Abstract of Statistics* 1961: 187, 1983: 211). Much of this massive increase came after 1960, and while 37 per cent of households had one or more cars in 1964 this proportion had risen to 61.8 per cent by 1980–81. By the latter date one quarter of households which owned a car had more than one. Falling car prices in the interwar years, together with the manufacture of smaller cars with low running costs, brought motor ownership within the reach of the growing middle classes. Before the First World War small and expensive specialist production had restricted motoring to the wealthy. But much greater growth came in the prosperous years after 1950 as full employment and rising incomes increased the number of potential buyers and as supply costs were kept down by the application of mass production techniques in Western Europe. So important has the motor car become that the state of the industry has frequently been invoked as the best barometer of economic well-being. The growing importance of private transport is indicated in the share of consumer expenditure on motor cars and motor cycles. In 1900 this was negligible, but by the end of the 1930s three per cent was spent on the purchase, running and maintenance of such vehicles, and by the mid 1960s nine per cent of expenditure was accounted for in this way. By 1980 vehicles and transport costs accounted for 14.6 per cent of consumer spending, while other durables accounted for 14.9 per cent (*Annual Abstract of Statistics* 1983: 279).

Increased national income and a more equitable distribution of that income have thus generated both substantial increases in consumer spending and major shifts in the allocation of that spending in the twentieth century. While expenditure has increased considerably on commodities like those just noted and, in the past decade, on holidays and recreational spending, there has been a relative fall in traditional spending areas. Food, drink and clothing have all received relatively less of family expenditure than in the nineteenth century, although home entertainment and fashion have had an offsetting effect. Even so, drink commands far less than the 18.9 per cent of consumer spending it had at the turn of the century, while public transport also takes a much smaller share of the household budget. Domestic service is now negligible although it accounted for over five per cent of spending at the end of Victoria's reign. By 1980, food, drink and tobacco accounted for only 30.5 per cent of total consumer spending, and housing, fuel and lighting a further 20.6 per cent. Much of the remaining half went on various forms of entertainment, tangible or otherwise.

IV

The increase in government spending as a share of national income has been a common feature in changing expenditure patterns in all advanced economies in the twentieth century. While public expenditure did not exceed 15 per cent of national income before the First World War, and averaged 19.9 per cent in the interwar years, its share greatly increased in recent decades to reach 45.6 per cent in 1979 (Peacock/Wiseman 164, Judge 28). For much of the twentieth century, provision for war and defence has been an important element in government spending, both in direct military expenditure and indirectly in paying off the national debt which had to be extended in order to finance the two world wars. Payment of the national debt, which had been about one per cent before 1914, rose to over four per cent after the war and remained at that share of GNP. Military spending rose to over seven per cent of GNP by the late 1930s and exceeded 11 per cent in the early 1950s. These two linked forms of public expenditure together accounted for 30–50 per cent of the total during the first half of the century

(Peacock/Wiseman 86). The other principal area of growth in spending in this period was on social services, increasing from 18.0 per cent of government spending in 1900 to 44.6 per cent by 1955, equivalent to 2.6 per cent and 16.3 per cent respectively of GNP. All the major components of social service spending increased, including education, health, housing and social security. Their growth, in turn, largely accounted for the big increase in local government expenditure.

In the very substantial increase in public expenditure since 1950, social services have been the principal areas of growth increasing from 16.1 per cent of GNP in 1951 to 28.3 per cent by 1979. Even the large defence component, although increasing in absolute terms, had fallen to 5.5 per cent of GNP by 1979. All the main elements of social service spending have increased substantially in the past three decades. Education and health spending increased threefold, in constant prices, but the greatest increase was in social security payments from £2,839 million in 1950 to £11,590 million in 1979. By the latter date, social security payments exceeded 11 per cent of national income (Judge 28, 30). Much, if not all, of this increased social expenditure resulted in increased personal consumption, so that the relative decline of consumers expenditure in national income should not be taken to indicate even relative decline in real consumer benefit. The growth of education and health provision confer obvious benefits to consumers whether they are provided through government agency or purchased directly in the market. Social security payments represent a substantial transfer payment in reallocating benefits, and a redistribution of consumer spending power. The necessity for such transfers does, of course, indicate that the growth of the consumer society has still not fully embraced all members of society.

The growth of public expenditure has attracted considerable interest, and several explanations have been developed to account for it. One line of argument is that successive wars contributed to the growth in social service provision by drawing attention to poor social conditions and stimulating the consensus needed to implement ameliorative policies. 'We must look, for example, for the birth of the National Health Service in the aftermath of the bombing of London which brought about the development of emergency state health measures on a large scale. We must view the plans for reconstruction after the war, especially the famous Beveridge plan, as a real part of the war effort' (Peacock/Wiseman 94). Similarly the exigencies of war made necessary and acceptable levels of taxation which had hitherto been regarded as intolerable or unattainable. Once established such taxation, and the public expenditure thereby made possible, has not been too difficult to maintain and even increase.

Several other hypotheses have been developed to explain the widespread growth in public expenditure in recent decades. Several have followed Wagner's Law which postulated that such increased expenditure was an inevitable concomitant of growth, operating through rising expectations amongst the populace and the difficulties encountered by the government in running an increasingly complex economy. Recently a Marxist explanation has emerged. This advances the thesis that the contradiction between social production and privately owned means of production, generates growth in state spending to the point of financial crisis. At advanced levels of capitalist development, it is argued, the private sector requires more and more state funded overheads, such as transport infrastructure or education, while extra social service provision is needed to make up the incomes of the labour force to a socially acceptable standard of living. Alternatively, public choice theory proposes that the provision of public services is given a continuous boost by the competitive 'advertising' of the different political parties, each raising the expectations of consumers as to acceptable levels of welfare provision without spelling out too closely the costs involved. Another manifestation of the same phenomenon has been the effect of Royal Commissions and other public and official enquiries into welfare provision arrangements. Such investigations have usually formulated a number of important but expensive improvements, as in the case of three major enquiries into education during the 1960s. All these theses, derived from extremely different basic premises, converge in that they conclude that public expenditure has developed with the aid of a substantial built-in growth component.

Pressures for a better provision of services have certainly met with some success as, for example, in education where expenditure per pupil has grown and the pupil/teacher ratio has fallen, while in the health service the patient/doctor ratio and the patient/dentist ratio have both fallen in the past few decades (*Social Trends* 1983: 48–50, 104). Some additional pressure for growth has been built into the system through demographic change. The proportion of the population not economically active has increased as a result of extended education for the young and the increase of the retired population, thus increasing the dependency ratio of non-workers to workers. Growth in the number of pensioners made a significant contribution to the massive increase in social security payments in the 1970s as, in the last few years, have unemployment benefit payments. Such spending is demand determined, rising with increasing dependency, and has proved extremely difficult to control by government. Furthermore, the slower rate of economic growth in the 1970s made it difficult to pay for such requirements out of increases in national income. This partly autonomous increase in public spending pushed outgoings beyond the limit of government revenue in the 1970s, thus giving some support to the Marxist prognostications. The gap had to be covered by an increase in government borrowing, the Public Sector Borrowing Requirement (PSBR). Prior to the 1970s such borrowing was modest, never exceeding five per cent of GDP in the previous decade. But between 1973–79, borrowing averaged 8.1 per cent of GDP (Surrey 549). The new Conservative administration elected in 1979 entered office committed to reducing the PSBR both as a means to stifle inflation and cut the size of the public sector. In spite of this, borrowing increased between 1979–83 and PSBR exceeded the target borrowing figure by a factor of two in the years 1980–82 (Greenaway/Shaw 374–5). The average annual size of PSBR exceeded £10 billion in 1979–83 compared to £8 billion in 1973–79 (*United Kingdom National Accounts 1984*: T13.14). The problem of controlling the PSBR indicates the strength of its autonomous component. Between 1966 and 1979 the number of state pensioners increased from 6.5 million to 8.8 million. Rising unemployment has added considerably to the growth of demand induced social security payments. Unemployment reduces the income from taxation and simultaneously increases the claims for benefit. One 1980 estimate suggested that an increase in the level of unemployment by 10,000 people cost £110 million in benefits. In the past five years, unemployment has increased by over two million people. Ironically, a government committed to supply side solutions to economic problems has found itself impeded by an element of autonomous demand. In the decade after 1973, government expenditure increased from 40.6 to 45.6 per cent of GNP, and three-quarters of that increase was caused by increased social security payments (*United Kingdom National Accounts 1984*: T9.4).

V

For much of the twentieth century the pressure of demand in the economy has been rather higher than before 1914, partly due to war and partly due to the golden age of growth 1951–73. In the latter phase there appeared for the first time a long-term shortage of labour. In the interwar period, however, pressure of demand was much less than before or after the wars which bounded it, and the level of activity was estimated at only 88.3 per cent (Matthews 304). As unemployment increased through the 1970s there was an obvious reduction in the pressure of demand. For much of the present century, therefore, demand has been insufficient to fully employ productive resources.

In spite of this the growth and diversification of demand to encompass the greater part of the population in the consumer society in the twentieth century has depended on economic growth. The fact that growth has been so slow and that demand pressure has been so moderate raises questions about the supply side of the economy which must be considered later. Growth and diversification of demand has depended in the last resort on the increase of affluence throughout the economy. But while greater growth and a strong shift towards greater income equality in the twentieth century has greatly expanded that prosperity in both worth and extensiveness, it has far from percolated down throughout all stratas of society. Recent decades have witnessed an increase in poverty through unemployment, one-parent families, retirement and the erosion in real terms of the benefits provided for such groups. Between 1960 and 1976, it was estimated, the number of people living in poverty rose from 4.6 million to 8.0 million (Townsend 908). The recent recession has increased considerably the number of those who depend on social security benefits, and while such payment comprised 9.0 per cent of household incomes in 1973, it has risen to 14.9 per cent a decade later (*Family Expenditure Survey* 1973: T37, 1983: T22). It is at the very bottom of the social order that the effects of low growth are most clearly shown and keenly felt.

9

Investment and the financial system

I

As the twentieth century brought economic growth at an unprecedented rate both in Britain and in the world economy, so it also brought a substantial increase in investment. After 1950 the ratio of investment to national income in Britain reached levels never before attained (Table 3.1). Before 1914 a substantial contribution to that investment came from the stimulus of foreign markets. After the First World War this was no longer the case and consequently the home market component of investment, as represented by the increase in gross domestic fixed capital formation, became far more important than hitherto. In the interwar years it was almost as high as in any earlier period and from 1950 onwards far exceeded earlier investment levels. Indeed during the past four decades, gross domestic fixed capital formation has been close to twice the level achieved in much of the two hundred years before 1914. The distribution of investment has also changed. Transport, a major component in Victorian capital formation, has absorbed relatively less in the present century. Conversely, there was a substantial increase in investment in dwellings, social and public services, public utilities, distribution, and in manufacturing and construction (Table 9.1). Twentieth-century investment growth was thus broadly based, with increases in most sectors, although in recent years there has been a decline in public utilities, manufacturing, and construction. But while the investment ratio has been very much higher in the twentieth century than it was earlier, in an international context it can be seen to have lagged well behind the investment ratios of other industrial countries (Rostow 1978a: 79–82).

II

The increased demand for investment in the twentieth century was reflected in the rising value of securities quoted on the London Stock Exchange from

164

Table 9.1 *Gross domestic fixed capital formation by sector (per cent of GDP)*

	Agriculture	Mining	Manufacturing/ construction	Distribution	Gas water, electricity	Transport/ communications	Social & public services	Dwellings	Transfer costs	Total
1882–1913			3.1		0.6	2.6	0.7	1.5	0.0	8.5
1913–1924			2.5		0.4	1.9	0.3	0.8	0.0	5.9
1924–1937	0.1	0.2	1.8	1.2	1.4	2.0	0.8	3.5	0.0	11.0
1937–1948	0.2	0.2	1.6	0.7	0.7	1.3	0.6	2.0	0.0	7.3
1951–1964	0.7	0.5	4.8	2.4	2.0	2.4	1.4	3.5	0.0	17.7
1964–1973	0.6	0.4	4.8	1.1	2.2	2.5	5.0	3.9	0.6	21.1
1973–1979	0.7	1.3	3.9	1.5	1.5	2.3	5.3	4.8	0.8	22.1
1979–1983	0.5	1.3	3.0	1.6	1.6	1.7	5.6	4.2	1.0	20.5

Sources: C. H. Feinstein, *Statistical Tables of National Income, Expenditure and Output of the UK 1855–1965* (Cambridge 1972) Tables 5, 42.
Central Statistical Office, *National Income and Expenditure 1963–73*, Tables 14, 57.
Central Statistical Office, *UK National Accounts 1984*, Tables 1.5, 10.7.

£1,215 million in 1853 to £11,262 million in 1913 and £45,139 million by 1968 (Morgan/Thomas 282–3). Impressive as the scale of this increase was, even more dramatic was the reorientation of investment, in the twentieth century, away from foreign investment and railways which had been so important before 1914. On the eve of that war, overseas investment had accounted for one third of all securities quoted in the London market while railway shares, home and abroad, were rather more than this. By the 1970s both types of share had fallen to a few percentage points of the total. In the context of considerable growth in investment, these two types of investment experienced both relative and absolute decline in the twentieth century.

The main area of growth in investment demand has been in government borrowing, generated by the two great stimuli of war and increasing state spending. British government stock increased from nine per cent of total investment on the eve of the First World War to 32.7 per cent by its close. Even greater was the effect of the Second World War, government borrowing reached a peak of 55.8 per cent of investment just after the war, declining relatively thereafter. In more recent years government borrowing has increased to pay for its social security obligations as its income has proved insufficient to cover its spending.

The other main increase in demand for institutional investment in the present century has come from industry and commerce. Such shares had accounted for only 8 per cent of the total in 1913 but increased to 25 per cent by the 1970s. In market rather than nominal terms the increase was greater than this, especially since the Second World War because faster economic growth and inflation affected equity shares more than government stocks. The majority of manufacturing and commercial firms before 1914 preferred to rely largely on private or internally generated sources of finance. Some were forced into the financial market because of their size and their consequent inability to supply their large capital requirements. This process continued in the twentieth century. By the 1920s, large firms like Imperial Chemical Industries (ICI), Morris, Ford, Thorn, Bowater and Beecham all sought public investment. By the 1970s, industrial, commercial and financial company shares together accounted for over half the market value of shares quoted on the London Stock Exchange. The growth in company demand for capital in the financial market has been much greater in recent decades. Capital issues by British companies in the interwar years ranged between £100 and £300 million. By the 1960s the range was £400–600 million, and increased considerably in the inflationary seventies (W. A. Thomas 1978: 27, 148–52).

The recourse of industry to the money markets for investment was not confined to the private sector. As the nationalized industries grew in number and size after the Second World War, so they too looked to the market for investment. Until the mid 1950s, nationalized industries obtained about one third of their capital needs from their own saving, a further 10–20 per cent from government loans and the rest from the money market. From the mid 1950s, the nationalized industries tended to borrow more from the Treasury than the market, usually in the form of long-term loans. By 1977, the amount outstanding in government advances stood at £11,310 million out of a total debt of £17,496 million (W. A. Thomas 1978: 297). This in turn contributed to the imbalance in the government's payments and stimulated its need to borrow. But the nationalized industries also obtained funds abroad by the 1970s, initially through public issues in West Germany, Switzerland and Luxemburg and later through the growing Eurodollar market. While only two per cent of borrowing was done abroad at the beginning of the 1970s, nearly one quarter of funds came from this source at the end of the decade, with electricity, gas, steel and the postal services providing the main demand for investment. This borrowing by the nationalized industries included a syndicated bank loan of one billion dollars raised in 1976 jointly by the Electricity Council, the Post Office, and the National Water Council. Such loans were usually obtained at lower rates of interest than public investment from the National Loans Fund, thus making considerable saving on interest charges. The increased financial deficit of the public corporations, the long-established local authority deficit and the new central government deficit which appeared in the 1970s, all contributed to the increase in government borrowing (Wilson Report 63–4).

While the main growth in institutional investment demand came from government and industry in the twentieth century, at the individual level it came primarily from a rising demand for owner occupied housing. At the end of the First World War, less than ten per cent of households were owner occupied. Eighty per cent were privately rented, and the remainder fell into the fairly new category of publicly provided housing (Boddy 2, 12). In the course of the century this balance has been completely changed. By the late 1970s private owner occupied housing comprised 54 per cent of all households, public sector housing accounted for a further 32 per cent and the privately rented sector had contracted to about 10 per cent. Several factors contributed to this. From the beginning of the century private renting became less attractive to landlords as building costs increased and statutory controls on rents eroded the returns on leasing. On the other hand, rising real incomes and, in the interwar years, falling real prices helped increase the demand for owner occupied housing. The housing boom of the 1930s was also helped by an increase in the length of the repayment period for mortgages up to 25 years. Borrowing was aided by the development of several schemes by which mortgages were made more widely available. Customarily in the 1930s building societies were reluctant to give loans greater than 70–75 per cent of the value of a property. But this proportion could be increased to 90–95 per cent by taking advantage of several optional schemes. Some insurance companies were prepared to provide a loan to cover the difference between the building society offer and the requirement of the putative purchaser, in return for the purchase of a single premium by the latter. Thus began an enduring and profitable relationship between building societies and insurance companies. Alternatively, advantage could be taken of the builders' pool. House builders deposited cash with building societies to the value of the 'excess' or the difference between the loan offered and the required sum, usually about 15–20 per cent of the purchase price. In the event of default by the borrower the building society could draw on this deposit. In this way the building societies obtained an additional guarantee against loss while the builder was able to sell his houses.

These strategies indicate the cautious and modest expansion of private housing in the interwar years. Since the Second World War this has been a major growth sector in the economy, both responding to increased affluence and acting as a manifestation of it. Some indication of the scale of increase is given by the growth of building society mortgage assets from £587 million in 1936 to £56,861 million in 1982 (Cleary 188, Coakley/Harris 155). The number of borrowers increased from 1.2 million in 1935 to 2.0 million in 1955 and 5.5 million in 1981. Full employment for much of the postwar period, rapidly rising real incomes, especially family incomes as female employment opportunities increased, and structural change in the economy in favour of professional white collar jobs, all brought home ownership within the financial reach of an increasing number of people. The growth of the economy and increased demand for funds for a variety of investments in the present century has developed a further and related increase in demand for financial services. Insurance was again in the forefront. Both the world wars increased insurance business. War obviously also increased risk, especially for marine and fire insurance. In the First World War this risk was offset by government guarantee, fixing marine insurance premiums and reinsuring each policy to the extent of 80 per cent of the risk. The State Insurance Office undertook to provide insurance for cargoes which remained commercially unacceptable. Within such an environment, insurance firms prospered. The London and Lancashire Insurance Company enjoyed a fivefold increase in premium income in the war, while overall marine insurance increased tenfold and fire insurance doubled, and even general accident premium income grew by fifty per cent. There were substantial although less dramatic increases in premium income in the Second World War (Francis 77, 95). The later war proved to be less lucrative because government regulations were more stringent. But the insurance companies acted as agents for the state assumed monopoly of insurance for war risks. As in the earlier war, marine and fire premiums increased substantially. The Royal Exchange Assurance gained about one million pounds worth of additional premium income from both fire and marine insurance in the First World War, quite a bit better than the increase in the later war (Supple 420–1, 517).

Apart from the peculiar situation of war, insurance business increased very considerably in the twentieth century from the expansion of established forms of insurance and the development of new branches. During the interwar years only marine insurance remained depressed as an obvious effect of the world-wide depression in shipping. Fire insurance increased, especially abroad through the extensive network of branch offices and agencies established by British firms before the war. Business remained concentrated in the United States, Canada, Australasia, and Western Europe. At home, growing middle class affluence generated an increase in ordinary life assurance premiums, and industrial insurance premiums doubled in the interwar years. But without doubt, the greatest impact upon insurance demand in the twentieth century came from the advent of motor insurance, as the spearhead of personal accident insurance, such that by 1927 it exceeded fire insurance in value of premiums. This form of general accident insurance increased, in terms of premiums, from £16 million in 1913 to £80 million in 1938 (Supple 428).

Demand for insurance services increased greatly after the Second World War. Increased affluence enabled people to allocate a larger share of income to insurance, and the premium income for life assurance alone increased from 2.1 per cent of personal disposable income in 1950 to 3.4 per cent in 1976. A greater and more widespread ownership of consumer durables, most obviously houses and cars, generated a related demand for insurance. Motor insurance, in particular, increased greatly as the number of vehicle licences increased from 1.4 million in 1944 to 12.6 million in 1968 and almost 19.8 million by 1982. Between the Second World War and the early 1970s, premiums on ordinary life insurance increased by over £1,000 million, fire insurance increased by almost as much and motor insurance increased by £600 million. Further demand came from abroad, and foreign business brought in about 10 per cent of premium income in the late 1960s (Clayton 211, 341–3).

A related provision for future security, characteristic of an increasingly affluent society, has been the growth of pension funds. While company pension schemes existed in the interwar period their growth since the 1950s has been quite spectacular. In the two decades prior to 1975, the number of contributors to occupational pension schemes increased from 7.7 million to 11.5 million people, and the number of people receiving such pensions increased from 1.0 to 3.4 million. Demand increased in the 1950s and early

1960s as more workers joined such schemes, but more recently growth has been generated through the provision of better and more extensive benefits for contributors, which in turn has increased the requisite payments. Half the national work force is now estimated to belong to a pension scheme, and by the 1980s about 80 per cent of British households had life assurance cover of some kind and some hundred million life assurance policies were active.

A major part of the growth of demand for financial services has fallen upon the banking system, both from individuals and from business. Not only has the number of people using bank accounts increased considerably, so has the use of bank borrowing facilities for the purchase of consumer durables and, recently, for mortgages. Business has continued to use bank loan and overdraft facilities sometimes on a large scale. In 1925 Lloyds Bank increased the overdraft of Beardmore, the Scottish engineering firm, from £500,000 to £650,000 and provided the firm with additional credit in the 1930s. The same bank financed the new integrated steel plant at Ebbw Vale in 1936 for Richard Thomas and Company (Winton 66). In much the same way in the previous century, the Swansea Bank had financed steel, coal and tinplate manufacture in South Wales (Cottrell 1980: 221–2). Overall loans from the main London clearing banks to industry remained static in the 1930s, ranging annually between £352–380 million. Investment advances to industry from the banks increased considerably in the 1950s, passing the £1,000 million mark in 1960 and reaching £5,500 million by 1974 (W. A. Thomas 1978: 78, 200–1). There was, in fact, a substantial shift in bank lending in the postwar period towards manufacturing at the expense of service investment and personal and professional loans. Since the early 1970s investment has shifted from manufacturing to service sector activities. The growth in bank borrowing by industry was a result of a fall in internally generated resources for expansion although it still remained at the high level of 80 per cent in the 1970s, so that the gap in investment filled by bank funds was still quite modest (Wilson Report 133).

III

As economic growth dispersed wealth more widely in the economy in the twentieth century so the importance of extremely wealthy investors as suppliers of capital declined. By the same process the number of people who contributed to investment supply, albeit indirectly, increased. Affluence increased the share of personal disposable income which could be saved, the average proportion rising from 1.4 per cent in 1950 to 14.9 per cent in 1976 (Franklin/Woodhead 23). For the great majority of people, funds for investment were provided through their subscription to institutions like building societies, pension funds and insurance companies. The building societies in particular derived the greater part of their funds from the personal sector, many people opening accounts as a means to saving for a deposit on a house while simultaneously gaining preferential treatment from that building society for a mortgage. The share of adults with building society accounts rose swiftly from 11 per cent in 1965 to 45 per cent by the late 1970s. Such deposits represented an increasing share of household assets, from about 20 per cent of the liquid assets of the personal sector in the early 1960s to over 45 per cent by the early 1980s, the gain being achieved partly through transfers from national savings (Boddy 1, 48, Coakley/Harris 156). Many of such investments are substantial, representing saving for retirement in a secure form. In 1975 over 70 per cent of these accounts were for sums over £10,000. The number of building society share holders, which had been 0.6 million before the First World War and 5.9 million in 1965, surged upward to 33.4 million by 1981 (Coakley/Harris 152).

The other major new institution created by personal saving in the twentieth century has been the pension fund. While they have shown a marked aggregate increase in assets, by some sixty billion pounds in the 1960s and 1970s, there have also emerged some exceptionally large individual funds. Many of the largest pension funds were those of nationalized industries and the biggest, the Post Office Staff Superannuation Fund had accumulated assets worth £5.2 billion by the early 1980s. The biggest building society, the Halifax, had assets worth only a fraction of this at £7.6 million. Insurance policies and, for the better off, investment trusts and unit trusts have also absorbed individual savings in the recent past, although the banks still hold about one third of the liquid assets of the non-institutional sector.

The accumulation of investible funds by a greater number of individuals in the present century, and the decline of extremely wealthy and sometimes unpredictable investors which the nineteenth-century nobility produced, has meant that capital has been drawn increasingly into the very large financial institutions. The combined assets of the insurance companies, pension funds, and investment trusts grew from £8.2 billion in 1957 to £154.2 billion in 1981. The supply of investment funds is powerfully influenced by the preferences of such institutions. Indeed, the largest insurance company, the Prudential Assurance, had assets worth £10.9 billion by 1981, sufficient to purchase at market price all the shares of General Electric Company (GEC) and half those of British Petroleum (BP) (Coakley/Harris 8).

The main shifts in demand for investment have therefore been met by the supply response of these major financial institutions, and the switch from government stock and overseas utilities to domestic manufacturing has produced a realignment of their investments, and given them a substantial influence on the funding of industry. The two world wars had an important influence in the shift of investment from overseas, and into government stock. This was effected by the subscription of war loans paid directly to the government, and in the sale or deposit of foreign securities with the Treasury. In the First World War, a large share of the £55 million overseas assets of the insurance companies was commandeered in this way to protect the exchange rate. Thus the insurance companies increased the share of their assets in government stock from one per cent to almost one third in the course of the 1914–18 war. While there was some shift away from gilts in the 1930s as interest rates fell, the repeated need for government lending in the Second World War pushed the share of insurance company investment in this stock to 36 per cent by the end of the war. Thereafter there was a steady fall in this relative share, although the stability of government stock makes it very attractive to cautious and conservative institutions.

But in the twentieth century there was a growth of investment in ordinary shares. Industry had never been popular as a source of institutional investment in the nineteenth century, and only four per cent of insurance company investments were so disposed in 1913. Apart from the fact that there existed an abundance of alternative and apparently more reliable investments, industry seldom looked for investment on a scale sufficient to interest institutions with very large sums to invest. The change in the twentieth century, especially after 1945, was due to the erosion of fixed interest rates by inflation. Since the value of ordinary company shares, unlike government securities, increase with inflation, diversification in this way became desirable and even necessary. But even when investing in company shares, the institutions were able to follow a risk-minimizing strategy by purchasing large blocks of high quality shares in major companies. By the late 1960s ordinary shares had increased to a quarter of insurance company investments. But these institutions have always favoured secure investments. In the eighteenth and nineteenth centuries, property, rent and land had been favoured for this reason. On the eve of the First World War the investments of British life assurance companies retained 9.2 per cent of funds in land, housing and ground rents and a further 22.6 per cent in mortgages (Supple 333). Such investments remained popular, and secure, in the twentieth century. Recent decades have seen the development of closer links between insurance companies and property companies. The Royal Exchange Assurance bought property subject to development and then either leased it back to the developers, or offered advances in return for a fixed interest return or a share in the equity of the property company (Supple 528).

The pattern of investment by pension funds and investment trusts has been very similar to that of the insurance companies. Investment trusts responded to postwar inflation by dispersing their investments from debentures, bonds and preference shares into ordinary shares. They too have shifted towards company securities and property and away from government securities in recent decades (Corner/Burton 84). Pension fund investments, controlled more by the insurance companies and banks than by the fund managers, have been similarly disposed. The building societies have differed from their larger institutional colleagues in investment strategy because most of their funds are held in mortgages on property. About one sixth of building society assets are maintained in liquid asset investments mainly in government and local authority securities and in certificates of deposit which mature within five years. This disposition of funds is prescribed by law to maintain the security of society assets.

Compared to the nineteenth century the major investing institutions, and especially the insurance companies, have had a much reduced commitment to foreign investment. Much of the change can be attributed to the sale of overseas assets in wartime. In part it has been a result of government restrictions on foreign investment. When such restrictions were eventually removed in 1979, there was a substantial responsive outflow of investment funds from the major institutions. Between 1979 and 1982, the share of insurance company and pension fund investment going abroad increased from 7.3 per cent to 25.3 per cent (Coakley/Harris 39). Whether this represents a process of adjustment and asset diversification which is now effectively complete, or the beginning of a major shift in investment, cannot yet be determined. Even the investment trusts, which had already a greater commitment to investing abroad, increased overseas investments from 32.0 per cent to 41.5 per cent of their total outlay in the years after the abolition of restrictions. Much will doubtless depend on the success of this upsurge in foreign lending, a great deal of which went to the Far East, to Japan, Australia, Singapore, and Hong Kong. The allocation of investment overseas came partly from newly acquired income and partly from the sale of government securities. It has not, as yet, made major inroads into investment in company securities. Pension funds and insurance companies together reduced their share of investment in gilts from 48.5 per cent to 27.3 per cent between 1979 and 1983, and their investment in company securities from 22.0 per cent to 19.8 per cent, as their foreign investment share rose from 5.2 per cent to 22.9 per cent.

The growth of the major financial institutions with a strong investment interest has placed them in a position of great importance in determining the allocation of investment between different ventures. By the early 1980s, the insurance companies, investment trusts, and pension funds together held 54.1 per cent of listed equity stock and 63.8 per cent of listed company bonds (Coakley/Harris 106–7). For their part, almost half the investments of these institutions were in company securities, and about 20 per cent in each of government securities and property. Any substantial change in investment, as in the transfer of investments abroad in recent years, must have a considerable effect on the supply of funds within the British economy.

IV

The structure of the British financial system was established by 1914 with a strong orientation towards international finance. It is hardly surprising, therefore, that the main changes in the City as a whole have been linked to international events. The loss of overseas links and the sale of foreign assets during the two world wars affected the banks as much as the insurance companies. They too substituted government securities for foreign investments. But the disruption of the international economy lasted well beyond the period of war. The boom and slump which followed the cessation of hostilities in 1918, together with the destabilizing effect of the peace treaty on European political and economic life, delayed any return to normal well into the 1920s. The Wall Street crash and subsequent depression soon cut that recovery short, and the result of the depression was a level of international trade, in the 1930s, far below that known in the previous century. Similarly, the effects of the Second World War lingered well into the 1950s. It is not surprising that the international aspects of British finance and investment were much diminished compared to the buoyant prosperity prevailing in such markets before 1914. Some of this, it has been suggested, was a manifestation of an ossified and conservative system resigned to gentle decline. 'During the nineteen-fifties there was little indication that London could again become a world financial centre: it seemed to offer a study of banking in decline. The London bankers were much more defensive and somnolent than the Americans, surveying their past more lovingly than their future . . . Visiting their mahogany parlours in the late fifties I found myself in a scene of butlers, silver salvers, and old claret which seemed to belong to a Victorian play: most of the cast of military and country-house characters turned out to be interconnected or intermarried and several were within the nexus of conservative interests which was then becoming known as "The Establishment" ' (Sampson 118).

Prior to 1914, there had been no attempt by the government to control or direct the flow of investment. But during and after the war, Treasury and Bank of England pressure was used to regulate the flow of funds abroad. This reflected a view that investment was more urgently needed at home, for housing in the 1920s, or to protect the sterling exchange rate when it was threatened, as in 1925, 1929 and 1931 (Atkin 333–4). By the 1930s, the internationalist trade and financial policies of Victorian Britain had been abandoned, and British trade followed by British investment became increasingly oriented towards the Empire. Thus there emerged the sterling area. This comprised countries which continued to link their currencies to sterling at a fixed rate of exchange after the abandonment of the gold standard in 1931. Such countries maintained their foreign exchange reserves in London and against that security they obtained long-term investment from the City. This system provided the City with a substantial volume of stable reserves and overseas holding of sterling doubled between 1931 and 1937. The members of the sterling area were mainly colonial and dominion countries, although there were others which had close trading links with Britain, such as the Scandinavian and later Middle East countries. The Second World War brought a massive increase in the sterling balances held in London. Britain financed the war by importing a substantial volume of goods from India, the Middle East and Commonwealth countries which was paid for in sterling credits in London. By the postwar years these deposits had grown to considerable size. Any large scale removal of such deposits, which for the most part were held in short-term credits, would have severely threatened the sterling exchange rate. Much of the stop-go cycle of the 1950s was a response to the need to protect the exchange rate and retain these sterling balances in London. A considerable proportion of investment overseas continued to flow to those countries which held sterling balances. Both the size of the sterling area and the role of sterling as a major reserve currency in international trade diminished in the 1950s. It was the restricted and then declining role of British finance in international investment which prompted the idea of permanent decline as expressed so graphically by Sampson.

But as the international economy recovered in the 1950s from a prolonged period of dislocation and depression which had lasted since the First World War, so the City of London found a new role at the very centre of that resurgence. In 1958 most of the countries of Western Europe returned to full convertibility of their currencies against the dollar. As the United States moved into a trade deficit that year, especially against European countries, so there was a substantial flow of dollar reserves into Europe. Since American interest rates were strictly controlled by the government Eurodollars (dollars held outside the United States) could generate greater interest abroad than at home. The growing, and soon booming, market in Eurodollars provided new international opportunities for the London financial institutions. In turn the City, with its expertise and tradition in international finance, provided an attractive venue for the hub of the Eurodollar business. The market tripled in size in 1959 and doubled again in 1960. The market was further boosted by the recovery of the Western European economy and the expansion of American multinational corporations. The adverse effects of the Vietnam War on the American balance of payments in the 1960s and the massive earnings generated by the Organization of Petroleum Exporting Countries (OPEC) oil price rise in the 1970s both fuelled the Eurodollar market.

In particular, it was the increase in oil revenues in the 1970s which caused a related increase in Eurodollars. Oil revenues accruing to Middle East states far exceeded requirements for consumption or reinvestment so that very large flows of income were placed on deposit in European banks, especially in London. Such deposits enabled the banks dealing in Euro-currencies to lend on a great scale to governments and international corporations. The net size of the Eurocurrency market, of which 75–80 per cent was in Eurodollars, increased from 60 billion dollars to 940 billion dollars between 1970 and 1982 (Coakley/Harris 52). Such an enormous flow of funds, and the central role played by the City as the main financial centre outside the United States, generated a vast increase in business for the banking institutions in London and drew into the City a great number and variety of foreign banks. By the early 1980s, 427 foreign banks had either a branch or a representative office in London, or were represented there through a holding in one of the main international banks. In 1960, the number of overseas banks with such a London office had numbered no more than 77.

The scale of the Eurodollar market allowed reinvestment on an impressive scale. This usually took one of two forms. Syndicated medium term credits comprised loans of dollars from banks outside the United States. Terms of repayment were fixed and the large loan was made up of contributions from several banks as part of a syndicate. This enabled them to handle business which would have been too great a risk for a single bank to undertake. Alternatively, the borrower could raise a Eurobond to obtain dollars from those institutions holding them, in this case without limit on the time scale of the loan. During the boom in the Eurodollar market in the 1970s, syndicated credits were much the more popular of the two modes of obtaining finance. About half the loans given went to industrializing countries either directly to the government or under conditions of government guarantee. Brazil, Argentina, Mexico and, exceptionally in the Soviet bloc, Poland all received such loans. Eurocurrency bank credits increased from 4.7 billion dollars in 1970 to 133.4 billion dollars in 1981. The City of London remained at the heart of this business, and the rate of interest on loans was calculated on the basis of the London inter-bank loan rate.

The growth of the Eurodollar market not only attracted many foreign banks to London, it also increased the degree of interrelatedness between the banks since lending between banks was a major feature of this market. Over half the gross size of the Eurocurrency market took the form of inter-bank lending. Much of the initiative for such business came from outside the traditional centres of British banking. But many of the long-established institutions were well placed in connections and professional skills to take advantage of the new opportunities. The main British banks had established subsidiaries which dealt in international finance. Lloyds had connections and interests in India and the Far East, and Barclays were similarly established in the Middle East and South Africa. The merchant bankers and stockbrokers retained their international links and traditions from the nineteenth century. By the beginning of the 1980s, the Barclay Group obtained almost 40 per cent of its gross profit from its international division. Thus the City has returned to its traditional international orientation in the past quarter of a century. 'The City of London became still more separate from the rest of Britain, like an offshore island in the middle of the capital. Even in the nineteenth century it had been cut off from the growth of British industry in the North: it made its money out of overseas trade rather than from domestic investment. Now the moat round the City was wider than ever. The young British bankers and their foreign counterparts earned much higher salaries, augmented with capital gains, than industrial managers in the provinces. The new international markets, together with Britain's own perilous boom, began to transform the style and pace of the City' (Sampson 125).

The swing back to internationalism in the City, and more recently the shift of the main investing institutions to a greater commitment to overseas markets, was not without effect on the domestic economy. In particular, changes in the distribution of investment in the highly mobile Eurodollar market can influence the exchange rate. Furthermore, the high degree of interrelationship between the financial institutions and their joint commitment to very large loans adds an element of instability. Over half the loans made by European banks to third world countries by the early 1980s were concentrated in six countries, namely Brazil, Argentina, Mexico, Venezuela, Indonesia and South Korea. One substantial defaulter could shake the entire system very severely. Even the more buoyant years of the early 1970s experienced the effects of instability, augmented by speculation, in the home market. Speculative lending fuelled the property boom of the early 1970s before it was suddenly cut short by the increase in bank lending rate. The collapse of property prices, most notably in the commercial sector, brought down those institutions and particularly the secondary banks. They had debts outstanding at high rates of interest which they could no longer cover with property which was rapidly losing value. The Eudorollar market brought this kind of instability to international financial markets since loans to sovereign states cannot be secured against property or by a third party guarantor. By the present decade, the international debts of the third world borrowers had grown to 300 billion dollars, and the mounting economic difficulties of many such countries had pushed up their debt service ratio to

20 per cent in a few years. Some of the largest borrowers had a substantially higher debt service ratio. Fears about the capacity of such countries to continue to repay their loans have increased in recent years. Furthermore, the competitive lending by the major international banks in more optimistic days drove them into a situation in which the ratio of outstanding loans against their capital reserves deteriorated, thus increasing even more their vulnerability to the effects of a default on one of the larger loans. By the 1980s, overseas assets and liabilities accounted for 75 per cent of the total debts and credits of British banks. Such a level of international commitment has placed these banks in an international rather than a national context to a degree unparalleled in any other part of the economy. 'This is yet another index of the City's entrepot role in international banking, its position as an enclave within Britain, acting as a stopover on international credit's flight round the world' (Coakley/Harris 122).

V

The major issue which has stirred debate with regard to the level of investment and its allocation before 1914 was the finance of industry, and specifically whether or not manufacturing and thence economic growth was obstructed by a shortage of investment. Much the same type of debate has characterized discussion of the twentieth century, and has been a constant source of investigation and public enquiry. While the investment ratio has increased considerably in the present century, particularly in relation to manufacturing, this has not been impressive in comparison to other advanced economies and in recent years, as part of spreading deindustrialization, capital formation in industry has declined (Table 9.1). In the past few years, it has been the growth of the services in general and the financial services sector in particular which has maintained the investment ratio.

Before 1914 the great bulk of industrial investment was generated by private borrowing or from undistributed profit. While some large firms raised money on the Stock Exchange in the late nineteenth century, it has been estimated that at least half the capital increase in industry came from undistributed profit (W. A. Thomas 1978: 6). The situation was similar in the interwar years, although there was an increase in the number of industrial share quotations on the new issue market. Since the last war there has, of course, been a great increase in industrial finance through the ordinary share market.

Obtaining industrial finance has not really been a problem for large and successful corporations. Indeed the growth of multinational corporations since 1945 has produced substantial flows of investment across national frontiers as direct investment. Multinational firms are not new, such institutions can be identified in English and Dutch trading companies in the six-teenth and seventeenth centuries. Many of present day multinational corporations established their first foreign branches and affiliated companies before 1914, but their greatest expansion has been a product of the recent past. As technology has become both more complex and specific in use, and as firms have become both larger and more diversified, so they have needed to operate on an international scale to achieve organizational and production economies appropriate to their size. Part of that process has been the growth of direct investment overseas. For Britain this has brought a substantial increase in direct investment flowing outward, from 10.8 billion dollars to 74.2 billion dollars between 1960 and 1980, as well as inward, from 5.0 billion dollars to 44.8 billion dollars over the same period (Stopford/Dunning 5–6, 12).

British direct investment abroad reflected both the type of multinational corporation which developed within the British economy while inward investment highlighted the gaps and weaknesses in the home manufacturing base. Outward flows of investment have been primarily in the less techno-logically advanced industries, although the past two decades have seen a shift away from investment in raw material exploitation towards manufac-turing, and hence away from less developed countries and towards Western Europe. In the 1970s, Britain was one of several countries whose multi-nationals invested very heavily in the United States because of the cheapness of American fuel prices and the low exchange value of the dollar. Grand Metropolitan Hotels, the Hanson Trust, BP, Pilkington, Beecham and Consolidated Goldfield all made direct investments in America by buying up companies (Stopford/Dunning 104–5). Several factors encouraged such investment, including the size and wealth of the American market, less attractive opportunities at home, and the fact that direct investment can enable firms to make a technological jump more easily by purchasing an existing concern than by developing branches on green field sites. Apart from the United States, there was British direct investment on a substantial scale in Western Europe and some limited advance into Japan, where British Oxygen bought a 43.5 per cent share in Osaka Oxygen in 1982. This kind of direct investment overseas has become a major part of the invest-ment commitment of British firms, 60 per cent of the total in 1981.

Nearly all the direct investment into Britain during the past quarter of a century has come from the United States and Western Europe. Much has been associated with technologically advanced industries like electronics and most recently oil. But in the 1970s there was a marked increase in invest-ment in property, distribution and finance. Towards the end of that decade, however, American investment flows to Europe were shifting away from Britain. Inflation, industrial unrest, restrictive practices by trade unions, a social system which did not provide incentives to work, as well as better growth prospects elsewhere in Europe all contributed to this (Dunning 165).

It is not easy to determine whether direct investment represents a net advantage or disadvantage to the economy as a whole. An increase in the outward flow of investment might imply that firms have improved their competitive position abroad, or that expansion abroad provides better prospects than expansion at home. Similarly, an increase in the inward flow of direct investment could imply an improvement in the attractiveness of the home market because of the improved production performance of British based firms, or it might reflect the fact that these foreign owned companies were successfully taking the domestic market from home producers. Dunning has concluded that the effect of investment flows over the past two decades has been mainly beneficial for the British economy. British owned firms have improved their competitive position abroad, especially in Western Europe. Since inward flows of investment have been directed to industry with more advanced technology than the outflows, the resource allocation within Britain has been improved and some high technology manufactures introduced (Dunning 171–2).

Direct investment applies very largely to big business. The persistent question about British industrial investment has related in the main to the finance of small firms, the number of which fell by half between 1924 and 1963 (W. A. Thomas 1978: 114). Furthermore this decline was a result of a low birth rate of such firms, not a high mortality rate. The well known preference of the major institutional investors for fixed interest securities rather than equities, at least until the 1950s, and for quoted rather than unquoted securities, helped identify the Macmillan Gap. Small issues, up to £150,000, which failed to meet the principal requirements of the institutional investors experienced difficulty in securing funds, hence the 'gap' in the market. The identification of this phenomenon by the Macmillan enquiry of 1931 did obtain a response from the City. Several specialist institutions were formed specifically to provide such small scale investment. Most important of these were Credit for Industry, Leadenhall Securities and the Charterhouse Industrial Development Company. The latter was established in 1934 by the Charterhouse Investment Trust, the Prudential, and two major banks to provide loans up to £100,000 for small businesses. Leadenhall Securities was set up by the merchant bankers Schroeder and Company for the same purpose. Government sponsorship did not appear until 1945 when the Industrial and Commercial Finance Corporation was established with the major banks as reluctant principal shareholders. By 1975 loans outstanding amounted to £224.7 million, most in debentures and secured loans.

Since the Second World War the share of external investment in industry has fallen, both increased scale of activity and falling profits contributing to that trend. Bank borrowing by industry increased. But, as in earlier times, the banking sector provided less cash for British industry than was the case in most other industrial countries. Even as late as the decade 1964–73, the share of external finance in industry was only 15.5 per cent in British industry compared to 31.3 per cent in the United States and a similar level in Japan (W. A. Thomas 1978: 331). The low investment orientation of banks and investing institutions towards British industry has been a result of the more highly developed and specialized nature of the British financial system and its international orientation. In any event, the criticism of inadequate investment for industry has reappeared often. But most reports and commissions have concluded that the financial system does provide adequate provision for industry. Both the Radcliffe Report (1959) and the Wilson Report (1980) reiterated the views of the Macmillan committee that the real problem lay in 'not a limitation on the amount of available bank credit, but the reluctance of acceptable borrowers to come forward' (Wilson Report 20). Shortage of investment opportunity not shortage of funds was diagnosed as the key to the problem, as it had been before 1914.

This conclusion returns the problems of industrial finance to the locus of industrial performance. Even in the context of greater industrial growth generated in the twentieth century, successive investigations have identified only the small firm as falling through a gap in investment provision. So why do doubts persist about the financial system and its contribution to economic growth? The most likely explanation is that industry is perceived as the essence of economic growth and finance thus cast as a supporter of industry. But the peculiarity of the British financial system has been that it was always far more than a handmaiden of industry. Throughout the past three centuries it has made an important contribution to the creation of wealth through its international dealings which were largely unrelated to British industry. Certainly the specialization and scale of the financial system needed a world-wide context in which to operate, and that same degree of specialization kept it separate from the industrial sector. For much of the past two centuries it has done considerably better than industry in wealth creation. So it is an injustice to regard the financial system either as a failure or simply an ancilliary to the main economic activity, manufacturing. But there is another aspect to the dichotomy between the financial system and the provision of investment for the British economy which does give rise to problems. The specialization of finance and the scale of its operations has reiterated the verdict of Victorian investors that industry was too small and too risky. The really neglected area of investment in the present century has been the much overdue extensive modernization of plant and infrastructure. Such projects are seldom the most attractive of investments, and the markets have reflected that (Stout 103ff).

Perhaps the real nub of the problem lies in the failure of markets to behave other than as markets. In any free market system some projects will simply be too unattractive or risky to receive commercial backing, and infrastructure renewal is a likely candidate. This indicates not the failure of the system but simply that it has limitations. There has been much debate about the reconstruction of the financial system. The Wilson Committee was sufficiently divided to provide no less than three alternative strategies for providing industrial investment, and could not even agree about whether or not a new institution should be created to deal with it (Wilson Report 268–87). Even more radically, it has been argued that only the nationalization of the financial system to restructure it away from its international orbit and force it to invest in the domestic economy will provide the funds necessary for industry and infrastructure (Coakley/Harris). Certainly, it seems unlikely that the British economy will become much more attractive to investors without some intervention in the markets, but a major change in the financial system seems likely to diminish the earnings from international finance more surely than to regenerate British industry.

10

Aggregate supply:
production and productivity

I

The generally high rate of growth in GDP in the twentieth century was the result of a related increase in the growth rate of aggregate supply. There were considerable increases in capital input and productivity, although increases in the labour input were either very low or contracting throughout the century (Table 1.1). GDP per head grew at a faster rate from the end of the First World War until the late 1970s than it had before 1914. The weighted sectoral contributions to aggregate growth show that manufacturing made a much greater contribution than hitherto, to the growth in GDP, both in the interwar years and in the expansionary decades 1951–73. As the rate of growth of GDP fell sharply in the 1970s, and became almost static in the period 1979–83, so manufacturing exhibited an accelerating rate of output contraction (Tables 1.4 and 11.2). The manufacturing sector thus played an important role in effecting variations in the growth of GDP in the twentieth century. But the service sector also generated an increasingly important contribution to growth until the 1970s. While the service sector weighted growth rate fell in the 1970s, it was services in general, and commerce together with professional and public services in particular, which provided the greater part of GDP growth after 1973. The only other sector to make a substantial contribution to growth was mining, mainly offshore oil production, which fortunately coincided with the decline in manufacturing in the 1970s and 1980s.

Within the broad aggregated manufacturing and service sectors there has been considerable change in the present century. In manufacturing most growth, until the watershed of 1973, was generated in engineering, especially electrical engineering, vehicles, and chemicals. Each of these industries increased its share of manufacturing output. In contrast, established major sectors like textiles and clothing, shipbuilding, and the miscellaneous metal working industries were all in relative, and sometimes absolute, decline (Table 10.1). The extent of structural change in manufac-

Table 10.1 *Industrial output of selected sectors*

	A	B	C	D	E	F
1913–24	753	266	7,873	8,087	250.1	688
1924–38	613	266	6,135	8,476	230.4	469
1938–51	438	281	8,051	13,331	208.4	1,080
1951–64	308	295	13,215	20,409	211.4	1,390
1964–73	178	162	16,314	25,728	157.9	1,107
1973–79	110	107	13,324	21,925	121.9	1,110
1979–83	60	82	9,343	15,401	122.4	470

A: Raw cotton consumption, U.K. annual average (thousand metric tons)
B: Raw wool output plus net imports of raw wool, U.K. annual average (thousand metric tons)
C: Output of pig iron, U.K. annual average (thousand metric tons)
D: Output of steel, U.K. annual average (thousand metric tons)
E: Output of coal, U.K. annual average (million metric tons)
F: Tonnage of shipping built in U.K. (thousand tons)
Data to 1938 as Table 4.1. Data after 1938 for merchant shipping over 100 gross tons.

Sources: B. R. Mitchell, *Abstract of British Historical Statistics* (Cambridge 1962) pp. 116, 132–3, 137, 179, 192, 194, 222.
B. R. Mitchell and H. G. Jones, *Second Abstract of British Historical Statistics* (Cambridge 1971) pp. 66, 78, 80, 90, 93, 102.
Central Statistical Office, *Annual Abstract of Statistics*, 1972 pp. 175, 177, 181, 236; 1975 p. 214; 1984 pp. 150, 158–9, 162–3; 1985 pp. 149, 157–8, 160–1, 173.

turing output is reflected in the sectoral contributions to output (Table 11.2). Similar shifts have characterized the growth of services. Transport and communications, distribution, and miscellaneous personal services, have all experienced relative decline. But government and defence, professional and scientific services, and financial services have all increased. The supply of both goods and services in the twentieth century has thus been characterized by considerable variations in sectoral growth rates, substantial structural change, and marked variations in the rate of growth of GDP.

II

The pre-1914 input balance with emphasis on labour rather than capital was completely reversed in the twentieth century. Capital inputs contributed much more to growth in GDP in the twentieth century than hitherto, although there has been a decline in recent years (Table 1.1). Even so, capital increase has contributed only modestly to the growth of national income (Table 1.2). But the greater growth of capital is reflected in the considerably increased investment ratio since the First World War. Furthermore, the decline in foreign investment in the investment ratio, despite its revival during the past decade, meant that there was a marked increase in domestic investment, averaging between 17–22 per cent since 1951, compared to a maximum of 11 per cent in any earlier period (Table 3.1). During the periods of greatest increase in capital investment, manufacturing absorbed a substantial share. By the 1970s this share was falling, and the increases were located in mining and particularly in social and public services (Table 9.1). The outline pattern of the growth of capital inputs in the twentieth century reflects the two outstanding features of British aggregate growth, the increased growth and role of manufacturing compared to the nineteenth century, and the relatively lower growth achieved compared to most other advanced economies.

The increased level of investment and augmented growth in capital inputs were manifest in the increased size of businesses and the shift away from labour intensive production towards capital intensity. Even allowing for inflation, the major firms of the 1980s completely dwarfed their late Victorian ancestors. The main British firms, all multinational corporations, were still rather small compared to some of their American rivals, although British Petroleum with a capital of £28.9 billion in 1981 and the Royal Dutch/ Shell Group with £13.1 billion were amongst the largest multinational corporations in 1981. The other major British firms were ICI £5.2 billion, BAT £5.0 billion, Unilever £4.2 billion and GEC £4.0 billion. Most of these firms had been amongst the largest businesses at the beginning of the century, like Unilever, or were the result of amalgamations of major companies, like ICI. Not only were such firms considerably larger than their predecessors but their capital/labour ratios were considerably greater. ICI employed £39,358 per worker in 1981, Royal Dutch/Shell £79,422, and Unilever £12,382. Even the lagging engineering firms of 1905 had partly caught up. GKN had total assets of £12,652 per worker, and John Brown £50,256 while Coats, Courtaulds, Vickers, and the Imperial Group (previously Imperial Tobacco) all had an assets to labour ratio over £8,000 (Stopford). The shift away from labour intensity is emphasized by the fact that such major companies did not employ a massive labour force. Unilever had 343,000 workers in 1981, but most of the others had considerably fewer employees. Royal Dutch/Shell employed 166,000 and British Petroleum 153,300 and some of the major companies employed many less like Vickers with 29,100 and John Brown with a labour force of 11,700. Furthermore, as would be expected of multinational enterprises, not all this employment was located in the domestic economy. Home-based employment in British Petroleum was only 27 per cent, and in Royal Dutch/Shell only 19 per cent. Vickers, ICI, the Imperial Group and GEC employed between 56–77 per cent of their workers in Britain (Stopford). The growth of modern multinational industry marked a strong shift in production towards both capital intensity and the absorption within a single company of a multiplicity of products and places of manufacture. It marked a significant departure from the labour intensive production which had been such a basic characteristic of nineteenth-century industry.

III

Increased labour inputs contributed significantly to twentieth-century growth only in the interwar years (Table 1.2). But since the Second World War, labour input growth declined slowly until the late 1970s when it contracted sharply. But within the overall context of slow growth and eventual contraction, the labour force experienced considerable changes in the structural composition of employment. The rate of structural change was higher in the twentieth century than it had been in earlier periods (Table 1.5). Prior to the twentieth century there was little net loss in employment, the only sector to be affected to a substantial extent was agriculture. Structural change was thus determined by the differential addition of new labour to the various sectors of the economy. In the twentieth century, however, the precedent set by agriculture has been followed by many other employment sectors. Between 1911 and 1981, agriculture contracted further by over 1.1 million jobs, while mining employment fell by almost 0.8 million jobs. The other great Victorian employment sector, textiles and clothing, fell from over 2.4 million jobs in 1911 to 642,000 in 1981. Together the loss of employment in these three nineteenth-century 'staple' employment sectors fell by 3.5 million jobs between the First World War and the 1980s (Lee 1979, *Annual Abstract of Statistics* 1983: 113–16). Much of this employment contraction has been concentrated into recent decades. In textiles and clothing almost 700,000 jobs were lost between 1961 and 1981. This decline in employment reflects increased productivity requiring less labour per unit of output, but also decline in the face of successful foreign competition, as in the case of the textile industry. The substantial job losses in these traditional manufactures required a substantial increase in employment elsewhere in the economy simply to maintain the existing level of employment. Nor were job losses confined to these sectors. There was a modest decrease in employment in miscellaneous services, by some half a million jobs, in the twentieth century, although this concealed a substantial change within that sector as domestic service fell sharply but was partly replaced by increased employment in hotel and restaurant work and various forms of entertainment.

In most other sectors of the economy, employment increased between the First World War and 1971 so that there was a net increase in employment of almost 5.4 million jobs. Employment in engineering and vehicle production increased from 0.7 million to 1.9 million during this period, while instrument and electrical engineering increased from 0.1 million to 1.0 million during the same time. But the biggest increases in employment were attained in the service sector. Distribution increased from 1.68 million in 1911 to a peak of 3.19 million in 1961, while government and defence increased by over one million jobs between the First World War and 1971. The biggest increases were in banking and finance together with professional jobs. The number employed in these two sectors increased from 0.97 million in 1911 to 4.80 million in 1981.

In fact, these two sectors were the only employment categories to show a real increase in the 1970s although miscellaneous services and government and defence remained fairly stable. But elsewhere contraction was general, and for the first time probably for three centuries there was a large fall in total employment by just over three million jobs between 1971 and 1981. Some sectors contracted sharply, construction by half a million jobs and distribution by almost as much. Again the mixture of increased productive efficiency and declining market share explain the falling employment. Even the successful chemical industry cut its employment by some 17 per cent in that decade. The sharp reduction in mechanical engineering, shipbuilding and vehicle production as well as metal manufacture suggest a more wide-spread decline. Indeed the total manufacturing employment fell by almost three million in the 1970s, and this sector in 1981 employed only 72 per cent of the workforce it had ten years earlier.

IV

The structure of British industry in the twentieth century was, in part, inherited from the previous century. The main characteristics of Victorian industry lay in the generally small scale of production with modest capital investment and a labour-intensive orientation. This allowed specialization within a narrow product range in an environment of generally expanding markets. The cotton industry was not only a major branch of British industry but an extreme example of specialized production and the separation of manufacturing from distribution, even to the extent of the regional concentration of different activities. This specialization extended to the markets served, so that Blackburn cloth sold mainly in the Indian subcontinent while Burnley weavers made a narrower cloth for the Chinese market. The separation of spinning from weaving, and indeed the decline of vertical integration from the middle of the nineteenth century, was peculiar to the British branch of the industry and reflected its large and diverse international market which allowed such extreme specialization.

Other established branches of industry entered the twentieth century with characteristically small units of production. Like cotton, the coal industry grew through the proliferation of units of production. On the eve of nationalization in 1947, there were still some 1,630 pits in operation by 740 firms, although 83 per cent of the output of 184 million tons came from 538 large pits. But this contrasted sharply with Germany, where in 1928 152 million tons of coal had been produced by only 175 collieries. Steel production was also produced on a much smaller scale than in Germany or the United States. In 1937, annual output per blast furnace in Britain was 83,000 tons, a substantial improvement on the pre-1914 level, but still far below the American average of 210,000 tons or the German average of 125,000 tons (G. C. Allen 94). Even in 1916, an American manager observed the antiquated design of British steel plants, the small furnace sizes and the resultant output levels, which would have been scrapped years ago in the United States as being ridiculously inefficient (Pagnamenta/Overy 78).

Small scale production had prospered in the nineteenth century because effective demand was sufficiently strong to soften the effects of competition. In the twentieth century, commodity markets, both abroad and in Britain, became considerably more competitive and thus exposed the weakness inherent in small scale production. This was effective both in old established industries like cotton textiles and in the new 'staples' of the present century, such as the motor industry, chemicals or electrical engineering. Several types of structural change emerged in response to increased competitiveness. One response was, of course, not to make structural adjustments but to ride out depressions in the same fashion as before 1914 by reducing labour, or by attempting to reduce the cost of labour by imposing wage cuts which generated considerable labour trouble in the interwar years. Others preferred to continue to compete within the traditional structure. Thus the motor industry, a new product in the twentieth century but manufactured in small product runs by small firms which had little regard for standardization, achieved some concentration of production through competition. Many smaller firms were forced out of business in the 1920s leaving Morris, Austin and Singer with 75 per cent of the market between them at the end of the decade. But their traditional reliance on craft skills rather than assembly line mass production, and the production of a great diversity of models each for a relatively small market, prevented them from turning their market advantage to profit by generating economies of scale (Church 200, 204).

The increased competitiveness faced by industry, in the twentieth century, presented structural problems in two main forms. In the case of industries fighting to hold markets, or to regain markets lost during the First World War, or facing a prolonged stagnation in demand, this was manifest in the form of excess capacity. For those industries which enjoyed a rather more buoyant demand for their products, the problem was primarily one of achieving sufficiently large-scale production to obtain the optimum possible economies of scale. In each case, the traditional small scale of production as a result of many small firms and extreme specialization was a major obstacle to the development of an appropriate industrial structure. Excess capacity was the basic problem in industries like cotton and woollen textiles. The scale of contraction was great. The number of spindles in operation in the British cotton industry in 1914 was almost 60 million. By 1961 this had fallen to 9 million and by 1981 was only 1.25 million. In the weaving section of the industry loom capacity fell from 805,000 in 1914 to 22,000 in 1981 (Porter 38, G. C. Allen 261, Blackburn 49). The woollen industry, by contrast, fared better and contracted only gradually during the twentieth century, although this too implied excess capacity. While textiles sought to adjust to falling sales after the collapse of the 1919–20 boom in the usual manner of reduced working hours and cuts in the wage rate, such short-term palliatives were no longer adequate to deal with the problem of excess productive capacity. As before the problem was approached through the establishment of combinations, although authentic mergers and amalgamations were not favoured in an industry in which rivalry between firms extended several generations into the past. The most important of the new combinations established in the interwar years was the Lancashire Cotton Corporation, registered in 1929, and which embraced 106 mills with 9.5 million spindles and 20,118 looms. Even this represented only one quarter of the total spinning capacity and a small proportion of weaving capacity. Half the spinning capacity taken over was abolished by the end of the 1930s. The reduction in loom capacity by 300,000 between 1924 and 1938 was the result primarily of attrition in the market. But the reduction in capacity did not foster large-scale production or allow investment in new machinery. Indeed the financial arrangements in the industry as a result of recapitalization or conversion to public companies in the post 1918 boom militated against foreclosure. When firms were unable to repay loans or the interest on them, responsibility for their affairs was transferred to the creditors. Rather than force a firm out of business, and thus incur a certain loss, creditors usually opted to allow it to continue to trade in the hope of events taking a turn for the better.

The opposition to conventional rationalization, by reductions in capacity or the amalgamation of firms into units large enough to be able to afford to re-equip, was revealed in divisions in the government working party set up to consider the problems of the cotton industry after the Second World War. While one group favoured such a strategy an alternative school of thought prevailed, arguing that there was no evidence that large scale production would increase efficiency and that the industry should be left to the decisions of individual firms. The government set up the Cotton Board as a central body to co-ordinate developments in the industry, and provided a subsidy for re-equipment of spinning machinery to the value of 25 per cent of the total cost, but it was available only to firms with a spindleage in excess of half a million. Structural change remained slow, although there was a limited return to vertical integration of spinning and weaving. A further attempt was made to reduce surplus capacity and spur re-equipment in the 1959 Cotton Industry Act. Again the stimulus came from a subsidy, two-thirds of which was provided by the Treasury while the industry itself contributed the rest through a levy. A substantial amount of plant was scrapped, much of which was idle anyway, but re-equipment was very limited and new investment amounted only to £53 million, well short of the estimated requirement of £80–95 million (Cable 73).

A more extensive restructuring of the industry than hitherto was effected in the 1960s through a series of mergers as the two major manufacturers of artificial fibres, Courtaulds and ICI, sought to extend their interests in textile manufacture. This, at last, provided firms large enough to embark on a process of acquisition by merger, and by outsiders who were not traditional rivals. Many established combines disappeared from the industry, including the Lancashire Cotton Corporation, the Fine Cotton Spinners and Doublers, Combined English Mills, the Bradford Dyers Association, Tootal, and the British Van Heusen Corporation. Securing the future of the Lancashire cotton industry was important to both purchasers. Courtaulds needed an outlet for its viscose rayon staple and acrylic fibre, while ICI was similarly committed to safeguard its nylon, terylene and dyestuff production. By the early 1970s these two firms dominated the cotton industry. The industry appeared to be in a much stronger position than a decade earlier, sales being four times the value of pre-merger days (Blackburn 47). But the accelerating contraction of the industry in the 1970s, indicated that its troubles were not over and that they were not due to structural factors alone.

The same problem of excess productive capacity linked to the need to renew equipment was characteristic of the steel and shipbuilding industries. Again traditional rivalries and the desire to retain control of established small firms inhibited rationalization. Old steel making plant comprised few integrated manufacturing systems, and the exhaustion of iron ore supplies undermined the rationale of the location of many steel firms in places such as Cleveland and the West Midlands. But the establishment of new plant in more favourable locations was dogged by local rivalries and political constraints. Thus the new strip mill built at Ebbw Vale in 1936 was chosen because of the high level of unemployment locally in preference to a site in Lincolnshire close to cheap ore supplies and its intended market, the motor industry. In Ebbw Vale both construction costs and transport were expensive. Similarly a scheme to establish an entirely new plant at Jarrow, producing steel 25 per cent more cheaply than elsewhere, was stopped in deference to opposition from local steel companies. More famous still was the blatantly political decision imposed in 1958 to split the intended new steel works at Llanwern into two smaller plants, the second being at Ravenscraig in Scotland. Thus there were two new plants both half the minimum economic size. As a result of the industry's reluctance to embrace change, together with the distortions effected by political interference for non-economic reasons, the industry remained in locations which made pro-vision of ore supplies very costly and operated on a scale far below its com-petitors. In 1965, there were still 41 steel plants in Britain, three-quarters of which produced less than one million tons per annum. A report written in 1952 suggested that an integrated steelworks should obtain economies of scale at production runs from 750,000 to 1,000,000 ingot tons per annum. At that time the average British steel plant capacity was only 325,000 tons. By the mid 1960s it had risen to 850,000 tons and there were fifteen plants making over one million tons. But the Japanese were constructing plant capable of making eight to ten million tons yearly (G. C. Allen 102).

Excess capacity was a chronic problem in shipbuilding after the First World War, which had stimulated a 25 per cent increase in British capacity. The slump in international trade in the interwar years naturally depressed the shipbuilding industry. In the 1930s, the industry and the government together established the National Shipbuilders Security Ltd which levied a toll on new ships and used the proceeds to pay for the closure of idle yards. One million tons of capacity was thus scrapped, but the scheme did not extend to mergers or re-equipment in the remaining yards, as did the equivalent scheme in Germany. Another boom brought by the Second World War followed by the recovery of international shipping in the 1950s enabled the industry to put aside thoughts of restructuring. Small concerns remained the norm, and expansion was often impossible because most yards were hemmed in by housing and other businesses. As late as the mid 1960s there remained 62 yards in operation, and regrouping was achieved only with government pressure and funds. Five major operations were estab-lished, helped by an investment of £160 million. Even this was unable to prevent the accelerating decline of the industry.

Faced with intensified competition and the need to reduce capacity and create larger units of production, the small family firms characteristic of Victorian industries showed little inclination for change. Indeed they were often very effective in opposing restructuring (Buxton 1979: 553). Typically, in the coal industry owners blamed the workforce for non-cooperation, a poor work rate, and a low number of hours worked, and their representa-tives argued that improved competitiveness in the 1920s depended on longer working and lower wages. The miners, in their turn, blamed inefficient management, poor living conditions in the tied cottages and pit villages, and the high rate of accidents in the mines. The recommendation of the 1919 Royal Commission that the industry be nationalized was quietly shelved. The Coal Mines Act of 1930 sought to secure price stability by setting a minimum price and output quotas for each pit. Since even the smallest pit received a quota, the act effectively prevented the elimination of the less productive concerns. Not until nationalization in 1947 was rationalization possible within this industry. Between that date and the early 1970s, the number of pits was reduced from 980 to under 300, and the closure pro- gramme has continued to operate through the past decade. Ironically, opposition to closure now comes from the workforce concerned about disappearing job opportunities.

What restructuring did occur in the contracting Victorian industries in the present century came from either market attrition as firms were forced out of business or from externally imposed solutions, by government schemes or take-over bids from outside the industry. The industries themselves were largely hostile to change and in any event unable to achieve it by agreement between traditional rivals. The effectiveness of structural change was thus heavily dependent on government involvement. This was sometimes ineffectual, as in the cotton industry, and occasionally highly successful, as in the creation of ICI. The merger which created this firm in 1926 had strong government support, mindful of the way in which weaknesses in the chemical industry had been exposed in the First World War and of the threat imposed by the establishment of the German chemical giant, I. G. Farben. This firm had a capital of £54 million which was greater than that of the four major British chemical firms. ICI united the four main producers, with an issue capital of £57 million, and strengths in several areas of chemical manu- facture. Brunner Mond and United Alkali were strong in traditional alkali production, Nobles brought an expertise in explosives, and the British Dye- stuffs Corporation contributed what had been the weakest element of the British industry before the war. Thus was created a British company sufficiently large not only to achieve scale economies in production but to operate on a world scale and develop into a successful multinational corporation.

Industries attracted government aid and attention either because they were in difficulty, like coal or shipbuilding, or because there was some per- ceived national interest involved, as in the ICI merger. Structural change elsewhere was left to the firms themselves. The motor industry is a manu- facture in which economies of scale are particularly important. As the indus- try has grown the level of production required to achieve optimum economies of scale has increased. It has been estimated that the minimum efficient size of production was 150,000 units per annum in the late 1940s, rising to 750,000 by 1960 and to two million by the early 1980s (Dunnett 23). As for individual models, at present, it is estimated that 200,000 represents a minimum product run and that ideally not less than one million units per annum should be produced (Bhaskar 54). To manufacture below such levels makes a substantial difference to production costs. Bhaskar estimated that the cost of manufacturing only 250,000 units per year over a four or five year model life could add between 6–20 per cent to total costs. The historical development of the British car industry produced a structure which was inimical rather than conducive to production on this scale. A wide variety of models manufactured by several specialist producers, and a home market conditioned to expect a wide range of choice despite the smallness of that home market, had produced a tradition from the earliest days of the industry of small production runs of numerous models. As late as 1960 seven firms contributed to British car production, including three with less than 10 per cent of the market, and two more only just above that level. Production was thus highly fragmented, and even the biggest manufacturer fell well below the minimum efficient scale of production. In 1947, production was 60,000 units compared to the efficient minimum of 150,000, by 1960 it was 486,000 against 750,000, and by 1977 it was 651,000 against 2,000,000 (Dunnett 23). By the latter date production had been concentrated into a single firm, BL, but even this production level fell well below the minimum for efficiency. The cost of low volume production in the 1970s amounted to six per cent of the price of a British saloon car and represented a major source of uncompetitiveness since British models sold little more than half the volume of their main European competitors.

Many of the problems of the British motor industry in recent decades can be attributed to the failure to restructure in order to achieve scale production. There were mergers. In 1952, the two major British firms in the industry, Austin and Morris, formed the British Motor Company (BMC). But while the new company expanded production substantially in response to the great increase in demand for cars in the postwar prosperity, it not only retained the full range of models in deference to established customer loyalty, but also retained the plants and organizational structures of the original firms. Like the cotton industry mergers of the 1890s, it was a merger without any real amalgamation or rationalization. As in the case of so many other British industries, the motor industry was near to collapse when it was effectively nationalized in 1975. By that time its failure to generate minimum scale economies meant that the problem was one of survival rather than lack of success.

The difficulty encountered by many British industries and firms in making structural adjustments necessary for effective competition in the twentieth century reflects many of the weaknesses often highlighted by investigations and reports. At the heart of the problem lay the small firm, family tradition, often limited funds and managerial competence, and a vested interest in opposing change which would reduce control by admitting outsiders or external funds.

V

By comparison with its own historical experience, British productivity growth was relatively high in the twentieth century, especially in the period 1951–73. Total factor productivity increase made a significant contribution to growth of GDP in most of the phases of the present century, in the war-time periods, in the boom of 1951–73 and in the recent deflationary phase (Tables 1.1 and 1.2). The contribution of manufacturing to aggregate productivity was considerably greater than it had been in the Victorian period, although commerce too increased by a significant amount (Matthews 229). But when compared with the productivity growth in other advanced economies, the British performance in the twentieth century has not been particularly impressive. For most of the recent past Britain has been well below the Organization for Economic Co-operation and Development (OECD) average and, with an annual rate of productivity increase of 2.2 per cent between 1953–79, performed worst of the Western European countries (Boltho 22).

The low overall rate of productivity increase was repeated at sectoral level. In the cotton industry, output per man hour was far below that in the United States industry in the late 1930s, American manufacturers having a 61–72 per cent advantage in spinning and 150–160 per cent advantage in weaving so that overall productivity levels were double those in Britain (Porter 37). Productivity in the coal industry in the 1930s was also well below that of other major European producers like Poland and Germany and output per man shift ranged from 0.53 tons in the Bristol coalfield and 0.76 tons in South Wales to 1.47 tons in Nottinghamshire and 1.67 tons in Leicestershire on the eve of nationalization. Even after the Second World War when productivity in Britain increased there were serious differences between home and foreign productivity levels in major industries. In the motor industry, the British Motor Corporation had a productivity record in the 1960s such that even an increase from seven to nine vehicles per worker compared unfavourably with the dozen produced by Ford and Vauxhall workers (Williams 221).

The low productivity of the British economy was, of course, closely related to the antiquity of much of the productive capacity and the structure of industry in which there were so many small firms. The weight of the past lay heavily on production methods in the coal industry. The peculiarity of the law regarding mineral rights meant that the underground layout of mines had to follow the boundaries which separated properties on the surface. Thus many of the roadways in the mines were not only narrow because they were so old, but often followed tortuous roundabout routes from shaft to coalface in order to conform to property laws. This inhibited the improvement of haulage systems underground. Further, as is well known, the exploitation of the easiest seams before 1914 meant that many mines worked narrow and geologically difficult seams, unsuitable for the application of coal-cutting machinery rather than manual extraction. Even so the proportion of coal which was mechanically cut increased from 8 per cent in 1913 to 55 per cent by 1936 (Buxton 1979: 60). Both productivity and safety increased after 1947 since nationalization brought a substantial and overdue increase in investment in the industry. Roadways were widened and strengthened so that new and mechanized haulage systems could replace the traditional pit pony, while timber pit props were replaced by steel, and winding gear was electrified. Productivity was also increased by reductions in the labour force which accelerated after nationalization. British labour productivity in mining compared well in a European context by the late 1960s, bettered only by West Germany (Pryke 133). But variations in the efficiency of pits held down the overall productivity level. In the early 1980s, after the closure of many weaker pits, some old pits in South Wales produced coal at a loss of £16 per ton, in sharp contrast to the highly efficient pits in the Yorkshire coalfield.

Low productivity was often the result of traditional practices and the vested interests of management and labour in sticking to them. Shipbuilding was long established as an industry dependent on skilled manual labour and extreme specialization of function. It was also an industry in which employment was highly insecure. The high and sustained unemployment in the industry in the interwar years confirmed the workers in their defensive stance, distrusting change and strongly defending the demarcation of jobs between different trades and unions. Shipyard owners were similarly reluctant to give up the labour-oriented production process which kept down fixed costs, and the low profitability of the depression years precluded increased investment. Furthermore, the practice in the industry was to build ships on a cost-plus basis so that the cost of overmanning and low productivity could be passed to the customer in the final price without cutting into the desired profit margin. As a result, British ships were some 10–40 per cent more expensive than foreign vessels by the 1960s, and their monopoly of the domestic market for ships was swiftly eroded. Some of the slowness in adopting new methods was the result of distrust. As Sir Leonard Redshaw recalled an experience during the Second World War, 'We were struggling to build submarines as fast as we could. We wanted to weld them in part or in full, but the Ministry would not agree. Then one day they brought into Barrow a German submarine they'd captured, plonked it in front of us, and it was all welded. Then, of course, there was a tremendous change of attitude, but the irony was that I had worked on all welded submarine parts in Germany in 1935 but they wouldn't listen to me' (Pagnamenta/Overy 139). Even after 1945 welding spread only slowly in shipyards. Similarly British manufacturers were slow to turn to new types of ship, like bulk carriers and tankers. Such large and technically unsophisticated vehicles were best constructed on green field sites with ample space and using a capital intensive technology requiring relatively unskilled labour. Japanese shipbuilders responded to shifting demand by moving to new locations and adopting the appropriate technology. Their share of the market increased accordingly. Most British yards were confined to the cramped waterside locations which had been adequate for the much smaller nineteenth-century ships, building on slipways made obsolete by the new techniques whereby large sections of a ship were moved into sheds on massive cranes to be welded together.

Traditional attitudes militated against new practices, while poor profitability inhibited reorganization and re-equipment. Traditional hostility soured management-labour relations and obstructed change. As a management spokesman observed, 'It was the British disease, the trade unions. Their attitudes towards progress were really lamentable. Simple things – the Swedes invented a small portable hand-welding machine where one man could easily work four machines, and in Sweden four machines were worked by one man, ditto in Germany, ditto in France. In Britain one man to one machine and that took a long time because the fact that it was automatic was objected to.' To this comment, came the response of a Clydeside shop steward 'If they had been given better job security, sick pay, pensions, better working conditions, and that was possible with the vast profits they made, then in my opinion they would have won the cooperation of the workers' (Pagnamenta/Overy 148). Such charges and countercharges could easily be multiplied for most sections of British industry, and a great many could be justified. The real cost of Victorian manufacturing practices, treating labour as a variable cost which must bear the main pressure of trade depression, was paid in the appalling industrial relations of the twentieth century, and the reluctance to change on all sides. Changing market conditions did not allow the status quo to endure. By the 1980s the only substantial remaining part of British shipbuilding was naval work.

But it was not only inbuilt attitudes and traditional modes of working which inhibited the changes which could increase productivity. The great expansion of the Victorian cotton industry with many small manufacturers had necessarily generated an extreme vertical specialization. The tech-

nology used was appropriate to that structure and to labour intensive manufacture. Newer forms of machinery like the ring frame in spinning and the
automatic loom for weaving were devised for integrated production and
used high quality cotton to avoid breakages as a labour saving method.
Apart from the cost of new machinery, the adoption of such machinery by
British manufacturers would have required a considerable restructuring of
the industry. The introduction of ring frames was inhibited by the fact that
neither spinner nor weaver was willing to accept the cost of the bobbins on
which the yarn was sent to the weaver. The adoption of ring spinning would
have necessitated a higher quality of cotton, making more risky the practice
of buying cotton in small quantities in the Liverpool market. Further along
the line of production, the adoption of automatic looms would have been
possible only if a more reliable yarn quality, from ring spindle manufacture,
could be obtained from the spinner. The extreme separation of function thus
tied each section of the industry together and bound them all to the
Victorian technology.

As a consequence of the structure of the industry, British manufacturers
were very slow to change from the mule to ring frame spinning. As late as
1954, Britain had 59 per cent of spindleage capacity on mule frames, and a
very large share of the total world mule spinning capacity. Not until the early
1970s did the mule frame actually disappear. Similarly in weaving, the
Lancashire loom still exceeded the productive capacity of the automatic
loom in the British industry at the end of the 1970s (Lazonick 1983: 198,
202). The adoption of new technology had taken place much faster
elsewhere. In the United States all production was based on the ring frame
and the automatic loom by the middle of the century, indeed the ring frame
had constituted 87 per cent of American spinning capacity before the First
World War. The shift back to vertical integration in the British industry after
1945 made possible the switch to ring frame and automatic loom production.
This, in turn, increased the productivity of the British industry and forced
some firms out of business.

By this time, rising labour costs were undermining the basis of the traditional manufacture and full employment deprived the industry of its
customary reserve of surplus labour for increasing production. But even the
scrapping of excess capacity, the introduction of new machinery and a shift
to vertical integration which realised productivity increases in the 1960s of
40 per cent in output per man hour in spinning and 25–30 per cent in
weaving, were not enough to prevent the continued decline of the industry.
Productivity levels were still well below those being realised abroad, both in
Western Europe and further afield. From the early 1950s production continued to contract, exports fell badly and, from the mid 1960s, imports
increased sharply (Lazonick 1983: 221).

The cotton industry provides an extreme example of a very common problem faced by the British economy in the twentieth century in seeking to increase productivity and hence competitiveness. Since the Victorian economy had relied so heavily on labour intensive production many industries were overmanned. As trade unions increased their power, especially after 1950 in the quarter of a century of full employment, it became more difficult to dispense with workers. But the main route to productivity increase for many sectors of industry, like cotton, lay in labour reducing innovation. In prosperous times it was far more expedient to avoid conflict and disruption by sticking to old machinery and methods. Hence the steel industry only manufactured 20 per cent of its output by the BOS (Basic Oxygen Steel) process in the 1960s, although this method produced in thirty-five minutes what the old open hearth process needed twelve hours to accomplish. Sir Robert Shone related that, 'United States Steel were very impressed with the British labour record because we had had no strikes for over fifty years. So they sent their Labour Director over to examine the British situation. And he reported to the United States Steel Corporation: "Yes, indeed, excellent relations there, but for God's sake don't follow their example, the only reason they have had no strikes is they face no issues." And this was the reason we hadn't got the efficiency, because we hadn't faced up to the issues' (quoted in Pagnamenta/Overy 92).

The problem of low productivity was not peculiar to industries trapped in nineteenth-century industrial structures. The motor industry, in particular, experienced considerable difficulties in increasing productivity. The motor industry, a classic product of the twentieth century, was a manufacture in which economies of scale could be obtained principally by mass production using capital intensive technology. This had been demonstrated very early in the century by American manufacturers like Ford. But this industry, too, demonstrated all the structural weaknesses of British manufacturing. A tradition of small firms competing against each other with a diversity of products mainly in the home market did not generate enough profits for investment on a scale large enough to reap the necessary production economies. Even as late as 1974 British Leyland (BL) had an investment of £920 per worker in fixed assets, compared to £2,657 in Ford UK and £3,632 in Volkswagen (Dunnett 126). But even in the expansive 1950s and 1960s, when production greatly increased and merger produced BMC as Austin and Morris were brought together, and later BLMC as British Leyland was added, there was neither rationalization of production nor investment to increase productivity. Thus BMC increased output from 300,000 units in the early 1950s to a peak of 886,000 in 1964–5 without a commensurate increase in investment. Existing plant was re-equipped and duplicated, an extension and more intensive use of existing processes, but no new plant was opened, nor was there restructuring to allow production on a much greater scale. That was left to competitors such as Volkswagen. Like the defensive mergers of the late Victorian period, the constituent companies retained their independent structure and model range. Even when a further amalgamation created BLMC in the late 1960s, there was little rationalization of production and trouble was avoided because there were no redundancies despite considerable overmanning. The low productivity was reflected in poor returns on capital which, in turn, made it difficult to raise investment in the financial markets. Return on capital in the British motor industry in the late 1960s was only 3.5 per cent, compared to 12.4 per cent in Germany and 6.8 per cent in France (Dunnett 125). As a result of this poor record, a projected £400 million investment in the second half of the 1960s was abandoned. By the mid 1970s BLMC losses were so great that only effective nationalization prevented total collapse. Even continued infusions of investments could not halt the rising deficit of BL and formed the background to the attempt to increase productivity by massive reductions in the labour force, which fell from 184,000 to 94,000 in the decade to 1981 (Williams 257). Whether this branch of British manufacturing can survive in an economically viable form still remains uncertain, and production is still far below the level required for an efficient large scale producer.

In spite of the difficulties of some sectors, there has been substantial advance in productivity in other parts of the economy. This has often been achieved in the context of expansion in a relatively new area of growth. Rising affluence after 1945 brought a great increase in distribution and made possible the growth of supermarkets and hypermarkets which reaped economies of scale by selling a wide variety of goods under a single roof at low prices, especially when the end of retail price maintenance in 1964 made price competition possible. Capital inputs and overheads could be kept low, and the mechanized handling of warehouse stock together with self-service reduced the workforce. Employment thus fell in the distributive trades in the 1970s as business boomed. Furthermore, skilled workers were replaced by semi-skilled operatives as traditional skills such as weighing, packaging, shop layout and selling itself were all superceded by standardized packaged goods, self-selected by the customer. Transport too has enjoyed increased productivity by reducing labour inputs. Recent decades have seen reduced manning levels on the railways, one-man operated bus services and, most spectacularly, the Tyneside Metro which has fully automated ticket offices and, apart from train drivers, an apparently unmanned transport system.

Since much of industry was too small to achieve merger by take-over followed by rationalization, an important role in generating productivity increase through reorganization or restructuring has been played by the state. Government intervention was vitally important in making available electricity on a sufficient scale to meet rapidly expanding demand from 1,976 Gwh in 1933 to 225,053 Gwh in 1980 (Hannah 1979: 427, 1982: 292). Not only was British production much smaller than other industrial countries early in the century, but production was controlled by small, independent producers. London alone, in 1914, enjoyed the benefit of 70 generating stations together with a variety of authorities and systems. The substantial production gap between Britain and countries such as the United States, Canada, France, Germany and Italy, is unlikely to have been bridged while production remained in the hands of small businesses using various frequencies and voltages. The Electricity (Supply) Act 1926 established a Central Electricity Board to control the supply side of the industry and sell electricity to authorized distributors. The entire system was to be standardized and linked to a national grid which was completed in 1933. Even so, the scale of production and investment needed after the Second World War necessitated the nationalization of production.

An even more impressive result of the positive intervention of government on productivity is found in agriculture. This industry which had been in increasing difficulties since the late nineteenth century was revived by the exigencies of the Second World War and flourished under state subsidy thereafter. The Agriculture Act of 1947 established guaranteed prices to be paid by the government to farmers determined at an annual review conducted jointly by the government and the farmers' union. The long term security provided by such support encouraged investment and there were substantial increases in productivity even though the area of land under cultivation fell. Another Agriculture Act in 1957 shifted support to grants given for specific improvements but covering a wide range of farming activities. As a result of this support, productivity increase was greater in agriculture in the 1960s and 1970s than in any other sector of industry. By 1981, wheat output per acre was 2.5 times the 1939 yield, and productivity in milk, potatoes, and sugar beet had doubled. Greater mechanization, improved fertilisers, and better organization all contributed as, indeed, did the subsidy because the industry received £358 million from the government in 1980 plus a further £1,570 million from the EEC which also subsidized agriculture. As in other industries increased productivity implied a reduction in the workforce, and agricultural employment fell from over 1.1 million in 1951 to 350,000 by 1981.

VI

The mixed record of productivity in the British economy in the twentieth century was representative of the mixed fortunes and varying performance of different sectors of production. A shift towards capital intensive production, and increases in investment and productivity, generated growth rates higher than were realised in the nineteenth century. But the low level of competitiveness of much of British industry led to loss of markets abroad and recently, in sectors like textiles and motor cars and consumer durables, to the severe erosion of their share in the home market. Some industries have collapsed and others have come close to it, with a result that in the past decade the level of unemployment has risen steadily then sharply.

The essence of the problem of competitiveness lies in the structure of much of industry, small firms, independently owned and run, but lacking the resources to operate on a scale large enough to produce at maximum efficiency. This kind of structure was characteristic of much of Victorian industry, but also formed the model for twentieth-century industries like motor manufacturing and some branches of electrical engineering. So the structural problem is not simply a Victorian left-over or an overcommitment to the wrong industries. It is endemic in the tradition of the family firm. It is also a characteristic of a means of production which relies on skilled labour as a variable cost and as a way of limiting capital inputs. Thus firms retain control by not having to seek outside finance, and pass the effects of trade variation onto their workers. This can only endure so long as markets remain buoyant and/or competition remains ineffective. But in the intensified competition of the present century and the greater capital and technological orientation of modern industry, the small family firm is ludicrously outdated in most industries. It cannot generate profits sufficient to invest on a scale large enough for optimum production, its product is likely therefore to be expensive and, perhaps if the best technology cannot be afforded, of poorer quality than its competitors. Further, as Chandler has pointed out, family control often retains management in the hands of the unprofessional, even incompetent. Certainly management as a skilled activity has never been taken seriously by many British companies although in the United States and elsewhere it has long been recognized and treated as such.

In the present century many firms have retained their traditional loyalties and rivalries, and kept trading through the good times without bothering to re-equip or reorganize (Pagnamenta/Overy 40–1). They have hung on until forced out of business. Apart from developing an industrial structure unsuitable for the present century, the British manufacturing tradition has fostered exceptionally bad labour relations, principally by treating workers in such a fashion that they bore the brunt of trade recession. Further the heavy emphasis on craft skills made both sides of industry reluctant to change practices or to adopt new technology. From the perspective of the owners such technology was costly and its purchase would make them shoulder a greater risk. From the viewpoint of the workers such technology represented another threat to employment and the possibility of dilution of labour skill. As in the more recent past industries have sought to increase competitiveness by more efficient working, this has meant in most cases a reduction in the workforce. Accordingly it has been resisted by the labour force, often bitterly and to the mutual disaster of all sides of industry.

The only way out of this malaise has been, for the most part, through the influence of outside agencies since traditional loyalties and practices have usually ruled out rationalization through merger, and even those mergers which were achieved were often in practice emasculated. There have been three major external influences which have changed British industry. Competition, sometimes referred to grimly as market attrition, has forced some firms and even industries out of business. There have been some real mergers, such as the creation of ICI in 1926 and GEC in 1968 which have been effective in creating multinational companies which engaged in real reorganization. ICI was one of the few British companies to adopt a structure appropriate to a modern business corporation in the interwar years, with functionally specialized divisions providing proper managerial and financial services (Hannah 1974: 264). Both of these multinationals are amongst the most successful British firms although they are not beyond attracting criticism (Williams 166). Indeed GEC has been accused of the reluctance to invest in new ventures and poor market judgement often levelled against less august enterprises. Multinationals do pose a problem for national economies in that they can switch their operations between many countries. Thus ICI decided to close its polythene plant at Wilton and concentrate production for the British market in its Dutch plant in 1980. Both ICI and GEC have reduced their British labour force in the past two decades, the former from 131,000 to 84,000 in the three decades after 1951 and the latter from 268,000 to 189,000 between 1968 and 1981.

The third influence on industrial performance and change has been that of government. This has been both positive, in helping the creation of ICI or providing support for agriculture, or establishing the national electricity grid as well as less helpful in other situations. The problem with government involvement is, of course, that political and social considerations become intermixed with economic decisions, and they are not always easily compatible. Restructuring of the steel industry and the establishment of new plants, both in the 1930s and 1950s, were determined by political considerations and created plants which were economically feeble from the beginning. Similarly the closure of steel capacity in recent years has been influenced by political expediency rather than economic rationality. Successive governments have been accused of subjecting the car industry to a kind of guerilla warfare since 1945, by generating fluctuations in demand through stop-go policies, by failing to provide an adequate road system, by distorting the structure of the industry by its regional policies which dispersed the industry away from the West Midlands, and by inhibiting the rescue of BL by subsidizing Chrysler UK in the 1970s (Dunnett). Certainly the record of many administrations has been less than impressive in regard to industry, giving priority to short-term considerations and giving preference to political rather than economic considerations.

But it would be unrealistic to place the problems of industrial performance at government's door. Equally it would be incorrect to depict productive performance of the economy in purely negative terms. As indicated in the aggregate growth rates, production and productivity have in general been rather better in the present century than hitherto. There have also been successes in terms of wealth creation, in the financial sector and in industries like chemicals and some branches of electronics. Two reasons underlay the emphasis on difficulty rather than success; the relatively low rate of growth compared to other advanced economies and the declining competitiveness of so many sectors which resulted, increasingly through the past decade, in rising unemployment.

11

Aggregate supply and economic growth

I

The two principal questions relating to the contribution of the supply side of the economy to twentieth-century growth reflect its two main features, the faster growth rate compared to Britain's pre-1914 past together with the lower growth rate compared to that of most other industrial nations. The measure often quoted by historians, the relative share of world industrial production, obviously continued to decline, from Britain's peak share of 22.9 per cent in 1880 to 4.1 per cent a century later (Bairoch 1982: 275). Given widespread industrialization elsewhere, this is hardly surprising and is not in itself an indicator of decline. Manufacturing output per head in Britain did grow more slowly than in several other advanced economies, so that its position in the manufacturing hierarchy fell from second in 1913 (to the United States) to twelfth in 1980. By this latter date Britain had fallen behind countries such as Hungary and Czechoslovakia as well as the more obvious industrial leaders like West Germany and Japan. By this latter date, British production had fallen below the European average (Bairoch 1982: 281, 286). Furthermore, this decline had occurred since the 1950s since in 1953 output per head was still second only to the United States. A similar conclusion is suggested by the comparative data for motor vehicle output, a popular twentieth-century index of industrial well-being (Table 11.1). British production was passed by West Germany in the 1950s, by France and Japan in the 1960s, and by Italy in the 1970s. By the 1980s British output was half that of France and West Germany and dwarfed by that of Japan and the United States.

But the growth of GDP in the interwar years and in the boom period 1951–73 reached unprecedented heights and was accompanied by a high rate of growth in manufacturing (Table 1.4). As manufacturing fell in the decade 1973–83 so too the aggregate growth of the economy exhibited a rapid deceleration. Does this suggest that the Kaldorian relationship between British growth and industrial production, which was not particularly strong

Table 11.1 *Motor vehicle production (annual average in thousands)*

	U.K.	France	Germany	Italy	Japan	U.S.A.
1907	12	25	5	3	44	
1912/13	34	45	18			485
1924–38	290	196	155	51	5	3,516
1938–51	369	136	91	57	28	3,772
1951–64	1,351	1,032	1,458	510	568	7,322
1964–73	2,169	2,449	3,366	1,591	4,251	10,330
1973–9	1,754	3,787	3,814	1,666	7,939	11,446
1979–83	1,285	3,793	4,050	1,537	10,638	8,713

Notes: Data for Germany and Italy in row 3 for period 1925–38. West Germany after 1945.
Sources: R. J. Overy, *William Morris, Lord Nuffield* (1976) p. 128.
J. P. Bardou, J. Chanaron, P. Fridenson and J. M. Laux, *The Automobile Revolution: The Impact of an Industry* (Chapel Hill, North Carolina 1982) p. 15.
B. R. Mitchell, *European Historical Statistics 1750–1975* (Cambridge 1981) pp. 488–90
B. R. Mitchell, *International Historical Statistics: Africa and Asia* (New York 1982) p. 349.
B. R. Mitchell, *International Historical Statistics: The Americas and Australasia* (1983) pp. 501–2.
United Nations, *Monthly Bulletin of Statistics*, (34) (January 1980) pp. 86–7, (39) (January 1985) pp. 85–6.

before 1914, was potent in the twentieth century? If so, why was there a sudden collapse in the 1970s?

II

Certainly the main increase in growth in GDP in the interwar years and, more forcefully, between 1951–73 was associated with a marked increase in manufacturing, construction and utilities. Indeed a comparison of the periods 1856–73 and 1951–73 shows that almost all the increase in GDP growth of 0.8 per cent was contributed by manufacturing and construction, the growth in services compensating for the decline in mining (Table 1.4). Since 1973 the sharp decline of growth in manufacturing has been attended by a simultaneous decline in the rate of growth of GDP. Only the revival of mining, through oil exploration, and the continued growth of the service sector ensured some growth.

This pattern of development is consistent with various econometric studies of advanced economies since 1950 which have found growth in GDP to be functionally dependent on the growth of manufacturing with coefficients of determination in the region of 0.9 (Cornwall 1977: 124). Kaldor's thesis, and his results are included, thus appears to stand up better in the post 1950 period than it does in the Victorian context. While

Stoneman's analysis did not show a strong causal relationship between GDP and manufacturing before 1914, these data too provide a strong relationship in the twentieth century. The functional relationship between GDP and manufacturing production in the recent past has been associated with Verdoorn's Law by scholars such as Kaldor and Cornwall. This holds that the rate of growth in manufacturing output determines the rate of growth of productivity. Econometric tests have supported this thesis with regard to labour productivity (Cornwall 1977: 127). The thesis has been extended to suggest that through linkages with other sectors increases in manufacturing output and productivity generate growth elsewhere in the economy. This is, of course, reminiscent of Rostovian explanations. Manufacturing not only produces a substantial proportion of final demand, it also embodies most of the application of technology. Advances in technology and increases in production in recent decades, in Britain and throughout the industrial nations, have been most apparent in industries such as chemicals, electronics, and machine tools (Table 11.2). Chemical manufacture has stimulated growth in other sectors by, for example, providing fertilisers and insecticides for agriculture. Electronics have improved most forms of radio communication and through products like computers and word processors generated widespread multiplier effects.

It has been argued that cause and effect run not from manufacturing output to productivity but in the opposite direction. Such a thesis must assume that technical advance is exogenous, a notion which has proved popular with many historians but has been less favoured by economists. The main evidence, though not unequivocal, suggests that technology should not be treated as exogenous (Stafford 35–6). Furthermore, the only study so far conducted which allows feed-back effects found a much stronger causal dependency of manufacturing employment on manufacturing output than in the opposite direction. This finding is also consistent with Kaldor's thesis (Parikh).

The drastic fall in the growth rate of GDP after 1973 together with the decline in manufacturing production is also starkly consistent with the thesis. The reduced rate of GDP growth and of productivity increase was common to the advanced economies from the early 1970s, as had been the earlier very high growth rates (Boltho 22, 34). Both before and after 1973 British rates of growth remained lower than those of almost all other industrial nations. The transition which emerged in the early 1970s introduced a phenomenon termed deindustrialization, which has been the subject of various definitions. Cornwall expressed it as the relationship between the rate of growth in manufacturing employment and the rate of growth in the ratio of labour employed in manufacturing to total employment. In common with Kaldor's thesis this assumes that the growth of manufacturing will draw

Table 11.2 *Weighted sectoral output growth rates in manufacturing (per cent per annum)*

	1924–37	1937–51	1951–64	1964–73	1973–79	1979–83
Food, drink, tobacco	0.40	0.20	0.27	0.29	0.08	−0.03
Chemicals	0.19	0.34	0.46	0.52	0.27	−0.10
Iron and steel	0.20	0.13	0.18	−0.01	−0.21	−0.34
Electrical engineering	0.28	0.38	0.50	0.56	0.07	0.07
Mechanical engineering and shipbuilding	0.21	0.53	0.37	0.54	−0.23	−0.45
Vehicles	0.48	0.34	0.48	0.08	−0.10	−0.31
Other metal industries	0.31	0.22	0.16	0.08	−0.31	−0.60
Textiles	0.21	0.03	0.01	0.19	−0.12	−0.20
Clothing	0.20	−0.10	0.10	0.07	0.01	−0.14
Paper, printing, publishing	0.21	0.21	0.32	0.22	−0.03	−0.29
Bricks, pottery, glass, cement	0.18	0.11	0.15	0.15 ⎫		
Timber, furniture	0.18	0.00	0.07	0.12 ⎬	−0.03	−0.21
Leather and other manufactures	0.15	0.11	0.13	0.19 ⎭		
Total manufacturing	3.20	2.50	3.20	3.00	−0.60	−2.60

Sources: R. C. O. Matthews, C. H. Feinstein, and J. C. Odling-Smee, *British Economic Growth 1856–1973* (Oxford 1982) pp. 239–40 (Cols. 1–4).
Central Statistical Office, *Annual Abstract of Statistics 1984* pp. 14, 254.
Central Statistical Office, *U.K. National Accounts 1984* Table 2.4 (Cols. 5–6). There is some lack of sectoral continuity of definition between the pre 1973 data and the later reclassified data.

labour away from other less productive sectors, thereby increasing productivity and growth during phases of substantive growth as in the 1950s and 1960s. When this attractive force weakens and the growth rate of manufacturing employment falls, then eventually deindustrialization will set in. This too has been a common experience of the industrial nations (Cornwall 1977: 154–5, 196–8).

According to the Kaldorian model, the most likely obstacle to the working of this relationship and the causes of its decline would be a shortage of labour available for industry. Indeed the Selective Employment Tax imposed in the 1960s in Britain was a Kaldorian device intended to 'shake' surplus labour out of the service sector. There was, by that time, little scope left in Britain for drawing labour from the agricultural sector. But it seems unlikely that labour shortage was the cause of the decline in manufacturing expansion, either in Britain or abroad. Nor was the transition to much lower levels of growth after 1973 the result of the massive increase in oil prices brought about by OPEC although that contributed. But the decline in industrial growth has been traced back to the late 1960s, and was in progress before the energy price crisis. Indeed the high growth of the preceding decades contributed to the eventual inflationary pressure which broke the boom. The full employment which was achieved in the decades of high growth necessarily led to labour shortages and helped the workforce to bid up rates of pay. For the first time in most employment sectors the balance of market power passed from employers to their employees. As a result wage rates rose, profit margins were squeezed, but in the buoyant market conditions producers were able to pass some of the increased cost incurred by paying wage rises to the customer in higher prices. This was generally thought a strategy preferable to engaging in conflict with organized labour and running the risk of disrupting production by strikes. The rigidities built into the labour market during expansion became obstacles to change later. The seeds for the retrenchment of the 1970s were thus inherent in the nature of the expansionary phase. Falling profits in much of industry inhibited new investment and the inflationary bias in expansion became so potent by the mid 1970s, aided by the energy price rise, that it forced governments to perceive inflation as the major problem and adopt deflationary policies in order to reduce it. This, in turn, stifled growth and generated unemployment on a scale unknown since before the Second World War.

While this experience was common to all industrial countries, the fragility of the British economy in boom and slump meant that its capacity to benefit from expansion or to weather deflation was less than most other economies. At an aggregate level, the relatively low investment ratio and scale of manufacturing production limited the productivity gains and hence the rate of growth of GDP. Failure to obtain production economies, such as those of scale, inhibited the accumulation of profit to fund investment. British industry was not immune to the effects of the rising power of organized labour, and the long history of poor labour relations and the many bad employers ensured that they would be treated with little sympathy and understanding now that industrial power had shifted. Inefficient production, augmented by the usual temporization in periods of business prosperity continued the downward trend of competitiveness in most of British industry. Since the home market is modest in size, especially in the context of the scale of production required for efficient manufacturing, this falling competitiveness was evidenced by the steady loss of overseas markets. This was not, of course, peculiar to the most recent past. British cotton goods were struggling in international markets from the First World War onwards. British yarn production fell by two thirds between 1914 and 1961, and by a similar proportion again in the following two decades. Piece goods in 1961 were less than one quarter of 1914 output, and fell by more than half again by 1981. By the early 1980s the industry was close to collapse, having been the undisputed world leader in the Victorian era. But this transformation took place within the context not of decline in the world cotton industry but of massive growth. World production of cotton goods increased from 3,162 million kilograms in 1900 to 14,138 million kilograms in 1977 and the total production of textiles, natural and man-made fibres, increased from 3,893 million kilograms in 1900 to 28,278 million kilograms in 1977 (Cable 1). It is in this context that British performance seems extremely poor. Initially the problem lay in the uncompetitiveness of British manufacturers in foreign markets. But by the 1960s the home market was being increasingly penetrated by cheap Asian goods and high quality European textiles, to bring the final collapse of the industry (Cable 53). In 1977 Courtaulds closed the Skelmersdale plant which had been one of the most modern in Europe with new machinery and a fully integrated system of manufacturing processes. It had been in production for less than a decade. Ironically the decline of the printing section of the industry and the inflexibility of structure brought by the massive combined firms of the 1970s probably inhibited the industry's response to the fashion changes of that decade and it was slow to develop new lines such as denim, corduroy and velvet.

British production fell in other industrial sectors in the twentieth century while worldwide output increased. In the interwar years, steel output declined as foreign markets were lost and as cheap European steel was imported. Between 1960 and 1982, British steel production fell from 24.7 million tons to 13.8 million tons while world output increased from 336 million to 708 million tons. In the 1970s, imported steel, as in other sectors, increased its share of the British market. Even more spectacular was the decline of merchant shipbuilding. In 1950 Britain still accounted for over one third of world shipbuilding tonnage completions. By 1981 output had fallen from 1,398 thousand to 213 thousand gross tons while world output had risen from 3,254 thousand to 16,932 thousand tons. By the latter date, British output had been exceeded by France, Denmark, West Germany, Italy, Norway, Sweden and Spain in Western Europe and by other major producers such as the United States, Brazil, South Korea and Japan. The problem for the traditional British manufacturing sectors was not simply that they were old, having existed for many decades even centuries, but that they were becoming less and less competitive in a rapidly expanding market.

Weak and diminishing competitiveness has not been peculiar to industries with a Victorian pedigree. British electrical engineering and electronics has always been oriented towards military production. Government spending on radar and radio during the Second World War together with rearmament in the subsequent Cold War provided an attractive and secure demand. Specialized defence research received ample investment funds from the state. Sales on a cost-plus basis to the Ministry of Defence, plus protection from foreign competition, boosted the business of those firms with contracts. Much the same situation obtained in the aircraft industry. But there was little diversification into consumer oriented electronics and the boom in consumer durables which grew through the 1960s was unanticipated to the advantage of foreign competitors. Even more reprehensible was the failure to exploit technological developments in which Britain was a leader. Most obvious was the slow commercial exploitation of computers, developed originally in the University of Manchester and funded partly by Ferranti. As was usual in British industry, several models were developed, each produced in small runs. The reluctance of British producers was not shared by their American counterparts. Some computer patents were bought by companies like International Business Machines (IBM) and they swiftly took advantage of the worldwide opportunities. By the 1960s, IBM had secured 60 per cent of the world computer market. Even in the 1970s, the major British electronics company, GEC, was sufficiently unenthusiastic about computers to sell its substantial shareholding in International Computers Limited (ICL). British firms were equally slow to develop the silicon chip, the essential miniature transistor required in microelectronics. 'Once again the basic concept was grasped in Britain at an early stage, but it was exploited faster and more efficiently in the United States. In Britain the Ministry [Defence] would not underwrite the further research necessary to put these ideas into practice, and Whitehall rules prevented joint exploitation of the idea with a British manufacturer. But the American Air Force paid Texas Instruments $2 million dollars to do the development work, and two years later they produced the first commercial integrated circuits' (Pagnamenta/Overy 256). The backwardness of the major British firms in commercial and technological terms encouraged many of the best technologists to move to American firms for better pay and greater opportunities to develop their ideas. Thus no British firm appeared amongst the major semiconductor producers in the late 1970s although the world turnover exceeded $10 billion.

In the motor industry too, British growth fell behind other major producers from the 1950s, and even in the general recession of the late 1970s the contraction of British production was greater than that of the other major manufacturers (Table 11.1).

The production of the British Motor Corporation and its successor BL fell from 800,000 units per annum in the late 1960s to 600,000 units a decade later. The slow growth of BMC relative to its competitors in the buoyant conditions of the post 1945 economy was a direct result of the poor export record of the company in Western Europe. This was hardly surprising as it did not even have a dealer network in either France or West Germany. In 1975 BLMC was able to sell only 7,204 cars in those countries out of a total market sale of 3.5 million (Williams 57). Imported cars took a growing share of the British domestic market, rising dramatically in the 1970s as tariffs against EEC member countries were reduced after British entry. In the 1970s imported cars took 40 per cent of the British market compared to only six per cent in the previous decade. As the motor industry became increasingly dominated by multinational corporations like Ford and General Motors, many 'British' cars were imported by the parent company from their workshops in Germany or Spain. At the same time, Britain's poor labour relations encouraged the same multinationals to shift production out of Britain to other parts of Western Europe. Thus the falling market share of BMC and its later corporate forms from 11.0 per cent in 1965 to 4.8 per cent in 1978 took place during a boom in sales in the British market. By the end of the 1970s, BL's market share was down to 23.5 per cent, while Ford had 24.6 per cent, General Motors 9.7 per cent and Japanese imports accounted for 11.0 per cent (Bhaskar 159, 189).

The decline of the motor industry in Britain had widespread effects on the rest of manufacturing. Apart from the fact that the industry was a major consumer of investment and provider of employment, and accounted for 11 per cent of industrial production in the 1960s and early 1970s, its sectoral linkages to other industries involved it in 27 per cent of total industrial production (Dunnett 12–13). The decline of the industry threatened a large share of manufacturing capacity and brought about the near collapse of what had previously been one of the most prosperous regions in the country, the West Midlands. The decline of the industry provided a dramatic indication of the long-term lack of competitiveness within the industry, the failure to standardize production or take full advantage of the various mergers and, consequentially, the failure to generate sufficiently large production runs to compete in the volume car market. The small cars and diversity of models which brought apparent success in the 1930s were peculiar to the home market which was never going to be large enough to sustain the growth needed for efficient production. Even the peculiarity of the home market and the support of a tax on engine size did not prevent American subsidiaries from expanding in the British market. General Motors established themselves in the 1920s through a subsidiary, Vauxhall, while the long established Ford developed a car specifically for the British market in the 1930s.

The slow growth and poor competitiveness of the motor industry was both cause and effect of the performance of the economy. Early in the twentieth century, car ownership per head of population in Britain was second only to that in the United States. From the 1960s the British ratio fell behind that of other advanced economies, as did national income. By 1979 there were 256 motor vehicles per thousand people in Britain compared to 527 in the United States, 357 in West Germany, 355 in France and 303 in Italy (Bardou 70, 112, 197).

As a result of deindustrialization, employment in manufacturing fell by

450,000 in the 1960s and by almost three million in the 1970s. Indeed, two million such jobs were lost in the two years after June 1979 with the adoption of a severely deflationary policy by the new administration (Thirlwall 1982: 22, 26). Virtually all sectors of production have been affected, ranging from long-established manufactures like textiles and clothing to expanding sectors like electronics and chemicals. The mixture of labour saving productivity and industrial decline had the same effect of reducing the need for labour. The common theme in many explanations of deindustrialization has been the failure of British industry to achieve a reasonable export record because of its poor competitive performance. Since the domestic market of a small economy can never be sufficient to sustain modern industry, this failure has been critical. The collapse of many British firms in the 1970s in face of import penetration in the home market represented a late phase in the process of industrial decline. Several scholars have drawn attention to the consequences of deindustrialization. Thirlwall accepted the export failure thesis and pointed out that the inevitable consequence must eventually be a balance of payments deficit. Deflationary policies designed to reduce that deficit by stifling the flow of imports, he argued, further reduced the level of activity within the British economy by diminishing demand and thus increasing unemployment further. In a similar analysis, Singh argued that deindustrialization was the measure of an economy's failure to generate export earnings sufficient to pay for the full employment level of manufactured imports. This is a rather different definition of the phenomenon than that offered by Thirlwall or Cornwall, but the pattern of cause and effect is very similar in all these analyses. Poor export performance leads to slow growth in manufacturing production, and hence in GDP, and leads to balance of payments problems while creating unemployment. All these elements of the equation appeared in the British economy during the 1970s to exercise successive governments.

III

The service sector continued to contribute to the growth of GDP in the twentieth century as it had before 1914. For most of the past century and a quarter, it has contributed one per cent or more to a rate of national income growth which has seldom exceeded two per cent and never reached three per cent for any sustained period. Public and professional services, and commerce, were the main contributors to GDP growth in the twentieth century (Table 1.4). Similarly, service sector growth has constituted the main area of employment increase, especially in the professions, finance and distribution. Employment in services increased by over five million jobs between

1911 and 1981 while the rest of the economy experienced a net loss of about three million jobs. Services have, therefore, provided all the growth in employment in the twentieth century and compensated for losses elsewhere.

As before 1914, the growth of services was a response to a variety of stimuli. One was the expansion of manufacturing, itself a more effective contributor to growth since the First World War. These linkages were both more extensive and more effective in the twentieth century. The great increase in housing, one of the major features of growth in the present century, generated work for the financial sector, influencing both the pattern of borrowing and of lending and creating, in the building societies, another body of major financial institutions. Furthermore, the expansion of new housing estates in suburban locations created demands for additional transport and distribution services. In the most recent decades increased ownership of motor cars has brought further changes in distribution in facilitating the development of supermarkets and hypermarkets away from the centre of cities. In the field of leisure, which has become big business in conjunction with the growth of affluence, the growth of manufacturing and services have been closely linked. Professional sport, theatre, radio and television are all branches of entertainment which have greatly expanded in recent decades. All exert a demand for equipment and facilities needed to provide their service. In recent years the burgeoning enthusiasm for fitness has impinged upon services, such as keep-fit classes and health studios, and for commodities, like track suits, training shoes and a wide range of fashionable paraphernalia. Tourism, too, appears to be an activity which requires, apart from the obvious services like hotels, restaurants and transport, a large amount of equipment including cameras, guide books, appropriate clothing and many oils and potions.

Besides the stimulus of manufacturing growth, services have increased with the growth in national income. This development has been the common experience of all high income economies. Affluence obviously enables the purchase of more and better services and thereby has a multiplier effect through the creation of employment and incomes. As before 1914, there remains a strong functional relationship between service provision and national or regional income. Thus health and educational provision have greatly increased, as have public services such as increased welfare provision through pensions and other transfer payments, and as have personal services privately purchased such as hairdressing, holidays and entertainment.

Finally, some service growth has been stimulated by the growth for financial services, as powerful a source of wealth creation as in the Victorian period. The revival of the fortunes of the City in recent decades has brought both business and foreign exchange and restored much of its earlier international specialization. As before 1914, the growth of the service sector cannot be explained solely in terms of its links with manufacturing, although this multiplier effect was probably greater in the twentieth century than earlier.

Historians of the eighteenth and nineteenth centuries have given pride of place to manufacturing, in their explanations of economic growth and thus, often implicitly, reduced services to a subsidiary role. A rather similar attitude can be identified in the view of some economists with regard to deindustrialization in recent decades. The Bacon/Eltis thesis drew a distinction between the market and non-market sectors of the economy rather than between industry and services, although much of the service sector falls, by the definition used, into the non-market sector. 'Almost everything that industry produces is marketed, that is, it is sold to someone. The private sector services are sold, so they are marketed. Defence, on the other hand, is not marketed . . . what the National Health Service provides, and most schools, is also not marketed, and the services provided by policemen and civil servants are not marketed; so they must spend their incomes on the marketed products of the rest of the community' (1978: 27). Some services, such as those of the financial and commercial sectors are marketed. So the non-market sector is, in effect, the public sector of the economy less the nationalized industries. The problem, argued Bacon/Eltis, lay in the fact that from the 1960s, possibly even earlier, the non-market sector grew faster than did the market sector and at the expense of the latter. Since the market sector creates the wealth of the entire economy, producing all exports and generating the investment and private consumption needs of society, the crowding out of the market sector causes difficulties. The growth of the non-market sector shifts resources to government. If this is at the expense of labour, say through increased taxation to pay for government services, labour will seek compensation and create wage inflation. If government tries to curb inflation by controlling the money supply the deflationary effect of this will increase unemployment. If the government sector grows at the expense of private industry, by taxation, the reduction in profits will lead to a cut in investment. Technical progress will, under such circumstances, be used to reduce labour costs rather than to increase production, reducing rather than creating employment. All these manifestations of crowding out have appeared in Britain in recent decades. From such a perspective it follows that economic success or regeneration must lie in increasing the level of investment in the market sector which is most easily achieved by increasing profits (Bacon/Eltis 1978: 110).

This thesis explains the growing difficulties of the British economy in recent decades as the effect of state funded activities, like education, health, social security and defence, crowding out both labour and capital from the manufacturing and exporting sectors of the economy. Interesting though it is, there are several difficulties inherent in the Bacon/Eltis thesis, not the least of which is the problem of identifying and measuring the market and non-market sectors (Hadjimatheou/Skouras, Bacon/Eltis 1979). There is no strong evidence to support the basic assumption that the growth of the non-market sector, as evidenced by the faster growth of service sector employment than manufacturing jobs in the 1960s and 1970s, has crowded out either labour or capital from manufacturing. There is no reason to believe, or evidence to suggest, that the decline in manufacturing employment was the result of workers being enticed into the non-market sector. Indeed in the 1970s and 1980s, rising unemployment demonstrated that this was not so. Nor is there any evidence of widespread starvation of investment in manufacturing, as a series of official investigations of the financial system have all testified during the past fifty years. The basic idea that growth is a simple direct function of the investment ratio, or that the investment ratio itself is a simple function of the non-market sector is far from certain. Indeed, econometric results obtained by Bacon/Eltis indicated a very poor functional relationship between the rate of growth of marketed output and the investment ratio of the market sector during the period 1955–73 (Stafford 39–40).

International comparisons have not proved to be helpful to the Bacon/Eltis thesis. Some of the fastest growing non-market sectors, like health and education, have grown just as swiftly in countries where they have been part of the market as in those where they have been in the non-market sector. Such services have grown in relation to growing national income, and not simply as a result of government profligacy. Nor did Britain actually generate government consumption at a rate faster than the growth rate of GDP in the period 1955–74 (Chrystal 154). The shift in spending from the private to the public sector in recent years has been a response primarily to growing unemployment and the obligation of the state to pay benefit even though income tax revenue is also eroded by unemployment. The Bacon/Eltis thesis thus touches on several economic problems which have arisen in the recent past, but without sustaining a comprehensive or convincing explanation for them.

IV

The twentieth century has been a period of enormous industrial and technological advance throughout the world. In Britain, as in many other economies, manufacturing has made a greater contribution to aggregate growth than it did before 1914. The functional relationship between manufacturing and the growth of GDP, as expounded by Kaldor, became more effective (Table 1.4). Most of British industry fared best in the domestic market, especially while foreign competition remained weak. The motor industry did well in the interwar years and in the 1950s producing small family cars for the home market. Shipbuilding continued to survive so long as it retained a near monopoly at home, although its prosperity remained uncertain. Since 1939 agriculture has revived and prospered under the protection of government subsidies and guaranteed prices. The nationalized industries have survived under state ownership, although shortage of investment has prevented some of them from performing well or enjoying prosperity.

Unfortunately, the British domestic market is too small to sustain modern industry, and even the introduction of protection during the First World War and its maintenance thereafter has not been sufficient to keep out imports. The central problem facing the supply side of the economy has, consequently, been the declining competitiveness of British manufactures. As a result, established industries like textiles and shipbuilding have declined even though international demand and production have greatly expanded. Relatively new industries, like motor vehicle manufacture, have failed to establish an export base and hence they too have declined. So great was the pressure of competition in the 1970s that British industry was obliged to fight, often unsuccessfully, to retain a major part of the home market. The disappearance of the motor cycle industry, and the near collapse of cotton textiles, shipbuilding, and motor vehicles indicate the severity of the crisis.

Most of Britain's economic problems in the twentieth century have developed from this steady erosion of industrial competitiveness, and its sharp acceleration since the 1970s. The low rate of industrial growth and small scale production prevented the realization of economies of scale and productivity increase. Economies of scale were not compatible with an industrial structure characterized by the small family firm owned by a few people who were generally unwilling to be merged into large conglomerates where they would lose control and identity. Most of them were too small or weak to absorb rivals. Full employment in the 1950s and 1960s, together with the increasing effectiveness of organized labour, removed the prop of cheap labour on which much of industry had traditionally relied to keep down costs. British prices tended to remain uncompetitively high in international markets. Poor technical education, lack of investment, and suspicion of new technology all militated against technological advance or expansion of production into new areas. Industry remained locked into long-established organizational structures, working practices, and attitudes. These became more and more outmoded as other countries increased investment in industry, improved technical education, adopted mass production, and paid better wages to a more highly trained and thus more productive workforce than did their British counterparts. They were thus able to oust British products from their traditional markets, keep them out of new ones and, in due course, make substantial inroads into the British market itself.

The consequence of the inability of British industry to gain new markets or hold old ones was a low rate of growth and productivity, and a slow rate of growth of GDP. Even in the best years, British industry's performance was moderate by international comparisons. As the basic problems remained unresolved, and some might add that they were not seriously tackled, so performance deteriorated. Industrial employment fell in the 1960s, and fell sharply in the 1970s and 1980s. By the 1980s industrial output was also falling in most sectors (Table 11.2). Not all manufacturing performed badly, nor did all sectors of the economy decline. As in the Victorian period, the service sector made a substantial and more enduring contribution to aggregate growth. But growth in these other sectors was unable to compensate for the effects of industrial decline. From the early 1970s, growth fell to late Victorian levels and unemployment moved steadily upwards. Not surprisingly, much attention was focused on the supply side as the source of British economic malaise.

The weakening performance of the supply side of the economy not only resulted in a falling rate of GDP growth. Declining industrial competitiveness adversely affected the balance of trade by failing to generate export earnings sufficient to pay for imports and by failing to keep foreign goods out of the home market. The relatively high rate of British inflation in the 1970s also attracted imports and inhibited export growth. The effects of deindustrialization were thus most seriously felt in the deterioration of the balance of payments.

12

Foreign trade and payments

I

British growth before the First World War was heavily influenced by the central and unique role of the economy within the developing international system to such an extent that it makes little sense to discuss the economy in isolation. Not only were all the major industries heavily oriented towards overseas markets, and in many cases dependent on imported raw materials, but the financial system was essentially international in its outlook and operations. Britain was thus able to combine the apparent contradiction of a deficit on commodity trade with a balance of payments surplus, by virtue of very large earnings from export services and income from investment abroad. The two most obvious aspects of the development of the international economy in the twentieth century brought considerable pressure to bear on the external relations of the British economy. Firstly, the rate of growth of the world economy in the present century and especially since the Second World War far exceeded pre-1914 development. This brought greater opportunities for export but also much more widespread and vigorous competition as industrialization spread. Secondly, the massive disruptions of the two world wars together with the depression of the interwar years and the problems of the inflationary 1970s brought a greater instability into the international economy and exerted a profound effect on Britain's financial role. The international dimension has been prominent in many of Britain's economic problems in the twentieth century.

II

For many observers, exports have constituted a fundamental problem for the economy since 1914. The ratio of exported goods to GDP fluctuated for much of the century at a rather lower level than had been achieved in the nineteenth century (Table 12.1). Only in the past decade has this export ratio reached and exceeded the best levels achieved in the Victorian period.

Table 12.1 *Trade: ratio of payments to GDP (annual averages per cent)*

	Export of goods	Import of goods	Net services	Balance of trade	Net income from abroad	Balance of payments
1855–73	17.9	20.9	4.7	1.7	2.8	4.5
1874–90	18.4	23.9	5.1	−0.4	5.4	5.0
1891–1913	17.7	23.8	4.3	−1.8	6.8	5.0
1921–29	18.2	23.3	2.2	−2.9	5.1	2.2
1930–38	10.9	16.9	0.9	−5.1	4.2	−0.9
1952–64	16.6	17.5	0.2	−0.7	1.3	0.6
1964–73	14.7	16.5	1.0	−0.8	1.1	0.3
1973–79	18.5	19.4	2.3	1.4	0.7	2.1
1979–83	20.5	20.1	1.7	2.1	0.4	2.5

Sources: R. C. O. Matthews, C. H. Feinstein and J. C. Odling-Smee, *British Economic Growth 1856–1973* (Oxford 1982) p. 442.
Central Statistical Office, *U.K. National Accounts 1984* Table 1.5.

In the depressed international conditions of the interwar years, exports of goods and services contracted. Since 1950 they have increased and, for the most part, grown faster than GDP. The growth of export services has continued to be a potent beneficial influence on this, although the net balance on trade in services has not been so large as it was in the unusual conditions prevailing before 1914.

The composition of exports has undergone a very considerable change in the present century. Nineteenth-century commodity exports were dominated by textiles and especially cotton goods. As late as 1913, when their share of exports was falling, textiles and clothing together accounted for 36.3 per cent of British exports, and cotton goods alone comprised 24.2 per cent (Mitchell 1962: 303–5). In that same year, iron and steel contributed 10.6 per cent of exports, coal 10.2 per cent and machinery, much of which was an offshoot of these sectors such as textile machinery and railway stock, made up a further 7.1 per cent. In the twentieth century most of these industries have experienced absolute as well as relative decline in exports. The textile industries were hit particularly hard in the interwar years. As the nineteenth century passed, cotton exports had shifted towards Asian markets and especially to India. The hiatus in British supplies caused by the First World War allowed Japanese cotton goods into the Indian market. By the interwar years they were not only established throughout Asia but were able to undercut British prices and thereby hold the market they had gained. Apart from Japanese competition, British manufacturers found themselves up against native cotton industries fostered by government import substitution policies. Britain suffered more from import substitution than any other industrial country in the interwar period because semi-industrial countries had comprised as much as 40 per cent of the British export market before 1914, a far greater proportion than any other industrial country. By 1937, textile exports had fallen to 23.3 per cent of total exports and cotton goods were down to 13.1 per cent. It was, in fact, the decline in cotton exports from £127.2 million in 1913 to £68.5 million in 1937 which reduced textile exports overall. Other established mainstays of export earnings, like coal and iron and steel also suffered an absolute decline in overseas earnings in the interwar years. The coal industry lost markets in Europe through import substitution, competition from alternative fuels, and from the more economical use of coal itself. British exports of machinery, for which Latin America had been an important outlet before the First World War, found their markets eroded by American firms which had moved into those markets during the war. Another feature of structural change in export composition was the decline in re-exports which had contributed 20 per cent of earnings from commodity exports in the late nineteenth century, principally in items such as cotton, wool, rubber, non-ferrous metals, oils, oil seed, gums and tallow. This fall in the interwar years to 14.4 per cent of commodity exports reflected shifts in international trade and the erosion of Britain's entrepot trade. The contraction was most apparent in cotton, rubber, coffee and oil products. The pattern of export contraction in these sectors, established in the interwar years, was continued after 1945. Re-exports accounted for only 4.6 per cent of total exports by 1956 as Britain ceased to be the trade buffer between the industrial countries and the raw material exporters. But the most obvious trend was the continued diminution of the textile industries which provided only 2.9 per cent of export earnings by 1981, while iron and steel contributed only 2.1 per cent (*Annual Abstract of Statistics* 1983: 249–50).

The considerable restructuring of exports necessitated by the decline of earnings in many of the sectors prominent in nineteenth-century trade placed a considerable burden on other manufactures. Chemicals, electrical goods and vehicles increased their share of exports in the interwar years, and were prominent in the twentieth century as the main expansion of trade has been in the exchange of manufactured goods between industrial countries. These same industries were at the very forefront of export growth after the Second World War. Chemicals accounted for 8.4 per cent of exports in the 1950s and 11.2 per cent by 1981. All types of electrical engineering product were important, and exports ranged from textile machinery, construction and earth moving equipment to office machinery, radio and electronic components, computers and radio equipment. The motor industry was, of course, a major export industry although its share of exports fell from 11.4 per cent in 1971 to 6.7 per cent a decade later.

The shift of export composition in the twentieth century away from low technology products to more sophisticated products entailed a redirection of exports. Before 1914 the main thrust of British exports had been in the markets of raw material producing countries, and eventually this pattern of trade became centred upon the Empire. The retreat into imperial preference in the 1930s with the introduction of tariffs discriminating in favour of such territories needed only a modest realignment of earlier export patterns. Indeed it may be regarded as an attempt to preserve the traditional structure under increasingly difficult circumstances. While trade with the sterling area countries remained very substantial through the 1950s, the principal growth of exports in the period after the Second World War was located in Western Europe. By 1971, still before Britain joined the European Economic Community, 28.6 per cent of exports went to member countries and a further 15.9 per cent to other Western European destinations. Less than one quarter of British exports went to primary producing countries. This trend was reinforced in the 1970s when Britain joined the EEC, and by 1980 43.4 per cent of exports went to fellow member countries. By that latter date, 57.7 per cent of exports were sold in Western Europe and 74.6 per cent to the advanced industrial nations (*Annual Abstract of Statistics* 1983: 253–4).

The changes in export performance influenced not simply the aggregate export income but the prosperity of the industries themselves. The fall in both relative share and absolute earnings from exports was disastrous for the cotton industry which had always depended so heavily on overseas markets. On the eve of the First World War over 80 per cent of cotton piece goods were exported. By 1937 exports by volume had fallen to little more than a quarter of the 1913 level, and the decline in production was entirely a result of falling exports, mainly sales of low quality goods in Asia. By the end of the 1930s protection had captured the Indian market for domestic producers and the British share of that market, which it had so recently dominated, was cut to four per cent. British exports of cotton piece goods to India fell from 2,507 million square yards in 1913 to a mere 356 million in 1937 (Robson 11). The collapse continued after 1945 as exports fell and the home market began to contract. Domestic sales were less than a quarter of the 1961 level by 1981. This represented the final phase of decline as low cost Asian fabrics and high quality goods from other advanced economies made extremely successive inroads into the British market. There was an increase in import penetration in all industrial countries for manufactured goods as their patterns of demand and supply converged and the increase in trade in such commodities accelerated. But in Britain the level of import penetration was greater than in most other countries. For the textile trades this had risen to one third by the mid 1970s and for clothing the ratio was only slightly less (Cable 53). The cotton industry in Britain was eventually destroyed by the same forces of international competition which had created it, shaped its growth and sustained its success. The same fate befell British shipbuilding and, to a lesser degree, steel and coal.

Export markets were equally important for the growth of the newer industries like motor manufacture. The general stagnation of the interwar years limited the scope for exporting, and only 20 per cent of the British motor industry output was sold abroad even in the late 1930s. Export development was, of course, essential in the post 1950 expansion both in order to achieve sufficient volume of output to reap economies of scale and to offset the unavoidable effects of import penetration. Inability to achieve this led, in the 1970s, to a dramatic decline in the British motor industry. So important has become the balance between export sales and import penetration that performance has been evaluated in terms of the ratio of export sales to total sales plus imports. Often a high ratio of exports is essential because of the internationalization of markets and thence an inescapable flow of imported goods. This was the case in instrument engineering, which exported 62 per cent of its product in 1980, while the equivalent export shares in other industries included 46 per cent in mechanical engineering, 43 per cent in vehicles, while over 30 per cent of output was exported in chemicals, electrical engineering, shipbuilding and textiles. For the manufacturing sector as a whole, the proportion of products exported was 26.1 per cent (*Annual Abstract of Statistics* 1983: 247–8, Wells/Imber 82–9).

Increasing competitiveness in international markets, the similarity of product composition amongst the advanced industrial nations, and the growth of import penetration partly as a result of EEC membership have all combined to make the export performance of the economy of prime concern. Several studies have sought to evaluate performance, and the widespread conclusion has been that it has been rather poor. Some extenuating circumstances have been suggested to reduce the degree of culpability of exporters, such as the loss of price competitiveness in Western Europe in the period between the initial formation of the EEC and the time Britain joined. Some market share was lost after 1950 to the United States as a result of the American practice of tying aid to trade. Foreign investment thus became conditional on the purchase of American goods by the recipient nation, a restriction imposed by both the federal government and American multinational corporations. Hence, it was calculated, if British prices had remained in line with those of their main rivals only half the loss in export trade suffered by Britain could have been avoided (Krause 222). In spite of this the tenor of comment has been critical and the principal theme has been that British goods lost competitiveness in international markets because their price was too high. British manufacturers have been criticized for failing to respond adequately to the requirements of potential customers and for providing poor styling, finish and salesmanship. In Britain, productivity increases fell behind wage increases so prices rose. But in many other industrial economies higher rates of productivity meant that wage increases could be absorbed without large increases in price (Wells 199). Criticism of British export performance increased in the 1970s, especially as competitive performance was weak in products which were growing fastest in international trade, like chemicals and sophisticated engineering products. Throughout the most buoyant phase of the postwar boom, the British export ratio for goods remained below its nineteenth-century level (Table 12.1). The near collapse of the motor industry in the 1970s was a result of poor export sales, and seemed to presage a future overshadowed by a more widespread collapse of exports. The increase in the export ratio in the decade 1973–83 appeared reassuring, but it reflected the slow down in the growth of GDP and the influence of sales of North Sea oil. The basic problem remains.

III

For most of the twentieth century, as in the Victorian period, the ratio of imports to GDP has exceeded that of exports (Table 12.1). The decline of re-export trade has had the effect of reducing the import ratio from the very high levels of late Victorian times, although it has begun to rise again during the past decade. There has also been a greater level of imported services in the twentieth century as the British hold over international freight and finance has been eroded. While there remains a net balance on services, it has been restricted throughout the present century to a level well below that attained before 1914. As a result there was a large deficit on balance of trade in the interwar years due to the collapse of exports of both goods and services. This was reduced to a modest deficit in the 1950s and 1960s as exports revived, and has become a trade account surplus since the early 1970s for the first time in over a century. Most of that increase can be attributed to the rise in the balance on services earned by the financial sector.

The changes in the structure of production and trade in the twentieth century have wrought a marked change in the composition of British imports. In the late nineteenth century, foodstuffs and raw materials were the main ingredients in imports although the share of manufactures, still modest, was increasing and pushing up the import ratio (Matthews 432). Since 1914 there has been a large relative decline in the import ratio of foodstuffs and raw materials. Conversely there has been a very large increase in the import ratio of manufactured goods, from 5.3 per cent in 1913 to 11.6 per cent by 1973, most of which increase occurred in the 1960s. There has also been a substantial increase in fuel imports, but this has been a steady growth through the century. But the main change has without doubt been the massive increase in the import of manufactured goods from 19.7 per cent of all imports in 1951 to 62.5 per cent thirty years later (*Annual Abstract of Statistics* 1960: 212, 1983: 251–2). The composition of such imports has been diversified to include machinery, office equipment, telecommunication equipment, consumer goods, motor cars, textiles and clothing, iron and steel and ships.

The shifting composition of imports has also been characterized by changes in the geographical pattern of imports. These changes have mirrored the changed distribution of exports although most of the change has happened since 1960. Before that date, trade with Asia and the imperial territories remained important and the Commonwealth still supplied over one third of imported goods in 1961. Sterling Area countries, mainly the Empire together with some Middle East countries, were important trading partners from the 1930s until the 1960s. This pattern of imports was a modification of the longer-term pattern. But in the past two decades, as manufactures have become a major component of imports, British imports have been drawn increasingly from the advanced industrial nations and especially from the EEC countries. By 1981, 42.2 per cent of imports came from these nations, a further 15.2 per cent from the rest of Western Europe and 14.8 per cent from North America. Altogether the developed world provided 79.6 per cent of British imports by the early 1980s, a complete transformation of the trade pattern prevailing during the two centuries prior to the Second World War.

In conformity with the general phenomenon of growing import penetration in manufactures throughout the advanced industrial nations, imports grew from 17.1 per cent of domestic demand in Britain in 1971 to 25.4 per cent by the end of the decade. But there were considerable variations in the extent of import penetration in different sectors, and in the speed of that penetration. By both criteria, import penetration in the 1970s was greatest in all types of engineering, metal manufacture, vehicles, textiles and clothing. By 1980 all these sectors had an import penetration level in excess of 30 per cent. Furthermore, this level had increased substantially in the course of the previous decade, from 15 to 39 per cent for vehicles, from 37 to 59 per cent for instrument engineering, and by over 15 per cent in metal manufactures, textiles, leather, clothing, and electrical engineering (Wells/ Imber 82–8, *Annual Abstract of Statistics* 1983: 247–8). Since there were large counterflows of exports at the same time these rather alarming ratios should be modified by expressing imports in terms of total home demand and exports. By this measure the overall ratio was 14.3 per cent in 1971 and 20.1 per cent in 1980.

The growth of imports of manufactures and its implications for trade performance has been much discussed. The Brookings Institution study noted the substantial increase in imports in the decade 1954–64, but did not draw adverse conclusions and simply regarded it as a result of trade liberalization common to all advanced countries (Denison). Such a trend was consistent with the 'variety hypothesis' which postulates that rising real income allows purchasers to buy and seek a greater variety of a given product. If the availability of foreign goods is unrestricted, the elasticity of total imports in relation to real incomes will be greater than unity or equal to it. Import elasticities computed for OECD countries in the 1950s and 1960s supported this thesis, and an analysis of British imports 1955–72 showed that 11 out of 32 sectors supported the hypothesis while only three ran counter to it (Barker 164–6).

While reflecting the general trend towards increasing import penetration, the growth of this phenomenon in Britain was greater than in most other advanced economies. Panic derived estimates which suggested that in 1957 and 1972 British imports relative to GDP were higher than in France or West Germany. Not only did Britain retain a greater dependence on imported food and raw materials than these countries but exhibited a much higher income elasticity of demand for manufactured imports. The estimated income elasticity of 3.09 for manufactures for Britain, compared to 2.14 for West Germany and 2.19 for France, contained the implication that an increase in real income would draw considerably more imports into the British market than it would in the other two countries.

For imports as a whole, an increase of 1.0 per cent in income in Britain would increase imports by 1.8 per cent, while a similar increase in income would boost West German imports by 1.3 per cent and French imports by 1.6 per cent (Panic 4, 6). The reason for these differences lay in the poorer performance of British manufacturers in competition in those sectors of industry which were growing fastest in international trade. 'The most likely explanation of this seems to be that the United Kingdom appears to be suffering, basically, from a structural disequilibrium. Owing to its relative slow growth since the last war, it has adjusted much more slowly to the changing patterns of domestic and international demand than other major industrial nations. Consequently, its external trade problems are becoming more and more akin to those of a developing country, though, of course, on a much smaller scale' (Panic 11–12).

Several other studies reiterated the same criticisms in the 1970s. Moore and Rhodes demonstrated that import penetration was much greater in manufactures in Britain in the period 1969–74 compared to other industrial countries, although there had been little difference in the period 1963–70. Import penetration continued unabated through the recession of 1975 whereas previously periods of depression had halted it. Several international comparative studies of income and price elasticity for imported goods found that the British predisposition to absorb imports was greater than elsewhere. Like many others, Singh concluded that 'the evidence outlined here suggests that there are serious weaknesses on the supply side in the UK manufacturing, which make it increasingly difficult for it to meet foreign competition in either home or overseas markets' (Singh 132). One measure of comparative trade performance compared the ratio of imports (Imports/Home Demand + Exports) to exports (Exports/Home Demand + Imports). In the early 1970s there was little difference between these two indices, although there was a large difference between sectors. Metal manufactures, textiles, shipbuilding, office machinery, broadcasting equipment and electronic computers fared badly, while chemicals and some branches of engineering did well. Electrical machinery, radio, radar, and electrical capital goods performed well, as did earth moving equipment, construction and, ironically, textile machinery. By the early 1980s, however, the import index exceeded that for exports, and there were some extremely high deficits, as in textiles, leather goods and clothing, food and drink, paper and printing, and timber and furniture. Chemicals and mechanical engineering almost alone remained strong international traders.

IV

Despite the problems attending Britain's trade performance, the decline in the balance of payments surplus and its occasional disappearance has been due largely to other factors. The two major elements in this were the fall in the surplus on invisibles and the contraction in the ratio of net income from abroad to GDP (Table 12.1). Throughout the Victorian era there was a net balance on services in international trade between four and five per cent of GDP; in the present century it has fallen, for the most part, below two per cent. The reason for this has been the faster growth of the previously small debit side of the account. Invisible earnings did fall in the interwar years as a result of the general depression in international trade but recovered in the postwar revival of trade to a similar level relative to GDP as was achieved before 1914, over 7.5 per cent (*Annual Abstract of Statistics* 1984: 232). Debits on invisible trade have increased throughout the century. Before 1914 such debits were usually less than 2.5 per cent of GDP. There was a small increase in the interwar years, but since the 1950s they have risen to six or seven per cent of GDP. The growth of debits on invisible trade reflects the inevitable erosion of the comparative advantage in shipping and the finance of trade held by Britain in the nineteenth century. A much greater share of world trade is now carried in ships and aeroplanes not owned by the British. Indeed in 1982 Britain had a deficit on sea transport payments, but a net credit on civil aviation services. Overseas travel has become another sector in which Britain has a net deficit, in spite of the successful tourist industry helped in recent years by a declining exchange rate. The government services account has also registered a net deficit recently. In fact, the net credit balance on services has been largely preserved by the success of financial services which had a credit balance of £5,066 million in 1982, while services as a whole had a net credit balance of £3,844 million.

The loss of this peculiar comparative advantage, obviously dependent on a degree of supremacy in international trade services which could not realistically be sustained, should not be regarded as indicative of failure in the twentieth century. Rather it is a reminder of the curious and fragile basis of nineteenth-century prosperity. But the weakening balance of trade in invisibles has increased the strain on the balance of payments. A similar trend has also been manifest in the present century in the payments of income to and from abroad. Here too the net surplus was very large in the nineteenth century, but has decreased markedly in the twentieth century until it has almost disappeared. Prior to 1914 there was little outflow of payments from Britain on this account, only equivalent to one per cent of GDP in 1913, while the extensive investments held abroad by the British generated a considerable inward flow of interest payments. In the present century the returns from investment abroad have declined relative to GDP from 9.6 per cent in 1913 to 3.1 per cent in 1972 before rising again to 4.7 per cent in 1982. During the same period there has been an increase in debits on this account. In 1982, for example, there was a total credit of £10,991 million for interest, dividends and profits and a debit of £9,414 million, thus covering a deficit of £800 million on the government account (*Annual Abstract of Statistics* 1984: 235). The shifts in returns on foreign investment in the twentieth century reflect both the diminution of Britain's massive pre-1914 overseas investment, partly as a result of the two world wars in which assets were sold off or lost, and the changes in international finance. The growth of multinational corporations has increased both the outflow and the inflow of such dividend payments. But the decline in the large surplus on foreign investment and trade in services in the twentieth century exerted a pressure on the balance of payments which had not been present in the Victorian period. As the surplus on balance of payments diminished and occasionally disappeared so attention was directed to the export performance and the scale of imports.

The decline of British supremacy in international trade, and the related weakening of the balance of payments has had extensive ramifications. As a result of British domination of world trade and international finance in the nineteenth century many countries used sterling as their main currency in international exchange. The gold standard was really the sterling standard before 1914. Overseas governments and institutions accumulated sub-stantial balances of money which they held in the form of sterling in London. It has been estimated that such balances were worth over £93 million by 1913. This sum included £28 million held by the Indian government, and £39 million held by the government and official banks of Japan. Such sterling balances far exceeded British official gold reserves, which amounted to £35 million in 1913, but were covered by a large volume of liquid assets. Altogether about £4,180 million was held in overseas assets by the British on the eve of the First World War (Drummond 288–9). The system was secure and stable, based on fixed exchange rates of currencies which were backed by gold, and founded on the stability of the pound sterling itself secured by the substantial balance of payments surplus.

The First World War badly disrupted this finely balanced network. Britain borrowed heavily to finance the war, including the war effort of many of her allies. War loans for the latter purpose had accumulated to £2,062 million by 1919. To pay for imports of produce from the United States, the British government borrowed £207 million in New York, selling assets worth £261 million in dollars to fund the loan. At a later stage in the war, American supplies were obtained for deferred payment, and thus a government debt of £1,122 million was incurred. Even so, the deficit on current account was not large until 1918. Drummond concluded, 'If all currencies had remained exchangeable for one another and if all the war-debt contracts had been honoured, the new superstructure of debt would not have mattered. Britain would have collected with one hand and paid out with the other. Her net worth had been depleted, but not by much – indeed, by less than the export surplus of a single pre-war year. Most of the assets had survived, and in the 1920s these provided an income that helped to keep Britain's current account in surplus' (Drummond 293).

But the war had shifted the balance of financial power, removing the long held supremacy of the pound over all other currencies as the dollar, backed by the immense and growing economic power of the United States, became increasingly acceptable and desirable to hold. The emergence of an alterna-tive currency to the pound increased the volatility of the sterling balances which became liable to conversion into whichever currency or financial centre offered the highest rate of interest. A portent of future difficulties appeared in 1927 when France, having built up a large accumulated holding of sterling, began systematically to convert those holdings into gold. By the end of the 1920s, sterling balances were worth considerably more than British reserves, the difference standing at £275 million to £146 million at the end of 1929. It was thus increasingly difficult to retain sterling balances in London and increasingly important to do so.

The international financial system remained fragile and unstable from the

Peace of Versailles to the successive bank crashes at the end of the 1920s which heralded the great depression. The final undermining of the position of sterling was delayed until 1931 and the collapse of several economies in Central Europe which owed liquid assets to Britain. Sterling balances were withdrawn by some countries in order to pay debts to the United States, while other withdrawals were occasioned by the attraction of apparently safer currencies like the dollar and the franc. Sterling holdings were reduced by £293 million in 1931 and Britain had to suspend the sale of gold at a fixed price. The era of the gold standard and the sterling standard thus ended.

A lower level of overseas investment in the 1920s, compared to the pre-war years, continued the run down of overseas assets. In the 1930s there were many fewer new issues for foreign investment, and the fact that repayments exceeded new issues brought a net inflow on the capital account. Furthermore, there were in that troubled decade some defaults on loans, some loans paid up and not renewed, and a fall in the rate of interest, all of which reduced the income generated from property investments abroad. But within the new protected sphere of imperial preference sterling balances continued to grow. Indeed they increased from £441 million in 1931 to £808 million by 1937. But the threat of war brought a substantial withdrawal of these balances, cutting them to £542 million by the middle of 1939. By the beginning of the Second World War reserves were higher than in 1914 but were supported by less in liquid assets. Reserves were falling and there remained a substantial sterling balance debt. The early years of the war obliged Britain to draw very heavily on these reserves, which fell from £305 million in the middle of 1939 to £70 million by 1941. In addition there was a large sale of dollar assets. Lend Lease from the United States was essential for the continuation of the war. Furthermore, supplies from the imperial countries during the war increased the sterling debt balance by £2,879 million. Reserves were run down further, overseas assets were reduced, and in total the loss of external assets in the war reached £4,198 million. With the loss of so many external illiquid assets went most of the property income from abroad which had, for so long, been important to the British balance of payments. While the war generated an addition to the government debt to other countries worth £650 million, postwar reconstruction required further large loans. The United States lent $3,750 million and Canada lent $1,250 million, while South Africa provided £80 million in gold. In addition, Britain required a full share of Marshall Aid.

The growth of the sterling balances in the war from £540 million to £3,700 million, a liability to pay which far exceeded Britain's reserves, created an obvious problem in the postwar period. Three main sources of difficulty have been identified, pressure on reserves occasioned by the withdrawal of sterling from London, speculation against the pound in expectation of a change in the rate of exchange, and the actions of government in response to these threats. Until the devaluation of the pound in 1967, government policy preference was always to take whatever measures were needed to protect the exchange rate. One implication of this was that priority had to be given to building up reserves, as through the export drive of the later 1940s, with a view to strengthening the balance of payments as much as possible. When there were large withdrawals of sterling balances, as in 1952 by Australia and by India in 1957, or when there were speculative runs against the pound the government responded by deflating the domestic economy even when the balance of payments was securely in credit. Thus the home economy was made to respond to economic events which bore no direct relationship to it, as for example when sterling balances were withdrawn because a sterling using country had a trade deficit with another country. This became more and more likely as the trading pattern of Britain diverged increasingly from that of the other sterling area countries. Between 1950–65 the share of British imports obtained from other sterling area countries fell from 40–31 per cent of the total while the share of Britain's exports to them fell from 51 to 38 per cent. In spite of this, the sterling balances remained fairly constant from the end of the war until the mid 1960s at aboaut £3,500 million. Large scale reductions in holdings, as by India and Pakistan, were made up by others, especially oil producing states like Kuwait.

The defence of the fixed exchange rate was only partly occasioned by the problem of the sterling debt. In part it represented an attempt to maintain the role of sterling as a major reserve currency, and was a manifestation of the internationalist outlook of the financial community of the City. Similarly it underlay the virulent opposition of the City to devaluation of the pound on the grounds that the loss of confidence thus engendered would cause a massive outflow of sterling holdings which could not be covered by existing reserves. To prevent withdrawals of such holdings by central banks, Britain obtained in 1968 a stand-by credit from the major non-sterling central banks which could be called upon in the event of withdrawals of sterling balances. Further, Britain guaranteed the dollar value of 90 per cent of the official reserves of overseas sterling area countries. By making these reserves effectively inflation-proof, it was hoped to prevent withdrawals and thereby limit financial fluctuations.

Through the 1970s the problem of sterling balances remained as official reserves of gold and foreign currency stayed well short of the total potential claims upon them. Sterling balances increased after the Basle credit agreement of 1968, and continued to grow until 1974. From 1972 the pound was allowed to float, within prescribed limits, in the hope that this would offset any speculative pressure as well as to protect the expansionary strategy of the current government. The exchange rate value of the pound continued to move down. This proved to be expensive since the 1968 guarantee of sterling holdings, which had been renewed annually, was replaced in 1973 by unilaterally agreed guarantees with the overseas sterling countries. The rising oil revenues generated by OPEC as a result of the massive price rise brought a rush of short-term funds into sterling in 1973–74. This was followed by an equally dramatic outflow in 1975–76 as the exchange rate of the pound continued to fall. Substantial and available OPEC funds allowed the government to borrow to protect both the exchange rate and the domestic economy from the effects of the rise in oil prices. But there was a further sharp drop in the value of sterling in 1976, aided if not caused by domestic inflation, and a sharp fall in sterling balances. In response to the liquidity crisis, the government negotiated a loan of record dimension from the International Monetary Fund, $3.9 billion. The conditions on which the loan was made available included the imposition of a severely deflationary package of policy measures on the British economy. Confidence was restored so swiftly that there was another increase in sterling balances in 1977, funds returning to London in anticipation of high interest rates. The external debt thus continued to increase, and efforts to convert short-term holdings into medium or long-term investments were unsuccessful. The basic problem thus remains. While a managed float of the currency provides the financial system with a greater degree of short-term flexibility than was possible with fixed exchange rates, the volatility of short-term capital movements in the 1970s, especially oil revenues, has created another source of instability. The sterling balances remain as a tangible and potent reminder of the inherent conflict between the interests of international finance, including the City of London, and the domestic economy as a whole and the industrial exporting sector in particular.

V

The functional relationship between economic growth and international transactions continues to be the subject of considerable debate, especially the causal direction of influence. There is a popular and respected version of the export-led growth thesis, applicable to mature economies, as expounded by Lamfalussy and Beckerman. Both have emphasized the reciprocal relationship between the rate of growth of exports and the growth of labour productivity. The former is regarded as the prime determinant of growth, but the latter has feedback effects allowing the achievement of greater efficiency and price competitiveness to give additional help to exports. In both versions the essential determinant of change is the relative competitiveness in prices. In the Lamfalussy model, export growth is sufficient although not necessary to generate sustained per capita growth in output. Beckerman argued that export growth was necessary to generate the requisite improvements in both productivity and competitiveness. Similarly, Kaldor advanced the hypothesis that exports are principally concentrated in sectors with a high productivity potential, as compared to the home market which provides an outlet for low productivity sectors like services and public utilities. Stressing the role of exports in generating growth implies that slow productivity growth, low investment, slow expansion of employment, and slow output growth, are all the result of demand limited by the inability to secure export markets (Stafford 90). Britain would thus represent a malfunctioning of the export-led growth stimulus. British concentration on the production of commodities for which world demand was not growing imposed a limit on effective demand and resulted in a poor export and growth performance.

It is, of course, possible to argue the other way, from productivity to export success. This hypothesis seems rather more plausible in the context of industries found in all the advanced industrial economies such as motor car manufacture, consumer durables based on electrical engineering and electronics, and even textiles. There can be little doubt that for a relatively small economy the export market is essential for any British industry. In an economy as open as Britain, the problem of the causal relationship between exports and productivity may appear rather academic. Britain has faced both problems in the twentieth century, limitation of export markets because of specialization in declining products and competitive difficulties because of low productivity with high costs resulting in high relative prices. Greater success has been achieved in structural changes to produce an appropriate range of products for international trade between advanced economies. British industry has been less successful in competing in those sectors because of high costs, poor quality, and ineffective marketing.

In spite of the widespread criticism of British trade and payments performance the latter has remained in surplus for most of the twentieth century. Considering the massive loss of foreign assets in the two world wars, 15 per cent of the total during the first and 28 per cent during the second, and the enormous foreign debt incurred at the same time, the balance of payments remains remarkably strong. Several of the problems which have emerged in the present century could not have been realistically avoided, such as the growth in invisible debits and the decline in the net income from overseas. Furthermore, since the late 1940s Britain has managed to restructure a trade pattern which was established in the peculiar circumstances of Victorian development and which became increasingly inappropriate and unsustainable in a twentieth-century context.

The criticism and anxiety about trade performance in recent decades has been concerned with the high propensity to import exhibited by the British economy since the 1950s. Export success generated growth throughout the economy but thereby drew in a greater value of imports and induced a deterioration in the balance of payments. It has been estimated that in periods of economic expansion the rate of growth of exports averaged 4.9 per cent annually while the rate of growth of imports averaged 7.9 per cent. Conversely in periods of relative stagnation the equivalent growth rates were 2.7 per cent for exports and 1.3 per cent for imports (Eltis 1969: 204). Thirlwall has supported this by illustrating the low elasticity of exports as against imports in relation to income. In a study of 113 industrial groups, he found that in 30 sectors Britain had an import elasticity over two between 1963–74. Only 11 sectors had so great an export elasticity and they were found in relatively insignificant industries (Thirlwall 1978: 30–1).

Thus it was feared that even an improvement in export performance would cause the balance of payments to deteriorate, and this certainly appeared to be justified by the experience of the 1950s and 1960s when the very rapid growth of GDP coincided with a weakening balance of payments position. One suggested solution to this dilemma has been import control. This has traditionally been rejected for fear of retaliation and a trade war. But the practicality of such a step is doubtful especially since British membership of the EEC precludes the imposition of tariffs against fellow members. The EEC is, of course, a major source of imports. A simpler means of controlling imports is to deflate the domestic economy. During the past decade a reduced rate of growth in GDP has coincided with a considerable improvement in the balance of payments. But deflation does not guarantee the avoidance of payments problems in future. Much of the improvement in the export of goods ratio since the early 1970s has been due to the windfall of oil which contributed 13.6 per cent of exports in 1980. Had fuel oil sales grown at the same rate as the rest of exports during the previous decade, the actual 1980 surplus on balance of payments of almost three billion pounds would have become a deficit of over two billion pounds. Security of the balance of payments surplus in future is likely to depend very much on the performance of export industries.

13

Government policy and the economy

I

Perhaps the single most outstanding phenomenon of twentieth-century economic change throughout the world has been the growth of the role of government. It is, of course, true that governments played an important part in earlier development even in free market economies like Britain. The requirements of British governments in the eighteenth century for funds to prosecute many costly wars was a major factor in the creation and growth of the London financial market. Indeed war, including the national debt which was primarily incurred by borrowing for war, and related administrative costs comprised 82 per cent of public expenditure at the end of the eighteenth century. By the eve of the First World War such obligations still amounted to almost half of all public expenditure. In the nineteenth century, public expenditure grew more slowly than national income. Even so, some of the developments which have become major trends in the twentieth century were emerging in the growth and distribution of public expenditure in the Victorian period. Spending increased from £1.2 per capita in 1790 to £5.5 by 1910, while the share of public expenditure accounted for by national debt payments fell from 39 per cent to 7 per cent. Conversely the share of spending on social, economic and environmental services rose from 18 per cent to over half the total expenditure (Veverka 119).

In the present century public spending has increased at a faster rate than the national income so that the ratio of public expenditure to GNP has increased from only 12 per cent in 1910 to a peak of 52 per cent in 1946. This reflects, of course, the massive increase in wartime spending in both world wars and the subsequent decline with the resumption of peace. By 1956 public spending had been reduced to 36 per cent of GNP, still higher than in the interwar years when it averaged a little over 25 per cent. But during the past three decades the trend has been sharply upwards, reaching 45.6 per cent by 1979. Nor has this pattern been peculiar to Britain. The British public expenditure ratio and the rate of growth of public expenditure during the

234

1960s and 1970s were both only slightly above the average rates for all OECD countries. By 1980, the public expenditure ratio of Britain was substantially below that of Sweden, Luxemburg, the Netherlands, Belgium and Denmark, as well as being lower than that of France, West Germany and Italy (Heald 30–1). The large increase in public spending in the twentieth century, both in absolute figures and relative to GNP, has been accompanied by substantial changes in the distribution of that spending. The greatest increase has been generated by the various forms of social spending.

The principal sources of government income required to finance this expenditure came from income tax, expenditure tax and the rates, although national insurance contributions and health contributions made up an increasing share in the course of the century. The ratio of government receipts to GNP rose as an obvious response to increasing spending. In 1900 this ratio stood at 8.8 per cent, but increased to 38.5 per cent by 1951. Between 1960 and 1980 taxation relative to GDP increased from 30.3 per cent to 40.4 per cent, much of this increase coming in the latter part of the 1960s. But within an international context the rate of taxaton and its increase was little greater than the OECD average. As in the case of public expenditure, Britain's tax ratio was lower than that of most of its partners in the EEC, including West Germany and France.

Not only has taxation increased faster than national income in the twentieth century, but there have been substantial shifts in the composition of government income. At the beginning of the century over 75 per cent of government receipts came from rates and expenditure tax. This share fell steadily through the century while income tax increased considerably as did national insurance and health contributions. Since the Second World War government revenue has greatly increased. Personal income tax and expenditure taxes have contributed a falling share necessitating a large increase in revenue from other sources. Social service contributions have increased substantially and payroll and corporation taxes introduced in the 1960s have made an important contribution. Compared to the composition of government income in the OECD countries as a whole, Britain takes relatively more in property tax, income tax and from payroll and corporate income but relatively less in tax on goods and services, and much less in the form of social service contributions (Heald 284). In the expansive 1950s and 1960s increased spending on services like health and education appeared to be an integral part of a benign cycle of expansion and increased welfare. In the past decade, public spending has been a subject of economic debate and political conflict as it has exceeded government revenue from which it was hitherto funded, in most of Western Europe as well as in Britain. Public sector borrowing, to make up the difference between spending and revenue, amounted to 10.7 per cent of GNP by 1975. Since then successive governments have sought to reduce both the borrowing and the deficit as a major aim of policy. This has been made difficult by the fact that much government spending is demand led as more people survive to the age of retirement and well beyond it and draw their pensions. Social security growth boomed in the 1970s with the increase in eligible claimants such as one-parent families, single parents, divorced women, and the growing number of the unemployed. The dependence created by economic stagnation inexorably increased the demand for such social services. Since they were protected by statute such transfer payments were hard for government to control. By the 1970s the long-accepted growth in public spending had become a major problem for public policy.

II

The considerable growth of public expenditure in the twentieth century does not, of course, mark the limit of government involvement in economic affairs which has become increasingly pervasive as the century has progressed. Nor indeed is it a new development. But prior to 1914 the role of government in Britain as far as economic matters were concerned was restricted to the maintenance of social and political stability at home, and an openness to trade appropriate to a major international and colonial power. In the nineteenth century these requirements were met by free trade, the maintenance of the gold standard as the basis for international financial stability, and a minimum amount of public spending. Fundamental to these requirements was a balanced budget at the lowest possible level of public expenditure.

The international orientation of the City and the most influential bodies of opinion in official circles has kept the commitment to maintaining the exchange rate at the centre of government policy for most of the present century. The First World War severely disrupted the patterns of trade and orderly international finance of the Victorian period. It also generated a massive increase in government spending and debt together with a doubling of the money supply. The economic policies established after the war were designed to restore the 'normalcy' of the prewar period. Central to that concern was a perceived need to return to the gold standard at the prewar parity to restore the keystone of the international financial system. The policy was formulated by the Cunliffe Committee established by the government to advise on economic recovery. It was a body heavily weighted in favour of international banking interests. So too was the Bank of England, itself greatly influential on policy matters. No less than 15 of the 26 members on the ruling court of the Bank were representatives of overseas banking interests, while a further five were connected with shipping and insurance in the mid 1920s. In sharp contrast, there was little representation of manufacturing interests (Pollard 1970: 13–14). The Bank of England had close links with the Treasury, where government economic policy tends to be formed, and their mutual inclination in the 1920s was to secure the gold standard and exchange rate as a means to a stable environment for international finance. Pollard, amongst others, has been highly critical of the overwhelming influence on policy possessed by a narrow sectional interest group. 'Here was a relic of bygone centuries, ages away from even the Northcote-Trevelyan reforms; a self-appointed corporation, recruiting its members neither by popular democratic election nor by ability and qualification, but by family descent and "interest" . . . The forcing through of the Cunliffe financial policy which dominated Britain in 1920–31 was largely due to the power and "expert" advice of the Bank of England which, in turn, depended and fed on the power of the City' (Pollard 1970: 25).

Certainly the decision to return to gold at the prewar parity and the attainment of that goal in 1925 had the strong approval of the City. It gave no assistance to exporters since it effectively overvalued the pound and hence exports by 10 per cent. Furthermore, high interest rates were essential to the policy both for the establishment of the old parity level and in order to persuade holders of short-term sterling debts to convert them into long-term assets. Even after the re-establishment of the gold standard interest rates had to be kept high to defend the exchange rate. Even so, the Wall Street crash and subsequent years of international financial disruption and economic depression drained the gold and currency reserves from London. It was an outflow which could not be staunched by raising the interest rate. Eventually, the severe loss of reserves as many European institutions collapsed and called in their outstanding debts forced Britain off the gold standard in 1931 and thence compelled the government to devalue the pound. The cheap money policy pursued in the 1930s was consistent with the stabilization of the exchange rate. The low rate of interest kept short-term funds out of London, previously attracted by the high interest rate, which by virtue of their volatility threatened the gold reserves and hence the exchange rate of the pound. The cheap money policy could only be sustained if the economy was protected from externally generated fluctuations and, to that end, the Exchange Equilisation Account was established in 1932. A substantial holding of gold, effectively sterilized from international credit, was thus provided to counter pressures applied against the sterling rate of exchange.

In spite of the prominence given to the advance of Keynesian economics and Beveridge's advocacy of full employment, the government policy after 1945 was primarily concerned with the balance of payments and the maintenance of the exchange rate. Indeed the traditional priorities of the City and the Treasury remained at the heart of policy from the 1920s until the floating of sterling in June 1972. In the 1920s emphasis on exchange rate policy reflected an attempt to recreate the international financial conditions which had proved so rewarding before 1914. In the 1930s and again after the Second World War, the immediate concern was related to the deterioration in the balance of payments. This was especially urgent after the war. The accumulation of sterling balances in London during the war, the growth of the national debt to finance the war, and the loss of trade incurred while fighting the war, all contributed to weaken the pound. So great was this that an immediate export drive to build up the reserves and restore some semblance of balance to Britain's international payments was imperative. The loan of five billion dollars from Canada and the United States, which was also imperative to cover the cost of imported raw materials needed to start the export drive, carried an obligation to restore the pound to full con-· vertibility against the dollar within a year, by July 1947. When that obligation was met, there was a massive run on the pound in favour of the extremely scarce dollar, with the result that British reserves were cut by 25 per cent in a year. The weakness of the reserves, the possibility that the pound or some other major currency might be revalued, and the growing deficit on trade which the other sterling countries accumulated against the dollar, created an environment from the late 1940s onwards in which speculative pressure against the pound was always a possibility and often was a reality. An early success of such pressure was the devaluation of 1949. When full convertibility was eventually secured in 1958, the defence of the exchange rate became more difficult, even though successive governments were fully committed to it in order to protect the advantages of sterling's role as a major reserve currency. But the reserves were never large enough to prevent speculative pressure, indeed it may be that no fund would have been large enough to do so. When full convertibility was restored and direct control by the Treasury withdrawn, the vulnerability of the exchange rate to such speculation, and the large debt in liquid assets owed to holders of sterling, meant that the interest rate had to be kept at a level higher than the rate in other financial centres in order to retain the funds. The growth of a large volume of liquid assets, held in private hands throughout the world, increased the possibility of destabilizing speculation and reduced the power of the financial authorities to resist effectively. In the event, the exchange rate of sterling was held at $2.80 from 1949 until 1967 when it was again devalued, the longest period in the century for which it remained unchanged. This could only be achieved, given the weakness of the reserve position and the frequency and severity of speculation, by putting it at the very top of policy priorities.

Speculative pressure could stem from several different causes. Weakness of the British balance of payments threatening a devaluation of the pound was one possibility, but the upward revaluation of another currency or its possibility could lead a flight from sterling, and further pressure could come simply from the trading weakness of other sterling countries against the dollar. Whatever the source of the pressure, the government response had to take the form of improving the balance of payments to strengthen reserves and thus signal that there was no need to revalue. The easiest and quickest way to achieve this was to reduce imports by deflating the economy and cutting consumer spending. This was usually achieved by the implementation of a deflationary fiscal package, typically pushing up purchase tax on consumer goods, imposing higher purchase restrictions or tightening those in force and reducing bank credit by means of an increase in the bank rate. Cuts in capital investment in nationalized industries were often part of this kind of deflation. As the crisis passed, and speculative pressure temporarily dissipated, the impositions of the deflationary policy package were removed or reversed to induce a modest reflation. Together this pattern of alternate deflation and reflation gained the title of the stop-go cycle and marked the ups and downs of the economy in the 1950s and 1960s. In spite of this, with the greatest reluctance and against the wishes of the City of London, the government further devalued the pound to $2.40 in 1967. It was accompanied by a severe deflationary package, bank rate increasing to a record level, increases in income tax, and cuts in public expenditure in the face of an accumulated foreign debt of £1.5 billion. Additional pressure on international exchange rates, including speculation against the dollar, led to the eventual abandonment of fixed exchange rates in 1972. Since then, the pound has been allowed to float and its exchange value has drifted gently downwards, including a sharp drop in 1976. The floating of the pound has not, as yet, brought the rate of exchange to a position of long-term equilibrium. But the continuing decline of the exchange rate during the past decade increased the price of imported goods and this, in turn, fuelled wage demands and other inflationary pressures. The rapid increase in inflation from the early 1970s has itself contributed to the decline in the exchange rate. While balance of payments problems have apparently fallen from representing the first priority of policy makers since the early 1970s, the overwhelming concern with inflation was very much part of the traditional preoccupation of twentieth century British governments.

The subjection of the economy to the effects of maintaining the rate of exchange has been widely criticized. 'It would appear that the meaning of British balance of payments policies during the two postwar decades was to maintain the sterling parity as a symbol of her former position in international monetary relations, and that the heavy weight assigned to the interest rate mechanism at the expense of the real sector of the economy was a reflection of the traditional sentiment of, or was actively intended to affirm, the superiority of finance over industry' (Fausten 151). In fact the orientation of policy in the 1950s and 1960s was no different from the long-term emphasis, reflecting the primacy of City interests and the close links in personnel and thought between the City and the Treasury. Just as the 1920s were primarily occupied in restoring sterling's international role the subsequent decades were primarily devoted to defending it in the face of a weakening balance of payments, a problem not encountered before 1914. The prosperity of the City was certainly bound to the strength of sterling in international markets. Ironically, since the early 1970s, the balance of payments has much improved by virtue of oil exports and Eurodollar business. So the City has continued to flourish despite the continued fall in the exchange rate of the pound and the continued exigencies of the domestic economy.

III

The maintenance of the fixed exchange rate had important and extensive effects on the economy. In fact, this was one facet of a dual policy designed to achieve stability of price in markets at home and abroad. Inflation was a major threat, at least it was perceived as such, to the smooth working of markets. Together with the aim of restoring the gold standard after the First World War, the government committed itself to balance the budget, to reduce the postwar inflation, and to restore confidence in the international economy. A heavy dose of deflationary pressure was applied by an increase in the bank rate, a reduction in the volume of money in circulation, an increase in taxation, and a sharp cut in government spending, the latter by means of the renowned Geddes Axe.

Fear of inflation has never disappeared from official circles at any time since the First World War and the Treasury has maintained a strong preference for deflation as a state in which the economy can be best controlled. It is also an environment in which the exchange rate and balance of payments can best be protected. Fiscal and monetary controls, restraint on public spending, a propensity to balanced budgets, and high interest rates have been common features of such deflationary pressure. Even in the interwar years such restrictions were applied. In an attempt to prevent the abandonment of the gold standard in 1931, the government made drastic cuts in public spending, including the reduction of the salaries of public employees, cut transfer benefits, and increased direct and indirect taxation. The hostility of the Treasury towards public spending as a means to reducing unemployment was based on the fear that such expenditure would be inflationary, especially if such spending was financed by government borrowing. With some prescience, the Permanent Secretary to the Treasury argued: 'If once expenditure can be incurred without the unpleasant necessity of imposing taxation to cover it, it would be impossible for the Chancellor of the Exchequer or the House of Commons to control public expenditure, especially if borrowing for current expenditure was advocated as the road to prosperity . . . Whatever may be thought by people outside, members of the House of Commons will realise how impossible it would be once we had abandoned the principle of paying our way to stop a rising tide of expenditure. Within a year or two (i.e. very near the next General Election) there would be the sort of situation we had in 1931, i.e. the need for new cuts and new taxes' (Sir Richard Hopkins; quoted in Middleton 1982: 59–60). Furthermore, as a Treasury report observed, any large scale borrowing by the government in the financial markets might generate apprehension as to the state of the national finances and thus oblige the Bank of England to keep interest rates at a high level (Peden 1984: 177–8). In fact the Treasury favoured the reduction of interest rates in the 1930s not so much to generate reflationary economic activity as to reduce the interest payments on the national debt accumulated in the First World War.

The strong deflationary instincts of the Treasury remained after the second major war of the century. Just as the maintenance of the exchange rate depended on the balance of payments, so the state of that balance could be tipped adversely by inflation. In view of the excess demand which existed at the end of the war, as a result of unspent wartime earnings, general shortages, and the further starvation of the home market in the 1940s export drive, inflation was a real threat. There was also the precedent of the post-war inflation in 1919. Full employment in the 1950s and 1960s promised more inflation although it was not until the following decade that the gravest fears were realised. Inflation in the 1950s and 1960s was modest, except for the effect of the Korean War in 1950–51 which greatly increased defence spending. Much like the other industrial economies, British inflation averaged 2.4 per cent between 1952–61 and 3.8 per cent between 1961–69. Thereafter the rate of inflation accelerated sharply upwards, averaging 8.0 per cent between 1969–73 and 15.6 per cent during 1973–79 (Allsopp 73, 79). While the British rate of inflation was close to the OECD average in the 1950s and 1960s, during the 1970s it moved well above that average and by the later years of the decade was exceeded only by that of Italy and Spain.

The main concern of government in the 1950s and 1960s, when productive resources were fully utilized, was to restrain the pressure of demand in order to prevent inflation caused by excess demand driving up prices. Demand was managed by adjusting consumers' expenditure through fiscal and monetary controls to keep demand steady and within the capacity of the supply side of the economy. Since the level of fluctuations was small there was no serious threat either from unemployment or destabilization until the 1970s (Dow 392, Blackaby 635). Nor was there any deficit spending on the public account. There was a substantial surplus on current account in the 1950s and 1960s, although capital expenditure for long-term projects did sustain a public sector borrowing requirement of 5–10 per cent of government expenditure (Tomlinson 1981b: 388). Thus it was possible, in these two decades, to reconcile full employment with low inflation and protect the exchange rate. The main deficiency of the policy has generally been regarded as its effect on investment. Frequent adjustments to demand conditions did not encourage the long-term view required for investment planning by the private sector. Further, as Pollard has argued, each deflationary package cut productive capacity by reducing capital expenditure or inhibiting the commissioning of new expenditure. Thus each reflationary phase was characterized by a shortage of productive capacity which boosted imports and prompted the next deflation (Pollard 1984: 48–50).

The escalating inflation of the 1970s appeared to realise the fears and justify the deflationary inclinations of the Treasury and the City. In part, the growth in inflation could be attributed to the abandonment of fixed exchange rates. Until the adoption of flexible rates in the early 1970s, European inflation moved in line with that in the United States as countries adjusted their domestic policies in order to maintain parity with the dollar. The American rate of inflation thus set the level for the rest of the advanced economies. When that restraint was removed by allowing exchange rates to float there was a much wider variety of inflation between countries than hitherto. A further traditional restraint which was abandoned in the 1970s was the balanced budget or rather the extent to which public spending should be balanced by government income. The Public Sector Borrowing Requirement was, in part, demand determined since government obligations to make social security payments increased under deflationary pressure as unemployment was pushed up and tax revenue fell. Both target growth rates for money supply and PSBR were exceeded in the severe deflation of the early 1980s (Greenaway/Shaw 375). Increased claims on the public purse for state pensions further increased spending in the 1970s. A further contributing factor to the inflation was the increasing growth of money supply, again a phenomenon common to much of Western Europe in the past decade. In part this may have been an attempt by governments to revive the growth rates of earlier decades and, by overestimating the amount of unused productive capacity, thereby creating inflation. Further, any increase in the PSBR will automatically increase the money supply unless some alternative arrangement is made to provide compensatory funds for that debt. Finally, the oil price increase of the 1970s added further to the pressure of inflation throughout the advanced industrial nations.

The response of the authorities to growing inflation was the traditional severe deflation, initiated by the Labour administration in the mid 1970s and continued by their Conservative successors after 1979. What has fashionably been portrayed as a radical new departure was, in fact, the assertion of a long-established strategy. The deflationary pressure encompassed cuts in public expenditure, increased taxation, and the usual range of fiscal and monetary controls. The severity of the deflation was reflected in the massive increase in the level of uncmployment on a scale unprecedented since the 1930s. While unemployment had averaged 600,000 per annum in the later 1960s, the one million mark was passed in 1975 and by 1983 it passed three million and did not include another million not entitled to benefit but possibly willing to work.

The attraction of policies able to halt the inflationary spiral and reduce the rate of inflation, and this was successfully achieved in the early 1980s, by means of market forces was great to neoclassical economists and political conservatives. The Treasury View had always given a major role to free market forces once the government had achieved price stability internally and internationally. By the later 1970s a strategy which could reduce inflation and maintain stable prices by means of monetary supply control was attractive because it sidestepped the problem of controlling incomes. In the event, both the money supply and the PSBR were very difficult to control and the real means by which inflation was reduced was the old fashioned deflationary package of suitable severity.

One effect of high growth rates and full employment in the 1950s and 1960s was to provide labour with a bargaining strength far greater than ever before. Fully exploiting that power, trade unions were able to force up wage ratcs. Some scholars have argued that this inflationary pressure was implicit in changes in the labour market which occurred before the First World War. From the 1890s labour costs rose faster than productivity and prices also moved upwards. There emerged a relative wage and price movement in which workers obtained the benefits of productivity increase through growth in money wages rather than in a fall in the price of goods produced (Cornwall 1983: 153). The power of organized labour, during full employment after the Second World War, enabled wage gains to be negotiated both on the basis of comparison between sectors and against the cost of living index. Shortages of labour in certain industries or regions, national wage bargaining, the increasing complexity of production which enabled a small group to stop an entire industry by going on strike, and the alternating phases of excess and shortage of demand in the stop-go cycle, all facilitated cost-push inflation. Given the buoyant market for most products in the 1950s and 1960s, firms and industries often found it expedient to succumb to wage demands in order to avoid any disruption of production through a strike, and maintained their profit margins by adding on the additional production cost to the selling price. Britain was especially susceptible to this type of pressure because industry was labour intensive, extreme specialization of function was usually matched by a diversity of different unions, and the long history of bitter labour relations left a legacy of mistrust and old scores to settle. As the rate of inflation accelerated, so wage claims increased to keep ahead of the cost of living and to maintain differentials over other groups or achieve comparability with them.

Attempts were made to control the inflationary pressure of wage increase from the Second World War until the late 1970s. The first attempt to control incomes, apart from the controls imposed from 1948–50, was a six months pay pause in the public sector introduced in 1961. During the following two decades there were a succession of similar attempts at restraint. They included compulsory and voluntary policies, short-term freezes on pay increases, the establishment of norms for pay increases, and the social contract agreed between the government and the trade unions in the mid 1970s. The degree of success in all these policies was confined largely to the very short run. In 1966–7 the six months freeze on wage increases, followed by a further six months of limited exceptional increases, was successful. But the return to a voluntary norm-based policy in 1967 brought a return to wage inflation fuelled by the attempts of workers to catch up ground lost during the period of restraint. Several features of the labour market created dissatisfaction with incomes policies. The use of productivity increase to justify wage increases proved difficult to interpret in a way which could be universally accepted. Attempts to help the low paid workers through incomes policies incurred the resentment of skilled workers as differentials were reduced. Obvious loopholes, such as increased payment in the form of fringe benefits, similarly created resentment and suspicion. Private sector and public sector workers each felt themselves treated relatively badly, the former because of the insecurity of their employment, the latter because of their relatively low pay. Most incomes policies set targets which were exceeded by a substantial margin, and pay norms became regarded as minimum increase levels. The voluntary restraint under the social contract of 1974–5 generated average increases in earnings of 25 per cent, while the 1977–8 voluntary agreement for a 10 per cent limit plus productivity agreements brought average increases of 19.0 per cent. The 1978–9 agreement established a voluntary norm of five per cent, but realised average increases of 12 per cent. The failure of this last policy, and the winter of industrial disruption which accompanied its failure, played a significant part in bringing the government down in 1979.

The British experience of incomes policies in the 1960s and 1970s was undoubtedly that they produced neither industrial peace nor industrial growth, and that they were quite ineffectual in controlling inflation. Hence the strong attraction of a policy package which could control inflation without relying on the powerful institutions of the economy such as the trade unions. Unfortunately this alternative, severe deflation, produced a different but equally unhappy effect in large scale unemployment.

IV

Apart from the balance of payments and the need to balance deflation against inflationary forces, the main problem that has intruded into government policy in the present century has been unemployment. This had been discussed and identified as a 'social problem' resulting from the deficiencies of the market system by Victorian economists (Winch). It had also become a charge on central government through the introduction of unemployment insurance in 1911 and its extension by the 1920s to most manual workers. As the level of unemployment remained high through the 1920s, so central government was increasingly involved in providing financial assistance. By 1930–1, this amounted to £14.9 million in direct payments and a further £56.7 million in loans. From the perspective of the Treasury, with its commitment to deflation, unemployment represented a source of financial drain on precious reserves. The Treasury pointed out to the Royal Commission on Unemployment Insurance in 1931 that the kind of expenditure proposed would upset the equilibrium of the budget on the basis of existing taxation (Tomlinson 1981a: 72). The same kind of threat was perceived in the activities of the Unemployment Grants Committee whose remit, from 1920 on, was to allocate funds from the Exchequer to public authorities to help finance public works schemes. In practice this too was extremely limited (Hancock). But the increase of financial obligations, which threatened to increase substantially and undermine the principal aims of the Treasury policy, led to the formulation of a list of specific objections to the expenditure on unemployment.

The argument was formulated in the 1920s on three main grounds. Firstly, the essence of the high level of unemployment lay in the fact that British goods were too expensive to compete effectively in overseas markets. This, in turn, was due to high costs especially labour costs. Thus the solution to both unemployment and the depression in the export industries lay in reducing wage rates. Secondly, the Treasury argued that if the government assumed responsibility for all economic problems it would lead to a loss of initiative and responsibility amongst the people. Finally, the argument postulated that any increase in government spending to increase employment, either by taxation or borrowing, would simply draw resources and employment from the private sector, thus transferring the unemployment rather than reducing it (Skidelsky 71–2). Implicit in this view of employment was the notion of a wage fund, a finite sum available to labour which could not be augmented by government action. Apart from these arguments of principle, the Treasury was worried that any increase in government spending to help reduce unemployment would interfere with their other, and more important, policies. Especially, it was argued, state borrowing would push up the interest rate increasing charges on the national debt and making it more difficult for industry to invest for recovery.

The official government view that developed in the interwar years was unsympathetic to public spending increases as an antidote to unemployment. Rather it envisaged a solution in terms of wage cuts. A similar line of argument has recently been advanced by two historians, developing the thesis that the relatively high ratio of unemployment benefit to wages allowed, even induced, workers to opt for unemployment to extend their search for a better paid job rather than take a poorly paid one. This effect, they argued, increased the level of unemployment from five to eight per cent (Benjamin/Kochin 468). Thus the unemployed in the 1930s constituted 'largely a volunteer army'. The logic of this analysis is that a reduction in unemployment benefits, apart from giving relief to the Exchequer, would have increased employment. It is hard to imagine that such an attractive thesis would have gone unnoticed by the Treasury had it been remotely feasible. In fact, the Benjamin/Kochin thesis has received much scholarly attention, most highly critical, and most of its statistical foundations have been undermined (Ormerod/Worswick).

In spite of Treasury reluctance, public spending did create some jobs in the 1930s, about half a million through public works at an estimated 4,000 jobs per million pounds and a multiplier effect of 1.5 (Glynn/Howells 34). But the enormity of the unemployment problem is indicated by the estimate that an expenditure of £532 million would have been needed in 1932 to provide work for the 2.8 million unemployed, a sum which represented about half the total level of current public authority spending (Glynn/Howells 42). The debate as to the potential effectiveness of government spending is by no means resolved. While Thomas derived modest multiplier effects which suggested a limited effectiveness for public spending boosts for employment, Hatton has produced estimates suggesting that a much greater potential increase in jobs would have been possible (T. Thomas; Hatton 1982: 23).

Political considerations prevailed and it was, as usual, the growth of defence spending, which increased threefold between 1935–8, which provided a major stimulus to employment. Rearmament created one million jobs and thus offset further reductions in employment. Certainly without this growth in state spending, and had the budget of 1938 been balanced, unemployment would have been substantially greater than it was. Further, the rearmament boom helped the most depressed industries and regions providing an additional 39,000 jobs in iron and steel and 30,700 in coal mining. Shipbuilding and engineering also benefitted, and the bulk of these new jobs were located in Wales, the South West, the midlands and, more modestly, in central Scotland, and north east England. From this emerged the conclusion that fiscal policy could have been a potent instrument for recovery in the 1930s and that the failure to adopt it, except for national security, represented a missed opportunity for economic recovery (M. Thomas 567–72).

The Treasury's resistance to public spending to reduce unemployment in the interwar years has been depicted as an early phase in the battle for Keynesian economic policy. In contrast, the period of full employment from the outbreak of the war until the early 1970s has been painted as the heyday of Keynesian economics, while the inflation of the past decade has raised the accusation that Keynesian economics has failed. Some economists have claimed to find evidence of Keynesian thinking penetrating official thinking in the 1930s, while others attribute it to the growth of government control of the economy during the war, and a recent explanation argues that the full adoption of Keynesian ideas was delayed until the attack on inflation in 1947 (Booth 1983: 123, 1984: 264).

Rather more convincing is the thesis that the Keynesian revolution in economic policy making was an event which never took place. The growth of national income accounting together with the increased budgetary control developed in the war, and the growth of government finance, all created the possibility of fiscal management after 1945 on a scale not possible in the 1930s. The commitment to full employment embodied in the 1944 White Paper became imperative in view of the popular support it carried and the political atmosphere after the war (Tomlinson 1981c: 133). But there is no evidence that Keynesian deficit financing was used to stimulate the economy in the period of full employment in the 1950s and 1960s. Government policy was more concerned to deflate demand to achieve price stability than to increase employment. Unemployment, after all, remained in those decades at a level below anything imagined in the Beveridge Report. The problem of unemployment re-emerged only in the 1970s. There is no substance to the claim that this arose, with inflation, because Keynesian policies had removed the sound basis of the fiscal constitution by encouraging deficits on public expenditure. The rising deficit was unintended and unwanted by each successive administration. Not only did the 1970s bring escalating unemployment it also heralded the end of the inverse relationship which had apparently existed between unemployment and inflation, thus enabling one to be traded off against the other. In the 1970s, however, the inverse relationship as described by the inverted 'J' shape of the Phillips Curve broke down as both inflation and unemployment grew (Allsopp 96). Now the inverted 'J' curve was upside down. Since the main preoccupation of the 1970s, and even more under the administration which came to power in 1979, lay in curbing inflation, unemployment was allowed to rise without correction as the lesser of the two evils. At no time in the twentieth century has the government used an increase in public spending, or an increase in the PSBR, as a major policy instrument in order to reduce unemployment. The problems and the inflation of the 1970s were the product of several factors, the floating of exchange rates, the oil price increase, and cost-push inflation from workers. The growth of the PSBR contributed too, but it stemmed not from the adoption of Keynesian deficits for policy purposes but from the unforeseen circumstances of state obligations undertaken to pay pensions and other social security payments. Nor indeed was the remedy novel. What the deflation of recent years has shown is both the continuity of government policy preferences through the century and the fact that, without some control on the growth of incomes, there will either be inflation or a massive deflation will be needed to prevent it.

V

The generation of economic growth, or the management of structural change, has not been accorded much attention by policy makers in the present century. Stabilization policy was primarily intended to provide a framework in which market forces could operate effectively and, thereby, produce growth. The priority given to the exchange rate and the high interest rates often required to protect it had an obvious effect on the supply side of the economy. As Keynes pointed out in the 1920s, the return to gold at the prewar parity overvalued the pound and placed exporters in a very unfavourable position. High interest rates discouraged investment in industry, as did the uncertainty generated by the stop-go cycle after the Second World War. The lower priority accorded to industry by policymakers thus created an unhelpful environment for manufacturers, as indeed had the maintenance of free trade until 1932 which exposed the home market to stiff import competition.

Direct government involvement in private industry has been occasional and variable in its effect. Some intervention has taken the form of attempts to improve competitiveness in industry, as in the legislation on monopolies in 1948 and against restrictive practices in 1956. An act of 1965 gave the government some control over mergers, and there has been some involvement in this area. The establishment of the Industrial Reorganization Corporation in 1966 brought into being a body intended to promote rationalization schemes in industry. But policy has often shifted with changes of government, and been marked by inconsistencies during most administrations. Thus the Conservative government abolished the Industrial Reorganization Corporation in the early 1970s, but then could not bring itself to allow market forces to bring about the collapse of Upper Clyde Shipbuilders or Rolls Royce. To avoid massive localized unemployment on Clydeside and in Derby, the government rescued both firms with public funds. The same concern underlay the resurrection of British Leyland as BL in the late 1970s and the rescue of Chrysler UK in 1975–6. In all these cases, the social and political costs of industrial collapse outweighed the economic market logic of allowing inefficient businesses to fail.

Government has also provided financial aid to industry on occasions. Subsidies to agriculture and the construction industry for house building were given in the interwar years. In the 1930s the Treasury offered loans to shipowners for the replacement of vessels on favourably low rates of interest. From such funds, Cunard obtained £8 million for two new transatlantic liners. Similarly the Industrial Expansion Act of 1968 provided investment for schemes approved by the government, and contributed to the construction of the QE2 liner and Concorde.

For some industries government has been of overwhelming importance even though they remained in the private sector. The aircraft industry provides the most clearcut illustration; the government has been the principal customer for both civilian and military aircraft. In fact, government demands for aircraft effectively created the industry in the First World War and revived the rather moribund industry in the mid 1930s. Defence commitments escalated after the Second World War and, on the grounds of national security, cost considerations were not of paramount importance. Technical excellence and a sustained high standard could be achieved since purchase was guaranteed and cost was secondary. The cost to the taxpayer was, however, very great and often well beyond the original estimates. The TSR2 fighter plane was originally estimated to cost £90 million, but £190 million had been spent by the time the plane made its test flight. At the time of cancellation the likely final cost was estimated at £750 million. The same Labour administration cancelled two other planes in the mid 1960s on which £42 million had been spent, while their predecessors had cancelled thirty projects over the previous decade which had cost £250 million without any aeroplane actually leaving the ground (Pagnamenta/Overy 68–9). The practice of building on a cost-plus basis, and the easy acceptance of optimistic completion dates and prices by the Ministry of Defence, allowed this profligacy with public funds.

The principal relationship between government and industry, at least in popular consciousness, has been within the context of nationalization. This has represented a development far more important in terms of political symbolism than economic effect, being envisaged alternatively as the means by which the people can reassume control of their heritage and as the thin end of the communist wedge. Throughout the period since 1945 the tide of nationalization has ebbed and flowed with changes in administration, so that steel was nationalized, denationalized and renationalized in less than twenty years. In recent years, the government has embarked on a policy of privatization as a means of returning industry to the people, or at least to the shareholders. Nationalized industries suffered both from changes in administration, given their politically controversial status, and from ambivalence in the attitude to them of successive administrations. The fundamental problem was whether state owned industry should be regarded as a commercial asset required to make profits or at least to cover costs, or whether it should be treated as a national asset to be used as part of a wider strategy and with regard also to social considerations. The coal industry strike of 1984–5 revealed the continuing absence of a consensus view on such issues. From the view of commercial viability the coal board strategy of closing pits, which made heavy operating losses, seemed obviously sensible. But if coal is a resource which should be husbanded to yield maximum output over a long period, then even uneconomic pits should be kept operational. Further, if consideration should be given to the creation of employment and the maintenance of mining communities, then again closure would not be warranted. Quite clearly, there is no way in which these opposing views, and the philosophies which underpin them, can be reconciled or brought to a compromise.

Apart from their position as a political battleground, the nationalized industries have been treated almost equally badly by administrations of all political colour. This has stemmed from the fact that the nationalized industries have remained in the forefront of public expenditure cuts during the past four decades. Capital spending in the public sector has always borne the brunt of deflationary strategies, even if these cuts have made little economic sense. British Rail responded to substantial cutbacks in 1979 by pointing out that 'we are meeting our financial targets and falling short of fulfilling our capability. The prospects have never been better, but under present financial stringencies we may be forced to contract in an expanding market' (quoted in Pollard 1984: 176). The failure to provide sufficient investment, and then to curtail the insufficiency, has generated both waste and inefficiency in the public sector. Pollard cited the case of London Transport forced to forego a plan to introduce automatic ticket machines at a cost of £90 million which would generate an income of £5–10 million per year in additional fares as well as make considerable savings in staff costs. By comparison, Paris invested three times as much in its, much superior, underground system in the same past decade.

The problems of the nationalized industries cannot be explained simply in terms of political manipulation and shortage of investment. Many of them were in a very poor state when originally nationalized, and this was part of the justification for taking them into public ownership. The railways had been starved of investment for half a century before nationalization, as well as being run down under wartime emergency conditions. Continued shortages of funds after nationalization continued the decline in performance and provided justification for those critical of state owned industry. But like the private sector, the performance in much of the state sector was poor and for similar reasons such as poor management, restrictive practices, and overmanning. As the inefficiencies of the private sector were passed on to the consumer in higher prices, so the inefficiencies of the public sector were passed to the taxpayer in losses. Such losses could be great indeed. A recent study has estimated that the cost to the taxpayer run up by the steel industry between its renationalization in 1967 and 1980 amounted to £7.6 billion, together with the loss of 131,000 jobs, the closure of several viable steel plants, and the relinquishing of four million tonnes per year of production to importers and the private steel producers (Bryer 3). Criticisms included an over-compensation payment to the former owners (by a Labour administration) of £1,255 million, loss of revenue from government restrictions on price increases which helped both importers and private steel firms, and substantial waste in capital investment undertaken by the British Steel Corporation (BSC). By nationalizing only the bulk steelmaking part of the industry and restricting BSC to it, the government enabled private producers and steel stockholders to make profits at the expense of the nationalized industry. Despite the fact that for most of the period with which this study deals a Labour government was in office, there was 'an apparently unbreakable constraint in both the formation and development of BSC . . . that the private sector should be allowed to flourish, no matter what the cost to BSC or its shareholders, the public' (Bryer 275). Neither the managers of the corporation, the civil servants or the ministers involved were subject to public accountability in any practical way. It is rather ironic, given the anxiety of the Treasury to control public spending, that there has been so much profligacy in the use of public funds, not just by some nationalized industries, but by major spending departments like the Ministry of Defence.

The same mixture of muddled economic and social aims, and frequent shifts of policy, have characterized the approach to regional development. Such policy has usually been activated by a concern about the wide variations in unemployment levels between different parts of the country, as the heavy manufacturing industries have declined. Much of this policy has had primarily a social amelioration objective, and has often run against economic efficiency. In the interwar years, regional policy took the form principally of taking workers to the work by facilitating migration from the areas of high unemployment to the south. In the context of postwar full employment this policy was reversed and firms were encouraged to shift location into areas with relatively high unemployment. Investment grants were provided for firms setting up in development areas, providing funds for plant and machinery together with free depreciation. In 1967 a subsidy was paid for each new worker employed in a development area. The other part of the same policy was the imposition of restrictions on new developments in regions like the South East where unemployment was relatively low. By such means the motor industry was induced to diversify production in the 1960s from the West Midlands and South East where it was concentrated and to establish plants in Central Scotland and on Merseyside. This move was later bitterly regretted by the manufacturers. Production was dispersed amongst plants several hundred miles apart, and the traditionally poor labour relations of the regions to which the industry moved, and their different work practices, led to industrial conflict.

But even this branch of economic policy was subject to frequent change. The definition of development areas within which financial incentives were provided was constantly changing. This inhibited firms from taking decisions to move into certain areas since the benefits might be withdrawn by the time a decision to move was translated into reality. Legislation passed in 1960 based development area status on local unemployment levels, about 4.5 per cent was the required target, but this meant that fluctuations in the level of unemployment around that figure could push some areas into and then out of the category fairly frequently (McCrone 124). Furthermore, there is no certainty that local unemployment levels represented the best basis for identifying potential growth areas. The criterion reflected the primacy of social considerations and political sensitivity about unemployment. But like other aspects of government policy, regional problems have been subject to the periodic requirement for cuts in public spending. Thus the Regional Employment Premium, which accounted for 40 per cent of regional incentive expenditure and was worth over £200 million annually, was abolished in 1976 in the public expenditure cuts (Nicol/Yuill 431). The Regional Development Grant was withdrawn from construction and mining at the same time. Even more severe reductions were imposed after 1979. Development areas were cut, so that they encompassed 43 per cent of the population in 1979 but only 30 per cent by 1982, and regional expenditure was cut by 40 per cent. By the 1970s and 1980s, the regional problem had become submerged by the general increase in unemployment in even the most prosperous areas, and this made any transfer of resources and jobs extremely sensitive. Regional assistance became increasingly concentrated on inner city problems and closely defined areas of special deprivation.

VI

Despite the growth of government involvement in economic affairs in the twentieth century through the great increase in public expenditure and macroeconomic management of the economy, there has been little attempt to devise policies to generate growth and bring about structural change. This has been left almost entirely to market forces. The only attempt to take a long view and develop a coherent strategy for growth, the National Plan of 1965, was soon ditched under pressure from exchange rate problems. The priority areas of policy, balance of payments stabilization, the protection of the exchange rate, and the control of inflation by deflationary fiscal and monetary instruments, were all essentially short-term adjustments with little regard for long-term problems. Indeed such a heavy concentration on the short term precluded any consideration of long-term development. It has been estimated that regional policies in the 1960s and, to a lesser extent, in the 1970s were successful in generating both employment and investment in the development areas at a considerably higher level than would have been achieved in their absence (Nicol/Yuill 438–9). But it is by no means certain that this represented a net contribution to national aggregate growth, or that it was more than a simple transfer of economic activity from other regions. If the complaints of the motor industry are to be believed, regional diversification brought a substantial loss in efficiency in that sector.

The speed with which successive governments cut spending in the public sector and pursued strategies adverse to the export and investment prospects of industry suggests that growth occupied a low priority status. As for structural change, it is difficult to think of any policy measure designed for such a purpose other than the Selective Employment Tax which was intended to flush out the excess labour hoarded in the service sector to compensate for imagined shortages in manufacturing. It is hard to disagree with those who argue that industry was regarded with contempt by those who formulated and applied British economic policy. While the internationalist perspective and deflationary orientation of policy might have been acceptable and effective if industry had been strong, in the context of a backward and weak industrial sector it was unlikely to arrest decline and certainly most unlikely to generate growth. As Pollard concluded his indictment of post 1945 policy, 'Virtually all our economic policies and all the major economic and political controversies surrounding them (with very few exceptions) have not been about how to improve the growth performance of the British economy, but how to slide down gracefully and elegantly rather than in ungainly or demoralizing lurches. Deflation, devaluation, tariffs and control of the money supply are all measures designed not to improve productivity or efficiency, but to find means of adjusting to their relative failure to improve' (Pollard 1984: 14).

14

Regional growth

I

The growth of the British economy in the twentieth century has been characterized by wide variations in growth and decline in different regions. The frequent juxtaposition of high unemployment against rapidly rising affluence has served to highlight the great social and economic gulf between the prosperous majority and the poor minority. The 'regional problem' has even intruded into the strategies of policy makers, albeit peripherally. Such differences in well-being between social groups and geographic areas have been common to all societies and all periods of history, and were certainly apparent in Britain in the eighteenth and nineteenth centuries. But the twentieth century has brought new growth on an unprecedented scale and affluence has become far more widely spread through society than it was before 1914. The twentieth century has also brought substantial and enduring economic decline in the contraction and decay of some sectors of the economy which had hitherto been prosperous. This mixture of growth and decline has been thrown into sharp relief by the fact that it has often coincided with differences in prosperity between the regions, and it has revived debates about north and south and the two nations.

II

The most obvious characteristic of change in the twentieth century has been the increased share of national population in the South East, East Anglia and South West, and the considerable relative loss in Scotland, Wales and the North West and North regions (Table 7.1). The changing distribution of national population has taken place within the context of a very low rate of population increase, the growth rate falling below that which prevailed from the mid eighteenth century until the First World War (Table 7.2). Much of the regional reallocation of population in the twentieth century was, therefore, the consequence of internal migration. During the interwar years, when half the total increase in national population was concentrated into London and the Home Counties, there was a net inward migration of over one million people into this area compared to a natural increase of three-quarters of a million people. In contrast, Wales lost about half a million people by migration, a number far greater than the natural increase in the principality. Scotland also lost substantially by migration in the 1920s, although the outward flow was halted in the following decade.

Since 1945 migration has continued to be the main medium through which regional population has changed. Scotland has lost particularly heavily. In the 1950s and 1960s substantial net outward migration limited net population increase to under two per cent. In the 1970s net outward migration was more than double natural increase and the total population fell. Wales and the North also lost heavily. There was an 'internal cascade from north to south' whereby each region lost migrants to all regions to the south of it but gained migrants from all those to its north. At the foot of the cascade, in the South East, the flow of population spilled over into the South West, East Anglia and even reached the East Midlands (A. J. Brown 258).

III

Regional income data, even the general estimates which have been derived for some benchmark years in the nineteenth century, are not available for the interwar years. But the post 1945 regional income data show considerable continuity with the estimates for the Victorian period (Table 14.1). In terms of regional income, as with most other indices, the South East remained far above the national average and all other regions. Indeed, the gap widened appreciably in the 1970s in spite of government attempts to implement regional policies which discriminated against the South East by diverting growth elsewhere. The remaining regions remained close to the mean income and, since 1950, have converged upon the mean. The small variation in average income between the regions outside the South East highlights the enormity of that principal dichotomy. Its continuity, the size of the South East, and the marked differences in wealth and economic structure which underlie the dichotomy, reflect its importance within the long-term growth of the national economy.

The distribution of regional GDP, available for recent decades, confirms the pattern depicted by the income data. There was no clear trend towards convergence during the two decades after 1960 although some regional GDP estimates shifted towards the average (East Anglia, South West and Scotland) while some shifted away from it (Yorkshire/Humberside, West Midlands and North West). But the most obvious feature of the data is the fact that the South East not only stood far above the national average and all

Table 14.1 *Index of regional income (per head)*

	1949/50	1959/60	1970/71	1976/77	1977	1983
South East	113	111	113	110	117	127
East Anglia	98	94	101	105	95	103
South West	99	97	102	99	94	102
West Midlands	104	106	105	104	103	94
East Midlands	103	101	101	105	99	101
North West	100	100	100	100	100	100
Yorkshire/Humberside	104	100	101	101	98	97
North	97	97	99	99	97	95
Wales	94	96	97	96	91	89
Scotland	100	95	101	96	99	103

Sources: C. M. Law, *British Regional Development since World War I* (Newton Abbot 1980)
   p. 80 [Cols. 2–5]
Central Statistical Office, *Regional Trends*, 15 (1980) p. 171 [Col. 6: GDP per head]
Central Statistical Office, *Regional Trends*, 20 (1985) pp. 118–19 [Col. 7: GDP per head]

other regions in GDP per capita, but that the gap increased. In 1961, the
GDP of the South East stood 11 per cent above the national average, by 1971
the gap was 13.7 per cent and in 1981 it was 15.9 per cent. Greater London
itself increased the gap between its GDP and the national average to reach
28.6 per cent in 1981 (*Regional Abstract* 1984: 108–9). By comparison the
differences between the other regions have been relatively modest.

The fact that there was a large gap between the South East and the rest,
and that there was not a large variation between other regions, explains the
apparent contradiction between the manifest and important differences
between regions in economic well-being and the fact that comparative
studies of regional variations amongst the advanced industrial nations place
Britain in a very low position on the comparative scale. Regional variations
in GDP per capita in Western Europe in 1977 showed a range in weighted
coefficient of variation from 0.37 (Portugal) to 0.09 (United Kingdom)
about an average of 0.22 (Nicol/Yuill 412). Even in terms of unemployment
British regional variations were low, although not at the bottom of the list.
But a comparison of the north/south divergence in Britain does reveal
significant and widening differences, and this has been especially obvious
with regard to unemployment in recent years (Table 14.2).

Regional variations in income, GDP, and unemployment have contributed to differences in the usual measures of relative prosperity. The
proportion of households living in owner occupied accommodation in 1981
showed substantial variations from 63 per cent in the South West to 47 per
cent in the North and 35 per cent in Scotland. Households with access to at

Table 14.2 *Regional unemployment (per cent)*

	1931	1951	1961	1971	1977	1983
South East	7.8	1.1	2.2	2.0	4.5	9.3
East Anglia	9.4	1.9	2.5	3.1	5.3	10.1
South West	8.1	1.8	2.4	3.4	6.8	11.1
West Midlands	12.0	1.3	2.1	2.9	5.8	15.5
East Midlands	9.6	1.2	2.0	2.9	5.0	11.6
North West	16.2	2.2	3.5	3.9	7.4	15.8
Yorkshire/Humberside	12.2	1.6	2.6	3.8	5.7	13.9
North	19.2	3.0	3.8	5.7	8.3	17.8
Wales	16.5	3.5	4.2	4.7	7.9	15.9
Scotland	16.1	3.5	4.5	5.8	8.1	14.8

Sources: C. M. Law, *British Regional Development since World War I* (Newton Abbot 1980) p. 77
Central Statistical Office, *Regional Trends*, 15 (1980) p. 109
Central Statistical Office, *Regional Trends*, 20 (1985) p. 99

least one car ranged from 69 per cent in the South West and East Anglia to only just over half in Yorkshire/Humberside, the North and Scotland. At a more basic level of comfort, 5.2 per cent of houses in Wales lacked an inside toilet compared to only 2.0 per cent in southern England.

The purchase of accommodation and private transport reflect differences in income and employment. State provision of welfare and transfer payments reduce other differentials but not to the point of elimination. Educational provision, in the state sector, showed similar pupil/teacher ratios in most regions. But there were considerable variations in the proportion of those eligible for higher education who actually took such courses. Participation in higher education was directly related to income (Regional Abstract 1984: 68). There were marked variations in the provision of health and dental treatment. The North, East Midlands and North West had relatively high patient/general practitioner ratios, while Scotland, the South West, Wessex and Wales had more favourable ratios. There was a greater diversity in the patient/dentist ratio. This ranged from 4,817 in the North and 4,760 in Trent to 2,344 in North West Thames and 2,571 in South West Thames. Other regions with a relatively poor provision of dental services included the North West, Wales, and Yorkshire, while the South West, South East Thames, and North East Thames did well (Regional Abstract 1984: 68).

These measures of welfare are rather crude generalizations since within each large region can be found considerable diversity at local level. Thus within Scotland can be found the extremes of deprivation characteristic of decayed mining and industrial areas in Strathclyde as compared to the affluence of Edinburgh, at least parts of it, and the prosperous north east. While the South East has remained generally extremely prosperous, even that region contains pockets of deprivation in inner London which are as bad as anywhere else in Britain. Similarly, Wales, which is a poor region by a number of important indicators, has more private housing than might be anticipated and a fairly high car access ratio. Even in the poorest regions with the highest unemployment and greatest deprivation, there is a substantial body of affluent people. It has been the bottom 20–30 per cent of income recipients who have borne the brunt of poor economic performance and poverty. This group, at the bottom of the social scale, has representatives in all regions. But they are found in greater number and as a larger part of their communities in the regions north of the hypothetical line often drawn from the Severn to the Wash.

IV

The economic structures which have produced these differences in regional affluence can be clearly discerned in regional employment composition and, for the most recent past, the structure of regional GDP. Variations in the growth of regional population in the twentieth century have been mirrored by changes in employment growth. While the labour force in the south of England and the two midland regions has increased substantially, there has been only a small increase in northern England, Wales, and Scotland. Two aspects of this have been differences in activity rates and unemployment. There has not been much difference between regions in male activity rates, and most regions have remained within two or three per cent of the national average throughout the century. But there have been wide divergences between female activity rates, as there were in the nineteenth century. Since female employment in the Victorian period had been largely restricted to domestic service and the clothing and textile industries, female employment was concentrated into affluent regions, like the South East, and the northern textile counties. By contrast, female activity rates were much lower in low income areas, such as mining communities, and in the rural counties, at least in terms of recognized paid employment. These differences were clearly delineated in 1921 when female activity rates ranged from 39.3 per cent in the North West and 34.1 per cent in the South East to 27.5 per cent in East Anglia, 22.4 per cent in the North and 21.1 per cent in Wales. One of the main economic trends in the twentieth century has been the great increase in employment for women, helped by the demonstration effect of the two world wars when women had to be mobilized into unfamiliar jobs and further stimulated by the labour shortages of the 1950s and 1960s. All female activity rates have increased in response to these demands and the much greater range of employment opportunities open to women, especially since 1950. By 1971 the national activity rate for women had increased to 42.6 per cent compared to 32.3 per cent in 1921. The greater range of employment opportunities and the universal growth of sectors using more female labour, such as distribution, brought some convergence in the regional variation in female activity rates. Even so, there remained a gap larger than 10 per cent between the highest and lowest rates, representing a considerable difference in employment and family income. By 1971, the range of female activity rates extended from over 44 per cent in the South East, West Midlands and North West to less than 40 per cent in the South West, East Anglia and North, while Wales registered only 35.6 per cent. Adding male and female activity rates together indicated that there was a difference of seven per cent in total activity rates between the highest and lowest regions.

Differential rates of growth in regional labour forces and activity rates in the twentieth century found a counterpart in the variations in unemployment. The interwar years witnessed not only large increases in unemployment but with very marked regional variations. Indeed, it was this phenomenon which suggested to commentators and historians that there was an emergent 'regional problem'. It is very difficult to compare twentieth-century unemployment with that prevailing in the Victorian period. In the nineteenth century casual employment and underemployment were the norm, thus making conventional modern notions about unemployment largely inapplicable. Such data which are available must also be treated in circumspect fashion. But the data derived for 1912–13 by Beveridge are of interest, especially as they show very low rates in the industrial regions. Thus Scotland had an unemployment level of 1.8 per cent, the North East and East Midlands 2.5 per cent, North West 2.7 per cent and West Midlands and Wales 3.1 per cent. All these regions were below the national average of 3.9 per cent. Conversely, London 8.7 per cent, South East 4.7 per cent and the South West 4.6 per cent were the highest rates (Beveridge 1909: 73).

By the interwar years a quite different distribution of unemployment from that depicted by Beveridge in 1912–13 had emerged (Table 14.2). Not only were the levels of unemployment higher but, by 1931, they were highest in the manufacturing regions. When unemployment rates rose again in the 1970s the pattern manifest in the interwar years reappeared. Rates of unemployment in Scotland, Wales, and northern England were much higher than in the regions of the south and west. By the 1970s, the West Midlands had joined the regions of high unemployment as the motor industry reduced its labour force. While the high unemployment rates of recent years are similar in percentage terms to those which prevailed in the 1930s, the much higher activity rate in society since 1945 means that the number of people actually in employment is still a much greater proportion of those of working age than was the case before the Second World War. Not surprisingly, regional variations in unemployment have been a major cause of internal migration in the twentieth century, a far more potent cause than variations in average regional income (A. J. Brown 259ff).

Regional variations in the growth of the labour force, activity rates, and unemployment have been largely the result of a single phenomenon, the great change in employment structure which has occurred since 1914 (Table 1.5). The considerable extent of regional employment specialization necessitated that such a large aggregate structural change must produce quite different effects in the various parts of the country. The greatest change was experienced by the North West, North, Wales, Scotland and, latterly, the West Midlands, that is by those regions which have been most affected by unemployment, outward migration, and slow growth in new employment.

Contraction in employment affected most of the 'staple' trades of the Victorian economy and was, therefore, highly localized. Mining reached a peak of employment in 1921, having enjoyed its last massive expansion in the wartime boom. In the following half century, mining employment contracted by over one million jobs and by the 1970s the industry was little larger, in terms of its workforce, than it had been at the beginning of Victoria's reign. While the industry had comprised 7.4 per cent of national employment in 1921 by 1971 its share had fallen to 1.7 per cent. Mining employment fell in all regions where the industry was established but the impact of decline fell most heavily on those regions with the greatest dependence on mining. In 1921 the industry accounted for 37.3 per cent of all employment in Glamorgan/Monmouth, 32.2 per cent in County Durham, 23.3 per cent in Central/Fife, 18.9 per cent in Northumberland, and 18.5 per cent in Nottinghamshire. Other regions with a substantial mining community were less dependent on the industry, including the West Riding with 11.4 per cent of employment in the industry, and Lancashire with 5.0 per cent (Lee 1979). A considerable loss of mining employment in an area like County Durham required a considerable creation of employment in other sectors simply to make good that loss. In the half century after 1921, Durham lost 121,460 mining jobs, equivalent to 23.9 per cent of employment in the county at the end of the First World War. Glamorgan/Monmouth lost 184,256 mining jobs during the same period, equivalent to 30.4 per cent of total regional employment in 1921. These regions, like the rest of the mining areas, possessed other specialized industries which contracted in the twentieth century. County Durham had substantial employment in shipbuilding, mechanical engineering, and agriculture, and together these sectors shed over 50,000 jobs in the half century after 1921. Between the First World War and 1971, County Durham gained 199,837 new jobs in expanding employment sectors. But against this increase must be set a loss of 179,661 jobs in the contracting sectors. The net increase in employment was accordingly very small. In Glamorgan/Monmouth and other mining regions the overall increase in employment was similarly small. Even in the days of their great expansion, mining regions had found difficulty in generating sufficient multiplier effects to create a diversified employment structure. In particular, mining areas generated a very low demand for services, indicative of low effective demand and modest average incomes. Thus service employment per head of population remained well below the national average. Not surprisingly, female activity rates remained well below the national average in such regions because much female employment has been created in the service sector. Failure to generate such demand not only prevents such regions compensating for job losses in declining industries but keeps them in the trap of high unemployment, low incomes and low activity rates. On all counts, Wales and the North have fared badly in the twentieth century.

The decline of mining areas as their natural resources have become exhausted has been paralleled by the collapse of the textile industries in the face of intense competition abroad and, recently, at home. Between 1911 and 1971, employment in textile manufactures fell by 706,571 while in the related clothing industry it fell by 673,509. By 1971 there were less jobs in textiles than there had been in 1841, and only slightly more in the clothing trade. In Lancashire, long associated with the cotton industry, the loss in employment between the First World War and 1971 in textiles and clothing exceeded half a million jobs and accounted for over half the contraction in employment in the county. The share of Lancashire employment in textiles and clothing fell from 29.9 per cent to 8.5 per cent. Overall, the county lost 870,000 jobs with the result that employment in the early 1970s was actually less than it had been on the eve of the First World War. Growth in other sectors was insufficient to make good such a huge loss (Lee 1980b: 263). In Tayside, where dependence on textiles was greater even than in Lancashire, the impact of contracting employment in the industry was even more severe. In this region textiles had accounted for one third of all employment at the beginning of the century. But textiles and clothing in 1971 employed only one quarter of the workers it had needed in 1901. Even substantial employment growth in the 1950s and 1960s was insufficient to prevent a net fall in employment. As in the mining regions, the size of the textile sector, which accounted for one quarter of all employment in both Lancashire and Tayside at the end of the nineteenth century, and the speed of its contraction was too great to allow these regions much chance of generating a net increase in employment.

Regions specializing in twentieth-century manufactures have proved to be equally vulnerable to the loss of comparative advantage. The vehicle industry, together with metal working and engineering, which provided components and ancilliary services to the motor industry, was strongly concentrated in the West Midlands even before the First World War. In the interwar years, this region represented an oasis of manufacturing prosperity and relatively full employment compared to the depressed textile and mining regions. Indeed, until the 1970s the prosperity of the motor industry seemed assured. In the West Midlands additional employment from the expansion of the motor industry and related sectors was sufficient to exceed by far the effect of contracting employment sectors in the region. The large increase in employment drew migrants from both the north and the west. By the early 1970s, the region was exhibiting the same scale of dependence on the motor industry for jobs that Durham had shown before 1914 on mining and Lancashire on textiles. By 1971, employment in vehicle manufacture accounted for 15.9 per cent of jobs in Warwickshire and the addition of metal manufacturing and engineering increased the proportion to 39.2 per cent. Similar concentrations were found in Oxford and Bedford. The loss of motor car markets in the 1970s, abroad and at home, stimulated the same kind of contraction of employment as had happened earlier in industries like mining and textiles. By 1981, the level of unemployment in the West Midlands was not only fourfold its level of a decade earlier but had become one of the highest rates in any region (Table 14.2).

One of the major characteristics of regional growth in the nineteenth century was the pre-eminence of the South East in wealth and growth. The experience of this region in the twentieth century has been very different from that of the beleagured manufacturing centres of the north. There was some contraction in employment in the South East, particularly in clothing and domestic service. In London and Middlesex about half a million jobs were lost between 1911 and 1971, but this was overshadowed by the creation of two million new jobs. Three-quarters of these new jobs were in services, with banking, finance and insurance, the professions, and government, together adding 900,000 new jobs. The supporting construction, transport, and distribution sectors contributed a further 450,000. In manufacturing there were significant additions in employment in chemicals, food processing, and electrical engineering. Much the same was the pattern of growth in the rest of the Home Counties. In the Home Counties as a whole there was an increase of 2.6 million new jobs between 1911 and 1971, to be set against a contraction of 0.9 million. Growth in the rest of the South East was even more impressive. Here there was a net increase of almost one million jobs, creating a labour force in 1971 which was 85 per cent larger than it had been in 1911. Mechanical and electrical engineering, vehicle manufacture, construction, the professions, and government service were all important growth sectors. The structure and growth of the outer South East was similar to that of the Home Counties and represented the continued expansion of the metropolitan economy from its eighteenth and nineteenth-century base.

The growth of the outer South East was largely a phenomenon of the post Second World War period. During the 1950s, employment in the Home Counties experienced considerable structural change. There were losses in textiles, clothing, shipbuilding and chemical manufacture but a net increase of 8 per cent was achieved by expansion of jobs in engineering, vehicles, printing and publishing and most of the services. In the 1960s no less than 19 of the 27 employment categories showed a decrease in the Home Counties. In order to compensate for this loss a substantial growth in three sectors was necessary. Banking and finance increased by 180,000 jobs, professional services by 169,000 and government by 60,000. Such was the concentration of such services that in 1971 the South East possessed 54.5 per cent of all employment in banking and finance, 40.2 per cent of all government employment, and 36.5 per cent of professional workers (Lee 1980b: 268–9). In the outer South East these sectors also increased, but there was a strong growth in manufactures such as electrical engineering and paper, printing and publishing.

The continued growth of the South East in the present century, latterly spreading into East Anglia and the South West to form an enlarged and very prosperous southern economy, has been mainly based on the expansion of those employment sectors which constituted its growth before 1914. Employment decline has been modest because the region did not have very much of its employment vested in those sectors which have contracted in the twentieth century, except for clothing and domestic service. This regional economy has not, therefore, had to contend with the restructuring on a massive scale which has been necessary in many other regions. Traditionally, the economy of the South East has been oriented towards services and consumer goods centred on the national capital which was a major centre of international trade and finance, seat of government and fashionable society.

Since the bulk of the growing middle-class occupations were in the South East, this region remained in the van of economic progress. The continued prosperity and regional pre-eminence of the south both in the twentieth century and earlier was rooted in the same comparative advantage and economic structure. If the British economy is divided into just two regions, the South East and the rest of the country, in the period 1851 to 1911 the South East gained 3.1 million new jobs and lost 0.1 million while the rest of Britain gained 6.4 million and lost 0.5 million. In the Victorian period, the South East thus gained about one third of the net national increase in employment. In the period 1911–71, the South East gained 3.8 million new jobs for the loss of 1.1 million, but the rest of Britain gained 6.2 million and lost 3.5 million. The net gain in employment in the twentieth century has thus been shared almost equally between the South East and the rest of the country.

The structural change in employment described above took place in the context of full employment and rapid economic growth in the postwar years. The 1970s intensified the problems of structural change as the balance of jobs lost exceeded that of jobs created. In the first half of the 1970s, the accelerating loss in manufacturing employment was covered by increased employment in the service sector, partly as a result of government spending. But the rate of increase of service job creation was declining and by the second half of the decade was no longer able to compensate for contraction elsewhere (Frost/Spence 90). The new government in 1979 was determined to exceed the zeal of their predecessors in curbing inflation and public spending. The severe deflation by which this was achieved both accelerated the decline of manufacturing employment, as weak firms were unable to survive high interest rates and a deflated market, and hit the service sector as public spending was sharply reduced.

The massive increase in unemployment affected the weaker regional economies most. One of the effects of regional policy in the early 1970s had been to create more jobs in the development areas and the intermediate areas than in prosperous regions in the south. But the effect of that bolstering of employment had virtually disappeared by the end of the decade (Frost/Spence 129). Even so, the main increases in employment in the 1970s were registered in East Anglia, the South West, and East Midlands. The deflationary policies adopted in the second half of the 1970s were felt everywhere, but most sharply in the weaker regions. By 1981 all regions other than East Anglia and the South West had fewer persons in employment than in 1975, and in all regions the number in work was less than in 1978. While the South East and East Midlands were only marginally worse off than in 1975, elsewhere the contraction in employment was substantial. In the North employment was down by 11.3 per cent, as it was by over seven per cent in the North West and West Midlands, and by over six per cent in Yorkshire/Humberside and Wales (*Regional Abstract* 1984: 83–4). The number of confirmed redundancies increased nationally from 7.8 per thousand people employed in 1977–9 to 22.2 in 1980–2. There was, as usual, a wide disparity in the rate in different regions. At the later date this ranged from 37.2 in Wales, 33.4 in the North West and 30.8 in the North to 12.4 in East Anglia and 11.9 in the South East (*Regional Abstract* 1984: 89). The greatest effects of the most recent deflation were found in those areas with low growth in new employment and a large loss of jobs in the 1950s and 1960s. Decline was greatest in Wales, the three northern and two midland regions of England. The more prosperous regions of the south were better able to ride out the economic storm.

Such emphasis has been placed on the discussion of structure in terms of employment because of the importance of variations in unemployment, but also because data on regional GDP are available only for the most recent past (Table 14.3). The composition of regional GDP confirms the pattern of employment and shows the main distinction to be that between the three regions of southern England and the rest of the country (A. J. Brown 55, Table 14.3). By 1983 the South East GDP was almost £1,000 per head greater than any other region, the only exceptions being East Anglia and Scotland. Furthermore, the West Midlands had fallen from second position in 1961 in regional GDP ranking to second lowest in 1983.

The composition of regional GDP illuminates this change. In the early 1960s regions such as Yorkshire/Humberside, North West, East Midlands and West Midlands obtained not only a higher share of their GDP from manufacturing than the southern regions but a substantially larger sum in money terms. By 1983 there was not very much difference between GDP per head in manufacturing in these regions and the South East and East Anglia. Obviously the regions of the south were more successful in maintaining their industrial base and developing new manufacturing activities. Of course, much of the light engineering and high technology industry is located in southern Britain. But the really large difference in regional structure in 1983 is found in income generated in financial and business services. In this sector the South East was at least £450 per head greater than any other region, and more than double that of the contribution to GDP made by this sector in any other region. In other words, half the difference between the GDP of the South East and other regions was explained by variations in this sector. Furthermore there were large and increasing differences between the South East, and to a lesser extent the South West and East Anglia, and the rest of the country in all other services. The long-term regional specializations in structure were more firmly established than ever by the early 1980s, but with greatly differing degrees of success.

V

The structure and growth of regional economies in Britain conform to the typologies identified in the development studies of Chenery/Syrquin. Small regions dependent on a major export, either a raw material like coal or some manufactured product such as textiles or motor cars are obviously extremely vulnerable to the loss of their particular comparative advantage. This can occur because a raw material resource is exhausted, as is now the case with

Table 14.3 Regional gross domestic product 1983 (£ per head)

	South East	East Anglia	South West	West Midlands	East Midlands	North West	Yorkshire/ Humberside	North	Wales	Scotland
Agriculture, forestry, fishing	53	281	171	83	137	40	101	82	126	142
Energy/water supply	185	142	167	197	371	223	410	367	389	272
Manufacturing	1,135	1,059	952	1,302	1,250	1,240	1,081	1,111	803	1,009
Construction	324	304	293	209	243	237	231	228	241	302
Distribution	755	644	635	527	549	596	563	516	488	598
Transport/communications	475	283	260	220	267	305	273	260	232	319
Financial and business services	933	418	455	386	351	431	359	334	287	421
Ownership of dwellings	375	275	288	277	254	259	210	223	196	188
Public administration/defence	379	326	420	240	268	250	252	238	335	326
Education/health	485	361	409	344	347	389	395	417	414	476
Other services	395	272	273	192	204	280	228	231	232	288
Adjustment for financial services	−343	−161	−176	−163	−137	−177	−145	−127	−116	−168
GDP per head	5,155	4,204	4,147	3,814	4,104	4,073	3,958	3,880	3,627	4,173

Source: Central Statistical Office, Regional Trends, 20 (1985) pp. 47, 118–19.

some of the coalfields of Britain as in South Wales, County Durham and Kent. For a manufacturing region loss of comparative advantage is more likely to reflect the fact that rival producers manufacture a commodity cheaper, or better, or both. The British textile industry has been hard hit in all markets by competition from cheap fabrics from the Far East, while the British motor industry is a victim of its own relative high prices and poor quality as compared to its rivals. The specialized production and 'export' orientation of most regional economies in Britain has exposed them to such external competitive pressures. The failures of much of British industry as chronicled above have thus had very severe consequences in most of the regions outside southern England.

The Chenery classification of economic types includes a large economy with relatively high per capita income. Such an economy is better able to sustain its affluence, partly by internally generated demand from high incomes and, by virtue of its size, create economies of scale and similar multiplier effects not possible in the small export economy. Size allows a wider range of products and services to be provided economically, and thus import substitution becomes a possibility. Such large, affluent economies are more self sufficient than the small export specialists. The classification, derived in terms of national economies, is pertinent at regional level. The South East provides a classic example of this latter typology. Throughout the twentieth century, and the previous two hundred years and more, this region enjoyed very high average incomes, was able therefore to sustain a very high provision of all kinds of services, and was able to sustain a strong demand for high quality consumer goods, the manufacture of which had always been a metropolitan speciality. In addition, the South East retained its specialized role as a centre of international investment, banking, and financial services. While the Eurodollar market provided a timely stimulus, it seems easier to retain a comparative advantage in an activity in which accumulated expertise and an appropriate institutional framework constitutes the basis of that advantage, that is in a service industry, rather than in manufacturing or raw material exploitation for which the past is a hindrance rather than an asset.

The pattern of British economic growth has been marked by the separation of industry from finance, by specialization in manufacturing or services, and by the divergent fortunes of these sectors in the long run. Given the extreme regional specialization which has also characterized British growth, it is hardly surprising that another manifestation of this development should be the juxtaposition of a wealthy and prosperous south against a poor and economically declining north throughout much of the twentieth century.

PART IV

Conclusion

15

Retrospect and prospect

The most outstanding feature of British economic growth during the past three centuries has been its extreme slowness (Maddison 44–5). As the British economy lost ground relative to the other industrial economies, which has been the situation for at least the past century, so its national income has fallen further behind those of its competitors. By 1982 British GNP per head ranked only fifteenth in the list of nineteen industrial market economies. The average per capita income of these countries stood 14.6 per cent above that of Britain, while West Germany was 29.0 per cent greater and France was 20.9 per cent greater (World Bank 219).

From this slow rate of growth, and the resultant relative poverty compared to the other industrial nations, have developed most of Britain's economic and social problems. A poor growth performance and relatively low average incomes obviously implies a lower standard of living. The ownership of a major consumer durable, private cars, per thousand people was 283 in Britain in 1981 compared to the EEC average of 325 and well below that of France and West Germany. But Britain did relatively well in less expensive durables like televisions and telephones (EEC 110). Low growth and incomes also inhibit welfare provision. The number of patients per doctor in Britain was 34 per cent above the EEC average in 1979. Educational provision, both an important welfare service and a vital investment for future economic progress, is relatively poor in Britain. In the context of the advanced industrial countries, the proportion of the appropriate age group in secondary education was seven per cent below the average in Britain while the share of the 20–24 age group in higher education was 17 per cent below the average in 1981 (World Bank 267).

The principal question concerning the history of the British economy must, therefore, be why the rate of growth has always been so slow, performance so consistently mediocre and why, even in the context of increasing and manifest relative poverty, the economy seems so unresponsive to change. Since the supply side of the economy and especially the manufacturing sector is usually regarded as central to aggregate growth, its structure and performance is crucially important. Recognizing this, economic historians have customarily described British economic development almost exclusively in terms of industrialization. Britain's role as a major centre of early industrial growth and the first industrial nation has always been stressed. Often historians have subscribed to the stronger thesis which explained the commencement of British and world economic modernization as the product of the first Industrial Revolution. Historical evidence does not support either the extravagant hyperbole sometimes adopted or the hypothesis that manufacturing began or even dominated British economic growth. The uniqueness of the British development experience, upon which all seem to be agreed, derived not from the novelty or dynamism of industrialization but from the relatively weak contribution to growth made by the industrial sector. Indeed the modest contribution to aggregate growth made by manufacturing, even if generous multiplier effects on the rest of the economy are assumed, provides a substantial part of the explanation for the slow rate of aggregate growth (Tables 1.3 and 1.4).

The limited contribution of manufacturing to growth was, in turn, largely a result of its unusual structure. In spite of the exaggerated importance attributed by some historians to the advent of factory production, the outstanding feature of British industrialization was that it embraced so many continuities. The basis of British manufacturing in the period before 1914 remained the labour force, sometimes highly skilled craft workers, as in shipbuilding, sometimes semi-skilled or unskilled as in textiles. Production remained heavily labour intensive and skill, when it was required, took the form of manual dexterity acquired by practical experience. The technical advances which were adopted were themselves the outcome of practical work, devised by skilled craftsmen for their peers. Capital, either in the form of productive capacity or investment in research, remained comparatively modest. Even the largest shipbuilding and armament combines, secure in their government defence contracts, had a very small capital per worker ratio at the close of the nineteenth century.

Labour intensive production with skill vested in manual operatives had a profound impact on British industry. It enabled expansion without very much recourse to the services of the financial sector. It enabled small family firms to survive, and owners to retain control. Any adjustment in favour of more capital intensive production would have increased the likelihood of outside investment being needed, and this would have reduced or even removed control of the firm from existing partners. Labour intensive production had a second advantage for manufacturers in that it enabled them to pass the costs of trade depressions to their employees by making them redundant. In a system which was more capital intensive such costs would have been borne by the manufacturers as plant and machinery they had paid for became idle. In the system of labour intensive production, variable costs (labour) were high in relation to fixed costs (machinery). The bitterness of British labour relations and the atmosphere of hostility and mutual distrust between employers and employees is a potent legacy of this type of industrial development.

The industries in which eighteenth and nineteenth-century Britain specialized were those most characteristic of early industrialization. They were thus susceptible to the development of industrialization in countries where even cheaper labour could undermine the British cost advantage. In the present century industries such as shipbuilding and textiles have contracted sharply in Britain, withered by competition from Asia initially in third markets and eventually in the British market itself. But the practices and structures of British industry established before the First World War were no better suited to new industries of the twentieth century such as motor vehicle manufacture. The prevalence of the small family firm with limited capital and often amateurish management, the continued reliance on manual craft skills and the consequent slow adoption of mass production techniques, prevented the achievement of optimum levels of production and hence cost efficiency. Pandering to the idiosyncrasies of the small domestic market provided some security until the 1970s, but prevented the generation of economies of scale which could only have been achieved by success in export markets. Failure to export in the twentieth century marked and compounded poor performance, and the weak competitiveness of much of British industry made it struggle in its home market by the 1970s. The motor cycle industry, once a great success, completely disappeared and so too might the motor industry without government support. Deindustrialization has been an experience common to the advanced industrial economies in recent years, as has the increase in unemployment which it brought. But in Britain the scale of industrial decline and the increase in unemployment were greater than elsewhere.

The structure of British industry and the attitudes of those within it were not amenable to change. The adoption of labour intensive production before 1914 was essentially a risk-avoiding strategy on the part of industrialists which belies the bold and aggressive image sometimes attributed to them by business historians. Under pressure, as in the interwar years, their response was to cut wages and reduce labour but not to invest in new machinery or research. Not surprisingly, Britain's internationally poor productivity record has been matched by a comparatively low investment ratio (Maddison 212). Even the creation of large firms through merger, a widespread phenomenon throughout industry during the past century, has seldom generated greater efficiency. Traditional loyalty to one of the original partners by members of the new board or simply the reluctance of management to face difficulties and contentious decisions were common features of such amalgamations. The soured industrial relations of the Victorian period have not eased twentieth-century industrial change. A long history of low wages and uncertain employment has persuaded workers to distrust their employers and predisposed them to resist change, especially as the demand for skilled manual workers has fallen. Since for manufacturers reducing costs by cutting the labour force still appears more attractive than retraining or increased investment, both sides of industry have been inclined to resist fundamental change. Rather they have joined in conflict over the distribution of existing funds. The past decade has brought to fruition most of the long-established weaknesses in the structure of industry and the attitudes of those within it.

This explains the slow growth and relatively poor economic performance of a large part of the economy, and the resultant low average incomes currently enjoyed by the British people. But it is far from the whole picture. Income and, even more, wealth are unevenly distributed in all societies so that while the majority of citizens have an income below the average a small minority have an income substantially above it. This has certainly been true of Britain throughout the past three centuries. There has existed, therefore, a section of society which has not only enjoyed considerable affluence but which has derived and sustained that affluence from sources other than British industry. Until the present century, and even then to a limited extent, the financial system in Britain has not been closely linked to manufacturing. It has nevertheless grown to a considerable size, manifest in the plethora of very large institutions, and made a notable contribution to the growth of national income. This has been the most unique aspect of British economic development. The financial system drew its stimuli for expansion from the landed wealth of the upper classes, the profits of metropolitan-based international commerce, the constant need for funds by the government and, in its periods of greatest expansion, from international investment and financial services. In this area of activity, Britain has been an international success.

The growth of the financial sector has been augmented by the spread of affluence, enabling more people to buy houses, take out insurance, become investors, and set funds aside for their retirement. The growth of British finance had three important influences on growth generally. Firstly, the long-established link between the financial institutions, landed society, government, and commerce bound together institutions, interests and sections of society which became known as 'the establishment', and which comprised the wealthiest and most influential groups in society. Secondly, the massive scale of the financial system as it developed in the mid nineteenth century was essentially international. The outlook of the City has remained international through the twentieth century, just as its interests have remained worldwide. Thirdly, the City and with it the establishment have never been closely involved with British industry and have never relied for their continued prosperity upon its success. Even the growth of the equity market since the Second World War has not been sufficient to tie the fortunes of the financial institutions to the performance of the manufacturing sector. Conversely the continued success of British finance sustains and justifies its acceptability to the establishment and ties the prosperity of the latter to it. Not surprisingly, successive governments throughout the twentieth century have followed policies suited to the needs of the City even when they were damaging to industry.

The division between finance and industry is, of course, far from a complete separation. Increased affluence has generated demand for a wide variety of goods and services which sustain and complement each other. But there has always been and still remains a considerable distinction between finance and industry in their activities and interests. This major fissure is but one of a number of divisions between economic activities, interest groups and areas of the country such that the notion of a national economy is rather chimerical. The economy is not a homogeneous entity, there is no common will or single national economic best interest. The sectional interests of finance and industry are often in conflict as, of course, are those of employers and employees. Another major division has emerged between the affluent and those economically less successful. The process of modern economic growth has extended economic prosperity to an increasing proportion of society. In the Victorian period the middle classes were the main beneficiaries of the spread of affluence beyond the rarefied heights of the upper classes. In the twentieth century the middle classes have continued to prosper, as have the very wealthy, and in recent decades full employment brought rising real incomes and greater prosperity to an even greater share of the population. The demands of such workers for consumer goods and services was also part of the stimulus for further economic expansion. But the recession of the past decade, marked by rising unemployment, has sharpened the gulf between the affluent employed and that substantial minority at the bottom of the social scale who depend on welfare support for their income. For those in employment the reduction of inflation in recent years has been welcomed for bringing a substantial increase in their real standard of living. The cost of the deflationary policies needed to curb inflation has been paid by the unemployed, large in numbers but a minority of the population.

The divergence between wealth and poverty has been exacerbated by its connection with another deep division in the economy, that between rich and poor regions. The difference between regions in economic activity, average income and unemployment encompasses the main fissures in the economy. In the South East, East Anglia, and South West the regional economic structures are strongly oriented towards services and consumer good manufactures. It is in the South East, of course, that the financial and commercial sectors have always been most strongly concentrated and where the greatest affluence has been found. The continued prosperity of these regions reflects the self-sustaining capacity of wealth and the continuing success of the international financial sector. In sharp contrast, much of the rest of the country enjoys considerably less prosperity. This is most obvious in those regions which are the home of declining industry where the loss of comparative advantage in shipbuilding, iron and steel, textiles, coal mining, and motor vehicle manufacture has left a legacy of dereliction, unemployment and poverty. Economic depression like economic growth is cumulative and self-reinforcing in its effects. Industrial decline reduces consumer spending power as employment falls and this cuts effective demand to give further impetus to the process of contraction. Depressed areas find it hard to attract new economic activities because they have an unattractive image, often justified by poor housing and amenities, the social problems related to poverty, and a workforce with redundant skills. The growth of the 'sunrise industries' in recent decades has been largely confined to the already prosperous and attractive parts of the country such as the Thames Valley. In stark contrast, many areas of northern England, South Wales, central Scotland and, latterly, the West Midlands, have levels of unemployment far above those in the prosperous regions and average incomes far below them.

The structure of the British economy and the unique pattern of its historical development has produced a society which finds change difficult. Furthermore, the many economic and social divisions within the system have created a situation in which some groups are prosperous and, therefore, have little incentive to generate or approve change. The interests of the internationally oriented financial sector desire a strong value for the pound in international markets, even if this necessitates that interest rates are kept at a high level, and freedom to invest their funds at home or abroad. Conversely, manufacturing wants low interest rates for cheap investment, a weak pound to help exports, and investment diverted from overseas to the domestic market. Despite the constant debate about what is required to improve economic performance, the diametrically opposed interests of various sectors preclude any consensus view. Opinions on the relative merits of curbing inflation and reducing taxation on the one hand or reducing unemployment and improving welfare provision on the other are polarized by income, region and occupational status.

There is considerable agreement amongst commentators as to the kind of changes needed to generate faster economic growth. Better manufacturing performance is widely regarded as central to this. While the growth of the service sector has been part of the process of development common to all industrial countries and not the drag on growth some suggested in the 1960s, services alone cannot generate either sufficient employment or export earnings to achieve a satisfactory aggregate growth rate. An improvement in manufacturing performance is crucial both to secure the balance of payments in credit and to make serious reductions in unemployment. Apart from changes in attitude on both sides of industry towards productivity and pay, it is also generally agreed that a substantial infusion of investment is required to modernize and extend productive capacity. Similarly, the need to renew infrastructure, improve road and rail links, replace decaying public utilities, and restructure and reorient education, are all widely recognized.

But there remain fundamental differences of opinion as to how this mobilization of resources for change should be accomplished, and what the nature of the current economic problem is. According to the optimistic view of the neoclassical school, Britain's current difficulties are part of a 'transition' in the international economy caused by the industrialization of countries in the Third World. Eventually readjustment will allow a resumption of higher growth rates (Beenstock). An optimistic Keynesian view is that a reflationary policy package could increase growth and cut unemployment without refuelling inflation (Godley). Those post Keynesians who believe that a restoration of full employment would inevitably reproduce inflation argue that only reflation linked to a strict incomes policy offers a credible alternative to the continuation of severe deflation and low growth (Cornwall).

But besides the mechanism for restoring growth, there remains the problem of paying for it. Ironically this problem has long exercised historians with regard to the eighteenth century. Could industrialization be funded from the surplus income generated by the process of growth itself or did it require a transfer of resources from consumption to saving? Historians are now agreed that eighteenth-century growth was achieved by the former means. But it was, of course, a very slow rate of growth which took a long time to make much of an impact on the living standards of most people and which did not achieve full employment. The same problem lies at the root of the British economic predicament at the end of the twentieth century. To generate the rates of growth sufficient to absorb unemployment, improve welfare provision to EEC standards, and achieve growth sufficient to refuel growth from newly created wealth rather than by redistribution will require a very long time if reliance is placed entirely on market forces. But the alternative course of speeding up the process by massive, if selective, investment in production can only be achieved by some redistribution from consumption to saving. Not only would such a course be politically sensitive, it would mark a fundamental change in British resource allocation preferences. Such a decision could only be taken and implemented by central government. Whether any political party would seek office on the basis of such a spartan programme, or secure office if it did, must be doubted. But without some substantial shift in social attitudes and in the allocation of economic resources the characteristic low rate of growth and the many divisions within Britain seem certain to persist.

Bibliography

This bibliography lists only those works to which reference is made in the text. In cases where there are joint authors, both are named in the text reference. Where there are more than two authors, only the first is named in the text. Except where stated, London is the place of publication.

Allen, G. C. 1970. *British Industries and their Organisation*.

Allen, R. C. 1979. 'International competition in iron and steel 1850–1913', *Journal of Economic History*, 39.

Allsopp, C. 1982. 'Inflation', in Boltho, A. (ed.), *The European Economy: Growth and Crisis*. Oxford.

Anderson, B. L. 1969. 'Provincial aspects of the financial revolution of the eighteenth century', *Business History*, 11.

Atkin, J. 1970. 'Official regulations of British overseas investment 1914–1931', *Economic History Review*, 2nd ser. 23.

Atkinson, A. B. 1972. *Unequal Shares: Wealth in Britain*
1983. *Social Justice and Public Policy*.

Atkinson, A. B. and Harrison, A. J. 1978. *Distribution of Personal Wealth in Britain*. Cambridge.

Bacon, R. and Eltis, W. 1978. *Britain's Economic Problem: Too Few Producers*.
1979. 'The measurement of the growth of the non-market sector and its influence: a reply to Hadjimatheou and Skouras', *Economic Journal*, 89.

Bairoch, P. 1973. 'Commerce international et genese de la Revolution Industrielle Anglaise', *Annales*, 28.
1982. 'International industrialisation levels from 1750 to 1980', *Journal of European Economic History*, 11.

Bardou, J. P., Chanaron, J., Fridenson, P. and Laux, J. M. 1982. *The Automobile Revolution: The Impact of an Industry*. Chapel Hill, North Carolina.

Barker, T. 1977. 'International trade and economic growth: an alternative to the neo-classical approach', *Cambridge Journal of Economics*, 1.

Beckerman, W. 1979. *Slow Growth in Britain: Causes and Consequences*. Oxford.

Beenstock, M. 1983. *The World Economy in Transition*.

Benjamin, D. K. and Kochin, L. A. 1979. 'Searching for an explanation of unemployment in interwar Britain', *Journal of Political Economy*, 87.

Berrill, K. 1960. 'International trade and the rate of economic growth', *Economic History Review*, 2nd ser. 12.

Beveridge, W. H. 1909. *Unemployment: A Problem of Industry*.
1944. *Full Employment in a Free Society*.

Bhaskar, K. 1980. *The Future of the World Motor Industry*.

Blackaby, F. T. 1978. *British Economic Policy 1960–1974*. Cambridge.

Blackburn, J. A. 1982. 'The vanishing UK cotton industry', *National Westminster Bank Quarterly Review*.

Blaug, M. 1960. 'The productivity of capital in the Lancashire cotton industry during the nineteenth century', *Economic History Review*, 2nd ser. 13.

Boddy, M. 1980. *The Building Societies*.

Boltho, A. 1982. 'Growth' in Boltho, A. (ed.), *The European Economy: Growth and Crisis*. Oxford.

Booth, A. 1983. 'The "Keynesian revolution" in economic policy-making', *Economic History Review*, 2nd ser. 36.

  1984. 'Defining a "Keynesian revolution"', *Economic History Review*, 2nd ser. 37.

Boswell, J. 1983. 'The informal social control of business in Britain 1880–1939', *Business History Review*, 57.

Bowley, A. L. 1920. *The Change in the Distribution of National Income 1880–1913*. Oxford.

Boyson, R. 1970. *The Ashworth Cotton Enterprise: The Rise and Fall of a Family Firm 1818–1880*.

Braudel, F. 1974. *Capitalism and Material Life 1400–1800*.

Brown, A. J. 1972. *The Framework of Regional Economics in the United Kingdom*. Cambridge.

Brown, R. D. 1978. *The Port of London*.

Bryer, R. A., Brignell, T. J. and Maunder, A. R. 1982. *Accounting for British Steel*. Aldershot.

Buckatzsch, E. J. 1950. 'The geographical distribution of wealth in England 1086–1843', *Economic History Review*, 2nd ser. 3.

Buxton, N. K. 1978. *The Economic Development of the British Coal Industry*.

  1979. 'Coalmining', in Aldcroft, D. H. and Buxton, N. K. (eds.), *British Industry between the Wars: Instability and Industrial Development 1919–1939*.

Byatt, I. C. R. 1979. *The British Electrical Industry 1875–1914: The Economic Return to a New Technology*. Oxford.

Cable, V. 1979. *World Textile Trade and Production*.

Cairncross, A. K. 1962. *Factors in Economic Development*.

Cameron, R. 1967. *Banking in the Early Stages of Industrialisation*. Oxford.

Campbell, R. H. 1980. *The Rise and Fall of Scottish Industry 1707–1939*. Edinburgh.

Cannadine, D. 1980. *Lords and Landlords: The Aristocracy and the Towns 1774–1967*. Leicester.

Cassis, Y. 1985. 'Bankers in English society in the late nineteenth century', *Economic History Review*, 2nd ser. 38.

Caves, R. E. 1971. 'Export-led growth and the new economic history', in Bhagwati, J. N. (ed.), *Trade, Balance of Payments and Growth*. North Holland.

Chalkin, C. W. 1974. *The Provincial Towns of Georgian England*.

Chandler, A. D. 1980. 'The growth of the transnational firm in the United States and the United Kingdom: a comparative analysis', *Economic History Review*, 2nd ser. 33.

Chapman, S. J. and Ashton, T. S. 1914. 'The sizes of businesses mainly in the textile industries', *Journal of the Royal Statistical Society*, 77.

Checkland, S. G. 1975. *Scottish Banking: A History 1695–1973*.

  1976. *The Upas Tree: Glasgow 1875–1975*. Glasgow.

Chenery, H. B. and Syrquin, M. 1975. *Patterns of Development 1950–1970*. Oxford.

Chrystal, K. A. 1979. *Controversies in British Macroeconomics*. Oxford.

Church, R. A. 1979. *Herbert Austin: The British Motor Car Industry to 1941*.

Cipolla, C. M. 1962. *The Economic History of World Population*.

Clapham, J. H. 1925, 1932, 1938. *An Economic History of Modern Britain*. (3 vols.) Cambridge.

Clark, G. N. 1953. *The Idea of the Industrial Revolution*. Glasgow.

Clayton, G. 1971. *British Insurance*.

Cleary, E. J. 1965. *The Building Society Movement*.

Coakley, J. and Harris, L. 1983. *The City of Capital*. Oxford.

Cole, W. A. 1973. 'Eighteenth century economic growth revisited', *Explorations in Economic History*, 10.

1981. 'Factors in demand 1700–80', in Floud and McCloskey, vol. 1.

Coleman, D. C. 1956. 'Industrial growth and industrial revolutions', *Economica*, N.S.

1969. *Courtaulds: An Economic and Social History*, vol. 1, Oxford.

Corner, D. C. and Burton, H. 1968. *Investment and Unit Trusts in Britain and America*.

Cornwall, J. 1977. *Modern Capitalism: Its Growth and Transformation*.

1983. *The Conditions for Economic Recovery*. Oxford.

Cottrell, P. L. 1975. *British Overseas Investment in the Nineteenth Century*.

1980. *Industrial Finance 1830–1914*.

Crafts, N. F. R. 1979. 'Victorian Britain did fail', *Economic History Review*, 2nd ser. 32.

1980. 'National income estimates and the British standard of living debate: a reappraisal of 1801–31', *Explorations in Economic History*, 17.

1983. 'British economic growth 1700–1831: a review of the evidence', *Economic History Review*, 2nd ser. 36.

1985. *British Economic Growth during the Industrial Revolution*. Oxford.

Crossick, G. J. 1976. *The Lower Middle Classes in Britain 1870–1914*.

Crouzet, F. 1980. 'Towards an export economy: British exports during the Industrial Revolution', *Explorations in Economic History*, 17.

1982. *The Victorian Economy*.

Cunningham, W. 1882. *The Growth of English Industry and Commerce in Modern Times*.

Dahrendorf, R. 1982. *On Britain*.

Daunton, M. J. 1977. *Coal Metropolis: Cardiff 1870–1914*. Leicester.

1978. 'Towns and economic growth in eighteenth-century England', in Abram, P. and Wrigley, E. A. (eds.), *Towns and Societies*. Cambridge.

Davis, L. E., Easterlin, R. A., Parker, W. N. *et al.* 1972. *American Economic Growth: An Economist's History of the United States*.

Davis, R. 1972. *The Rise of the English Shipping Industry*. Newton Abbot.

1979. *The Industrial Revolution and British Overseas Trade*. Leicester.

Deane, P. 1957. 'The output of the British woollen industry in the eighteenth century', *Journal of Economic History*, 17.

1973. 'The role of capital in the Industrial Revolution', *Explorations in Economic History*, 10.

Deane, P. and Cole, W. A. 1967. *British Economic Growth 1688–1959*. Cambridge.

Deaton, A. S. 1976. 'The structure of demand 1920–1970', in Cipolla, C. M. (ed.), *The Fontana Economic History of Europe, 5.1*. Glasgow.

De Cecco, M. 1974. *Money and Empire*. Oxford.
Defoe, D. 1727. *A Tour Through the Whole Island of Great Britain*.
Denison, E. F. 1967. *Why Growth Rates Differ*. Washington D.C.
Devine, T. M. 1975. *The Tobacco Lords*. Edinburgh.
De Vries, J. 1976. *The Economy of Europe in an Age of Crisis 1600–1750*. Cambridge.
Dickson, P. G. M. 1960. *The Sun Insurance Office 1710–1960*. Oxford.
  1967. *The Financial Revolution in England*.
Dow, J. C. R. 1964. *The Management of the British Economy 1945–60*. Cambridge.
Drummond, I. 1981. 'Britain and the World Economy 1900–45', in Floud and McCloskey, vol. 2.
Duesenberry, J. S. 1949. *Income, Saving and the Theory of Consumer Behaviour*. Cambridge, Mass.
Dunnett, P. G. S. 1980. *The Decline of the British Motor Industry*.
Dunning, J. H. 1981. *Industrial Production and the Multinational Enterprise*.
Eagly, R. V. and Smith, V. K. 1976. 'Domestic and international integration of the London money market 1731–1789', *Journal of Economic History*, 36.
Eatwell, J. 1982. *Whatever Happened to Britain?*
Edelstein, M. 1982. *Overseas Investment in the Age of High Imperialism: The United Kingdom 1850–1914*.
Ellison, T. 1886. *The Cotton Trade of Great Britain*.
Eltis, W. A. 1969. 'Economic growth and the British balance of payments', in Aldcroft, D. H. and Fearon, P. (eds.), *Economic Growth in Twentieth Century Britain*.
Engels, F. 1892. *The Conditions of the Working Classes in England*.
Engerman, S. L. 1971. 'The American tariff, British exports and American iron production 1840–60', in McCloskey, D. N. (ed.), *Essays on a Mature Economy: Britain after 1840*.
Eversley, D. E. C. 1967. 'The home market and economic growth in England 1750–1780', in Mingay, G. E. and Jones, E. L. (eds.), *Land, Labour and Population in the Industrial Revolution*.
Falkus, M. E. 1979. 'Modern British economic development: the Industrial Revolution in perspective', *Australian Economic History Review*, 19.
Farnie, D. A. 1979. *The English Cotton Industry and the World Market 1815–1896*. Oxford.
Fausten, D. K. 1975. *The Consistency of British Balance of Payments Policies*.
Feinstein, C. H. 1972. *Statistical Tables of National Income, Expenditure and Output of the U.K. 1855–1965*. Cambridge.
  1978. 'Capital formation in Great Britain', in Mathias, P. and Postan, M. M. (eds.), *Cambridge Economic History of Europe*, vol. 7, Part I. Cambridge.
  1981. 'Capital accumulation and the Industrial Revolution', in Floud and McCloskey, vol. 1.
Feinstein, C. H., Matthews, R. C. O. and Odling-Smee, J. C. 1982. 'The timing of the climacteric and its sectoral incidence in the U.K. 1873–1913', in Kindleberger, C. P. and Di Tella, G. (eds.), *Economics in the Long View: Essays in Honour of W. W. Rostow* (vol. 2).
Fisher, F. J. 1971. 'London as an engine of growth', in Bromley, J. S. and Kossman, E. H. (eds.), *Britain and the Netherlands*, vol. 4. The Hague.
Flinn, M. W. 1966. *Origins of the Industrial Revolution*.
Floud, R. C. 1976. *The British Machine Tool Industry 1850–1914*. Cambridge.

Floud, R. C. and McCloskey, D. N. (eds.), 1981. *The Economic History of Britain since 1700*. 2 vols. Cambridge.

Fores, M. 1981. 'The myth of a British industrial revolution', *History*, 66.

Francis, E. V. 1962. *London and Lancashire History*.

Franklin, P. J. and Woodhead, C. 1980. *The U.K. Life Assurance Industry*.

Fraser, W. H. 1981. *The Coming of the Mass Market 1850–1914*.

Frost, M. and Spence, N. 1984. 'The changing structure and distribution of the British workforce', *Progress in Planning*, 21.

Fulford, R. 1953. *Glyn's 1753–1953*.

Gaski, J. F. 1982. 'The cause of the Industrial Revolution: a brief "single factor" argument', *Journal of European Economic History*, 11.

Gerschenkron, A. 1968. *Continuity in History and Other Essays*, Cambridge, Mass.

Gilboy, E. W. 1967. 'Demand as a factor in the Industrial Revolution', in Hartwell, R. M. (ed.), *The Causes of the Industrial Revolution in England*.

Glamann, K. 1974. 'European trade 1500–1750', in Cipolla, C. M. (ed.), *Fontana Economic History of Europe*, 2.

Glynn, S. and Howells, P. G. A. 1980. 'Unemployment in the 1930s: the "Keynesian solution" reconsidered', *Australian Economic History Review*, 20.

Godley, W. 1984. 'Confusion in economic theory and policy – is there a way out?' in Cornwall, J. (ed.), *After Stagflation: Alternatives to Economic Decline*. Oxford.

Greasley, D. 1982. 'The diffusion of machine cutting in the British coal industry 1902–1938', *Explorations in Economic History*, 19.

Greenaway, D. and Shaw, G. K. 1983. *Macroeconomics*. Oxford.

Haber, L. F. 1958. *The Chemical Industry during the Nineteenth Century*. Oxford.

Hadjimatheou, G. and Skouras, A. 1979. 'Britain's economic problem: the growth of the non-market sector', *Economic Journal*, 89.

Hammond, J. L. 1925. 'Review', *New Statesman*, 21 March.

Hancock, K. J. 1962. 'The reduction of unemployment as a problem of public policy 1920–29', *Economic History Review*, 2nd ser. 15.

Hannah, L. 1974. 'Mergers in British manufacturing industry 1880–1918', *Oxford Economic Papers*, N.S. 26.

1979. *Electricity before Nationalisation*.

1982. *Engineers, Managers and Politicians*.

Harbury, C. D. and Hitchens, D. M. W. N. 1979. *Inheritance and Wealth Inequality in Britain*.

Harley, C. K. 1971. 'The shift from sailing ships to steamships 1850–1890: a study in technological change and its diffusion', in McCloskey, D. N. (ed.), *Essays on a Mature Economy: Britain after 1840*.

1974. 'Skilled labour and the choice of technique in Edwardian industry', *Explorations in Economic History*, 11.

1982. 'British industrialisation before 1841: evidence of slow growth during the Industrial Revolution', *Journal of Economic History*, 42.

Harrison, A. E. 1981. 'Joint stock company flotation in the cycle, motor-vehicle and related industries 1882–1914', *Business History*, 23.

Hartwell, R. M. 1971. *The Industrial Revolution and Economic Growth*.

Hatton, T. J. 1982. 'Unemployment in the 1930s and the "Keynesian solution": some notes of dissent', *Essex Economic Papers*, 197.

Hatton, T. J., Lyons, J. S. and Satchell, S. E. 1983. 'Eighteenth century British trade: homespun or Empire made?', *Explorations in Economic History*, 20.

Hausman, W. J. and Watts, J. M. 1980. 'Structural change in the 18th century British economy: a test using cubic splines', *Explorations in Economic History*, 17.

Heald, D. 1983. *Public Expenditure*.

Hicks, J. R. 1969. *A Theory of Economic History*. Oxford.

Hobsbawm, E. J. 1968. *Industry and Empire*.

Hollingsworth, T. H. 1957. 'A demographic study of the British ducal families', *Population Studies*, 11.

Holmes, G. J. (ed.) 1914. *The Investors' Blue Book for 1914*.

Hueckel, G. 1981. 'Agriculture during industrialisation' in Floud and McCloskey, vol. 1.

Hyde, C. K. 1977. *Technological Change and the British Iron Industry 1700–1870*. Princeton.

Irving, R. J. 1976. *The North East Railway Company 1870–1914*. Leicester.

John, A. H. 1950. *The Industrial Development of South Wales 1750–1850*. Cardiff.

Jones, E. L. 1965. 'The constraints on economic growth in Southern England 1650–1850', *Third International Conference on Economic History*. Paris.

  1981a. 'Agriculture 1700–80', in Floud and McCloskey, vol. 1.

  1981b. *The European Miracle*. Cambridge.

Judge, K. 1982. 'The growth and decline of social expenditure', in Walker, A. (ed.), *Public Expenditure and Social Policy*.

Kaldor, N. 1966. *Causes of the Slow Rate of Economic Growth in the United Kingdom*. Cambridge.

  1975. 'Economic growth and the Verdoorn law', *Economic Journal*, 85.

Kennedy, W. P. 1976. 'Institutional response to economic growth: capital markets in Britain to 1914', in Hannah, L. S. (ed.), *Management Strategy and Business Development*.

  1984. 'Notes on economic efficiency in historical perspective: the case of Britain 1870–1914', in Uselding, P. (ed.), *Research in Economic History*, 9.

Keynes, J. M. 1936. *General Theory of Employment, Interest and Money*.

Kirby, M. W. 1981. *The Decline of British Economic Power since 1870*.

Krause, L. B. 1968. 'British trade performance', in Caves, R. E. (ed.), *Britain's Economic Performance*.

Kravis, I. B. 1970. 'Trade as handmaiden of growth: similarities between the nineteenth and twentieth centuries', *Economic Journal*, 80.

Kuznets, S. 1966. *Modern Economic Growth: Rate, Structure and Spread*.

Lamfalussy, A. 1961. *Investment and Growth in Mature Economies*.

Landes, D. S. 1969. *The Unbound Prometheus*. Cambridge.

Law, C. M. 1981. *British Regional Development since World War I*.

Lazonick, W. H. 1980. 'Production relations, labour productivity and choice of technique: British and U.S. cotton spinning', *Journal of Economic History*, 41.

  1983. 'Industrial organisation and technological change: the decline of the British cotton industry', *Business History Review*, 57.

Lazonick, W. H. and Mass, W. 1984. 'The performance of the British cotton industry 1870–1913', in Uselding, P. (ed.), *Research in Economic History*, 9.

Lee, C. H. 1979. *British Regional Employment Statistics 1841–1971*. Cambridge.

  1980a. 'The cotton textile industry', in Church, R. A. (ed.), *The Dynamics of Victorian Business*.

  1980b. 'Regional structural change in the long run: Great Britain 1841–1971', in Pollard, S. (ed.), *Region and Industrialisation: Studies on the Role of the Region in the Economic History of the Last Two Centuries*. Gottingen.

1981. 'Regional growth and structural change in Victorian Britain', *Economic History Review*, 2nd ser. 33.

1983. 'Modern economic growth and structural change in Scotland: the service sector reconsidered'. *Scottish Economic and Social History*, 3.

1984. 'The service sector, regional specialisation, and economic growth in the Victorian economy', *Journal of Historical Geography*, 10.

Lenman, B. 1977. *An Economic History of Modern Scotland*.

Lewis, A. 1955. *The Theory of Economic Growth*.

Lindert, P. H. 1980. 'English occupations 1670–1811', *Journal of Economic History*, 40.

Lindert, P. H. and Trace, K. 1971. 'Yardsticks for Victorian entrepreneurs', in McCloskey, D. N. (ed.), *Essays on a Mature Economy: Britain since 1840*.

Lindert, P. H. and Williamson, J. G. 1982. 'Revising England's social tables 1688–1812', *Explorations in Economic History*, 19.

1983a. 'Reinterpreting Britain's social tables 1688–1913', *Explorations in Economic History*, 20.

1983b. 'English workers' living standards during the Industrial Revolution: a new look', *Economic History Review*, 2nd ser. 36.

Lipson, E. 1949. *The Growth of English Society*.

McBride, T. M. 1976. *The Domestic Revolution*.

McCloskey, D. N. 1970. 'Did Victorian Britain fail?', *Economic History Review*, 2nd ser. 23.

1973. *Economic Maturity and Entrepreneurial Decline: British Iron and Steel 1870–1913*. Cambridge, Mass.

1975. 'The economics of enclosure: a market analysis', in Parker, W. N. and Jones, E. L. (eds.), *European Peasants and Their Markets: Essays in Agrarian Economic History*. New Jersey.

1979. 'No it did not: a reply to Crafts', *Economic History Review*, 2nd ser. 32.

1981a. 'The Industrial Revolution 1780–1860: a survey', in Floud and McCloskey, vol. 1.

1981b. *Enterprise and Trade in Victorian Britain*.

McCrone, G. 1969. *Regional Policy in Britain*.

McKendrick, N. 1974. 'Home demand and economic growth: a new view of the role of women and children in the Industrial Revolution', in McKendrick, N. (ed.), *Historical Perspectives: Studies in English Thought and Society*.

McKendrick, N., Brewer, J. and Plumb, J. H. 1982. *The Birth of a Consumer Society*.

Maddison, A. 1982. *Phases of Capitalist Development*. Oxford.

Mantoux, P. 1928. *The Industrial Revolution in the Eighteenth Century*.

Mathias, P. 1959. *The Brewing Industry in England 1700–1830*. Cambridge.

1969. *The First Industrial Nation: An Economic History of Britain 1700–1914*.

Mathias, P. and O'Brien, P. K. 1976. 'Taxation in Britain and France 1715–1810: a comparison of the social and economic incidence of taxes collected for the central government', *Journal of European Economic History*, 5.

Marshall, A. 1890. *Principles of Economics*.

Matthews, R. C. O., Feinstein, C. H. and Odling-Smee, J. C. 1982. *British Economic Growth 1856–1973*. Oxford.

Meyer, J. R. 1955. 'An input-output approach to evaluating British industrial production in the late nineteenth century', *Explorations in Entrepreneurial History*, 8.

Michie, R. C. 1981. *Money, Mania and Markets*. Edinburgh.
  1985. 'The London stock exchange and the British securities market 1850–1914', *Economic History Review*, 2nd ser. 38.
Middleton, R. 1982. 'The Treasury in the 1930s: political and administrative constraints to acceptance of the "new" economics', *Oxford Economic Papers*, N.S. 34.
Miles, M. 1981. 'The money market in the early Industrial Revolution: the evidence from West Riding attorneys c. 1750–1800', *Business History*, 23.
Minchinton, W. E. 1954. 'Bristol – metropolis of the west in the eighteenth century', *Transactions of the Royal Historical Society*, ser. 4, no. 5.
  1973. 'Patterns of demand 1750–1914', in Cipolla, C. M. (ed.), *The Fontana Economic History of Europe*, 3.
Mingay, G. E. 1963. *English Landed Society in the Eighteenth Century*.
Mirowski, P. 1981. 'The rise (and retreat) of a market: English joint stock shares in the eighteenth century', *Journal of Economic History*, 41.
Mitchell, B. R. 1962. *Abstract of British Historical Statistics*. Cambridge.
  1973. 'Statistical appendix', in Cipolla, C. M. (ed.), *The Fontana Economic History of Europe*, 4.
  1976. 'Statistical appendix', in Cipolla, C. M. (ed.), *The Fontana Economic History of Europe*, 6.2.
  1981. *European Historical Statistics 1750–1975*. Cambridge.
  1982. *International Historical Statistics: Africa and Asia*. New York.
  1983. *International Historical Statistics: The Americas and Australasia*.
  1984. *Economic Development of the British Coal Industry 1800–1914*. Cambridge.
Mitchell, B. R. and Jones, H. G. 1971. *Second Abstract of British Historical Statistics*. Cambridge.
Mokyr, J. 1976. *Industrialisation in the Low Countries 1795–1850*. New Haven.
  1977. 'Demand vs. supply in the Industrial Revolution', *Journal of Economic History*, 31.
Moore, B. and Rhodes, J. 1976. 'The relative decline of the U.K. manufacturing sector', *Economic Policy Review*, 2.
Morgan, E. V. and Thomas, W. A. 1962. *The Stock Exchange*.
Morrah, D. 1955. *A History of Industrial Life Assurance*.
Morris, R. J. 1979. 'The middle class and the property cycle during the Industrial Revolution', in Smout, T. C. (ed.), *The Search for Wealth and Stability*.
Munn, C. W. 1981. *The Scottish Provincial Banking Companies 1747–1864*. Edinburgh.
Musson, A. E. 1976. 'Industrial motive power in the United Kingdom 1800–70', *Economic History Review*, 2nd ser. 29.
  1980. 'The engineering industry', in Church, R. A. (ed.), *The Dynamics of Victorian Business*.
Nicol, W. and Yuill, D. 1982. 'Regional problems and policy', in Boltho, A. (ed.), *The European Economy: Growth and Crisis*. Oxford.
Nishimura, S. 1971. *The Decline of Inland Bills of Exchange in the London Money Market 1855–1913*. Cambridge.
North, D. C. 1968. 'Sources of productivity change in ocean shipping 1600–1850', *Journal of Political Economy*, 76.
  1981. *Structure and Change in Economic History*.
North, D. C. and Thomas, R. P. 1973. *The Rise of the Western World*. Cambridge.
O'Grada, C. 1981. 'Agricultural decline 1860–1914', in Floud and McCloskey, vol. 2.

Ormerod, P. A. and Worswick, G. D. N. 1982. 'Unemployment in interwar Britain', *Journal of Political Economy*, 90.

Overy, R. J. 1976. *William Morris, Lord Nuffield*.

Pagnamenta, P. and Overy, R. J. 1984. *All Our Working Lives*.

Panic, M. 1975. 'Why the U.K.'s propensity to import is high', *Lloyds Bank Review*, 115.

Parikh, A. 1978. 'Differences in growth rates and Kaldor's law', *Economica*.

Payne, P. L. 1967. 'The emergence of the large-scale company in Great Britain 1870–1914', *Economic History Review*, 2nd ser. 20.

Peacock, A. T. and Wiseman, J. 1961. *The Growth of Public Expenditure in the United Kingdom*.

Peden, G. C. 1984. 'The "Treasury view" on public works and employment in the interwar period', *Economic History Review*, 2nd ser. 37.

Phelps Brown, H. 1977. *The Inequality of Pay*. Oxford.

Pollard, S. 1970. *The Gold Standard and Employment Policies between the Wars*.
   1980. 'A new estimate of British coal production 1750–1850', *Economic History Review*, 2nd ser. 33.
   1984. *The Wasting of the British Economy*.

Pollard, S. and Robertson, P. 1979. *The British Shipbuilding Industry 1870–1914*. Cambridge, Mass.

Porter, J. H. 1979. 'Cotton and wool textiles', in Aldcroft, D. H. and Buxton, N. K. (eds.), *British Industry between the Wars: Instability and Industrial Development 1919–39*.

Postan, M. M. 1972. 'Recent trends in the accumulation of capital', in Crouzet, F. (ed.), *Capital Formation in the Industrial Revolution*.

Powell, C. G. 1980. *An Economic History of the British Building Industry 1815–1979*.

Pryke, R. 1971. *Public Enterprise in Practice*.

Reader, W. J. 1979. *A House in the City*.

Redford, A. 1931. *The Economic History of England 1760–1860*.

Reed, M. C. 1975. *A History of James Capel & Co*.

Richards, E. 1973. *The Leviathan of Wealth*.
   1979. 'An anatomy of the Sutherland fortune: income, consumption, investment and returns 1780–1880', *Business History*, 21.

Richardson, H. W. 1965. 'Retardation in Britain's industrial growth 1870–1913', *Scottish Journal of Political Economy*, 12.
   1967. *Economic Recovery in Britain 1932–39*.
   1968. 'Chemicals', in Aldcroft, D. H. (ed.), *The Development of British Industry and Foreign Competition 1875–1914*.

Riley, J. C. 1980. *International Government Finance and the Amsterdam Capital Market 1740–1815*. Cambridge.

Robson, R. 1957. *The Cotton Industry in Britain*.

Rose, M. B. 1979. 'Diversification of investment by the Greg family 1800–1914', *Business History*, 21.

Rostow, W. W. 1960. *The Stages of Economic Growth*.
   1963. *The Economics of Take-Off into Sustained Growth*.
   1975. *How It All Began: Origins of the Modern Economy*.
   1978a. (with F. E. Fordyce) 'Growth rates at different levels of income and stages of growth: reflections on why the poor get richer and the rich slow down', in Uselding, P. (ed.), *Research in Economic History*, 3.
   1978b. *The World Economy: History and Prospect*.

Routh, G. 1980. *Occupation and Pay in Great Britain 1906–79*.

Rubinstein, W. D. 1977a. 'The Victorian middle classes: wealth, occupation and geography', *Economic History Review*, 2nd ser. 30.

1977b. 'Wealth, elites and the class structure of modern Britain', *Past and Present*, 76.

1980. *Wealth and the Wealthy in the Modern World*.

1981. *Men of Property: The Very Wealthy in Britain since the Industrial Revolution*.

Sampson, A. 1981. *The Money Lenders*.

Sandberg, L. G. 1974. *Lancashire in Decline*. Ohio.

Saul, S. B. 1962. 'The motor industry in Britain to 1914', *Business History*, 5.

1970. 'The market and the development of the mechanical engineering industries in Britain 1860–1914', in Saul, S. B. (ed.), *Technological Change: The United States and Britain in the Nineteenth Century*.

Sayers, R. S. 1957. *Lloyds Bank in the History of English Banking*. Oxford.

Shammas, C. 1983. 'Food expenditure and economic well-being in early modern England', *Journal of Economic History*, 43.

Shapiro, E. 1970. *Macroeconomic Analysis*. New York.

Shaw, C. 1983. 'The largest manufacturing employers of 1907', *Business History*, 25.

Singh, A. 1977. 'U.K. industry and the world economy: a case of deindustrialisation', *Cambridge Journal of Economics*, 1.

Skidelsky, R. 1981. 'Keynes and the Treasury view: the case for and against an active unemployment policy in Britain 1920–1939', in Mommsen, W. J. (ed.), *The Emergence of the Welfare State in Britain and Germany*.

Soltow, L. 1968. 'Long-run changes in British income inequality', *Economic History Review*, 2nd ser. 21.

Sperling, J. 1962. 'The international payments mechanism in the seventeenth and eighteenth centuries', *Economic History Review*, 2nd ser. 14.

Stafford, G. B. 1981. *The End of Economic Growth? Growth and Decline in the U.K. since 1945*. Oxford.

Stedman Jones, G. 1971. *Outcast London*. Oxford.

Stone, L. and Stone, J. C. F. 1984. *An Open Elite? England 1540–1880*. Oxford.

Stoneman, P. 1979. 'Kaldor's law and British economic growth 1800–1970', *Applied Economics*, 11.

Stopford, J. M. 1982. *The World Directory of Multinational Enterprises 1982–83*.

Stopford, J. M. and Dunning, J. H. 1983. *Multinationals: Company Performance and Global Trends*.

Stout, D. 1979. 'Capacity adjustment in a slowly growing economy', in Beckerman, W. (ed.), *Slow Growth in Britain: Causes and Consequences*. Oxford.

Streeten, P. 1959. 'Unbalanced growth', *Oxford Economic Papers*, N.S. 11.

Supple, B. 1970. *The Royal Exchange Assurance: A History of British Insurance 1720–1970*. Cambridge.

Surrey, M. 1982. 'The United Kingdom', in Boltho, A. (ed.), *The European Economy: Growth and Crisis*. Oxford.

Taylor, A. J. 1968. 'The coal industry', in Aldcroft, D. H. (ed.), *The Development of British Industry and Foreign Competition 1875–1914*.

Temin, P. 1964. *Iron and Steel in Nineteenth Century America*. Cambridge, Mass.

1966. 'The relative decline of the British steel industry 1880–1913', in Rosovsky, H. (ed.), *Industrialisation in Two Systems*. New York.

1974. 'The Anglo-American business cycle 1820–60', *Economic History Review*, 2nd ser. 27.

Thirlwall, A. P. 1978. 'The U.K.'s economic problem: a balance of payments constraint?', *National Westminster Bank Quarterly Review*.

1982. 'Deindustrialisation in the United Kingdom', *Lloyds Bank Review*, 144.

Thomas, B. 1973. *Migration and Economic Growth: A Study of Great Britain and the Atlantic Economy*. Cambridge.

1978. 'The rhythm of growth in the Atlantic economy of the eighteenth century', in Uselding, P. (ed.), *Research in Economic History*, 3.

Thomas, M. 1983. 'Rearmament and economic recovery in the late 1930s', *Economic History Review*, 2nd ser. 36.

Thomas, R. P. and McCloskey, D. N. 1981. 'Overseas trade and empire 1700–1860', in Floud and McCloskey, vol. 1.

Thomas, T. 1981. 'Aggregate demand in the United Kingdom 1918–45', in Floud and McCloskey, vol. 2.

Thomas, W. A. 1973. *The Provincial Stock Exchanges*.

1978. *The Finance of British Industry 1918–76*.

Thompson, E. P. 1963. *The Making of the English Working Class*.

Thompson, F. M. L. 1963. *English Landed Society in the Nineteenth Century*.

Tomlinson, J. 1981a. 'Why was there never a "Keynesian revolution" in economic policy?', *Economy and Society*, 10.

1981b. 'Economics of policy and public expenditure: a critique', *Economy and Society*, 10.

1981c. *Problems of British Economic Policy 1870–1945*.

Townsend, P. 1979. *Poverty in the United Kingdom*.

Toynbee, A. 1884. *Lectures on the Industrial Revolution of the 18th Century in England*.

Treble, J. H. 1980. 'The pattern of investment of the Standard Life Assurance Company 1875–1914', *Business History*, 22.

Vamplew, R. 1976. *The Turf: A Social and Economic History of Horse Racing*.

Veverka, J. 1963. 'The growth of government expenditure in the United Kingdom since 1790', *Scottish Journal of Political Economy*, 10.

Von Tunzelmann, N. 1981. 'Britain 1900–45: a survey', in Floud and McCloskey, vol. 2.

Walton, J. K. 1981. 'The demand for working-class seaside holidays in Victorian England', *Economic History Review*, 2nd ser. 34.

Ward, J. R. 1974. *The Finance of Canal Building in Eighteenth-Century England*. Oxford.

Ward, J. T. 1976. 'West Riding landowners and mining in the nineteenth century', in Benson, J. and Neville, R. G. (eds.), *Studies in the Yorkshire Coal Industry*. Manchester.

Wechsberg, J. 1966. *The Merchant Bankers*.

Wedgwood, J. C. 1929. *The Economics of Inheritance*.

Wells, S. J. 1964. *British Export Performance*. Cambridge.

Wells, J. D. and Imber, J. C. 1977. 'The home and export performance of United Kingdom industries', in Central Statistical Office, *Economic Trends*, 286.

Whitehead, D. 1970. 'The English Industrial Revolution as an example of growth', in Hartwell, R. M. (ed.), *The Industrial Revolution*. Oxford.

Wiener, M. J. 1981. *English Culture and the Decline of the Industrial Spirit 1850–1980*. Cambridge.

Williams, K., Williams, J. and Thomas, D. 1983. *Why are the British bad at manufacturing?*

Williamson, J. G. 1974. *Late Nineteenth Century American Development: A General Equilibrium Approach*. Cambridge.

1982. 'The structure of pay in Britain 1710–1911', in Uselding, P. (ed.), *Research in Economic History*, 7.

1984. 'Why was British growth so slow during the Industrial Revolution?', *Journal of Economic History*, 44.

1985. 'The historical content of the classical labour surplus model', *Population and Development Review*, 11.

Winch, D. 1969. *Economics and Policy: A Historical Study*.

Winton, J. R. 1982. *Lloyds Bank 1918–1969*. Oxford.

Wordie, J. R. 1983. 'The chronology of English enclosure 1500–1914', *Economic History Review*, 2nd ser. 36.

Wright, G. 1973. 'An econometric study of cotton production and trade 1830–60', in Temin, P. (ed.), *New Economic History*.

Wrigley, E. A. 1967. 'A simple model of London's importance in changing English society and economy 1650–1750', *Past and Present*, 37.

Yotopoulos, P. A. and Nugent, J. B. 1976. *Economics of Development*.

Official publications

Business Statistics Office, *Census of Production*. Annually from 1970.
   Historical Record of the Census of Production 1907–70. 1978.
Central Statistical Office,
   Annual Abstract of Statistics.
   Monthly Digest of Statistics.
   Regional Abstract. Annual.
   Regional Trends. Annual.
   Social Trends. Annual.
   United Kingdom National Accounts. Annual.
   U.K. National Income and Expenditure 1963–73.
Department of Employment, *Family Expenditure Survey*. Annual.
General Register Office, *Census of Population 1841–1981*.
Inland Revenue, *Report of the Commissioners of H.M. Inland Revenue*. Annual.

Parliamentary reports

National Plan 1965. Cmnd 2764.

Committee on Currency and Foreign Exchanges after the War 1918. (Cunliffe Committee)

Committee on Finance and Industry 1931. (Macmillan Committee)

Committee on the Working of the Monetary System 1959. (Radcliffe Report) Cmnd 827.

Committee to Review the Functioning of the Financial Institutions 1980. (Wilson Report) Cmnd 7937.

Royal Commission on the Distribution of Income and Wealth. Report No. 1 (1975) Cmnd 6171. Report No. 5 (1977) Cmnd 6999. Report No. 7 (1979) Cmnd 7595.

International institutions

European Economic Community, *Eurostat Review 1973–82*. 1984. Luxemburg.
World Bank, *World Development Report 1984*. Oxford.
United Nations, *Monthly Bulletin of Statistics*. New York.

Index